The Illustrated Directory of

FIGHTING
AIRCRAFT

OF WORLD WAR II

Bill Gunston

MBI Publishing Company

This edition first published in 1998 by MBI Publishing Company, 729 Prospect Avenue, PO Box 1, Osceola, WI 54020-0001 USA

MBI Publishing Company books are also available at discounts in bulk quantity for industrial or sales-promotional use. For details write to Special Sales Manager at Motorbooks International Wholesalers & Distributors, 729 Prospect Avenue, PO Box 1, Osceola, WI 54020-0001 USA.

Library of Congress Cataloging-in-Publication Data Available.

Author: Bill Gunston, former Technical Editor of *Flight International,* Assistant Compiler of *Jane's All the World's Aircraft,* contributor to many Salamander illustrated reference books.

Editor: Ray Bonds
Designer: Lloyd Martin
Color and line drawings:
© Pilot Press Ltd.

ISBN 0-7603-0722-9

Printed in Slovenia

ALLIED
FIGHTERS
OF WORLD WAR II

Contents

Aircraft are arranged alphabetically by manufacturers' names, within national groups

FRANCE

During the 1930s French aircraft companies flew some 150 different types of military aircraft. Many were notorious for their ugliness, but from 1935 the Gallic designers created increasingly competitive designs which could have been the basis for airpower that not even Hitler could have scorned.

Sadly, the morale of France was poor. In 1936 a newly elected Left-Wing government nationalised all defence industries, ripping all the old companies apart and forming giant conglomerate groups on a purely geographical basis. Far from increasing output, it caused chaos; and the excellent designs that remained with the tattered surviving private firms were denied essential parts and suffered delay of a year or more. Even the nationalised projects were surrounded by malcontents and saboteurs who crippled production despite increasingly desperate efforts by the dedicated majority.

Another important factor was that available engines were hardly powerful enough to make French fighters adequate when the stern test came. Lorraine and Farman virtually gave up. Hispano-Suiza had a basically good vee-12 which by 1935 was type-tested at 860hp and in World War II was to be the basis for over 100,000 engines made in the Soviet Union at up to 1,650hp. But the only fighter available to the Armée de l'Air in really large numbers in 1939, the M.S. 406, was stuck with 860hp, so that when it met the Bf 109E it was shot down in droves.

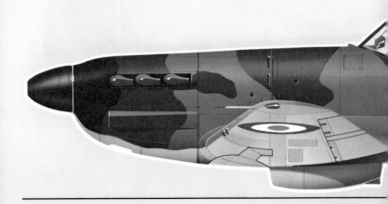

Gnome-Rhône, from 1921 a licensee of Bristol, purchased a licence for the British company's 1,375hp Hercules sleeve-valve radial, but never got into wartime production. Instead all it could offer in production was a radial that was hard-pressed to give 1,000hp, and this was fitted to the basically formidable Bloch 151 series. The power was simply not enough, and one of the enduring memories of the Bloch was of the number that managed to limp back shot to ribbons but unbowed. Ability to take punishment is desirable in a fighter, but not the way to win.

Apart from the splendid prototypes by engineers Vernisse and Galtier at the Arsenal de l'Aéronautique, which did not reach the squadrons, the best homegrown fighter of World War II is judged to have been the Dewoitine 520. This had the Hispano vee-12 at 910hp, and was small, light and agile enough to do well. If only the workers had "pulled their finger out" a year earlier the Luftwaffe's 109s would not have had quite such an easy time over France.

As it was, the frantic French government had by 1938 turned elsewhere for fighters and placed massive orders in the USA. One type, the Curtiss Hawk 75, reached the squadrons in significant numbers and even managed to achieve near-parity with the 109 despite a poorer flight performance. By the time the other US types were in their crates, France had fallen.

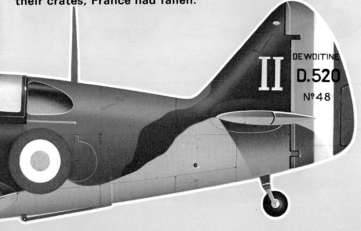

Bloch MB-152C-1
MB-150 to 157 (data for 152)

Origin: SNCASO.
Type: Single-seat fighter.
Engine: 1,080hp Gnome-Rhône 14N-25 14-cylinder radial.
Dimensions: Span 34ft 6¾in (10·5m); length 29ft 10in (9·1m); height 13ft 0in (3·95m).
Weights: Empty 4,453lb (2020kg); loaded 5,842lb (2650kg).
Performance: Maximum speed 323mph (520km/h); climb to 16,400ft (5000m) in 6 minutes; service ceiling 32,800ft (10,000m); range 373 miles (600km).
Armament: Two 20mm Hispano 404 cannon (60-round drum) and two 7·5mm MAC 1934 machine guns (500 rounds each); alternatively four MAC 1934.
History: First flight (MB-150) October 1937; (MB-151) 18 August 1938; (MB-152) December 1938; (MB-155) 3 December 1939; (MB-157) March 1942.
Users: France (Armée de l'Air, Vichy AF), Greece, Romania.

Development: Like so many French aircraft of the time, the Bloch monoplane fighter story began badly, got into its stride just in time for the capitulation and eventually produced outstanding aircraft which were unable to be used. The prototype 150 was not only ugly but actually failed to fly, the frightened test pilot giving up on 17 July 1936. It was only after redesign with more power and larger wing that the aircraft finally left the ground. Bloch had been absorbed into the new nationalised industry as part of SNCASO and five of the new group's factories were put to work making 25. But the detail design was difficult to make, so the MB-151 was produced with the hope that 180 would be made each month from late 1938. Orders

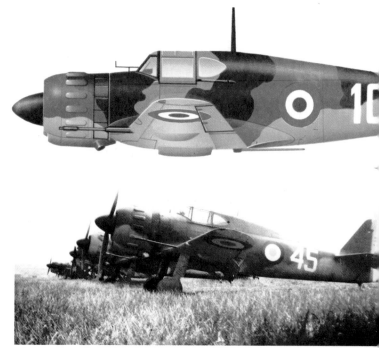

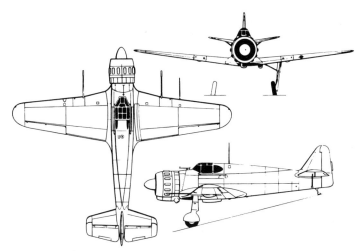

Above: MB-152; note the canted engine to reduce engine torque.

were also placed for the slightly more powerful MB-152, but by the start of World War II only 85 Blochs had been delivered and not one was fit for use; all lacked gunsights and most lacked propellers! Eventually, after overcoming desperate problems and shortages, 593 were delivered by the capitulation, equipping GC I/1, II/1, I/8, II/8, II/9, II/10, III/10 and III/9. The Germans impressed 173 surviving Bloch 151 and 152 fighters, passing 20 to Romania. The MB-155 had a 1,180hp engine and was used by Vichy France. The ultimate model was the superb MB-157, with 1,580hp 14R-4 engine and 441mph (710km/h) speed, never put into production. By this time the firm's founder had changed his name to Dassault.

Left: 152-C1 (C1 = chasse, 1 seat) flying with GC II/1 (GC = Groupe de Chasse) in May 1940. Bloch delivered 140 MB-151 and 488 MB-152, the serial numbers on the tail running unbroken.

Below left: A line-up of 152s; by the French collapse Bloch fighters had gained 188 air-combat victories for the loss of 86 pilots killed, wounded or missing.

Below: First production example of the longer-ranged MB-155, flown in April 1940.

Dewoitine D 520

D 520S

Origin: SNCA du Midi.
Type: Single-seat fighter.
Engine: One 910hp Hispano-Suiza 12Y-45 vee-12 liquid-cooled.
Dimensions: Span 33ft 5¾in (10·2m); length 28ft 8½in (8·75m); height 11ft 3in (3·4m).
Weights: Empty 4,630lb (2100kg); loaded 6,173lb (2800kg).
Performance: Maximum speed 329mph (530km/h); initial climb 2,362ft (720m)/min; service ceiling 36,090ft (11,000m); range 777 miles (1240km).
Armament: One 20mm Hispano-Suiza 404 cannon, with 60 rounds, firing through the propeller hub, and four 7·5mm MAC 1934 machine guns, each with 500 rounds, in wings.
History: First flight (520–01) 2 October 1938; (production, 520-2) 3 December 1939; service delivery 1 February 1940.
Users: Bulgaria, France, Italy (RA), Romania.

Development: Few people have ever disputed that this neat little fighter was the best produced in France prior to the Armistice; it was certainly the best to reach the squadrons. Unlike so many other hopeful types which just failed to be ready in time, the D 520 made it — but only just. The great Marcel Doret did not help when, having made a splendid first test flight, he forgot

Above: The D 520 was adopted by the collaborative Vichy government as its standard fighter, and saw service against the Allies, as well as with Axis air forces. This example was No 147, delivered prior to France's capitulation in 1940.

Right: Production of the D 520 resumed in 1941 when, under German control, the SNCA du Midi was merged into SNCASE, and manufacture picked up again at Toulouse-Blagnac. This example is fresh off the line.

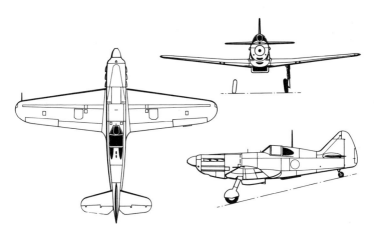

Above: Standard D 520 with folded ventral radio mast.

about the retractable landing gear on 27 November 1938 and put the first prototype out of action. The new fighter was a direct development of the 500 series and though it was very small it was hoped to fit an engine of 1,300hp — but nothing suitable was available. The first prototype had an open cockpit and the second still had a curved windscreen, tailskid and two drum-fed machine guns, as did the first production machine. But the second was up to production standard. The Dewoitine plants had vanished into the nationalised SNCA du Midi under the law of 1936 and these were meant to deliver ten in September 1939 and 30 in October. Actually timing ran about three months late, but with the panic in 1940 industry went mad. In May 1940 101 were delivered and by June the output had reached ten per day, a figure seldom exceeded by any aircraft plant in history. GC I/3 was first to go into action, followed in late May by GC II/3, with III/3, III/6 and II/7 following before the capitulation. These groups were credited with 147 kills for the loss of 85 fighters and 44 pilots. Subsequently the Vichy government restored the D 520 to production, 740 being built in all. In 1942 the Luftwaffe seized 411, passing many to Italy, Romania and Bulgaria. But in 1944 GC I/8 was re-formed under Doret and, after painting out the German insignia, went into action against the last German pockets in southern France.

Morane-Saulnier M.S.406

M.S.405, M.S.406C-1

Origin: Aeroplanes Morane-Saulnier; also assembled by SNCAO at St Nazaire-Bouguenais; variant built under licence by Dornier-Werke, Switzerland.

Type: Single-seat fighter.

Engine: One 860hp Hispano-Suiza 12Y-31 vee-12 liquid-cooled.

Dimensions: Span 34ft 9¾in (10·60m); length 26ft 9¼in (8·16m); height 9ft 3¾in (2·83m).

Weights: (406) empty 4,189lb (1900kg); loaded 5,364–5,445lb; maximum loaded 6,000lb (2722kg).

Performance: Maximum speed 302mph (485km/h); initial climb 2,789ft (850m)/min; service ceiling 30,840ft (9400m); range (without external tanks) 497 miles (800km).

Armament: One 20mm Hispano-Suiza HS-9 or 404 cannon with drum of 60 rounds, and two 7·5mm MAC 1934 in wings each with 300 rounds.

History: First flight (405) 8 August 1935; (production 405) 3 February 1938; (production 406) 29 January 1939; service delivery (406) 1 March 1939.

Users: Croatia, Finland, France, Germany, Turkey; ordered by China, Lithuania and Poland but for various reasons never in service with these countries.

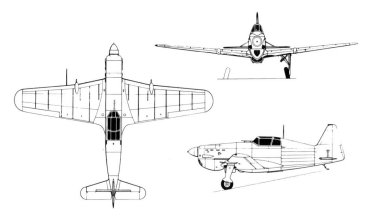

Above: M.S.406-C1, with ventral aerial folded.

Development: After their unbroken series of parasol monoplanes Morane-Saulnier built the M.S.405 secretly to meet a 1934 specification of the Armée de l'Air. Compared with other fighters at the start of World War II it was underpowered, lacking in performance and somewhat lacking in firepower. On the other hand its early start meant it was at least available, while other French fighters were mainly a vast collection of prototypes. ▶

Left: The 704th production M.S.406-C1, serving in early 1940 with 1e Escadrille, GC I/2 at Nîmes. The radiator between the landing gears could be wound in or out (in the picture below it is fully extended) and the ventral radio aerial was extended vertically down, in the air.

Below: One of the first operational units to be equipped with the M.S.406 was GC I/7, which began conversion in 1938. They went to North Africa in 1939, and this 1940 photograph shows them in the Lebanon.

Above: Fodder for 109s, a Battle of the Advanced Air Striking Force visits a Groupe de Chasse equipped with Moranes in 1940.

Altogether 17 M.S.405 were built, most becoming prototypes of proposed future versions and ultimately giving rise to the Swiss D-3800 series of fighters which, unlike most 405s, did not have a retractable radiator. An unusual feature was the fact that, except for the fabric-covered rear fuselage, most of the covering was Plymax (light alloy bonded to plywood). The M.S.406 was the 405 production version incorporating all the requested modifications. The production was shared out among the nationalised groups (Morane retaining only a small part of the work), with production lines at Bouguenais and Puteaux. By the time of the collapse in June 1940 no fewer than 1,081 had been completed, despite a desperate shortage of engines. In May 1940 the 406 equipped 19 of the 26 French combat-ready fighter groups. One who flew them said they were "free from vices, but too slow to catch German aircraft and too badly armed to shoot them down. Poorly protected, our own losses were high". The Vichy government fitted 32gal drop tanks to Moranes sent to Syria to fight the RAF. Many were used by Finland, fitted with skis and often with Soviet M-105P engines of higher power (the so-called LaGG-Morane).

Below: Moranes of a Free Polish unit (aircraft No 1031 is nearest the camera). Previously Moranes had been shipped to Poland.

Above: This 406-C1 shows the radiator fully extended, sloping main wheels and crude ring-and-bead auxiliary gunsight.

Potez 63 series
630, 631, 633, 637 and 63·11

Origin: Avions Henri Potez.
Type: (630, 631) two- (sometimes three-) seat day and night fighter; (633) two-seat light attack bomber; (63.11) three-seat army co-operation and reconnaissance.
Engines: (630) two 725hp Hispano-Suiza 14AB 14-cylinder two-row radials; all other versions, two 700hp Gnome-Rhône 14M of same layout.
Dimensions: Span 52ft 6in (16m); length 36ft 4in (11·07m); (63·11 only) 36ft 1in; (11m); height 11ft 9¾in (3·6m).
Weights: Empty (630, 631, 633) typically 5,730lb (2600kg); (637) 6,390lb (2900kg); (63·11) 6,912lb (3205kg); maximum loaded (631) 8,235lb (3735kg); (633, 637) 9,285lb (4210kg); (63·11) 9,987lb (4530kg).
Performance: Maximum speed (630, 631, 633) 273mph (440km/h); (637) 267mph (430km/h); (63·11) 264mph (425km/h); initial climb (typical) 1,800ft (550m)/min; service ceiling (630, 631) 32,800ft (10,000m); (others, typical) 26,250ft (8000m).
Armament: See "Development" text.
History: First flight (Potez 63) 25 April 1936; (production 630) February 1938; (prototype 63·11) December 1938.
Users: France, Germany (Luftwaffe), Greece, Romania, Switzerland.

Development: Winner of a 1934 competition for a C3 (three-seat fighter) for the Armée de l'Air, the Potez 63 was a clean twin-finned machine powered by two of the new Hispano slim radials. It soon branched into a host of sub-variants, including many for foreign customers. The first 80 production aircraft were 630s, but they were soon grounded due to severe engine failure after only a few hours. The 631, however, was more successful and 208 were delivered (121 in May 1940 alone), equipping five fighter squadrons, two Aéronavale squadrons and many other units and shooting down 29 German aircraft (12 by the navy squadrons) in the Battle for France. Most had two (some only one) 20mm Hispano 9 or 404 cannon, one or two 7·5mm MAC in the rear cockpit and, from February 1940, six MAC faired under the outer wings. The 633 had only two machine guns, one forward-firing and the other in the rear cockpit, and the profusion of export variants had several different kinds of gun. Maximum bomb load was 1,323lb (600kg), including 880lb (400kg) internal. Many 633s had a busy war, Greek examples fighting with the Allies and Romanian examples fighting the Russians. The 637 was used in numbers in May 1940 but was only a stop-gap for the 63·11, with glazed nose and humped rear canopy, which was used in large numbers by the Luftwaffe, Vichy French, Free French and others. Over 900 were built, bringing the total for the 63 family to more than 1,300.

Below: Mass-produced three-seat reconnaissance Potez 63.II, No 831, which joined the Allies in North Africa.

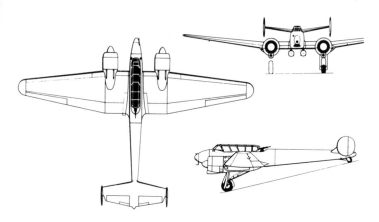

Above: The Potez 633 bomber, used mainly by export customers.

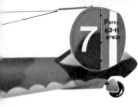

Above: Two photographs of a Potez 631 twin-engined fighter of 4° Escadrille, GCN II/3, one of the world's first dedicated night-fighter units since 1918. Note the six machine guns under the outer wings, just visible in the upper view. After the Armistice all Vichy aircraft were painted with prominent red/ yellow stripes over their engines and tail units, ostensibly to indicate neutrality.

GREAT BRITAIN

Apart from Italy, Britain was the only country to see the famed Schneider Trophy races through to the bitter end. The final winner was Reginald Mitchell's Supermarine S.6B seaplane. It is often held that this led to his Spitfire, but similarities are almost non-existent. Far more important was the fact that the thrashing of its special engine greatly assisted Rolls-Royce to develop the PV.12 from which stemmed the Merlin, and though this was small by comparison it had just enough power to keep abreast of the big Daimler-Benz in the Bf 109. (One thing it lacked was direct fuel injection, which allowed the German pilots to do negative-g manoeuvres without the engine cutting out.)

One cannot over-emphasize the importance of the Merlin, which in the Hurricane won the Battle of Britain. The Spitfire, one of the first British aircraft to adopt modern stressed-skin construction, came later. The Hurricane was strong and easy to repair, but had to be flown with great dash and skill to beat a 109, whereas the Spit could outfly the enemy in almost all respects but would have benefited from a shell-firing cannon or long-range gun earlier in the war. Later it was to be discovered that, possibly by chance, its odd elliptical wing had a cross-section which enabled it to dive faster than any other aircraft, to at least Mach 0.92. In fact, during the 1950s it was realised that it was a much better wing than the later "laminar-flow" wing that

One major fault of pre-war RAF procurement was belief in the fighter armed only with a turret. This example is a Defiant I as flown by the CO of the first squadron, No 264.

replaced it on the Spiteful and jet Attacker.

High-Mach performance was of limited relevance to fighting the Luftwaffe, however, and the chief importance of the Spitfire was its incredible ability to develop with more power, more fuel, more cannon, more bombs, naval equipment and everything else which, if it did not include the kitchen sink, did include full-size beer barrels flown on the belly racks to troops in the Normandy beachhead! The ''Spit'' was more important than all other British fighters combined, and it might have helped the Allied cause if all other British fighters had been cancelled except the long-range radar-equipped Mosquito.

Sydney Camm's Typhoon was a disappointment as a fighter, but very useful for catching hit-and-run raiders at low level and bagging them in a straight chase. Later it was even more valuable as a ground-attack aircraft with bombs and rockets. The Tempest, with a better airframe, was the top killer of flying boats, and the Mosquito was a superb night fighter that did more than any other aircraft to sap the morale of the Luftwaffe by night. In 1940 the Beaufighter – like the Mosquito the product of persistence by designers, not any order by the RAF – at last combined radar with good performance and devastating firepower, while in July 1944 the first batch of 16 Meteor Is joined a flight of 616 Sqn, the first regular turbojet unit in the world.

Blackburn Skua and Roc

Skua II, Roc I

Origin: The Blackburn Aircraft Company, Brough; Roc production assigned to Boulton Paul Aircraft, Wolverhampton.

Type: (S) two-seat carrier fighter/dive bomber; (R) two-seat carrier fighter.

Engine: 905hp Bristol Perseus XII nine-cylinder sleeve-valve radial.

Dimensions: Span (S) 46ft 2in (14·07m), (R) 46ft 0in (14·02m); length (S) 35ft 7in (10·85m), (R) 35ft 0in (10·67m); height 12ft 5in (3·79m).

Weights: Empty (S) 5,490lb (2490kg), (R) 6,121lb (2776kg); maximum (S) 8,228lb (3732kg), (R) 8,800lb (3992kg).

Performance: Maximum speed (S) 225mph (362km/h), (R) 196mph (315km/h); service ceiling 20,200ft (6157m); range (typical) 800 miles (1287km).

Armament: (S) four 0·303in Browning fixed in wings, one 0·303in Lewis or Vickers K in rear cockpit, 500lb (227kg) bomb on hinged arms under fuselage, light bombs under wings; (R) four 0·303in Browning in power dorsal turret, light bombs under wings.

History: First flight (S) 9 February 1937, (R) 23 December 1938; service delivery (S) November 1938, (R) April 1939.

User: UK (RN).

Development: The Skua was designed to a 1934 specification, O.27/34, for a naval dive bomber. Two prototypes powered by 840hp Mercury engines looked sleek against the Navy's fabric-covered biplanes, and eventually 190 were built to a later requirement (25/36), to enter service as the Fleet Air Arm's first monoplane and first with v-p propeller or retractable landing gear. During the first year of war the Skuas worked hard, and made many gallant attacks on German capital ships. On 26 September 1939

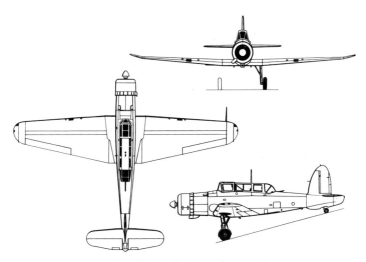

Above: Blackburn Skua II, the dive-bomber version.

Skuas of 803 Sqn from *Ark Royal* shot down a Do 18, the first Luftwaffe aircraft destroyed by Britain. But the basic aircraft was underpowered, and by 1941 the Skua was becoming a target tug and trainer. Likewise the 136 turreted Rocs were even less capable of surviving, let alone acting as fighters. The 136 built, to O.30/35, never served on a carrier and were soon withdrawn. A few were seaplanes, with Shark-type floats.

Below: A fine study of the 28th Roc, which despite retaining its turret was used as a testbed for the sleeve-valve engine.

Boulton Paul P.82 Defiant

Defiant I and II (data for I)

Origin: Boulton Paul Aircraft, Wolverhampton.

Type: Two-seat fighter.

Engine: I, 1,030hp Rolls-Royce Merlin III vee-12 liquid-cooled; II, 1,260hp Merlin 20.

Dimensions: Span 39ft 4in (12m); length 35ft 4in (10·75m); height 12ft 2in (3·7m).

Weights: Empty 6,000lb (2722kg); loaded 8,350lb (3787kg).

Performance: Maximum speed 303mph (488km/h); initial climb 1,900ft (579m)/min; service ceiling 30,500ft (9300m); range, probably about 500 miles (805km).

Armament: Hydraulically operated dorsal gun turret with four 0·303in Browning machine guns, each with 600 rounds.

History: First flight (prototype) 11 August 1937; (production Mk I) 30 July 1939; first delivery December 1939.

User: UK (RAF).

Development: By 1933 military staffs were intensely studying the enclosed gun turret, manually worked or power-driven, either to defend a bomber or to arm a fighter. A primitive form was seen on the Hawker Demon in 1936, while in France the *Multiplace de Combat* class of aircraft were huge fighters with turrets all over. The Defiant was a bold attempt to combine the performance of the new monoplanes with a powered enclosed turret carrying four 0·303in Brownings, each with 600 rounds. The gunner, behind the pilot, had a control column moved left/right for rotation, fore/aft for depression and elevation and with a safety/firing button on top. The Defiant itself was a clean and pleasant aircraft, but rather degraded in performance by carrying a crew of two and the heavy turret. No 264 Sqn went into action on 12 May 1940 in desperate fights over the Low Countries. On the 13th six escorted Battle bombers, and only one returned; it seemed the ▶

Right: As it carried a second crew-member the Defiant was judged a good basis for a dedicated night fighter, with airborne-interception radar. From the start of the "night Blitz" many Defiants, particularly those of 141 and 264 Sqns, operated by night but without radar. In 1941 no fewer than seven squadrons received Defiants with radar, including this Mk IA with AI.V.

Below: Without radar but a later aircraft, AA436 was a Defiant II serving with one of the world's first (1917 with Sopwith Camels) night-fighter squadrons, No 151. Note the two ventral radio aerial masts which were retracted prior to landing.

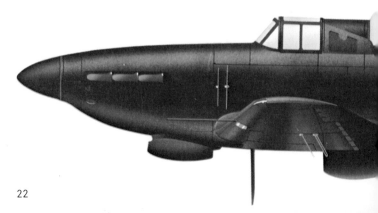

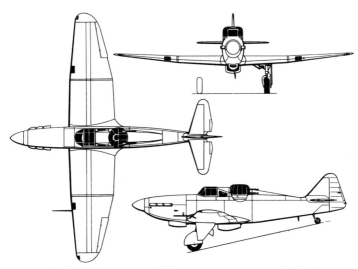

Above: Defiant I with turret fairings raised and masts folded.

Defiant was a failure against the Bf 109E. But seven days later remnants of 264 shot down "17 Messerschmitts without loss" and later on the same day destroyed eleven Ju 87s and 88s. Once the enemy were familiar with the Defiant it had had its day by daylight, but it did well in 1940—41 as a night fighter and was later fitted with radar. Most of the 1,064 built served as night fighters, target tugs and in air/sea rescue in Britain, the Middle East and Far East. Defiants carried the Mandrel jamming system to confuse German defences.

Right: This black-painted Defiant II was the subject for the profile drawing at the foot of the preceding pages. In this late-1942 photograph the rear radio mast is retracted and the rear turret fairing is in the lowered combat-ready position. For full turret usage round 360° the pilot had to shut his hood and the gunner then retracted the forward fairing as well. The oil cooler and radiator of the Mk II were both deeper than on the Mk I aircraft, but manoeuvrability remained poor.

Below: In its heyday: 264 Sqn in March 1940, just ready for ops.

Bristol Type 156 Beaufighter
Beaufighter I to TF.X (data mainly Mk X)

Origin: Bristol Aeroplane Company, Filton and Weston-Super-Mare; also Department of Aircraft Production, Australia.

Type: Two-seat torpedo strike fighter (other marks, night fighters, target tugs).

Engines: Two 1,770hp Bristol Hercules XVII 14-cylinder sleeve-valve radials; (Mk II) 1,250hp R-R Merlin XX; (other marks) different Hercules; (one-offs had R-R Griffons and Wright GR-2600 Cyclones).

Dimensions: Span 57ft 10in (17·63m); length 41ft 8in (12·6m) (II, 42ft 9in); height 15ft 10in (4·84m).

Weights: Empty 15,600lb (7100kg) (I, II, 13,800lb; VI, XI, 14,900lb); loaded 25,400lb (11,530kg) (most other marks 21,000lb, 9525lb).

Performance: Maximum speed 312mph (502km/h) (fighter marks, 330mph, 528km/h); initial climb 1,850ft (564m)/min; service ceiling 26,500ft (8077m) (fighters, 30,000ft, 9144m); range 1,540 miles (2478km).

Armament: Four 20mm Hispano cannon fixed in underside of forward fuselage (initially hand loaded with 60-round drums, later with belt feed), and one 0·303in Vickers K aimed by observer (fighters, also six 0·303in Brownings, two fixed in outer left wing and four in right. One 1,605lb (728kg) torpedo on centreline or 2,127lb (954kg) and wing racks for eight rocket projectiles or two 1,000lb (454kg) bombs.

History: First flight (Type 156 prototype) 17 July 1939; (production Mk I) May 1940; service delivery 27 July 1940; first flight (Mk 21, Australia) 26 May 1944; last delivery from new (UK) September 1945, (Australia) October 1945.

Users: Australia, Canada; New Zealand, South Africa, UK (RAF), US (AAF); other countries post-war.

Development: During the critical years 1935—39 the most glaring gap in the RAF's armoury was the lack of any long-range fighter, any cannon-armed fighter and any fighter capable of effective bomber escort and night fighting. Leslie Frise and engine designer Fedden talked at length of the possibility of creating a single type out of the Blenheim and Beaufort

Right: R2059 was the seventh production aircraft, delivered (minus the AI Mk IV radar, fitted later) in August 1940. It served with 25 Sqn at North Weald, north-east of London. Aircraft of these early batches lacked the wing machine guns, which again were fitted later. The first 400 also had cannon which had to be laboriously reloaded with 60-round drums by the observer.

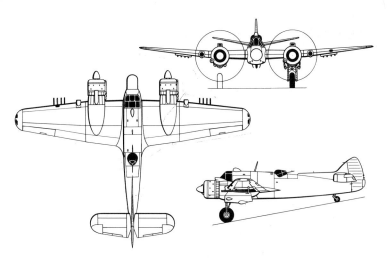

Above: Beaufighter TF.X with rear gun, radar and rocket rails.

families that could meet all demands, but no official requirement was forthcoming — other than the strange F.11/37 Specification for a fighter with a heavily armed cannon turret. Eventually the two Bristol leaders did the obvious thing: they proposed a new twin-Hercules two-seater carrying enough armament to blast anything in front of it out of the sky. By using the wing, tail, landing gear, systems and jigs of the Beaufort it could be put into production quickly. The Air Ministry was enthusiastic and the first of what was to be an historic war-winning aeroplane took the air only six months later. A snub-nosed battleship, it was immensely strong, surprisingly manoeuvrable and a great basis for development. Almost its only operational shortcoming was a tendency to swing on takeoff or landing, and instability at low speeds, which later addition of a large dorsal fin and dihedral tailplane did not fully cure.

Early models barely exceeded 300mph with low-power Hercules and, in the absence of Griffon engines, 450 were fitted with Merlins, but these were ▶

Left: A much later "Beau", this was one of the first batch of Coastal TF.X built at Weston. Serving with 455 Sqn, it is shown with rear defence gun (a belt-fed Browning in this mark) and underwing rockets. Later the Mk X supplemented the dihedralled tailplane with a large dorsal fin to improve asymmetric handling and reduce swing on takeoff and landing. All TF (torpedo/fighter) aircraft had provision for either the British 18-inch or US 22.5-inch torpedo.

Above: A fine picture of a Mk VIC of RAF No 455 Sqn firing its underwing rockets — probably just for the benefit of the photographer, since the aircraft is flying straight and level.

less powerful and accentuated instability. Speed was soon judged less important when the need for night fighters to beat the Blitz became urgent. Equipped with AI Mk IV radar the early deliveries to 25 and 29 Sqns were a major reason for the Luftwaffe giving up the Blitz on Britain. Eventually the "Beau" served on all fronts, having thimble-nose AI Mk VII in 1942, torpedoes in 1943, rockets in 1944 and a spate of special installations in 1945. A total of 5,564 were built in England and 364 in Australia, the last fighter and torpedo versions serving with Coastal Command, the Far East Air Force and the RAAF until 1960. To the Luftwaffe it was a feared opponent even 500 miles out in the Atlantic; to the Japanese it was "Whispering death", so named because of the quietness of the sleeve-valve engines. It was sheer luck the "Beau" could be produced in time.

Left: Probably taken in Tunisia in early 1943, this photograph shows a war-weary Mk VI, with structural provision for AI.VIII radar but nothing actually fitted except the forward-ident lamp.

Below: Red-doped fabric covers the muzzles of this Mk IF taxiing on Malta; it also has outer-wing bomb racks, but no radar

De Havilland 98 Mosquito

D.H.98 Mosquito I to 43

Origin: The de Havilland Aircraft Company, Hatfield and Leavesden; also built by Airspeed, Percival Aircraft and Standard Motors (Canley); de Havilland Aircraft Pty, Australia; de Havilland Aircraft of Canada.

Type: Designed as high-speed day bomber, see text for subsequent variants.

Engines: (Mks II, III, IV and early VI) two 1,230hp Rolls-Royce Merlin 21 or (late FB.VI) 1,635hp Merlin 25; (Mk IX) 1,680hp Merlin 72; (Mk XVI) Merlin 72 or 1,710hp Merlin 73 or 77; (Mk 30) 1,710hp Merlin 76; (Mk 33) 1,640hp Merlin 25; (Mks 34, 35, 36) 1,690hp Merlin 113/114. Many other variants had corresponding Merlins made by Packard.

Dimensions: Span (except Mk XV) 54ft 2in (16·5m); length (most common) 40ft 6in (12·34m); (bombers) 40ft 9½in; (radar-equipped fighters and Mks 34–38) typically 41ft 9in; (Mk 39) 43ft 4in; height (most common) 15ft 3½in (4·66m).

Weights: Empty (Mks II–VI) about 14,100lb; (Mks VIII–30) about 15,200lb; (beyond Mk 30) about 15,900–16,800lb; maximum gross (Mks II and III) around 17,500lb; (Mks IV and VI) about 22,500lb; (later night fighters) about 20,500lb (but HF.XV only 17,395lb); (Mks IX, XVI and marks beyond 30) typically 25,000lb (11,340kg).

Performance: Maximum speed, from 300mph (TT.39 with M4 sleeve) to 370mph (595km/h) for early night fighters, 380mph (612km/h) for III, IV and VI, 410mph (660km/h) for IX, XVI and 30, and 425mph for 34 and 35; service ceiling, from 30,000ft (9144m) for low-rated naval versions to 34,500ft (10,520m) for most marks, to around 40,000ft (12,190m) for high-blown versions, with Mk XV reaching 44,000ft (13,410m); combat range, typically 1,860 miles (2990km), with naval TFs down at 1,260 miles and PR.34 up to 3,500 miles.

Armament: See text.

History: See text.

Users: Australia, Belgium, Canada, China, Czechoslovakia, France, Jugoslavia, New Zealand, Norway, Soviet Union, Turkey, UK (RAF, RN, BOAC), US (AAF). *continued* ▶

Right: Last and most formidable of all the wartime fighter marks, the NF.XXX (NF.30) had high-blown engines and paddle-blade propellers giving performance superior to anything in the Luftwaffe except the jets, at all heights up to over 35,000 feet.

Below: In contrast, the first fighter version was the F.II, seen here defending Malta with 23 Sqn in 1942. Most had AI.IV radar.

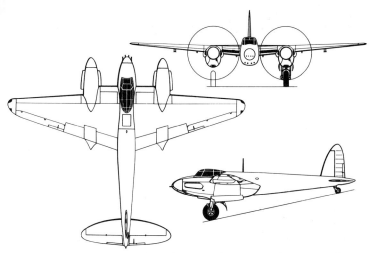

Above: The FB.VI fighter/bomber was the most numerous variant.

Development: The de Havilland Aircraft Co planned the Mosquito in October 1938 as a high-speed unarmed day bomber, with the added attraction of wooden construction to ease the strain on Britain's hard-pressed materials suppliers. The Air Ministry showed no interest, suggesting instead the Hatfield plant should make wings for existing heavy bombers. In 1940, with extreme reluctance, it was agreed to allow the firm to proceed, the only role thought possible for an unarmed aircraft being reconnaissance. The first prototype, built secretly at Salisbury Hall by a team which grew from 12 in January 1940 to 30 in the summer, was flown painted yellow on 25 November 1940. From it stemmed 7,781 aircraft, built in Britain, Canada and Australia, of the following types;

PR.I Unarmed photo-reconnaissance, with span lengthened from 52ft 6in of prototype to 54ft 2in but still with short engine nacelles.

F.II Night fighter, with pilot and observer side by side, flat bullet-proof windscreen, extended nacelles (as in all subsequent aircraft, with flaps divided into inner and outer segments) and armament of four 20mm Hispano cannon with 300 rounds each under the floor and four 0·303in Brownings with 2,000 rounds each in the nose. First flew 15 May 1941; subsequently fitted with AI Mk IV or V radar or Turbinlight searchlight.

T.III Dual-control trainer, first flown January 1942 but produced mainly after the war (last delivery 1949).

B.IV Unarmed bomber, carrying four 500lb (227kg) bombs internally; first delivered to 105 Sqn at Swanton Morley November 1941, making first operational sortie (Cologne, the morning after the first 1,000-bomber night attack) on 31 May 1942. Some later fitted with bulged bomb bays for 4,000lb (1814kg) bomb.

FB.VI Fighter-bomber and intruder, by day or night; same guns as F.II but two 250lb (113kg) bombs in rear bay and two more (later two 500lb) on wing racks; alternatively, 50 or 100 gal drop tanks, mines, depth charges or eight 60lb rockets. Some fitted with AI radar. Total production 2,584, more than any other mark.

B.VII Canadian-built Mk IV, used in North America only.

PR.VIII Reconnaissance conversion of B.IV with high-blown Merlin 61.

Mk IX Important advance in bomber (B.IX) and reconnaissance (PR.IX) versions; high-blown two-stage engines, bulged bomb bay for 4,000lb bomb or extra fuel, much increased weight, paddle-blade propellers and new avionics (Rebecca, Boozer, Oboe or H_2S Mk VI).

NF.XII Conversion of F.II fitted with new thimble nose containing AI Mk VIII céntimetric radar in place of Brownings.

NF.XIII Similar to Mk XII but built as new, with thimble or bull nose and same wing as Mk VI for drop tanks or other stores; flew August 1943.

Above: A fine portrait of a Mosquito FB.VI. NT193 was a Hatfield-built example of this prolific mark, though many others were built by shadow factories and in Canada and Australia, with minor differences. The universal wing was plumbed for drop tanks but is seen here fitted with pylons for stores such as 500 lb (227 kg) bombs. Radar was not fitted.

NF.XV High-altitude fighter with wings extended to 59ft, pressurised cockpit, lightened structure, AI Mk VIII in nose and belly pack of four 0·303in Brownings to combat Ju 86P raiders.

Mk XVI Further major advance with two-stage Merlins, bulged bomb bay and pressurised cockpit. PR.XVI flew July 1943; B.XVI in January 1944, over 1,200 of latter being used for high-level nuisance raids with 4,000lb bombs.

NF.XVII Night fighter with new AI Mk X or SCR.720 (some with tail-looking scanner also); four 20mm each with 500 rounds.

FB.XVIII Dubbed Tse-Tse Fly, this multi-role Coastal Command fighter had low-blown engines and carried a 57mm six-pounder Molins gun with 25 rounds plus four Brownings, as well as eight 60lb rockets or bombs.

NF.XIX Mk XIII developed with AI.VIII or X or SCR.720 in bulged Universal Nose and low-blown Merlin 25s.

B.XX Canadian-built B.IV (USAAF designation F-8).

FB.21 to T.29, Canadian marks with Packard V-1650 (Merlin) engines, not all built.

NF.30 Night fighter with two-stage engines, paddle blades, AI Mk X and various sensing, spoofing or jamming avionics; based on Mk XIX.

PR.32 Extended-span reconnaissance version with Merlin 113/114.

Mk 33 First Royal Navy Sea Mosquito version, with power-folding wings, oleo main legs (in place of rubber in compression), low-blown engines driving four-blade propellers, arrester hook, four 20mm cannon, torpedo (or various bomb/rocket loads), American ASH radar and rocket JATO boost.

PR.34 Strategic reconnaissance version, with 113/114 engines, extra-bulged belly for 1,269 gal fuel (200gal drop tanks) and pressure cabin.

B.35 Equivalent bomber version, with PR and target-tug offshoots.

NF.36 Postwar fighter, with 113/114 engines and AI Mk X.

TF.37 Naval torpedo-fighter; basically Mk 33 with AI/ASV Mk XIII.

NF.38 Final fighter, mainly exported; AI Mk IX, forward cockpit.

TT.39 Complete rebuild by General Aircraft as specialised target tug.

FB.40 Australian-built Mk VI, with PR.40 as conversions.

PR.41 Australian-built derivative of PR.IX and Mk 40.

T.43 Australian trainer; all Australian production had Packard engines.

Fairey Firefly

Firefly I to 7 and U.8 to 10

Origin: The Fairey Aviation Company.

Type: Originally two-seat naval fighter; later, see text.

Engine: I, up to No 470, one 1,730hp Rolls-Royce Griffon IIB vee-12 liquid-cooled; from No 471, 1,990hp Griffon XII; Mks 4–7, 2,245hp Griffon 74.

Dimensions: Span (I-III) 44ft 6in (13·55m), (4-6) 41ft 2in (12·55m), (7) 44ft 6in (13·55m); length (I-III) 37ft 7in (11·4m); (4-6) 37ft 11in (11·56m); (7) 38ft 3in (11·65m); height (I-III) 13ft 7in (4·15m); (4-7) 14ft 4in (4·37m).

Weights: Empty (I) 9,750lb (4422kg); (4) 9,900lb (4491kg); (7) 11,016lb (4997kg); loaded (I) 14,020lb (6359kg); (4) 13,927lb (6317kg) clean, 16,096lb (7301kg) with external stores; (7) 13,970lb (6337kg).

Performance: Maximum speed (I) 316mph (509km/h); (4) 386mph (618km/h); initial climb (I) 1,700ft (518m)/min; (4) 2,050ft (625m)/min; service ceiling (I) 28,000ft (8534m); (4) 31,000ft (9450m); range on internal fuel (I) 580 miles (933km); (4) 760 miles (1223km).

Armament: (I) four fixed 20mm Hispano cannon in wings; underwing racks for up to 2,000lb (907kg) of weapons or other stores; (4 and 5) usually similar to I in most sub-types; (6) no guns, but underwing load increased to 3,000lb and varied; (7) no guns, but underwing load remained at 3,000lb and equipment changed.

History: First flight 22 December 1941; first production F.I 26 August 1942; production FR.4, 25 May 1945; final delivery of new aircraft May 1955.

User: UK (RN); other countries post-war.

Development: Before World War II Fairey designed a light bomber, P.4/34, from which evolved the Fulmar naval two-seat fighter to Specification O.8/38. A total of 600 of these slender carrier-based aircraft served during the war with various equipment and roles. The Firefly followed the same formula, but was much more powerful and useful. Designed to N.5/40 — a merger of N.8/39 and N.9/39 — it was a clean stressed-skin machine with folding elliptical wings housing the four cannon and with the trailing edge provided with patented Youngman flaps for use at low speeds

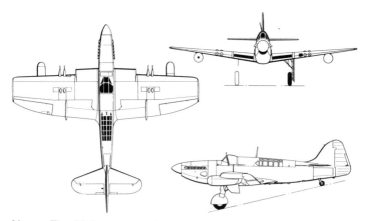

Above: The FR.5 was one of many post-war variants.

and in cruise. Unlike the installation on the Barracuda, these flaps could be recessed into the wing. The pilot sat over the leading edge, with the observer behind the wing. The main wartime version was the Mk I, widely used from the end of 1943 in all theatres. Fairey and General Aircraft built 429 F.Is, 376 FR.Is with ASH radar and then 37 NF.2 night fighters. There followed the more powerful Mk III, from which derived the redesigned FR.4 with two-stage Griffon and wing-root radiators. There were 160 of these, 40 going to the Netherlands and the rest serving in Korea, with the 352 Mk 5s with folding wings. There were FR, NF and AS (anti-submarine) Mk 5s, and they were followed by the 133 specialised AS.6 versions with all role equipment tailored to anti-submarine operations. The 151 AS.7s rounded off production, this being a redesigned three-seater, with new tail and wings and distinctive beard radiator. More than 400 Fireflies were rebuilt in the 1950s as two-cockpit T.1s or armed T.2s, or as various remotely piloted drone versions (U.8, U.9, U.10). Some were converted as target tugs and for other civil duties.

Below: Deck parties aboard fleet carrier (probably *Illustrious*) fold the wings of a Firefly I after an attack on Japanese installations. Some aircraft were fitted with underwing rocket rails.

Fairey Fulmar

Fulmar I and II

Origin: Fairey Aviation Co, Hayes.
Type: Carrier fighter bomber.
Engine: (I) 1,080hp Rolls-Royce Merlin VIII vee-12 liquid-cooled; (II) 1,300hp Merlin 30.
Dimensions: Span 46ft 4½in (14·14m); length 40ft 2in (12·24m); height 10ft 8in (3·25m).
Weights: Empty (II) 7,015lb (3182kg); normal loaded (II) 9,672lb (4387kg); maximum 10,200lb (4627kg).
Performance: Maximum speed (II) 272mph (440km/h); service ceiling (II) 27,200ft (8300m); range 780 miles (1255km).
Armament: Eight 0.303in or (some aircraft) four 0.5 in Browning fixed in outer wings (some also 0.303 in Vickers K manually aimed from rear cockpit), with underwing racks for two 250lb (113kg) bombs.
History: First flight 4 January 1940; service delivery 10 May 1940.
User: UK (RN).

Development: Based on the P.4/34 light bomber first flown in January 1937, the Fulmar was designed by a team under Marcel O. Lobelle to meet the Admiralty's urgent need for a modern shipboard fighter. Specification O.8/38 was drawn up around the Fairey design, stipulating eight guns and a seat for a navigator. Development and clearance for service was amazingly rapid, and 806 Sqn equipped with the new fighter in July, reaching the Mediterranean aboard *Illustrious* in August 1940. Later 14 FAA squadrons used the Fulmar, most seeing intensive action in the Mediterranean or aboard CAM (catapult-armed merchant) ships in Atlantic convoys (a Fulmar was shot from a CAM ship as early as August 1941). Against the Regia Aeronautica the Fulmar did well, having adequate performance, good handling and fair endurance. After building 250 Mk I Fairey delivered 350 of the more powerful Mk II, the last in February 1943.

Above: A standard Fairey Fulmar I (eight 0.303in guns).

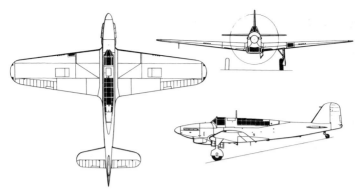

Above: N1858, the fifth Fulmar I. The prototype, N1854, flew in January 1940, and a production Fulmar was delivered in May.

Below: A superb photograph of a Fulmar I landing along the port (left) side of the deck of a fleet carrier in November 1940.

Gloster Gladiator

S.S.37 Gladiator I and II and Sea Gladiator

Origin: Gloster Aircraft Company.

Type: Single-seat fighter; (Sea Gladiator) carrier-based fighter.

Engine: One 840hp Bristol Mercury IX or IXS nine-cylinder radial; (Gladiator II) usually Mercury VIIIA of similar power.

Dimensions: Span 32ft 3in (9·85m); length 27ft 5in (8·38m); height 10ft 4in (3·17m).

Weights: Empty 3,450lb (1565kg); (Sea Gladiator) 3,745lb; loaded 4,750lb (2155kg); (Sea Gladiator) 5,420lb.

Performance: Maximum speed 253mph (407km/h); (Sea Gladiator) 245mph; initial climb 2,300ft (700m)/min; service ceiling 33,000ft (10,060m); range 440 miles (708km); (Sea Gladiator) 425 miles.

Armament: First 71 aircraft, two 0·303in Vickers in fuselage, one 0·303in Lewis under each lower wing; subsequent, four 0·303in Brownings in same locations, fuselage guns with 600 rounds and wing guns with 400.

History: First flight (S.S.37) September 1934; (Gladiator I) June 1936; (Sea Gladiator) 1938; service delivery March 1937; final delivery April 1940.

Users: Belgium, China, Egypt, Finland, Greece, Iraq, Ireland, Latvia, Lithuania, Norway, Portugal, South Africa, Sweden, UK (RAF, RN).

Development: Air Ministry Specification F.7/30 recognised that future fighters would have to be faster and better armed, but the delay in placing an order extended to a disgraceful 4½ years, by which time war clouds were distantly gathering and the fabric-covered biplane was swiftly to be judged obsolete. Folland's S.S.37 was built as a very late entrant, long after the competition to F.7/30 ought to have been settled. Though less radical than most contenders it was eventually judged best and, as the Gladiator, was at last ordered in July 1935. Features included neat single-bay wings, each of the four planes having small hydraulically depressed drag flaps; cantilever landing gear with Dowty internally sprung wheels; four guns; and, in the production aircraft, a sliding cockpit canopy. Most early production had the Watts wooden propeller, though performance was better with the three-blade metal Fairey-Reed type. The Mk II aircraft introduced desert filters, auto mixture control and electric starter from internal battery. The Sea Gladiator had full carrier equipment and a dinghy. Total production amounted to at least 767, including 480 for the RAF, 60 Sea Gladiators and

Right: This Gladiator I, seen in service with No 73 Sqn just before the war, was one of the second production batch, K7892-8077. K7939 was the first to be fitted with the Browning gun in place of the Vickers/Lewis combination. All this batch had the Watts propeller, very like that fitted to the pre-1940 Hurricane I. Sea Gladiators could be distinguished by the belly dinghy fairing.

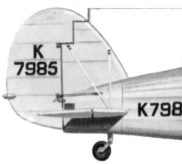

216 exported to 12 foreign countries. Gladiators of the Auxiliary Air Force intercepted the first bombing raid on Britain, over the Firth of Forth in September 1939, and these highly manoeuvrable biplanes were constantly in heroic action for the next three years. Aircraft from the torpedoed *Glorious* operated from a frozen lake in Norway and three Sea Gladiators defended Malta against the Regia Aeronautica from 11 June 1940.

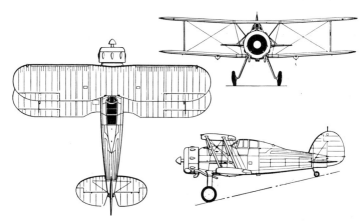

Above: Gloster Gladiator I (Mk II almost identical).

Below: This Gladiator destined for Latvia was one of 14 export versions, some of which saw action during World War II.

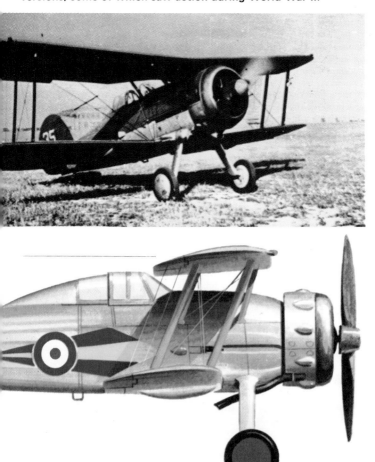

Gloster G.41 Meteor

G.41 Meteor I and III

Origin: Gloster Aircraft Company; (post-war, other builders).
Type: Single-seat fighter.
Engines: Two Rolls-Royce centrifugal turbojets (sub-types, see text).
Dimensions: Span 43ft 0in (13·1m); length 41ft 4in (12·6m); height 13ft 0in (3·96m).
Weights: Empty 8,140lb (3693kg); loaded 13,800lb (6260kg).
Performance: Maximum speed (I) 410mph (660km/h); initial climb (I) 2,155ft (657m)/min; service ceiling 40,000–44,000ft (12,192–13,410m); range on internal fuel about 1,000 miles at altitude (1610km).
Armament: Four 20mm Hispano cannon on sides of nose.
History: First flight (prototype) 5 March 1943; squadron delivery (F.I) 12 July 1944.
Users: UK (RAF), US (AAF, one, on exchange); (post-war, many air forces).

Development: Designed to Specification F.9/40 by George Carter, the Gloster G.41 was to have been named Thunderbolt, but when this name was given to the P-47 the Gloster twin-jet became the Meteor. The first Allied jet combat design, it was surprisingly large, with generous wing area. Though this made the early marks poor performers even on two engines, it proved beneficial in the long term, because marvellous engine development by Rolls-Royce transformed the Meteor into a multi-role aircraft with outstanding speed, acceleration and climb and, thanks to its ample proportions, it could be developed for such challenging roles as advanced dual training, long-range reconnaissance and two-seat night fighting. Initial development was protracted, not because of the revolutionary engines but because of the ailerons, tail and nosewheel. Several engines were used. First flight was with two Halford H.1, later called de Havilland Goblin; second, on 12 June 1943, was with Rolls-Royce Welland (W.2B/23); third, on 13 November 1943, was with Metrovick F.2 axials. The Welland, rated at 1,700lb, was chosen for the first batch of 16 Meteor Is, which entered service on 12 July 1944 with one flight of 616 Sqn, the pilots having previously converted. This was eight days before the first nine Me 262s of KG51 entered service. The first task of the new jet was to chase flying bombs, and even the Meteor I soon showed that it was formidable (though the guns jammed on the first encounter and F/O Dean finally succeeded by daringly tipping the missile over with his wing tip). The first major production version was the F.III, with 2,000lb Derwent 1s, extra tankage, sliding canopy and, on the last 15, longer nacelles. The Mk 4 introduced the redesigned Derwent 5 of 3,500lb thrust, with bigger nacelles on a wing whose tips were clipped to improve speed and rate of roll. In 1945 a Mk 4 set a world speed record at 606mph, raised the following year to 616mph. There were many post-war versions.

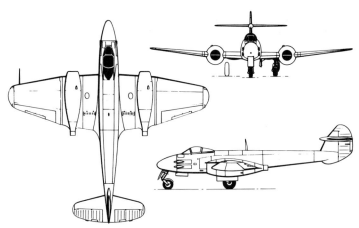

Above: Gloster Meteor F.III (Welland or Derwent engines similar).

Below left: An original Meteor F.I fighter with 616 Sqn in July 1944. Provision was made for six cannon, two being omitted.

Below: The Meteor F.III is distinguished from the F.I by its neat sliding canopy. From No 15 (EE245) the engine was the Derwent.

Hawker Hurricane

Hurricane I to XII, Sea Hurricane IA to XIIA

Origin: Hawker Aircraft Ltd; also built by Gloster Aircraft, SABCA (Belgium) and Canadian Car & Foundry Inc.

Type: Single-seat fighter; later, fighter-bomber, tank buster and ship-based fighter.

Engine: One Rolls-Royce Merlin vee-12 liquid-cooled (see text for sub-types).

Dimensions: Span 40ft (12·19m); length 32ft (9·75m); (Mk I) 31ft 5in; (Sea Hurricanes) 32ft 3in; height 13ft 1in (4m).

Weights: Empty (I) 4,670lb (2118kg); (IIA) 5,150lb (2335kg); (IIC) 5,640lb (2558kg); (IID) 5,800lb (2631kg); (IV) 5,550lb (2515kg); (Sea H.IIC) 5,788lb (2625kg); loaded (I) 6,600lb (2994kg); (IIA) 8,050lb (3650kg); (IIC) 8,250lb (3742kg); (IID) 8,200lb (3719kg); (IV) 8,450lb (3832kg); (Sea H. IIC) 8,100lb (3674kg).

Performance: Maximum speed (I) 318mph (511km/h); (IIA, B, C) 345–335mph (560–540km/h); (IID) 286mph (460km/h); (IV) 330mph (531km/h); (Sea H. IIC) 342mph (550km/h); initial climb (I) 2,520ft (770m)/min; (IIA) 3,150ft (960m)/min; (rest, typical) 2,700ft (825m)/min; service ceiling (I) 36,000ft (10.973m); (IIA) 41,000ft (12,500m); (rest, typical) 34,000ft (10,365m); range (all, typical) 460 miles (740km), or with two 44 Imp gal drop tanks 950 miles (1530km).

Armament: (I) eight 0·303in Brownings, each with 333 rounds (Belgian model, four 0·5in FN-Brownings); (IIA) same, with provision for 12 guns and two 250lb bombs; (IIB) 12 Brownings and two 250 or 500lb bombs; (IIC) four 20mm Hispano cannon and bombs; (IID) two 40mm Vickers S guns and two 0·303in Brownings; (IV) universal wing with two Brownings and two Vickers S, two 500lb bombs, eight rockets, smoke installation or other stores.

History: First flight (prototype) 6 November 1935; (production Mk I) 12 October 1937; (II) 11 June 1940; (Canadian Mk X) January 1940; final delivery September 1944.

Users: (Wartime) Australia, Belgium, Canada, Czechoslovakia, Egypt, Finland, India, Iran, Iraq, Ireland, Jugoslavia, New Zealand, Poland, Portugal, Romania, South Africa, Soviet Union, Turkey, UK (RAF, RN).

continued ▶

Above: This Mk I, seen in the markings of No 73 Sqn based at Rouviers, France, in 1939, was one of a batch of 500 built by Gloster. P2682 of this batch was the first with the Rotol propeller.

Right: A much later Hurricane, this Mk IIC, HL716, was one of a batch of 388 built in 1942. Note Vokes filter, drop tanks and Pacific-area markings.

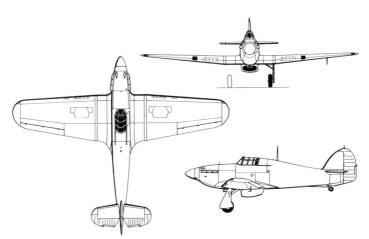

Above: Hawker Hurricane I with stressed-skin wings.

Above: The original Hawker F.36/34 prototype, flying from Brooklands in 1935. Obvious changes to produce the Hurricane included removal of the tailplane strut and addition of the rear underfin, radio and guns, but in fact the largest modification was redesign of the engine installation because of a major change in the Merlin. The official title of K5083 was Hawker High-Speed Monoplane.

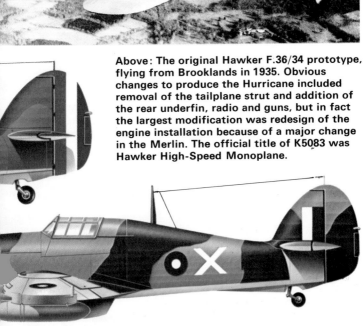

Development: Until well into 1941 the Hurricane was by far the most numerous of the RAF's combat aircraft and it bore the brunt of the early combats with the Luftwaffe over France and Britain. Designed by Camm as a Fury Monoplane, with Goshawk engine and spatted landing gear, it was altered on the drawing board to have the more powerful PV.12 (Merlin) and inwards-retracting gear and, later, to have not four machine guns but the unprecedented total of eight. The Air Ministry wrote Specification F.36/34 around it and after tests with the prototype ordered the then-fantastic total of 600 in June 1936. In September 1939 the 497 delivered equipped 18 squadrons and by 7 August 1940 no fewer than 2,309 had been delivered, compared with 1,383 Spitfires, equipping 32 squadrons, compared with 18½ Spitfire squadrons. Gloster's output in 1940 was 130 per month. By this time the Hurricane I was in service with new metal-skinned wings, instead of fabric, and three-blade variable pitch (later constant-speed) propeller instead of the wooden Watts two-blader. In the hectic days of 1940 the Hurricane was found to be an ideal bomber destroyer, with steady sighting and devastating cone of fire; turn radius was better than that of any other ▶

Below: Belgian MK I (armament, four 0.5in FN Browning) of 2 Esc ''Le Chardon'' of Regiment I/2 at Diest, 1940.

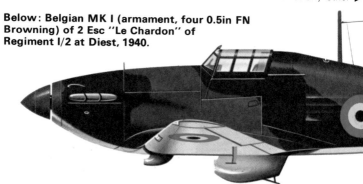

Above: Pilots of No 257 Sqn race over a snowy Martlesham Heath towards their Hurricanes in early 1941.

Below: An idyllic study of a Hurricane I (one of a batch of 600 built by Gloster) with two Spitfire IIs from a batch of 1,000 built at Castle Bromwich, all with an Operational Training Unit, 1942.

Above: A Hurricane I for Yugoslavia being factory-tested near Brooklands in early 1939. Many of the Yugoslav Hurricanes saw action against the Luftwaffe in early 1941.

Right: another export customer for this great warplane was Finland, a dozen being sent freely to help in the Winter War in late 1939. Survivors later become Britain's enemies.

Below right: "Last of the Many", the final Hurricane (PZ865, a IIC bomber) delivered in September 1944.

monoplane fighter, but the all-round performance of the Bf 109E was considerably higher. The more powerful Mk II replaced the 1,030hp Merlin II by the 1,280hp Merlin XX and introduced new armament and drop tanks. In North West Europe it became a ground-attack aircraft, and in North Africa a tank-buster with 40mm guns. While operating from merchant-ship catapults and carriers it took part in countless fleet-defence actions, the greatest being the defence of the August 1942 Malta convoy, when 70 Sea Hurricanes fought off more than 600 Axis attackers, destroying 39 for the loss of seven fighters. The Hurricane was increasingly transferred to the Far East, Africa and other theatres, and 2,952 were dispatched to the Soviet Union, some receiving skis. Hurricanes were used for many special trials of armament and novel flight techniques (one having a jettisonable biplane upper wing). Total production amounted to 12,780 in Britain and 1,451 in Canada (after 1941 with Packard Merlins) and many hundreds were exported both before and after World War II.

Above: BE485 was a Mk II bomber built at Langley in 1941. The revelation that the Hurricane could carry bombs was a small fillip to morale at a dark period of the war. At first only the 250-pounder could be carried (as here); later the wing hardpoint took 500-pounders, or eight rockets, drop tanks, SBCs (small bomb containers), 40mm anti-tank guns or smoke apparatus.

Hawker Tempest

Tempest V and VI

Origin: Hawker Aircraft Ltd; Mk II, Bristol Aeroplane Company.
Type: Single-seat fighter bomber.
Engine: (V) one 2,180hp Napier Sabre II 24-cylinder flat-H sleeve-valve liquid-cooled; (VI) one 2,340hp Sabre V.
Dimensions: Span 41ft (12·5m); length 33ft 8in (10·26m); height 16ft 1in (4·9m).
Weights: Empty 9,100lb (4128kg); loaded 13,500lb (6130kg).
Performance: Maximum speed (V) 427mph (688km/h); (VI) 438mph (704km/h); initial climb 3,000ft (914m)/min; service ceiling, about 37,000ft (11,280m); range (bombs, not tanks) 740 miles (1191km).
Armament: Four 20mm Hispano cannon in outer wings; underwing racks for eight rockets or up to 2,000lb (907kg) bombs.
History: First flight (prototype Mk V) 2 September 1942; (Mk I) 24 February 1943; (production V) 21 June 1943; (Mk II) 28 June 1943; (prototype VI) 9 May 1944; (production II) 4 October 1944.
Users: New Zealand, UK (RAF).

Development: The Typhoon was noted for its thick wing — occasional erratic flight behaviour at high speeds was traced to compressibility (local airflow exceeding the speed of sound), which had never before been encountered. In 1940 Hawker schemed a new laminar-flow wing with a root thickness five inches less and an elliptic planform rather like a Spitfire. This was used on the Typhoon II, ordered in November 1941 to Specification F.10/41, but there were so many changes the fighter was renamed Tempest. Fuel had to be moved from the thinner wing to the fuselage, making the latter longer, and a dorsal fin was added. The short-barrel Mk V guns were buried in the wing. Though the new airframe could take the promising Centaurus engine it was the Sabre-engined Mk V that was produced first, reaching the Newchurch Wing in time to destroy 638 out of the RAF's total of 1,771 flying bombs shot down in the summer of 1944. After building 800 Mk Vs Hawker turned out 142 of the more powerful Mk VI type with bigger radiator and oil coolers in the leading edge. After much delay, with production assigned first to Gloster and then to Bristol, the Centaurus-powered Mk II — much quieter and nicer to fly — entered service in November 1945, and thus missed the war. A few Mks 5 and 6 (post-war designations) were converted as target tugs.

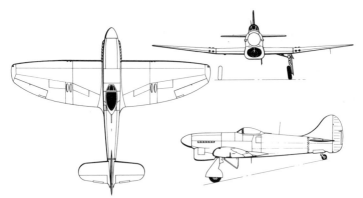

Above: Hawker Tempest V, the first version in service.

Above: The first production Tempest, JN729 (a Mk V, Series 1) on test from Langley, near Slough. It first flew in June 1943, but by now its wing has become well scuffed by boots and the fuselage blackened by exhaust.

Left: NV768 was built as a Mk V Series 2, and then modified with wing-root oil coolers like a MkVI and used for experiments with annular radiators and even giant ducted spinners.

Hawker Typhoon

Typhoon IA and IB

Origin: Hawker Aircraft Ltd; built by Gloster Aircraft Company.
Type: Single-seat fighter bomber.
Engine: (Production IB) one 2,180hp Napier Sabre II, 24-cylinder flat-H sleeve-valve liquid-cooled.
Dimensions: Span 41ft 7in (12·67m); length 31ft 11in (9·73m); height 15ft 3½in (4·66m).
Weights: Empty 8,800lb (3992kg); loaded 13,250lb (6010kg).
Performance: Maximum speed 412mph (664km/h); initial climb 3,000ft (914m)/min; service ceiling 35,200ft (10,730m); range (with bombs) 510 miles (821km), (with drop tanks) 980 miles (1577km).
Armament: (IA) 12 0·303in Brownings (none delivered); (IB) four 20mm Hispano cannon in outer wings, and racks for eight rockets or two 500lb (227kg) (later 1,000lb, 454kg) bombs.
History: First flight (Tornado) October 1939; (Typhoon) 24 February 1940; (production Typhoon) 27 May 1941; final delivery November 1945.
Users: Canada, New Zealand, UK (RAF).

Development: The Typhoon's early life was almost total disaster. Though the concept of so big and powerful a combat aircraft was bold and significant, expressed in Specification F.18/37, the Griffon and Centaurus engines were ignored and reliance was placed on the complex and untried Vulture and Sabre. The former powered the R-type fighter, later named Tornado, which ground to a halt with abandonment of the Vulture in early 1941. The N-type (Napier), named Typhoon, was held back six months by the desperate need for Hurricanes. Eventually, after most painful development, production began at Gloster Aircraft in 1941 and Nos 56 and 609 Sqns at Duxford began to re-equip with the big bluff-looking machine in September of that year. But the Sabre was unreliable, rate of climb and performance at height were disappointing and the rear fuselage persisted in coming apart.

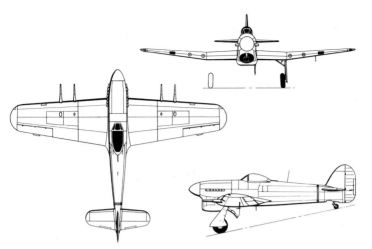

Above: Hawker Typhoon IB with sliding canopy and whip aerial.

There was much talk of scrapping the programme, but, fortunately for the Allies, the snags were gradually overcome. In November 1942 the Typhoon suddenly sprang to favour by demonstrating it could catch and destroy the fastest fighter-bombers in the Luftwaffe which were making low-level hit-and-run raids. In 1943 "Tiffy" squadrons shot-up and blasted everything that moved in northern France and the Low Countries, and in the summer of 1944 the hundreds of Typhoons — by now thoroughly proven and capable of round-the-clock operation from rough forward strips — formed the backbone of 2nd Tactical Air Force attack strength, sending millions of cannon shells, rockets and heavy bombs into German ground forces and in a single day knocking out 175 tanks in the Falaise gap. Gloster built 3,315 of the 3,330 Typhoons, the final 3,000-odd having a clear bubble hood instead of a heavy-framed cockpit with a car-type door on each side. ▶

Above left: MN304 was one of a batch of 800 Mk IBs (all of them made by Gloster) with sliding canopy, faired guns (like all Typhoons depicted here) and rocket rails. The serial is repeated in white on the fin.

Above: JP853, an early Mk IB.

Left: An early MK IB, seen bombed-up, with 198 Sqn, based at Martragny, France, July 1944.

Above: JR128 came earlier in a production batch of 600 than JR371, illustrated on the previous page, yet it has the later type of canopy (a vast improvement inspired by the canopy of the Fw 190). Final batches of Typhoons had four-blade propellers.

Right: In an exceptional blast-proof dispersal, a Mk IB of 175 Sqn is serviced between flights and bombed up with 500-pounders. The photograph was probably taken in 1943, long before the use of D-Day "invasion stripes" which appeared on 5 June 1944 on all Allied combat aircraft. The Typhoon was thought to be easily mistaken for an Fw 190, and so was adorned with black and white stripes!

Supermarine Spitfire and Seafire

Mks I to 24 and Seafire I, III, XV, XVII and 45-47

Origin: Supermarine Aviation Works (Vickers) Ltd; also built by Vickers-Armstrongs, Castle Bromwich, and Westland Aircraft; (Seafire) Cunliffe-Owen Aircraft and Westland.

Type: Single-seat fighter, fighter-bomber or reconnaissance; (Seafire) carrier-based fighter.

Engine: One Rolls-Royce Merlin or Griffon vee-12 liquid-cooled (see text).

Dimensions: Span 36ft 10in (11·23m), clipped, 32ft 2in, or, more often, 32ft 7in (9·93m), extended, 40ft 2in (12·24m); length 29ft 11in (9·12m), later, with two-stage engine, typically 31ft 3½in (9·54m), Griffon engine, typically 32ft 8in (9·96m), final (eg Seafire 47) 34ft 4in (10·46m); height 11ft 5in (3·48m), with Griffon, typically 12ft 9in (3·89m).

Weights: Empty (Mk I) 4,810lb (2182kg); (IX) 5,610lb (2545kg); (XIV) 6,700lb (3040kg); (Sea.47) 7,625lb (3458kg); maximum loaded (I) 5,784lb (2624kg); (IX) 9,500lb (4310kg); (XIV) 10,280lb (4663kg); Sea.47) 12,750lb (5784kg).

Performance: Maximum speed (I) 355–362mph (580km/h); (IX) 408mph (657km/h); (XIV) 448mph (721km/h); (Sea.47) 451mph (724km/h); initial climb (I) 2,530ft (770m)/min; (IX) 4,100ft (1250m)/min; (XIV) 4,580ft (1396m)/min; (Sea.47) 4,800ft (1463m)/min; range on internal fuel (I) 395 miles (637km); (IX) 434 miles (700km); (XIV) 460 miles (740km); (Sea.47) 405 miles (652km).

Armament: See "Development" text.

History: First flight (prototype) 5 March 1936; (production Mk I) July 1938; final delivery (Mk 24) October 1947.

Users: (Wartime) Australia, Canada, Czechoslovakia, Egypt, France, Italy (CB), Jugoslavia, Netherlands, Norway, Poland, Portugal, South Africa, Soviet Union, Turkey, UK (RAF, RN), US (AAF).

Development: Possibly the most famous combat aircraft in history, the Spitfire was designed by the dying Reginald Mitchell to Specification F.37/34 using the new Rolls-Royce PV.12 engine later named Merlin. It was the first all-metal stressed-skin fighter to go into production in Britain. The following were main versions.

I Initial version, 450 ordered in June 1936 with 1,030hp Merlin II, two-blade fixed-pitch propeller and four 0·303in Browning guns. Later Mk IA with eight guns, bulged canopy and three-blade DH v-p propeller and Mk IB with two 20mm Hispano and four 0·303. Production: 1,566.

II Mk I built at Castle Bromwich with 1,175hp Merlin· XII and Rotol propeller. Production: 750 IIA (eight 0·303), 170 IIB (two 20mm, four 0·303).

III Single experimental model; strengthened Mk I with many changes.

Below: This Mk IIA, flown by S/L Don Finlay, CO of 41 Sqn at Hornchurch in 1940, was the gift of members of the ROC.

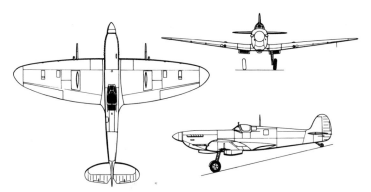

Above: Supermarine Spitfire F.IX.

IV Confusing because Mk IV was first Griffon-engined, one built. Then unarmed Merlin photo-reconnaissance Mk IV delivered in quantity. Production: 229.

V Like PR.IV powered by 1,440hp Merlin 45, many detail changes, main fighter version 1941–42 in three forms: VA, eight 0·303; VB, two 20mm and four 0·303; VC "universal" wing with choice of guns plus two 250lb (113kg) bombs. All with centreline rack for 500lb (227kg) bomb or tank. Many with clipped wings and/or tropical filter under nose. Production: VA, 94; VB, 3,923; VC, 2,447.

VI High-altitude interim interceptor, 1,415hp Merlin 47, pressurised cockpit, two 20mm and four 0·303. Production: 100.   ***continued*** ▶

Above: Basically tougher and more powerful than the Mks I and II, the V was the standard version in production in 1941. More were built (6,464) than any other single mark. R6923 was one of many built as a Mk I and converted to a VB. It went to the first user of this mark, 92 Sqn, in March 1941. Below about 15,000 feet it could hold its own, but the Fw 190 was so superior at altitude that the Spitfire IX had hurriedly to be produced, mating the two-stage Merlin with the Mk V airframe.

Above: BL479 was a Spitfire LF.VB, with clipped wings which, with the low-blown Merlin 45 or 50 series engine, produced a fighter mediocre above 20,000 feet but formidable at low level. It was one of a batch of 1,000 built at Castle Bromwich in 1941.

Left: BR195 was one of more than 2,000 Mk V series to be tropicalised by the addition of a Vokes sand filter. The basic Mk V was not particularly sprightly, and with the filter became slower than any mark except the early Seafires. These Spits are seen with 417 Sqn RCAF in Sicily in 1943. They are Mk VCs with the universal wing able to carry any armament fit or various loads of external stores (but the only drop-tank location was on the centreline).

VII High-altitude, extended wing-tips, new 1,660hp Merlin 61 with two-stage supercharger (and symmetrical underwing radiators); retractable tailwheel, later broad and pointed rudder. Pressurised cockpit. Production: 140.

VIII Followed interim Mk IX, virtually unpressurised Mk VII in LF (low-altitude, clipped), F (standard) and HF (high-altitude, extended) versions. Production: 1,658.

IX Urgent version to counter Fw 190, quick lash-up of V with Merlin 61; again LF, F and HF versions, plus IXE with two 20mm and two 0·5in. Production: 5,665.

X Pressurised photo-reconnaissance, Merlin 77, whole leading edge forming fuel tank. Production: 16.

XI As X but unpressurised, 1,760hp Merlin 63A or 1,655hp Merlin 70. Mainstay of Photo Reconnaissance Unit 1943—45. Production: 471.

XII Low altitude to counter Fw 190 hit-and-run bomber, 1,735hp Griffon III or IV, strengthened VC or VIII airframe, clipped. Production: 100.

XIII Low-level reconnaissance, low-rated 1,620hp Merlin 32, four 0·303. Production: 16.

XIV First with two-stage Griffon, 2,050hp Mk 65 with deep symmetric radiators and five-blade propeller, completely redesigned airframe with new fuselage, broad fin/rudder, inboard ailerons, retractable tailwheel. F.XIV, two 20mm and four 0·303; F.XIVE, two 20mm and two 0·5in; FR.XIVE, same guns, cut-down rear fuselage and teardrop hood, clipped wings, F.24 camera and extra fuel. Active in 1944, destroyed over 300 flying bombs. Production: 957.

XVI As Mk IX but 1,705hp Packard Merlin 266; LF.IXE, E-guns and clipped, many with teardrop hood, extra fuel. Production: 1,054.

XVIII Definitive wartime fighter derived from interim XIV, extra fuel, stronger, F and FR versions, some of latter even more fuel and tropical equipment. Production: 300.

XIX Final photo-reconnaissance, 2,050hp Griffon 65 and unpressurised, then Griffon 66 with pressure cabin and increased wing tankage; both option of deep slipper tank for 1,800 mile (2900km) range. Made last RAF Spitfire sortie, Malaya, 1 April 1954. Production: 225.

21 Post-war, redesigned aircraft with different structure and shape, 2,050hp Griffon 65 or 85, four 20mm and 1,000lb (454kg) bombs. Production: 122.

22 Bubble hood, 24-volt electrics, some with 2,375hp Griffon 65 and contraprop. Production: 278.

24 Redesigned tail, short-barrel cannon, zero-length rocket launchers. Production: 54. Total Spitfire production 20,334.

Seafire IB Navalised Spitfire VB, usually 1,415hp low-rated Merlin 46. Fixed wings but hook and slinging points. Conversions: 166.

IIC Catapult spools, strengthened landing gear, 1,645hp Merlin 32 and four-blade propeller. Various sub-types, Universal wing. Production: 262 Supermarine, 110 Westland.

III Manual double-fold wing, 1,585hp Merlin 55M, various versions. Production: 870 Westland, 350 Cunliffe-Owen.

XV (Later F.15) 1,850hp Griffon VI, four-blade, asymmetric radiators, cross between Seafire III and Spitfire XII. Production: 390.

XVII (F.17) Increased fuel, cut-down fuselage and bubble hood. Production: (cut by war's end): 232.

45 New aircraft entirely, corresponding to Spitfire 21; Griffon 61 (five-blade) or 85 (contraprop); fixed wing, four 20mm. Production: 50.

46 Bubble hood like Spitfire 22. Production: 24.

47 Navalised Spitfire 24, hydraulically folding wings, carb-air intake just behind propeller, increased fuel. Fought in Malaya and Korea. Production: 140. Total Seafires: 2,556.

Left: When the Mk IB and IIB appeared with two 20mm Hispanos the fact was obvious to German pilots from the long faired barrels and the blisters over the ammunition drums. They found the Mk IX, however, hard to tell from a Mk V at a distance, and from 1942 had to respect all Spitfires due to the Merlin 61.

Below: Post-war models included the F.21 (LA217) and F.22 (PK312).

Westland Whirlwind

Whirlwind I, IA

Origin: Westland Aircraft Ltd.
Type: Single-seat day fighter (later fighter-bomber).
Engines: Two 885hp Rolls-Royce Peregrine I vee-12 liquid-cooled.
Dimensions: Span 45ft (13·72m); length 32ft 9in (9·98m); height 11ft 7in (3·52m).
Weights: Empty (I) 7,840lb (3699kg); (IA) 8,310lb (3770kg); maximum loaded 10,270lb (4658kg); (IA) 11,388lb (5166kg).
Performance: Maximum speed (clean) 360mph (580km/h), (with bombs) 270mph (435km/h); initial climb (clean) 3,000ft (915m)/min; service ceiling (clean) 30,000ft (9144m); range, not recorded but about 800 miles (1290km).
Armament: Standard, four 20mm Hispano Mk I cannon in nose, each with 60-round drum; IA added underwing racks for bomb load up to 1,000lb (454kg).
History: First flight 11 October 1938; service delivery June 1940; final delivery December 1941.
User: UK (RAF).

Development: At the outbreak of World War II the gravest deficiency of the RAF was in the field of twin-engined high-performance machines for use as long-range escort or night fighters. This was precisely the mission of

Below: Though flown in 1938 the distinctive Whirlwind was kept secret from the British public for nearly four years, though it was known to be included in Luftwaffe recognition handbooks in 1940. This Mk I was operated from Exeter by 263 Sqn in 1941, occasionally venturing on "Rhubarb" offensive sweeps over France.

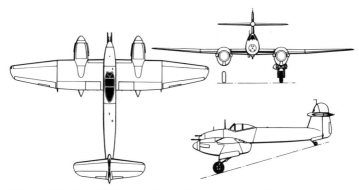

Above: Westland Whirlwind I, without bomb racks.

the Whirlwind, designed to a specification as early as F.37/35. It was a fine and pleasant machine, and in its slender nose was an unprecedented punch. Yet its development was delayed by engine troubles, the Peregrine being an unhappy outgrowth of the reliable Kestrel; another trouble was that, despite Fowler flaps, the landing speed was 80mph which was incompatible with short grass fields. Eventually only 263 and 137 Sqns used the type, which in combat showed much promise. In August 1941 No 263 escorted Blenheims to Cologne in daylight! Only 112 were built, ending their days as "Whirlibombers" on cross-Channel "Rhubarb" sorties strafing and bombing targets of opportunity.

Below: Specification F.37/35 did not stipulate use of two engines but it did call for armament of four 20mm cannon. At the time this was a tremendous armament, and it was most successfully carried into effect by the Westland company. The Achilles heel of the Whirlwind was its weak and unreliable engine. With Merlins it could have been a real world-beater, especially with handed propellers. With Peregrines it was useless, and the last 88 of the 200 ordered were cancelled. Their only effective use was as bombers, after conversion in late 1941.

SOVIET UNION

When Hitler's terrible war machine was unleashed against the USSR on 22 June 1941 the plan was to wipe out almost all the Red Army and VVS (air force) in a matter of weeks. The plan almost came off; even the Russians admitted the loss of over 1,200 aircraft in the first nine hours, and after a week more than 90 per cent of the Soviet front-line strength had ceased to exist.

So secretive had the Russians been that the world learned of their aircraft from pictures put out by the Germans. The only two fighters were thought to be the Chato biplane and Rata monoplane, and the names were uncomplimentary ones bestowed by Franco's pilots in Spain! Not until about 1960 did students of Soviet airpower really begin to piece together the impressive story of what had been accomplished by the Soviet OKBs (design bureaus).

Numerically the Chato and Rata (actually the I-15 and I-16) had indeed been the chief fighters in 1941, but much better machines were in production. The LaGGs, MiGs and Yaks were destined to be produced in quantities fantastic by any yardstick, despite the need in the autumn of 1941 to evacuate most of the original plants and set up new production facilities far to the east. Gradually, and at horrific cost, the command of the sky on the Eastern Front was to be wrested from the

The LaGG-3 was one of several indifferent Russian types whose main assets were robustness and simplicity. This one, with an unusual enlarged tail wheel, was captured by the Finns in 1942.

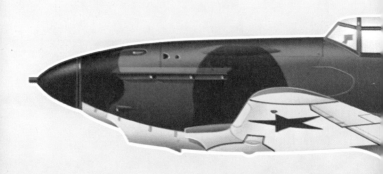

enemy. A small part was played by fighters sent from the USA and Britain, and by non-Russian pilots (notably Poles, Czechs and Frenchmen). It is significant that the élite among these foreign units chose Russian aircraft.

By Western standards the Soviet fighters were crude, small and poorly armed. In fact they were designed with painstaking care, to do the best they could in the harsh environment. In 1941 their structures were wood, because aluminium supplies were far from secure. By 1943 light-alloy primary structure, notably in the wings, had provided more room for fuel. By 1944 airframes were all stressed-skin, and greater power allowed the installation of heavier firepower.

More than 90 per cent of the nearly 70,000 fighters made during World War II to Lavochkin or Yakovlev design had just one cannon and two machine guns. The philosophy was: make fighters small, agile and able to outfly the enemy; what use is firepower if it cannot be brought to bear? A weakness of this argument is that it works well only with experienced pilots. In the Luftwaffe the aces often flew the Bf 109F, with Russian-style armament, and racked up scores topping 200 or even 300. The common herd preferred more guns; and most of the Russian pilots did not last long enough to rise above the common herd.

Lavochkin La-5 and La-7

La-5, -5FN, -7 and -7U

Origin: The design bureau of S. A. Lavochkin.
Type: Single-seat fighter (-7U, dual-control trainer).
Engine: (Original La-5) one 1,330hp Shvetsov M-82A or M-82F 14-cylinder two-row radial; (all other versions) one 1,700hp M-82FN.
Dimensions: Span 32ft 2in (9·8m); length 27ft 10¾in (8·46m); height 9ft 3in (2·84m).
Weights: Empty, no data; loaded (La-5) no data; (La-5FN) 7,406lb (3359kg); (La-7) 7,495lb (3400kg).
Performance: Maximum speed (La-5) 389mph (626km/h); (La-5FN) 403mph (650km/h); (La-7) 423mph (680km/h); initial climb (La-5FN) about 3,600ft (1100m)/min; (La-7) about 3,940ft (1200m)/min; service ceiling (La-5FN) 32,800ft (10,000m); (La-7) 34,448ft (10,500m); range (La-5) 398 miles (640km); (La-5FN) 475 miles (765km); (La-7) 392 miles (630km).
Armament: (La-5, -5FN) two 20mm ShVAK cannon, each with 200 rounds, above engine; optional underwing racks for light bombs up to total of 330lb (150kg); (La-7) three faster-firing ShVAK (one on right, two on left); underwing racks for six RS-82 rockets or two 220lb (100kg) bombs.
History: First flight (re-engined LaGG-3) January 1942; (production La-5) June 1942; (La-5FN) late 1942; (La-7) about June 1943.
User: Soviet Union.

Development: Though the LaGG-3 was a serviceable fighter that used wood rather than scarce light alloys, it was the poorest performer of the new crop of combat aircraft with which the VVS-RKKA (Soviet Military Aviation Defence Forces) sought to halt the German invader. It was natural that urgent consideration should be given to ways of improving it and during 1941 Lavochkin's team converted one LaGG-3 to have an M-82 radial engine. Despite its fractionally greater installed drag (a matter of 1%) it offered speed increased from 353 or 373mph and, in particular, improved all-round performance at height. The liquid-cooled fighter was cancelled in May 1942, all production switching to the new machine, designated LaGG-5. But within a matter of weeks this in turn was replaced on the assembly line by a further improvement, tested as a prototype early in 1942, with a new fuselage ▶

Right: The La-7 was aerodynamically cleaned-up compared with the otherwise similar La-5FN, the most obvious change being relocation of the supercharger duct in the left wing root. This example was Moscow-built, with two ShVAK guns.

Below: Unusual because of its shorter supercharger air inlet duct above the engine, this La-5FN is typical of about 15,000 fighters of this type flown by pilots from at least nine Allied countries.

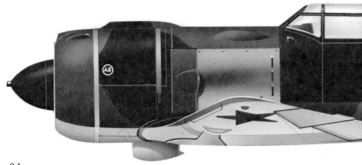

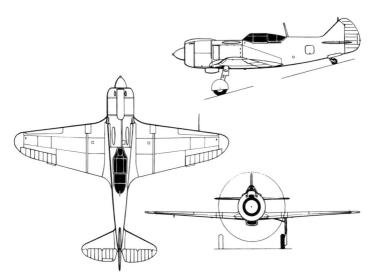

Above: Lavochkin La-5FN with standard twin-ShVAK armament.

containing two 20mm guns and having a lower rear profile behind a canopy giving all-round vision. This was the La-5 which proved to be 28mph faster than a Bf 109G-2 at below 20,000ft. But the German fighter could outclimb it and efforts were made to reduce weight. The resulting La-5FN had an FN (boosted) engine, lighter wing with metal spars and overall weight 379lb (presumably on both empty and gross weight) less. Thousands of -5FNs participated in the huge battles around Kursk and throughout the Eastern front in 1943, demonstrating that Soviet fighters could be more than a match for their opponents. The La-5UTI was a dual trainer. Further refinement led to the harder-hitting La-7, with reduced weight (partly by reducing fuel capacity) and much reduced drag. The -7 and -7U trainer retained the slats and big ailerons that made the Lavochkin fighters such beautiful dog-fighters and were the choice of most of the Soviet aces (Ivan Kozhedub's aircraft is in the Central Soviet Air Force Museum).

Right: A standard La-5FN, distinguished from the La-5 externally by the air duct extended to the front of the engine cowl (the profile drawing on the preceding pages shows an alternative, shorter La-5FN duct unlike that on the original La-5).

Below: Inscribed "In the name of Hero of the Soviet Union Lt-Col N. Koniev", this La-5FN was flown by top-scoring ace Ivan Kozhedub in 1944. Later that year, with 176 IAP, he changed to a white La-7.

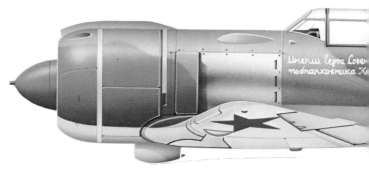

Below: La-5FNs of the 1st Czech (Partisan) IAP operating from Preborsk in 1943.

Lavochkin LaGG-3

I-22, LaGG-1, I-301, LaGG-3

Origin: The design bureau of S. A. Lavochkin, in partnership with Gorbunov and Gudkov.

Type: Single-seat fighter.

Engine: (-1) one 1,050hp Klimov M-105P (VK-105P) vee-12 liquid-cooled; (-3) one 1,240hp M-105PF with improved propeller.

Dimensions: Span 32ft 2in (9·8m); length 29ft $1\frac{1}{4}$in (8·9m); height 8ft 10in (3·22m).

Weights: Empty (-1) 5,952lb (2700kg); (-3) 5,764lb (2620kg); maximum loaded (-1) 6,834lb (3100kg); (-3) 7,257lb (3300kg).

Performance: Maximum speed (-1) 373mph (600km/h); (-3) 348mph (560km/h); initial climb (both) 2,953ft (900m)/min; service ceiling (-1) 31,496ft (9600m); (-3) 29,527ft (9000m); range (both) 404 miles (650km).

Armament: Very varied; typically, one 20mm ShVAK firing through propeller hub, with 120 rounds, two 12·7mm BS above engine, each with 220 rounds, and underwing racks for six RS-82 rockets or various light bombs; LaGGs on Il-2 escort had three 12·7mm and two 7·62mm; some had a 23mm Vla cannon and various combinations of machine guns.

History: First flight (I-22) 30 March 1939; (production LaGG-1) late 1940; (production LaGG-3) 1941; final delivery June 1942.

User: Soviet Union.

continued ▶

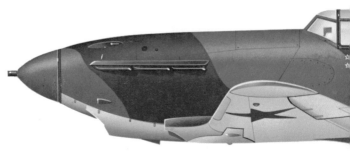

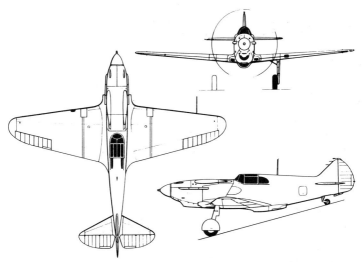

Above: The LaGG-1, which was not fitted with wing slats.

Above: Early LaGG-3 fighters had a prominent horn balance above and below the rudder. This example was operated by an unknown fighter regiment on the Ukrainian front in mid-1942.

Left: A later LaGG with the cleaned-up rudder.

Below: This LaGG-3 was one of those still operational in 1944. It was flown by Yuri Shchipov of 9 IAP, Black Sea Fleet, in the Novorossisk earlier. The lion's head was his personal emblem.

Above: This LaGG-3 had a horn balance at the top of the rudder only. Thickly coated with wax to smooth the exterior, it was flying with the Baltic Fleet when it was shot down over Finland on 6 March 1942. Two-figure numbers were usually the last two digits of the construction number, in this case 070171.

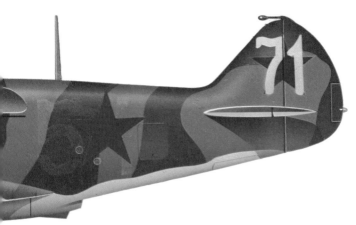

Below: An interesting photograph taken at a winter ceremony at a LaGG-3 regiment. Not only are the aircraft burdened by under-wing RS-82 rockets and 22-GAU (100 litre) drop tanks, but they have ski landing gears which could not retract completely. Performance must have been poor.

Development: Semyon Alekseyevich Lavochkin headed a design committee which included V. P. Gorbunov and M. I. Gudkov in creating the very unusual I-22 fighter prototype of 1938–39. Though outwardly conventional, it was rare among the world's new crop of streamlined monoplane fighters not to have metal stressed-skin construction; instead it was built of wood, except for the control surfaces, which were light alloy with fabric covering, and the flaps which, to avoid damage, were all-metal. The ply skinning was both impregnated and bonded on with phenol-formaldehyde resin, which at the time seemed quaint but today is very widely used for this purpose. The result was a neat, clean and manoeuvrable fighter, which later showed outstanding robustness and resistance to combat damage. On the other hand it was inferior to other Russian fighters in all-round performance. Several hundred had been delivered, as the LaGG-1, when production was switched to the LaGG-3. This had a better engine, leading-edge slats, and improved armament options. By 1942 all LaGG fighters had internally balanced rudder, retractable tailwheel and wing fuel system for two 22gal drop tanks. Further development led to the switch to an air-cooled radial, from which stemmed all Lavochkin's later piston-engined fighters.

Right: Under test in Japanese hands at Harbin (now Shenyang), this LaGG-3 was flown to a ploughed field in Manchuria by a Russian deserter in 1942. The Japanese were most unimpressed.

Below: This aircraft was built at Plant 153 at Novosibisk, and the non-standard black/green camouflage was paint left over from the tractors previously built there! This aircraft served in the summer of 1942 with the 6th Fighter Aviation Division in the Moscow Corps Command of the IA-PVO.

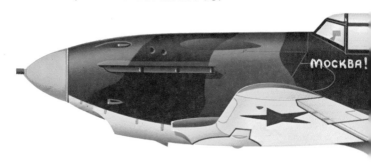

Below: Another LaGG of the 6th Fighter Aviation Division, in this case portrayed in winter camouflage in 1942-3. This was the aircraft of one of the few really successful LaGG-3 pilots, Capt (Col) Gerasim A. Gregoryev, who at this time had 15 confirmed victories. He must have been both skilled and lucky.

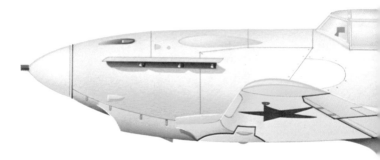

Mikoyan MiG-3

MiG-1 (I-61), MiG-3, MiG-5 and MiG-7

Origin: The design bureau of Mikoyan and Gurevich.
Type: Single-seat fighter.
Engine: (-1) one 1,200hp Mikulin AM-35 vee-12 liquid-cooled; (-3) one 1,350hp AM-35A; (-5) one 1,600hp ASh-82A 14-cylinder radial; (-7) one 1,700hp VK-107A vee-12.
Dimensions: Span (all) 33ft 9½in (10·3m); length (-1, -3) 26ft 9in (8·15m); (-5) about 26ft; (-7) not known; height (-1, -3) reported as 8ft 7in (2·61m).
Weights: Empty (-1) 5,721lb (2595kg); (others) not known; maximum loaded (-1) given as 6,770lb and as 7,290lb; (-3) given as 7,390lb and 7,695lb (3490kg); (-5) normal loaded 7,055lb (3200kg); (-7) not known.
Performance: Maximum speed (-1) 390mph (628km/h); (-3) 398mph (640km/h), (also given as 407mph); (-5) over 400mph; (-7) probably over 440mph; initial climb (-1) 3,280ft (1000m)/min; (-3) 3,937ft (1200m)/min; (-5, -7) not known; service ceiling (-1, -3) 39,370ft (12,000m); (-5) not known; (-7) 42,650ft (13,000m); range (-1) 454 miles (730km); (-3) 776 miles (1250km); (-5, -7) not known.
Armament: (-1, -3) one 12·7mm BS and two 7·62mm ShKAS all in nose, later supplemented as field modification by underwing pods for two further unsynchronised BS; underwing rails for six RS-82 rockets or two bombs up to 220lb (100kg) each or two chemical containers; (-5) as above except four 7·62mm ShKAS disposed around cowling, no BS guns; (-7) not known but probably included 20mm ShVAK firing through propeller hub.
History: First flight (I—61) 5 April (also reported as March) 1940; (production MiG-1) September 1940; (MiG-3) about May 1941; final delivery (MiG-3) late 1941; first flight (-5) 1942; (MiG-7) 1943.
User: Soviet Union.

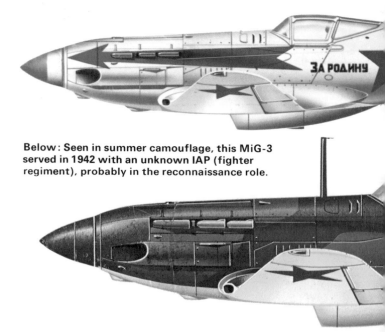

Below: Seen in summer camouflage, this MiG-3 served in 1942 with an unknown IAP (fighter regiment), probably in the reconnaissance role.

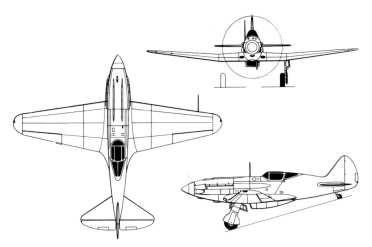

Above: Most MiG-3s had a cockpit canopy and radio mast.

Development: There were probably several new Soviet fighter prototypes in 1938–40, but apart from the Yak-1 information is available on only one other, the I-61 designed by the new partnership of Artem I. Mikoyan and Mikhail I. Gurevich. Though handicapped by its long and heavy engine, which held the armament to a poor level, the mixed wood/metal fighter was a fair performer and went into production as the MiG-1, its only serious vice being an extreme tendency to swing on take-off and landing. In view of the amazing rapidity of its development this was an acceptable penalty and 2,100 are said to have been delivered before it was replaced in production by the refined MiG-3 with more powerful engine, new propeller, additional ▶

Left: One of the few early MiGs to be familiar outside the Soviet Union from wartime photographs, this winter-painted example served in December 1941 with No 34 IAP based at Vnukovo, today one of Moscow's airports and at that time location of the MiG production factory, Zavod 1. IAP 34 was part of the Moscow Western Sector of the IA-PVO, fighter-aviation air defence of the homeland. The inscription meant "For the Fatherland".

fuel tank, increased dihedral and sliding canopy. "Several thousand" are said to have been delivered, but despite adding extra guns they were no match for Luftwaffe fighters and by 1942 were being used for armed reconnaissance and close support. The MiG-5 was used in only small numbers, and few details are available of the all-metal high-altitude MiG-7 with pressurised cockpit.

Below: A winter-painted MiG-3 also seen in the foreground of the photograph, which was taken in early 1942 when the operating unit, 12 IAP, converted from the Yak-1 and was awarded the coveted "Guards" title. Based in Moscow Military District, this unit had wings painted red on the upper surfaces to assist rescue in winter.

Polikarpov I-15 and 153

TsKB-3, I-15, I-15bis, I-153

Origin: The design bureau of Nikolai N. Polikarpov.
Type: Single-seat fighter (15bis, 153, fighter-bomber).
Engine: (15) one 700hp Shvetsov M-25 (Wright Cyclone); (15bis) 750hp M-25B; (153) 1,000hp M-63, all nine-cylinder radials.
Dimensions: Span 29ft 11½in (9·13m); (bis) 33ft 6in; (153) 32ft 9¾in; length 20ft 7½in (6·29m); (bis) 20ft 9¼in; (153) 20ft 3in; height 9ft 7in (2·92m); (bis) 9ft 10in; (153) 9ft 3in.
Weights: Empty 2,597lb (1178kg); (bis) 2,880lb; (153) 3,168lb; maximum loaded 3,027–3,135lb (1370–1422kg); (bis) 4,189lb; (153) 4,431lb.
Performance: Maximum speed 224mph (360km/h); (bis) 230mph; (153) 267mph; initial climb (all) about 2,500ft (765m)/min; service ceiling 32,800ft (10,000m); (bis) 26,245ft; (153) 35,100ft; range 450 miles (720km); (bis) 280 miles; (153) 298 miles.
Armament: Four (sometimes two) 7·62mm DA or ShKAS in fuselage; (bis) as 15, plus two 110lb (50kg) or four 55lb bombs or six RS-82 rockets; (153) as 15bis but two 165lb bombs.
History: First flight (TsKB-3) October 1933; service delivery 1934; service delivery (bis) 1937; (153) 1939.
Users: China, Finland (captured Soviet), Soviet Union, Spain (Republican).

Development: One might jump to the conclusion that these Polikarpov biplanes were superseded by the I-16 monoplane (p. 186). In fact the I-16 flew before any of them, was in service first and, in 1939, was replaced in Mongolia by the more agile I-153! Polikarpov's bureau began work on the TsKB-3 in 1932, when the earlier I-5 was in full production. Unlike the I-5 the new fighter had a small lower wing and large upper gull wing curved down at the roots to meet the fuselage. As the I-15 the highly manoeuvrable fighter gained a world altitude record before serving in very large numbers (about 550) in Spain, where it was dubbed "Chato" (flat-nosed). It even served against the Finns and Luftwaffe, but by 1937 was being replaced by the I-15bis with continuous upper wing carried on struts. Over 300 of these served in Spain, and many were used as dive bombers against the Germans in 1941. The ultimate development was the powerful 153, with retractable landing gear, either wheels or skis folding to the rear. Some

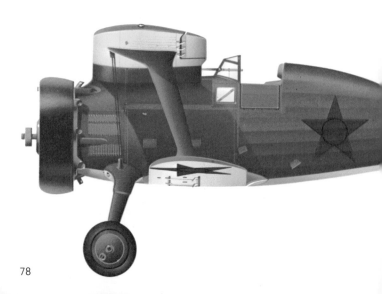

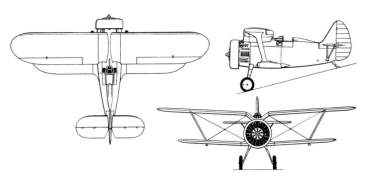

Above: Polikarpov I-15, with guns shown as white dots in front view.

thousands served in the Far East, Spain, Finland and on the Eastern Front. Later sub-types had variable-pitch propellers and drop tanks well outboard under the lower wings. continued ▶

Above: The Luftwaffe estimated the VVS (Red Air Forces) lost 2,200 I-15, 15bis and 153 type fighters in the first week of the German invasion in June 1941. Luftwaffe intelligence officers paid attention to all wrecks discovered. This almost undamaged I-153 has eight RS-82 rocket rails under the outer wings. Extremely agile, the 153 was produced after 1939 at a higher rate than the monoplane I-16.

Left: An I-15 in typical VVS summer livery of the mid-1930s, at which time it was not uncommon for a black circle to be inscribed within the national insignia. Almost all I-15s had light bomb carriers under the lower wings, though RS-82 rocket rails were seen mainly on the later versions. Points of interest include multiple exhaust stubs, Aldis gunsight and small windows on each side at the front of the cockpit.

Right: Even more bizarre than a biplane fighter in production in World War II with retractable landing gear is a fighter of such form with jet propulsion! Ivan Merkulov was one of the Russian pioneers of simple ramjet engines, and this I-153 was one of at least two Polikarpov biplane fighters (the other being an I-152 or I-15bis in early 1940) used as a testbed. In this aircraft the units were designated DM-4, DM standing for "auxiliary motor"; the ramjets were intended simply to boost the speed of fighters for brief periods. In October 1940 this I-153 was measured at 273 mph (440 km/h) at 6,560 ft (2,000 m), compared with a maximum at this height on piston engine alone of 241 mph (388 km/h).

Below: Even in peacetime Soviet fighters had lived rough, seldom having the luxury of a permanent airfield or hangar. This I-153 was photographed in 1942. Note the Hucks engine-start truck.

Polikarpov I-16

I-16 Types 1, 4, 5, 10, 17, 18, 24, SPB and UTI

Origin: The design bureau of Nikolai N. Polikarpov.
Type: Single-seat fighter (except SPB dive bomber and UTI two-seat trainer).
Engine: (Type 1) one 480hp M-22 (modified Bristol Jupiter) nine-cylinder radial; (Type 4) 725hp M-25A (modified Wright Cyclone) of same layout; (Types 5, 10, 17) 775hp M-25B; (Types 18 and 24) 1,000hp Shvetsov M-62R (derived from M-25).
Dimensions: Span 29ft 6½in (9·00m); length (to Type 17) 19ft 11in (6·075 m); (18, 24 and UTI) 20ft 1¼in (6·125m); height (to 17) 8ft 1¼in (2·45m); (18, 24) 8ft 5in (2·56m).
Weights: Empty (1) 2,200lb (998kg); (4, 5, 10) 2,791lb (1266kg); (18) 3,110lb (1410kg); (24) 3,285lb (1490kg); loaded (1) 2,965lb (1345kg); (4) 3,135lb (1422kg); (5) 3,660lb (1660kg); (10) 3,782lb (1715kg); (17) 3,990lb (1810kg); (18) 4,034lb (1830kg); (24) 4,215lb (1912kg) (24 overload, 4,546lb, 2062kg).

Below: This Type 24 served on the Central Sector in 1941. Slogan is "For Stalin!"

It was service for Republican Spain that brought the I-16 to the notice of the outside world. This type 10 is seen in Nationalist markings after the Republican defeat in 1939.

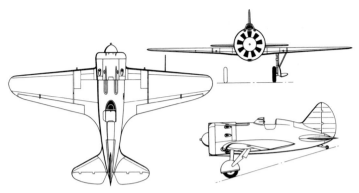

Above: An I-16 Type 24; the ailerons also formed split flaps.

Performance: Maximum speed (1) 224mph (360km/h); (4–18) 280–288 mph (450–465km/h); (24) 326mph (525km/h); initial climb (4–24, typical) 2,790ft (850m)/min; service ceiling (typical) 29,500ft (9000m); range (1–18) 500 miles (800km); (24) 248 miles (400km), (with two 22gal drop tanks, 435 miles, 700km).   *continued* ▶

Below: Many I-16s served with the Chinese; This Type 10 was with the 4th Wing, Chiangkiakow.

Above: A pair of late (M-62 engined) I-16
fighters recorded in a propaganda film made
on the Eastern Front in autumn 1941.

Armament: (1, 4, 5) two 7·62mm ShKAS machine guns in wings; (10) two ShKAS in wings, two in top decking of fuselage; (17) two ShKAS in top decking, two 20mm ShVAK cannon in wings; (18) as 10 or 17; (24) as 17; SPB, various guns plus external bomb load of 220lb (100kg). Many versions were later fitted with underwing rails for two RS-82 rockets.

History: First flight (I-16-1) 31 December 1933; production delivery (1) autumn 1934; (4) autumn 1935; final delivery (24) probably early 1942.

Users: China, Soviet Union, Spain (Republican).

Development: Possibly influenced by the Gee Bee racers of the United States, the TsKB-12, or I-16, was an extremely short and simple little fighter which — perhaps because of its slightly "homebuilt" appearance — was almost ignored by the West. Nobody outside the Soviet Union appeared to notice that this odd fighter, with wooden monocoque body and metal/fabric wing, was a cantilever monoplane with retractable landing gear and v-p propeller, which in its first mass-produced form was 60–75mph faster than contemporary fighters of other countries. It suddenly came into prominence when 475 were shipped to the Spanish Republicans, where its reliability, 1,800 rounds/min guns, manoeuvrability and fast climb and dive surprised its opponents, who called it the "Rata" (rat). A few old Type 10 remained in Spanish use until 1952. Hundreds of several types fought Japanese aircraft over China and Manchuria, where many I-16s were fitted with the new RS-82 rocket. The final, more powerful versions were built in far greater numbers than any others, about one in 30 being a UTI trainer with tandem open cockpits (and in some versions with fixed landing gear). Total production of this extremely important fighter is estimated at 7,000, of which probably 4,000 were engaged in combat duty against the German invader in 1941–43. Heroically flown against aircraft of much later design and often used for deliberate ramming attacks, the stumpy I-16 operated on wheels or skis long after it was obsolete yet today is recognised as one of the really significant combat aircraft of history.

Left: This early (Type 6) I-16 was operational with the 4a Escuadrilla, Grupo núm 31, of the Spanish Republican air force in 1936. Dubbed Mosca by its users, it became better known by the name given it by its Nationalist foes, Rata (rat).

Below: An I-16 Type 24 with skis, though still in dark summer camouflage. This landing gear retracted, but some ski arrangements were fixed.

Yakovlev Yak-1

Ya-26, I-26, Yak-1, Yak-7

Origin: The design bureau of A. S. Yakovlev.
Type: Single-seat fighter.
Engine: Initially, one 1,100hp VK-105PA (M-105PA) vee-12 liquid-cooled, derived from Hispano-Suiza 12Y; later, 1,260hp VK-105PF.
Dimensions: Span 32ft 9¾in (10m); length 27ft 9¾in (8·48m); height 8ft 8in (2·64m).
Weights: Empty (early I-26) 5,137lb (2375kg); maximum loaded 6,217lb (2890kg).
Performance: Maximum speed 373mph (600km/h), 310mph (500km/h) at sea level; initial climb 3,940ft (1200m)/min; service ceiling 32,800ft (10,000m); range, 582 miles (850km).
Armament: (I-26) one 20mm ShVAK cannon, with 120 rounds, firing through propeller hub and two 7·62mm ShKAS machine guns, each with 375 rounds, above engine. (Yak-1, late 1941) one 20mm ShVAK, with 140 rounds, one or two 12·7mm Beresin BS above engine, each with about 348 rounds, and underwing rails for six 25lb (12kg) RS-82 rockets. Some, wing racks for two 110lb or 220lb (50 or 100kg) bombs.
History: First flight March 1939; service delivery (pre-production) October 1940; (production) July 1941.
User: Soviet Union.

continued ▶

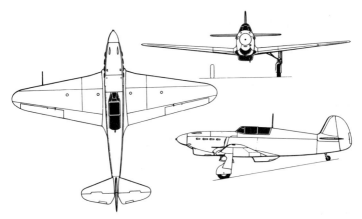

Above: A standard Yak-1, similar in general outline to the Yak-7A.

Left: Seen in winter camouflage, this Yak-1 operated on the Central Sector in January 1942. Note the different type of rear-view windows (instead of a completely transparent rear decking) and absence of a radio mast. The different rear windows appeared after the evaucation of production to Kamensk-Uralsk in late 1941 and is seen on about one-quarter of Yak-1s.

Below: Thousands of women flew combat aircraft in the Soviet Union in World War II, the top-scorer being Lt Lily Litvyak of No 73 IAP (third from left).

Development: In 1939 the Soviet government announced specifications for a new fighter. Surprisingly, the best of four rival prototypes was that from young Alexander S. Yakovlev, who had previously designed only gliders and sporting machines. His Ya-26 earned him fame and riches, and in June 1941 was cleared for production as the chief Soviet fighter. At this time the designation was changed from I-26 to Yak-1, in conformity with the new policy of designation by design bureau rather than by function. In the same month the German hordes swept in from the West and the entire production line was moved 1,000 miles eastwards to Kamensk-Uralsk.

Below: Yak-1, with the inscription "Death to Fascists" near the 27 victory stars, as flown in 1942 by Lt M. D. Baranov of 183 Fighter Regiment.

Despite this there was a delay of only about six weeks, and about 500 Yak-1 were in action by the end of 1941. With a wooden wing and steel-tube body it was a solid and easily maintained machine, with excellent handling. In parallel came the UTI-26 trainer, with tandem seats, which went into production as the Yak-7V. In late 1941 this was modified with lower rear fuselage to improve view and this in turn led to the Yak-7B fighter which in early 1942 supplanted the Yak-1 in production. Such was the start of the second-biggest aircraft-production programme in history, which by 1945 had delivered 37,000 fighters.

Bottom: A Yak-7A fresh off the line at Kamensk-Uralsk, probably in August 1942.

Yakovlev Yak-3

Yak-1M and -3

Origin: The design bureau of A. S. Yakovlev.
Type: Single-seat fighter.
Engine: (-1M) one 1,260hp Klimov VK-105PF vee-12 liquid-cooled; (-3) 1,225hp VK-105PF-2; (final series) 1,650hp VK-107A.
Dimensions: Span 30ft 2¼in (9·20m); length 27ft 10¼in (8·50m); height 7ft 10in (2·39m).
Weights: Empty (VK-105) 4,960lb (2250kg); maximum loaded 5,864lb (2660kg).
Performance: Maximum speed (VK-105) 404mph (650km/h); (VK-107) 447mph (720km/h); initial climb (105) 4,265ft (1300m)/min; (107) 5,250ft (1600m)/min; service ceiling (105) 35,450ft (10,800m); range (105) 506 miles (815km).
Armament: One 20mm ShVAK, with 120 rounds, and two 12·7mm BS, each with 250 rounds.
History: First flight (-1M) 1942; (-3) spring 1943; service delivery (-3) about July 1943; (-3 with VK-107) not later than January 1944.
Users: Czech, French and Polish units, and Soviet Union.

Development: As early as 1941 Yakovlev was considering means whereby he could wring the highest possible performance out of the basic Yak-1 design. As there was no immediate prospect of more power, and armament and equipment were already minimal, the only solution seemed to be to cut down the airframe, reduce weight and reduce drag. In the Yak-1M the wing was reduced in size, the oil cooler replaced by twin small coolers in the wing roots, the rear fuselage cut down and a simple clear-view canopy fitted, the coolant radiator duct redesigned and other detail changes made. The result was a fighter even more formidable in close combat than the -1 and -9 families, though it landed faster. The production -3 was further refined by a thick coat of hard-wearing wax polish, and after meeting the new fighter during the mighty Kursk battle in the summer of 1943 the Luftwaffe recognised it had met its match. Indeed by 1944 a general directive had gone out to Luftwaffe units on the Eastern Front to "avoid combat below 5000m with Yakovlev fighters lacking an oil cooler under the nose"! To show what the Yak-3 could do when bravely handled, despite its ►

Right: Derived from the Yak-1M (which, except for a single example, had the original size of wing) the Yak-3 was a nimble dogfighter with a smaller wing and other changes to reduce drag, including wing-root oil coolers and a long radiator duct.

Below: Yak-3 as flown by Maj Gen Zakharov, CO of the 303 Fighter Aviation Division, 1944, sporting the Order of the Red Banner (Military) emblem on the engine cowling and his personal emblem under the cockpit.

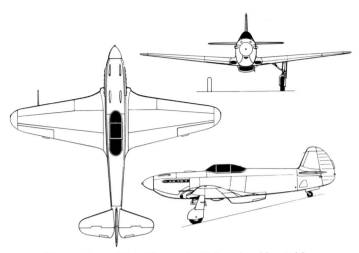

Above: Three-view of Yak-3 (some had hinged rudder-tab).

Above: Yak-3s of an unidentified IAP probably in the summer or autumn of 1944. Apart from the small wing and clean lower cowl the Yak-3 could be identified by the two-piece landing-gear fairings, which were not seen on other Yaks since the Yak-1.

armament – which was trivial compared with that of the German fighters – on 14 July 1944 a force of 18 met 30 Luftwaffe fighters and destroyed 15 for the loss of one Yak-3. Small wonder that, offered all available Soviet, British or American fighters, the Normandie-Niemen Group changed from the Yak-9 to the Yak-3 and scored the last 99 of their 273 victories on these machines. It was natural that the more powerful VK-107 engine should have been fitted to the Yak-3, though the designation was not changed. After prolonged trials in early 1944 the Soviet test centre judged the 107-engined aircraft to be 60–70mph faster than either a Bf 109G or an Fw 190, but the re-engined aircraft was just too late to see action in World War II. As in the case of the Yak-1 and -9, there were various experimental conversions of the Yak-3, the best-known being the mixed-power Yak-3 ZhRD of early 1945, which reached at least 485mph (780km/h) on a VK-105 and a liquid-propellant rocket. A more radical installation was the Yak-7VRD with two large ramjets under the wings. Total production of the Yak-1, -3, -7 and -9 was not less than 37,000. These fighters may have been smaller and simpler than those of other nations in World War II but they served the Soviet Union well in its hour of great need. They conserved precious material, kept going under almost impossible airfield and maintenance conditions and consistently out-performed their enemies.

Below: One of the first production Yak-3s, which gave the Axis fighter pilots on the Eastern Front an unpleasant shock around May 1944. Later its performance was further enhanced by fitting the VK-107 engine; this variant, the Yak-3U, was all-metal.

Yakovlev Yak-9

Yak-9, -9D, -9T, -9U and -9P

Origin: The design bureau of A. S. Yakovlev.
Type: Single-seat fighter (some, fighter-bomber).
Engine: (-9, D and T) one 1,260hp Klimov VK-105PF vee-12 liquid-cooled; (U, P) one 1,650hp VK-107A.
Dimensions: Span 32ft 9¾in (10m); length (-9, D, T) 28ft 0½in (8·54m); (U, P) 28ft 6½in (8·70m); height 8ft (2·44m).
Weights: Empty (T) 6,063lb (2750kg); (U) 5,100lb (2313kg); maximum loaded (T) 7,055lb (3200kg); (U) 6,988lb (3170kg).
Performance: Maximum speed (9) 373mph (600km/h); (D) 359mph (573km/h); (T) 367mph (590km/h); (U) 435mph (700km/h); (P) 416mph (670km/h); initial climb (typical, 9, D, T) 3,795ft (1150m)/min; (U, P) 4,920ft (1500m)/min; service ceiling (all) about 34,500ft (10,500m); range (most) 520–550 miles (840–890km); (D) 840 miles (1350km); (DD) 1,367 miles (2200km).
Armament: (Most) one 20mm ShVAK, with 100 rounds, and two 12·7mm BS, each with 250 rounds, plus two 220lb (100kg) bombs; (B) internal bay for 880lb (400kg) bomb load; (T) gun through propeller changed to 37mm NS-P37 with 32 rounds; (K) this changed for 45mm cannon; certain aircraft had 12·7mm BS firing through hub.
History: First flight (7DI) June 1942; (9M) about August 1942; (D, T) probably late 1943; (U) January 1944; (P) August 1945; final delivery (P) about 1946.
Users: (Wartime) France, Poland, Soviet Union.

Development: The Yak-7DI introduced light-alloy wing spars and evolved into the Yak-9, most-produced Soviet aircraft apart from the Il-2. Able to outfly the Bf 109G, which it met over Stalingrad in late 1942, the -9 was developed into the anti-tank -9T, bomber -9B, long-range -9D and very long-range -9DD. The DD escorted US heavy bombers, and once a large group flew from the Ukraine to Bari (southern Italy) to help Jugoslav partisans. The famed Free French Normandie-Niemen Group and both free Polish squadrons used various first-generation -9s. With a complete switch

Below: French Normandie-Niemen regiment Yak-9.

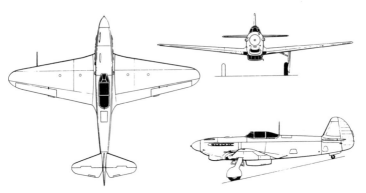

Above: Standard Yak-9; long-range -9D and -9DD externally similar.

to stressed-skin structure and the VK-107 engine there was a dramatic jump in performance, the -9U entering service in the second half of 1944 and flying rings round the 109 and 190. The U could be identified by the smooth cowl, the oil coolers being in the wing root; the post-war -9P, encountered in Korea, had a DF loop under a transparent cover in the rear fuselage.

Above: Yak-9Ds of a Guards IAP over the Crimea in 1944; nearest the camera the aircraft of Col Avdyeyev (15 victories).

Below: A Yak-7B, derived from Yak-1, but in technology and appearance closer to the Yak-9.

USA

Remote geographically from any evident potential
enemies, the mighty USA devoted only modest sums to
warplanes until war in China, Spain and then Europe
forced the giant to stir in the late 1930s. By this time,
despite an industry second to none in its engineering
skills, technology and production potential, the nation
had slipped markedly in fighter design and had nothing
to match the Bf 109E or Spitfire. This is the more
remarkable when it is realized that Americans led the
world in stressed-skin structures, variable-pitch
propellers, flaps and pressurization, and had fiercely
competing engine builders who before World War II
were offering engines of 1,500hp.

One of the classic stories of procurement relates how,
in November 1939, North American Aviation was asked
by Britain to build the Curtiss P-40 for the RAF.
"Dutch" Kindelberger, the company's president, replied
NAA could design a much better fighter from scratch.
The P-40, though mediocre, was a known quantity,
whereas NAA had no experience with fighters. The
British wasted six months before finally giving their
consent; even then they did nothing to ensure the
resulting NA-73 had a Merlin engine. Named Mustang,
the NA-73 was a masterpiece, with superior speed,
superb handling and three times the range of a Spitfire.
Later, with a two-stage Packard Merlin, it mastered the
Luftwaffe even over distant Berlin.

One of the best Allied fighters, the Merlin-Mustang, did not see
action until 1944, yet accounted for almost 14,000 of the 15,586
Mustangs built. This P-51B was flown by ace Don Gentile.

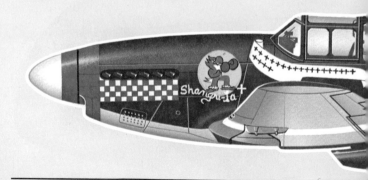

The unorthodox P-38 was a fine long-range fighter and good bomber, but with a 52-foot wingspan it rolled too slowly for dogfighting. The mighty P-47 was possibly the war's greatest ground-attack aircraft, but the mass-produced P-39 and P-40 were also-rans used mainly and successfully as fighter-bombers.

One area where the United States excelled was in naval aircraft. Though the Brewster F2A is best forgotten, its rival, the Grumman F4F, held the fort over Allied oceans almost single-handed until in 1943 the formidable F6F and F4U (and the British Seafire) made their presence felt. Thanks to Pratt & Whitney's R-2800, a sheer package of power, the F6F and F4U could move their ponderous bulk better than their smaller and much lighter enemies. The F6F was more numerous among Pacific fighter squadrons, and did far more than any other aircraft to destroy Japan's command of the air. But the bent-wing F4U, at first judged tricky and unfit for carrier operation (a belief disproved by the British Fleet Air Arm even with baby carriers), was finally recognised as possibly the greatest fighter of the entire war. It outflew such doughty opponents as the P-47M, P-51H and Japan's Ki-84!

America built a wealth of fighter prototypes during the war, some of them bizarre in design. That none saw production is testimony to such machines as the P-51 and F4U, two of the most successful fighters in history.

Bell P-39 Airacobra

P-39 to P39Q Airacobra (data for P-39L)

Origin: Bell Aircraft Corporation.

Type: Single-seat fighter.

Engine: 1,325hp Allison V-1710-63 vee-12 liquid-cooled.

Dimensions: Span 34ft 0in (10·37m); length 30ft 2in (9·2m); height (one prop-blade vertical) 11ft 10in (3·63m).

Weights: Empty 5,600lb (2540kg); loaded 7,780lb (3530kg).

Performance: Maximum speed 380mph (612km/h); initial climb 4,000ft (1220m)/min; service ceiling 35,000ft (10,670m); ferry range with drop tank at 160mph (256km/h) 1,475 miles (2360km).

Armament: One 37mm cannon with 30 rounds (twice as many as in first sub-types), two synchronised 0·5in Colt-Brownings and two or four 0·30in in outer wings.

History: First flight of XP-39 April 1939: (P-39F to M sub-types, 1942); final batch (P-39Q) May 1944.

Users: France, Italy (CB), Portugal, Soviet Union, UK (RAF, briefly), US (AAF).

Development: First flown as a company prototype in 1939, this design by R. J. Woods and O. L. Woodson was unique in having a nosewheel-type landing gear and the engine behind the pilot. The propeller was driven by a long shaft under the pilot's seat and a reduction gearbox in the nose, the latter also containing a big 37mm cannon firing through the propeller hub. Other guns were also fitted in the nose, the first production aircraft, the P-39C of 1941, having two 0·30in and two 0·5in all synchronised to fire past the propeller. Britain ordered the unconventional fighter in 1940 and in June 1941 the first Airacobra I arrived, with the 37mm gun and 15 rounds having been replaced by a 20mm Hispano with 60. Two 0·303in Brownings in the nose and four more in the wings completed the armament. No 601 Sqn did poorly with it and failed to keep the unusual aircraft serviceable, but the US Army Air Force used it in big numbers. Altogether 9,588 were built and used with fair success in the Mediterranean and Far East, some 5,000 being supplied to the Soviet Union, mainly through Iran. Biggest production version was the P-39Q, of which over 4,900 were built. The P-39 was succeeded in production in 1944 by the P-63 Kingcobra.

continued ▶

Below: This P-39L, an interim model with Curtiss propeller, flew with the 91st FS, 81st FG.

Right: Disproving the wartime joke about the "P-400 – a P-40 with a Zero in its tail", this really was designated P-400. These were ex-RAF aircraft with 20mm Hispano still fitted and British serial unerased.

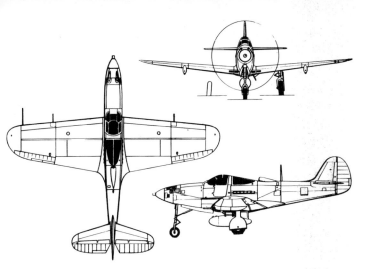

Above: Bell P-39Q, the most numerous model, with drop tank.

Above: Many Allied nations used Airacobras, notably the Soviet Union which liked the US fighter for its ground-attack capability. This example, a P-39N, is shown operating with the Italian Co-Belligerent AF, which was busy in Balkan airspace in 1944.

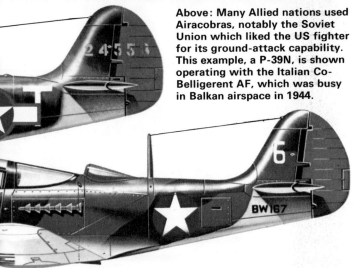

Part of a US Army Air Corps formation of P-39D Airacobras, probably in 1942. This model saw action in the Pacific in the course of that year.

Another 1942 photograph, showing one of the first P-39Ds, the first model judged combat-ready. Note the masking tape round the radio door, and the red star-centres painted over to avoid confusion with the Japanese Hinomaru.

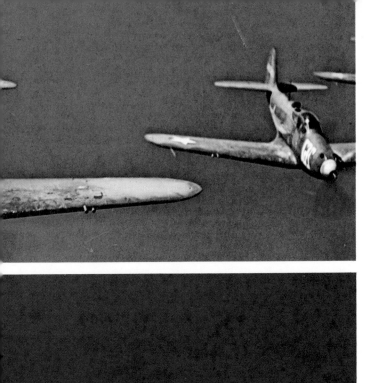

Bell P-59 Airacomet

YP-59, P-59A and XF2L-1

Origin: Bell Aircraft Corporation.
Type: Single-seat jet fighter trainer.
Engines: Two 2,000lb (907kg) thrust General Electric J31-GE-3 turbojets.
Dimensions: Span 45ft 6in (13·87m); length 38ft 1½in (11·63m); height 12ft 0in (3·66m).
Weights: Empty 7,950lb (3610kg); loaded 12,700lb (5760kg).
Performance: Maximum speed 413mph (671km/h); service ceiling 46,200ft (14,080m); maximum range with two 125 Imp gal drop tanks 520 miles (837km) at 289mph (465km/h) at 20,000ft (6096m).
Armament: Usually none, but some YP-59A fitted with nose guns (eg one 37mm cannon and three 0·5in) and one rack under each wing for bomb as alternative to drop tank.
History: First flight (XP-59A) 1 October 1942; (production P-59A) 7 August 1944.
Users: US (AAF, Navy); (one UK in exchange for Meteor I).

Development: In June 1941 the US government and General "Hap" Arnold of the Army Air Corps were told of Britain's development of the turbojet engine. On 5 September 1941 Bell Aircraft was requested to design a jet fighter and in the following month a Whittle turbojet, complete engineering drawings and a team from Power Jets Ltd arrived from Britain to hasten proceedings. The result was that Bell flew the first American jet in one year from the start of work. The Whittle-type centrifugal engines, Americanised

Below: The 16th P-59A, without armament fitted and bearing the red-outlined national marking of 1942—43. Pleasant to fly, the basic type was simply too big for the low thrust engines, and was inferior in performance to a P-51.

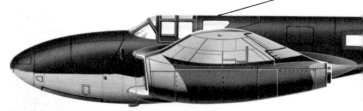

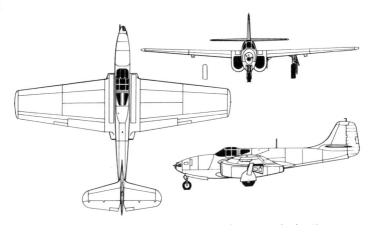

Above: Bell P-59A with broader but cut-down vertical tail.

and made by General Electric as the 1,100lb (500kg) thrust 1-A, were installed under the wing roots, close to the centreline and easily accessible (two were needed to fly an aircraft of useful size). Flight development went extremely smoothly, and 12 YP-59As for service trials were delivered in 1944. Total procurement amounted to 66 only, including three XF2L-1s for the US Navy, and the P-59A was classed as a fighter-trainer because it was clear it would not make an effective front-line fighter. But in comparison with the fast timescale it was a remarkable achievement, performance being very similar to that attained with the early Meteors.

Below left: Devoid of any tail number, this is one of the original three XP-59 prototypes, pictured at Lake Muroc. The designation P-59 had previously been that of a Bell piston-engined fighter, and as a security cover the first XP-59 was fitted with a dummy propeller.

Below: Another view of an early Airacomet, in this case a YP-59, seen being towed across the apron.

103

Bell P-63 Kingcobra

P-63A to E and RP-63

Origin: Bell Aircraft Corporation, Buffalo, NY.
Type: Single-seat fighter-bomber.
Engine: One Allison V-1710 vee-12 liquid-cooled, (A) 1,500hp (war emergency rating) V-1710-93, (C) 1,800hp V-1710-117.
Dimensions: Span 38ft 4in (11·68m); length 32ft 8in (9·96m); height 12ft 7in (3·84m).
Weights: Empty (A) 6,375lb (2892kg); maximum (A) 10,500lb (4763kg).
Performance: Maximum speed (all) 410mph (660km/h); typical range with three bombs 340 miles (547km); ferry range with three tanks 2,575 miles (4143km).
Armament: Usually one 37mm and four 0·5in, plus up to three 500lb (227kg) bombs.
History: First flight 7 December 1942; service delivery October 1943; final delivery early 1945.
Users: Brazil, France, Italy, Soviet Union, US (AAF).

continued ▶

Almost three-quarters of the 3,303 Kingcobras went to the Soviet Union. This photograph, taken in late 1943, shows P-63As awaiting collection at the Buffalo plant.

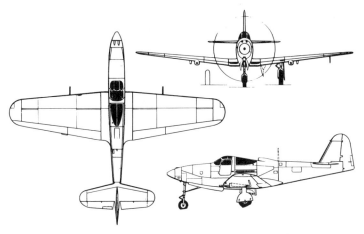

Above: Bell P-63A with outboard bomb racks and radio mast.

Development: Though it looked like a P-39 with a different tail, in fact the P-63 was a completely different design, greatly improved in the light of painful combat experience. It fully met a February 1941 Army requirement, but air war developed so fast that – though Bell did a competent job to a fast schedule – the P-63 was outclassed before it reached the squadrons. It never fought with the US forces, but 2,421 of the 3,303 built went to the Soviet Union where their tough airframes and good close-support capability made them popular. At least 300 went to the Free French, in both A and C variants (both of which had a wealth of sub-types). The D had a sliding bubble canopy and larger wing, and the E extra fuel. The only USAAF Kingcobras were 332 completed or modified as heavily armoured RP-63A or C manned target aircraft, shot at by live "frangible" (easily shattered) bullets. Each hit made a powerful lamp light at the tip of the spinner.

Left and below: Two aircraft from the same late production block of P-63As (delivered unpainted), with outboard wing racks, four-blade Aeroproducts propeller and radio mast. Armament comprises a 37mm gun (in this model the M10, which did not project externally, with ammunition magazine enlarged from 30 to 58 rounds) and four 0.5in.

Brewster F2A Buffalo

F2A-1 (239), F2A-2 (339), F2A-3 and 439 Buffalo 1 (data for F2A-2)

Origin: Brewster Aircraft Company, Long Island City.
Type: Single-seat carrier or land-based fighter.
Engine: 1,100hp Wright R-1820-40 (G-205A) Cyclone nine-cylinder radial.
Dimensions: Span 35ft (10·67m); length 26ft 4in (8m); height 12ft 1in (3·7m).
Weights: Empty 4,630lb (2100kg); loaded 7,055lb (3200kg) (varied from 6,848–7,159lb).
Performance: Maximum speed 300mph (483km/h); initial climb 3,070ft (935m)/min; service ceiling 30,500ft (9300m); range 650–950 miles (1045–1530km).
Armament: Four machine guns, two in fuselage and two in wing, calibre of each pair being 0·30in, 0·303in or, mostly commonly, 0·50in.
History: First flight (XF2A-1) January 1938; first service delivery April 1939; termination of production 1942.
Users: Australia, Finland, Netherlands (E. Indies), New Zealand, UK (RAF), US (Navy, Marines).

Development: The Brewster company was established in 1810 to build carriages. In 1935 it plunged into planemaking and secured an order for a US Navy scout-bomber. It also entered a competition for a carrier-based monoplane fighter and won. Not surprisingly, it took almost two years – a long time in those days – to fly the first prototype. Yet one must give the team their due, for the F2A-1 was confirmed as the Navy's choice for its first monoplane fighter even after Grumman had flown the G.36 (Wildcat). In June 1938 a contract was placed for 54 of these tubby mid-wingers, then armed with one 0·50in and one 0·30in machine guns. Only 11 reached USS *Saratoga*; the rest went to Finland, where from February 1940 until the end of World War II they did extremely well. The US Navy bought 43 more powerful and more heavily armed F2A-2 (Model 339), and then 108 F2A-3 with armour and self-sealing tanks. Of these, 21 in the hands of the Marine Corps put up a heroic struggle in the first Battle of Midway. In 1939 bulk orders were placed by Belgium and Britain, and the RAF operated 170 delivered in 1941 to Singapore. Another 72 were bought by the Netherlands.

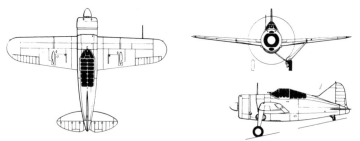

Above: Brewster F2A-3, the final US Navy production version.

Above: The wartime censor has obliterated the RAF code letters on this Buffalo squadron pictured over Malaya in 1941 in company with a Blenheim IV. Totally outclassed by the rival A6M Zero, the RAF did its best to increase performance by replacing the 0·5-inch guns by 0·303-inch, reducing ammunition to 350 rounds and fuel to a mere 84 gallons. The Brewster remained inferior.

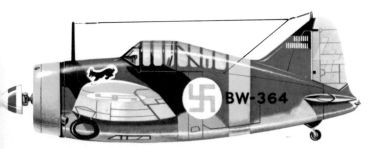

Above: As described in the text, most of the initial production version, the F2A-1, were diverted to Finland, where their robust manoeuvrability made them quite popular. They equipped two squadrons of LeR 2, this particular machine serving with the 3rd Flight of No 24 Squadron based at Römpötissa as late as 1942.

Left: Though it failed to reach customers in Belgium and the Dutch East Indies, the F2A did see action with the British Commonwealth air forces, Fleet Air Arm and (in the F2A-3 form illustrated) with a Marine Corps fighter squadron. The unit was VMF-221, and it suffered heavy casualties at Midway in 1942.

Curtiss Hawk family

A: Hawk 75A, P-36A, Mohawk IV
B: Hawk 81A, P-40C, Tomahawk IIB
C: Hawk 87D, P-40F, Kittyhawk II
D: Hawk 87M, P-40N, Kittyhawk IV

Origin: Curtiss-Wright Corporation.

Type: (A) single-seat fighter, (B) single-seat fighter, reconnaissance and ground attack; (C, D) single-seat fighter bomber.

Engine: (A) P-36A, 1,050hp Pratt & Whitney R-1830-13 Twin Wasp 14-cylinder two-row radial; Hawk 75A and Mohawk, 1,200hp Wright GR-1820-G205A Cyclone nine-cylinder radial; (B) 1,040hp Allison V-1710-33 vee-12 liquid-cooled; (C) 1,300hp Packard V-1650-1 (R-R Merlin) vee-12 liquid-cooled; (D) 1,200hp Allison V-1710-81, -99 or -115 vee-12 liquid-cooled.

Dimensions: Span 37ft 3½in (11·36m); length (A) 28ft 7in (8·7m), (B) 31ft 8½in (9·7m); (C) 31ft 2in (9·55m) or 33ft 4in (10·14m); (D) 33ft 4in (10·14m); height (A) 9ft 6in (2·89m), (B, C, D) 12ft 4in (3·75m).

Weights: Empty (A) 4,541lb (2060kg), (B) 5,812lb (2636kg), (C) 6,550lb (2974kg), (D) 6,700lb (3039kg); loaded (A) 6,662lb (3020kg), (B) 7,459lb (3393kg), (C) 8,720lb (3960kg), (D) 11,400lb (5008kg).

Performance: Maximum speed (A) 303mph (488km/h), (B) 345mph (555km/h), (C) 364mph (582km/h), (D) 343mph (552km/h); initial climb (A) 2,500ft (762m)/min, (B) 2,650ft (807m)/min, (C) 2,400ft (732m)/min, (D) 2,120ft (646m)/min; service ceiling (all) about 30,000ft (9144m); range on internal fuel (A) 680 miles (1,100km), (B) 730 miles (1175km), (C) 610 miles (976km), (D) 750 miles (1207km).

Armament: (A) P-36A, one 0·50in and one 0·30in Brownings above engine; P-36C, as P-36A with two 0·30in in wings; Hawk 75A/Mohawk IV, six 0·303in (four in wings); (B) six 0·303in (four in wings); (C, D) six 0·50in in wings with 281 rounds per gun (early P-40N, only four); bomb load (A) underwing racks for total of 400lb (181kg); (B) nil; (C) one 500lb on centreline and 250lb (113kg) under each wing; (D) 500 or 600lb (272kg) on centreline and 500lb under each wing.

History: First flight (Model 75 prototype) May 1935; (first Y1P-36) January 1937; (first production P-36A) April 1938; (XP-40) October 1938; (P-40) January 1940; (P-40D) 1941; (P-40F) 1941; (P-40N) 1943; final delivery (P-40N-40 and P-40R) December 1944.

Users: Argentina, Australia, Belgium, Bolivia, Brazil, Canada, China, Colombia, Egypt, Finland, France, Iraq, Italy (CB), Netherlands, New Zealand, Norway, Peru, Portugal, S. Africa, Soviet Union, Turkey, UK (RAF), US (AAC/AAF).

Development: In November 1934 Curtiss began the design of a completely new "Hawk" fighter with cantilever monoplane wing, backwards retracting landing gear (the wheels turning 90° to lie inside the wing) and all-metal ▶

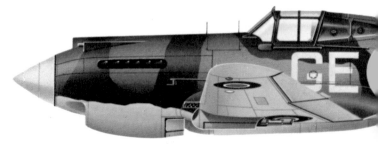

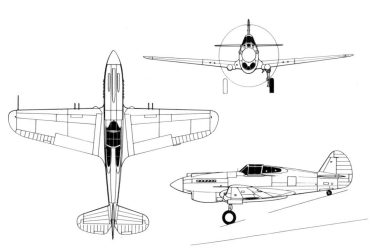

Above: Curtiss P-40C (Hawk 81A and Tomahawk II similar).

Below: Two of the many variants of Hawk 75 that saw action in World War II were the Hawk 75A-7 of the Netherlands East Indies (R-1820 Cyclone) and the Hawk 75-C1 (maker's designation, 75A-1) of the Armée de l'Air (R-1830 Twin Wasp). Other sub-types saw action with the RAF (India), Finland, and USAAF (Hawaii).

Left: AH972 was a Tomahawk IIA (Hawk 81A-2), one of the first Hawks supplied on UK account instead of being diverted from a French order. Basically similar to the P-40B it had two 0.5in guns on the cowling and two 0.303in in the wings. The much more numerous Tomahawk IIB had an armament of six 0.303in. This machine served with 349 (Belgian) Sqn RAF at Ikeja, Nigeria.

stressed-skin construction. After being tested by the Army Air Corps this design was put into production as the P-36A, marking a major advance in speed though not in firepower. Successive types of P-36 and its export counterpart, the Hawk 75A, had different engines and additional guns and the Hawk 75A was bought in large numbers by many countries and made under licence in several. Biggest customer was the French Armée de l'Air, which began to receive the H75A in March 1939. Five groups — GC I/4, II/4, I/5, II/5 and III/2 — wrote a glorious chapter over France in May 1940, invariably outnumbered and usually outperformed, but destroying 311 of the Luftwaffe, more than the total H75A strength when France fell. The rest of the French orders were supplied to the RAF as Mohawks, serving mainly on the Burma front.

More than 1,300 radial-engined models were delivered, but the real story began with the decision in July 1937 to build the P-40, with the liquid-cooled Allison engine. This was a novel and untried engine in a land where aircraft engines had become universally air-cooled, and teething troubles were long and severe. Eventually, towards the end of 1940, the P-40B and RAF Tomahawk I were cleared for combat duty and the process of development began. The rest of the aircraft was almost unchanged and in comparison with the Bf109 or Spitfire the early P-40 showed up badly, except in the twin attributes of manoeuvrability and strong construction. Eventually the RAF, RAAF and SAAF took 885 of three marks of Tomahawk, used as low-level army co-operation machines in Britain and as ground attack fighters in North Africa. Many hundreds of other P-40Bs and Cs were supplied to the US Army, Soviet Union, China and Turkey.

With the P-40D a new series of Allison engines allowed the nose to be shortened and the radiator was deepened, changing the appearance of the aircraft. The fuselage guns were finally thrown out and the standard armament became the much better one of six "fifties" in the wings. The RAF had ordered 560 of the improved fighters in 1940, and they were called ▶

Above: A fine picture of Kittyhawk IIIs of the Desert Air Force returning with empty bomb racks in Tunisia in early 1943. At advanced airfields it was standard practice for an ''erk'' to ride on a wingtip and guide the pilot past potholes and obstructions.

Below: Field maintenance for a P-40F Warhawk, with Packard Merlin whose carb-air inlet was on the underside, not above.

Kittyhawk I. When the US Army bought it the name Warhawk was given to subsequent P-40 versions. The Merlin engine went into production in the USA in 1941 and gave rise to the P-40F; none of the 1,311 Merlin P-40s reached the RAF, most going to the Soviet Union, US Army and Free French. Most Fs introduced a longer fuselage to improve directional stability. Subsequent models had a dorsal fin as well and reverted to the Allison engine. Great efforts were made to reduce weight and improve performance, because the whole family was fundamentally outclassed by the other front-line fighters on both sides; but, predictably, weight kept rising. It reached its peak in the capable and well-equipped P-40N, of which no fewer than 4,219 were built. Some of the early Ns had all the weight-savings and could reach 378mph (608km/h), but they were exceptions. Altogether deliveries of P-40 versions to the US government amounted to 13,738. Though it was foolhardy to tangle with a crack enemy fighter in close combat the Hawk family were tough, nimble and extremely useful weapons, especially in close support of armies.

Right: A 1942 photograph of a P-40E with the anti-swing dorsal fin of the P-40K. Note armament of six "point-fifties".

Right: This P-40K is one of the later K-10 or -15 production blocks with the fuselage length increased from 31ft 2in to 33ft 4in, as in most of the Merlin-engined P-40Fs. This particular example, seen with very necessary drop tank, was designated Kittyhawk III and operated by the RNZAF on Guadalcanal in the closing months of 1942.

Below: Seen in this case operating with the Army Air Corps 77th Fighter Sqn, 20th Pursuit Group, Hamilton Field, California, in 1941, the P-40C usually had two wing guns.

Below: Hawks served in every theatre in World War II, and though inferior as dogfighters against their best enemies they did as much as any other Allied type in the role of tactical fighter-bomber. This USAAF P-40K is about to depart on an interception mission after the alert had sounded at Dobodura, New Guinea, in May 1943. Its unit is the 7th Fighter Group.

115

Grumman F4F/FM Wildcat
G-36, Martlet, F4F-1 to -4 and Eastern Aircraft FM-1 and -2

Origin: Grumman Aircraft Engineering Corporation; also built by Eastern Aircraft.

Type: Single-seat naval fighter.

Engine: (XF4F-2) one 1,050hp Pratt & Whitney R-1830-66 Twin Wasp 14-cylinder two-row radial; (G-36A, Martlet I (Wildcat I)) one 1,200hp Wright R-1820-G205A Cyclone nine-cylinder radial; (F4F-3) 1,200hp R-1830-76; (F4F-4 and FM-1 (Wildcat V)) R-1830-86; (FM-2 (Wildcat VI)) 1,350hp R-1820-56.

Dimensions: Span 38ft 0in (11·6m); length 28ft 9in to 28ft 11in (FM-2, 28ft 10in, 8·5m); height 11ft 11in (3·6m).

Weights: Empty (F4F-3) 4,425lb; (F4F-4) 4,649lb; (FM-2) 4,900lb (2226kg); loaded (F4F-3) 5,876lb; (F4F-4) 6,100lb rising to 7,952lb (3607kg) with final FM-1s; (FM-2) 7,412lb.

Performance: Maximum speed (F4F-3) 325mph (523km/h); (F4F-4, FM-1) 318mph (509km/h); (FM-2) 332mph (534km/h); initial climb, typically 2,000ft (610m)/min (3,300ft/min in early versions, 1,920 in main production and over 2,000 for FM-2); service ceiling, typically 35,000ft (10,670m) (more in light early versions); range, typically 900 miles (1448km).

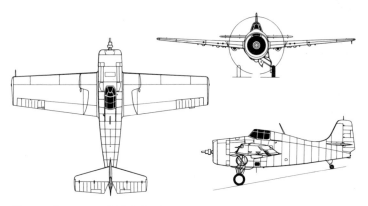

Above: Grumman F4F-4 (FM-1 similar but only four 0·50-in guns).

Armament: (XF4F-2) two 0·5in Colt-Brownings in fuselage; (F4F-3) four 0·5in in outer wings; (F4F-4 and subsequent) six 0·5in in outer wings; (F4F-4, FM-1 and FM-2) underwing racks for two 250lb (113kg) bombs.
History: First flight (XF4F-2) 2 September 1937; (XF4F-3) 12 February 1939; production (G-36 and F4F-3) February 1940; (FM-2) March 1943; final delivery August 1945.
Users: France (FFL), Greece, UK (RN), US (Navy, Marines). *continued* ▶

Left: A US Navy F4F-4 Wildcat in late-war markings (post September 1943 with blue-bordered insignia). This model had a Twin Wasp engine and six guns; this particular aircraft has a vertical radio mast, normally fitted only to the later FM-2.

Below: A Cyclone-powered Martlet IV (later renamed Wildcat IV to fall into line with the name selected by the US Navy) after recovery aboard a Royal Navy Fleet Carrier, probably in 1943. This variant, with four guns, saw much action, particularly with 811 and 882 Sqns.

Development: Designed as a biplane to continue Grumman's very successful F3F series of single-seat carrier fighters, the XF4F-1 was re-planned on the drawing board in the summer of 1936 as a mid-wing monoplane. Though this machine, the XF4F-2, lost out to the Brewster F2A Buffalo, Grumman continued with the XF4F-3 with a more powerful engine and in early 1939 received a French Aéronavale order for 100, the US Navy following with 54 in August. The French aircraft were diverted to Britain and named Martlet I. Production built up with both Twin Wasp and Cyclone engines, folding wings being introduced with the F4F-4, of which Grumman delivered 1,169 plus 220 Martlet IVs for the Fleet Air Arm. Eastern Aircraft Division of General Motors very quickly tooled up and delivered 839 FM-1s and 311 Martlet Vs, the British name then being changed to the US name of Wildcat. Grumman switched to the Avenger, Hellcat and other types, but made F4F-7 reconnaissance versions, weighing 10,328lb and having a 24-hour endurance, as well as a floatplane version. Eastern took over the final mark, the powerful and effective FM-2, delivering 4,777 of this type (including 340 Wildcat VI) in 13 months. A Martlet I shot down a Ju 88 on Christmas Day 1940, and an F4F-3 of VMF-211 destroyed a Japanese bomber at Wake Island on 9 December 1941. Each event was the first of thousands of furious actions from which this quite old fighter emerged with a splendid reputation. Wildcats were especially valuable for their ability to operate from small escort carriers, the pioneer work having been done with British Martlets based in November 1940 on the 5,000 ton captured German vessel *Audacity* on which a flat deck had been built. Noted for their strength and manoeuvrability. Wildcats even sank Japanese submarines and a cruiser.

Above: A 1944 photograph of F4F-4 Wildcats over the Pacific. By this time the Wildcat was no longer holding the fort by itself.

One of the first F4F-4s to reach the US Navy, this example is seen with VF-41, the first squadron to be equipped in November 1941 (when the white star still had a red centre). Though this Pratt & Whitney-engined version, the first with a folding wing, was in production only a year, it equipped every US Navy carrier-based fighter squadron at the start of 1943.

Grumman F6F Hellcat

F6F-1 to -5 Hellcat

Origin: Grumman Aircraft Engineering Corporation.
Type: Single-seat naval fighter; later versions, fighter-bombers and night fighters.
Engine: Early production, one 2,000hp Pratt & Whitney R-2800-10 Double Wasp 18-cylinder two-row radial; from January 1944 (final F6F-3 batch) two-thirds equipped with 2,200hp (water-injection rating) R-2800-10W.
Dimensions: Span 42ft 10in (13·05m); length 33ft 7in (10·2m); height 13ft 1in (3·99m).
Weights: Empty (F6F-3) 9,042lb (4101kg); loaded (F6F-3) 12,186lb (5528kg) clean, 13,228lb (6000kg) maximum, (F6F-5N) 14,250lb (6443kg).
Performance: Maximum speed (F6F-3, -5, clean) 376mph (605km/h); (-5N) 366mph (590km/h); initial climb (typical) 3,240ft (990m)/min; service ceiling (÷3) 37,500ft (11,430m); (-5N) 36,700ft (11,185m); range on internal fuel (typical) 1,090 miles (1755km).
Armament: Standard, six 0·5in Brownings in outer wings with 400 rounds each; a few -5N and -5 Hellcats had two 20mm and four 0·5in. Underwing attachments for six rockets, and centre-section pylons for 2,000lb of bombs.
History: First flight (R-2600) 26 June 1942; (same aircraft, R-2800) 30 July 1942; (production F6F-3) 4 October 1942; production delivery (F6F-3) 16 January 1943; final delivery November 1945.
Users: UK (RN), US (Navy, Marines).

Development: Though pugnacious rather than elegant, the Hellcat was a truly war-winning aircraft. It was designed and developed with great speed, mass-produced at a rate seldom equalled by any other single aircraft factory and used to such good effect that, from the very day of its appearance, ▶

Right: Part of a formation put up by one of the first US Navy squadrons to be equipped with the new F6F-3 (probably VF-8) in early 1943. F4F pilots found conversion relatively painless.

Below right: A Hellcat makes a free takeoff from USS *Enterprise* in 1945. Note the solid phalanx of 40mm and 20mm guns providing devastating firepower all round the ship against Kamikazes.

Below: One of the first F6F-3 Hellcats to have a vertical radio mast, this aircraft was one of those in action at Marcus Island on 31 August 1943, a mere 13 months after the first flight!

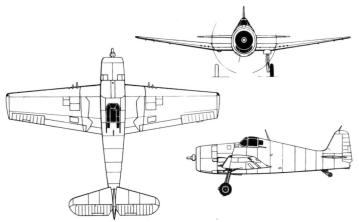

Above: The original F6F-3 variant with F4F-type sloping mast.

Above: One of the first production block of F6F-3 Hellcats. photographed in October 1942 within three months of first flight. It was a pity the F4U could not have rivalled this pace.

Below: This F6F-3, waiting to start engines before an interception mission in 1944, may be the aircraft depicted in the colour profile (with 1942-43 red-bordered markings) at the foot of p. 120.

Above: A fine study of an early F6F-3 about to hit the board deck of a fleet carrier in the Pacific. Note the batsman at right.

Right: An F6F-5 gets a wave-off from an escort carrier and goes round again as the preceding Hellcat disengages from the wire.

the Allies were winning the air war in the Pacific. It began as the XF6F-1, a natural development of the F4F Wildcat with R-2600 Double Cyclone engine. Within a month the more powerful Double Wasp had been substituted and in the autumn of 1942 the production line took shape inside a completely new plant that was less advanced in construction than the Hellcats inside it! This line flowed at an extraordinary rate, helped by the essential rightness of the Hellcat and lack of major engineering changes during subsequent sub-types. Deliveries in the years 1942–45 inclusive were 10, 2,545, 6,139 and 3,578, a total of 12,272 (excluding two proto-types) of which 11,000 were delivered in exactly two years. These swarms of big, beefy fighters absolutely mastered the Japanese, destroying more than 6,000 hostile aircraft (4,947 by USN carrier squadrons, 209 by land-based USMC units and the rest by Allied Hellcat squadrons). The Fleet Air Arm, which originally chose the name Gannet, used Hellcats in Europe as well as throughout the Far East. Unusual features of the F6F were its 334 sq ft of square-tipped wing, with a distinct kink, and backward-retracting landing gear. The F6F-3N and -5N were night fighters with APS-6 radar on a wing pod; the -5K was a drone and the -5P a photographic reconnaissance version. After VJ-day hundreds were sold to many nations.

Grumman F7F Tigercat

F7F-1 to -4N Tigercat

Origin: Grumman Aircraft Engineering Corporation.
Type: Single-seat or two-seat fighter bomber or night fighter (-4N for carrier operation).
Engines: Two Pratt & Whitney R-2800-22W or -34W Double Wasp 18-cylinder two-row radials each rated at 2,100hp (dry) or 2,400hp (water injection).
Dimensions: Span 51ft 6in (15·7m); length (most) 45ft 4in or 45ft 4½in (13·8m); (-3N, -4N) 46ft 10in (14·32m); height (-1, -2) 15ft 2in (4·6m); (-3, -4) 16ft 7in (5·06m).
Weights: Empty (-1) 13,100lb (5943kg); (-3N, -4N) 16,270lb (7379kg); loaded (-1) 22,560lb (10,235kg); (-2N) 26,194lb (11,880kg); (-3) 25,720lb; (-4N) 26,167lb.
Performance: Maximum speed (-1) 427mph (689km/h); (-2N) 421mph; (-3) 435mph; (-4N) 430mph; initial climb (-1) 4,530ft (1380m)/min; service ceiling (-1) 36,200ft; (-2N) 39,800ft (12,131m); (-3) 40,700ft; (-4N) 40,450ft; range on internal fuel (-1) 1,170 miles (1885km); (-2N) 960 miles; (-3) 1,200 miles; (-4N) 810 miles.
Armament: Basic (-1) four 0·5in Browning each with 300 rounds in the nose and four 20mm M-2 cannon each with 200 rounds in the wing roots; outer-wing pylons for six rockets or two 1,000 lb (454kg) bombs; alternatively, one 21in torpedo on fuselage centreline. (-3), nose guns only; (-2N, -3N, -4N) wing guns only.
History: First flight (XF7F-1) December 1943; first service delivery October 1944; final delivery, December 1946.
Users: UK (RN), US (Navy, Marines).

Development: Ordered on the same day as the F6F Hellcat prototypes in June 1941 the F7F was one of the boldest designs in the history of combat aircraft. During the preceding two years the US Navy had keenly studied air war in Europe and noted that the things that appeared to count were the obvious ones; engine power, armament and protective armour and self-

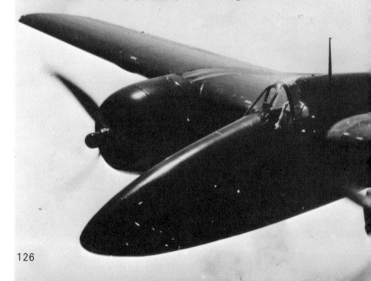

Seen here on factory test over Long Island, the F7F-3 was the final wartime Tigercat variant, with slightly more fuel and engines giving greater power at high altitudes.

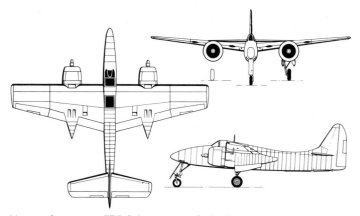

Above: Grumman F7F-3 (post-war -3s had radar or photo noses).

sealing tanks. At a time when the average US Navy fighter had 1,000hp and two machine guns the Bureau of Aeronautics asked Grumman to build a fighter with more than 4,000hp and a weight of fire more than 200 times as great. The company had embarked on a venture along these lines in 1938 with the XF5F, which remained a one-off prototype that was judged not worth the cost and incompatible with Navy carriers. In contrast the F7F was planned on a basis of knowledge and though dramatically heavier and faster than any previous carrier aircraft it was matched with the deck of the large Midway class carriers then under construction. Most, however, were ordered for the Marine Corps for use from land. The F7F-1 of which 34 were built, were single seaters with APS-6 radar in a wing pod. The 66 F7F-2Ns followed, with nose radar in place of guns and the observer in place of the rear fuel tank. The -3 introduced the -34W engine and so had a larger tail; most of the 250 built were -3N night fighters or -3P photographic aircraft. The final models were strengthened -4s, cleared for carrier use, the whole batch being -4Ns. Tigercats arrived at a time when emphasis was rapidly switching to the jet.

Lockheed P-38 Lightning

XP-38 to P-38M, F-4 and F-5, RP and TP conversions

Origin: Lockheed Aircraft Corporation.

Type: Single-seat long-range fighter (see text for variations).

Engines: Two Allison V-1710 vee-12 liquid-cooled; (YP-38) 1,150hp V-1710-27/29 (all P-38 engines handed with opposite propeller rotation, hence pairs of engine sub-type numbers); (P-38E to G) 1,325hp V-1710-49/52 or 51/55; (P-38H and J) 1,425hp V-1710-89/91; (P-38L and M) 1,600hp V-1710-111/113.

Dimensions: Span 52ft (15·86m); length 37ft 10in (11·53m); (F-5G, P-38M and certain "droop-snoot" conversions fractionally longer); height 12ft 10in (3·9m).

Weights: Empty, varied from 11,000lb (4990kg) in YP to average of 12,700lb (5766kg), with heaviest sub-types close to 14,000lb (6350kg); maximum loaded, (YP) 14,348lb (6508kg); (D) 15,500lb; (E) 15,482lb; (F) 18,000lb; (G) 19,800lb; (H) 20,300lb; (L, M) 21,600lb (9798kg).

Performance: Maximum speed (all) 391—414mph (630—666km/h); initial climb (all) about 2,850ft (870m)/min; service ceiling (up to G) 38,000—40,000ft; (H, J, L) 44,000ft (13,410m); range on internal fuel 350—460 miles (563—740km); range at 30,000ft with maximum fuel (late models) 2,260 miles (3650km).

Armament: See "Development" text.

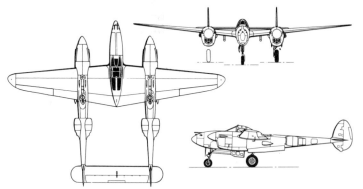

Above: Lockheed P-38J, the mass-produced definitive version.

History: First flight (XP-38) 27 January 1939; (YP-38) 16 September 1940; service delivery (USAAC P-38) 8 June 1941; (F-4) March 1942; (P-38F) September 1942; final delivery September 1945.
Users: France, UK (RAF, briefly), US (AAC/AAF)

Development: In February 1937 the US Army Air Corps issued a specification for a long-range interceptor (pursuit) and escort fighter, calling for a speed of 360mph at 20,000ft and endurance at this speed of one hour. Lockheed, which had never built a purely military design, jumped in with ▶

Left: The first really good and fully combat-ready variant was the P-38F; this P-38F-5 (not to be confused with the F-5 photo variant) served on Guadalcanal with the 347th FG, detached from the 13th Air Force in February 1943.

Below: The F-5E was one of the later series of unarmed photo-reconnaissance Lightnings, based on the P-38J (as here) or the similar L.

both feet and created a revolutionary fighter bristling with innovations and posing considerable technical risks. Powered by two untried Allison engines, with GEC turbochargers recessed into the tops of the tail booms, it had a tricycle landing gear, small central nacelle mounting a 23mm Madsen cannon and four 0·5in Brownings firing parallel directly ahead of the pilot, twin fins, Fowler flaps, cooling radiators on the flanks of the booms and induction intercoolers in the wing leading edges. This box of tricks ran into a ditch on its first taxi test, and two weeks after first flight undershot at Mitchell Field, NY, and was demolished. What made headlines, however, was that it had flown to New York in 7hr 2min, with two refuelling stops, demonstrating a performance which in 1939 seemed beyond belief. The enthusiasm of the Air Corps overcame the doubts and high cost and by 1941 the first YP-38 was being tested, with a 37mm Oldsmobile cannon, two 0·5s and two Colt 0·3s. Thirteen YPs were followed on the Burbank line by 20 P-38s, with one 37mm and four 0·5, plus armour and, in the 36 D models, self-sealing tanks. In March 1940 the British Purchasing Commission had ordered 143 of this type, with the 37mm replaced by a 20mm Hispano and far greater ammunition capacity. The State Department prohibited export of the F2 Allison engine and RAF aircraft, called Lightning I, had early C15 engines without turbochargers, both having right-hand rotation (P-38s had propellers turning outward). The result was poor and the RAF rejected these machines, which were later brought up to US standard. The E model adopted the British name Lightning and the RAF Hispano gun. Within minutes of the US declaration of war, on 7 December 1941, an E shot down an Fw 200C near Iceland, and the P-38 was subsequently in the thick of fighting in North Africa, North West Europe and the Pacific. The F was the first to have inner-wing pylons for 1,000lb bombs, torpedoes, tanks or other stores. By late 1943 new G models were being flown to Europe across the North Atlantic, while in the Pacific 16 aircraft of the 339th Fighter Squadron destroyed Admiral Yamamoto's aircraft 550 miles from their base at Guadalcanal. The J had the intercoolers moved

Above: A fully operational khaki-drab P-38F on test from Burbank in 1942. This was the first variant with drop tanks.

under the engines, changing the appearance, providing room for 55 extra gallons of fuel in the outer wings. Later J models had hydraulically boosted ailerons, but retained the wheel-type lateral control instead of a stick. The L, with higher war emergency power, could carry 4,000lb of bombs or ten rockets, and often formations would bomb under the direction of a lead-ship converted to droop-snoot configuration with a bombardier in the nose. Hundreds were built as F-4 or F-5 photographic aircraft, and the M was a two-seat night fighter with ASH radar pod under the nose. Lightnings towed gliders, operated on skis, acted as fast ambulances (carrying two stretcher cases) and were used for many special ECM missions. Total production was 9,942 and the P-38 made up for slightly inferior manoeuvrability by its range, reliability and multi-role effectiveness.

Below: The "droop-snoot" Lightnings were P-38Js converted in England to carry a bombardier with a Norden precision sight in a glazed nose. They were lead-ships for large formations of Lightnings which released their bombs when they saw the lead do so.

North American NA-73 P-51/A-36 Mustang

P-51 to P-51L, A-36, F-6, Cavalier 750 to 2500, Piper Enforcer and F-82 Twin Mustang

Origin: North American Aviation Inc, Inglewood and Dallas; built under licence by Commonwealth Aircraft Corporation, Australia (and post-war by Cavalier and Piper).

Type: (P-51) single-seat fighter; (A-36) attack bomber; (F-6) reconnaissance; (post-war Cavalier and Piper models) Co-In; (F-82) night fighter.

Engine: (P-51, A, A-36, F-6A) one 1,150hp Allison V-1710-F3R or 1,125hp V-1710-81 vee-12 liquid-cooled; (P-51B, C, D and K, F-6C) one Packard V-1650 (licence-built R-R Merlin 61-series), originally 1,520hp V-1650-3 followed during P-51D run by 1,590hp V-1650-7; (P-51H) 2,218hp V-1650-9; (Cavalier) mainly V-1650-7; (Turbo-Mustang III) 1,740hp Rolls-Royce Dart 510 turboprop; (Enforcer) 2,535hp Lycoming T55-9 turboprop; (F-82F, G, H) two 2,300hp (wet rating) Allison V-1710-143/145.

Dimensions: Span 37ft 0½in (11·29m); (F-82) 51ft 3in (15·61m); length 32ft 2½in (9·81m); (P-51H) 33ft 4in; (F-82E) 39ft 1in (11·88m); height

Below: Merlin-engined P-51B-15, with Malcolm bubble hood in place of the earlier hinged pattern, of the top-scoring outfit the 4th Fighter Group (334th FS) based at Debden, Essex.

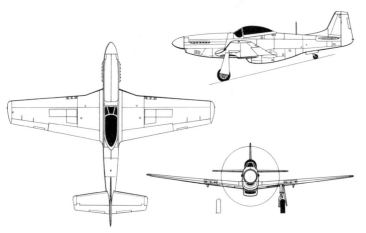

Above: North American P-51D with dorsal fin (P-51K similar).

(P-51, A, A-36, F-6) 12ft 2in (3·72m); (other P-51) 13ft 8in (4·1m); (F-82) 13ft 10in (4·2m).
Weights: Empty (P-51 early V-1710 models, typical) 6,300lb (2858kg); (P-51D) 7,125lb (3230kg); (F-82E) 14,350lb (6509kg); maximum loaded (P-51 early) 8,600lb (3901kg); (P-51D) 11,600lb (5,206kg); (F-82E) 24,864lb (11,276kg). *continued ▶*

Below left: An early Merlin-Mustang, from the P-51B-15-NA production block, in olive drab and red-bordered markings in early 1943. These P-51s had only four 0.5in guns.

Below: Most famous of all Mustangs, *Shangri-La* was the personal mount of Capt Don Gentile, top-scorer of the famed 4th FG. His final revised score was 21.8 in the air (more than half gained in the month of March 1944) and 6 in ground strafing. He crashed this aircraft beating up Debden!

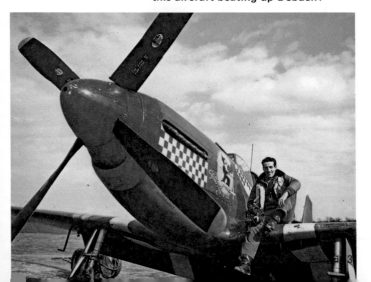

133

Performance: Maximum speed (early P-51) 390mph (628km/h); (P-51D) 437mph (703km/h); (F-82, typical) 465mph (750km/h); initial climb (early) 2,600ft (792m)/min, (P-51D) 3,475ft (1060m)/min; service ceiling (early) 30,000ft (9144m); (P-51D) 41,900ft (12,770m), range with maximum fuel (early) 450 miles (724km); (P-51D) combat range 950 miles, operational range 1,300 miles with drop tanks and absolute range to dry tanks of 2,080 miles; (F-82E) 2,504 miles.

Armament: (RAF Mustang I) four 0·303in in wings, two 0·5in in wings and two 0·5in in lower sides of nose; (Mustang IA and P-51) four 20mm Hispano in wings; (P-51A and B) four 0·5in in wings; (A-36A) six 0·5in in wings and wing racks for two 500lb (227kg) bombs; (all subsequent P-51 production models) six 0·5in Browning MG53-2 with 270 or 400 rounds each, and wing racks for tanks or two 1,000lb (454kg) bombs; (F-82, typical) six 0·5in in centre wing, six or eight pylons for tanks, radars or up to 4,000lb weapons.

History: First flight (NA-73X) 26 October 1940; (production RAF Mustang I) 1 May 1941; service delivery (RAF) October 1941; first flight

Above: As Inglewood and Dallas poured out the war-winning P-51D, so did Allied airpower swell in every theatre. These served with the 8th AF's 361st FG, in early 1944 based at Bottisham but later at St Dizier, France (ship 2106811 is a P-51B).

(Merlin conversion) 13 October 1942; (P-51B) December 1942; final delivery (P-51H) November 1945; first flight (XP-82A) 15 April 1945; final delivery (F-82G) April 1949.

Users: (Wartime) Australia, Canada, China (and AVG), Netherlands, New Zealand, Poland, South Africa, Soviet Union, Sweden, UK (RAF), USA (AAC/AAF).

Development: In April 1940 the British Air Purchasing Commission concluded with "Dutch" Kindelberger, chairman of North American Aviation, an agreement for the design and development of a completely new fighter for the RAF. Designed, built and flown in 117 days, this silver prototype was the start of the most successful fighter programme in history. ▶

The RAF received 620 Mustang I, 150 IA and 50 II, while the US Army adopted the type with 500 A-36A and 310 P-51A. In 1942 the brilliant airframe was matched with the Merlin engine, yielding the superb P-51B, bulged-hood C (Mustang III) and teardrop-canopy D (Mustang IV), later C and all D models having six 0·5in guns and a dorsal fin. The final models were the K (different propeller) and better-shaped, lighter H, the fastest of all at 487mph. Total production was 15,586. Mustang and P-51 variants served mainly in Europe, their prime mission being the almost incredible one of flying all the way from British bases to targets of the 8th AF deep in Germany — Berlin or beyond — escorting heavies and gradually establishing Allied air superiority over the heart of Germany. After the war the Mustang proved popular with at least 55 nations, while in 1947—49 the US Air Force bought 272 examples of the appreciably longer Twin Mustang (two Allison-powered fuselages on a common wing), most of them radar night fighters which served in Korea. In 1945—48 Commonwealth Aircraft of Australia made under licence 200 Mustangs of four versions. In 1967 the P-51 was put back into production by Cavalier for the US Air Force and other customers, and the turboprop Turbo III and Enforcer versions were developed for the Pave Coin programme for Forward Air Control and light attack missions. Many of the new or remanufactured models of 1968—75 are two-seaters.

Right: Until late 1943 the only variants in service had the Allison engine; this example is a cannon-armed P-51 (NA-91).

Below: Deadly sight for a Jap was this swarm of P-51Ds of the 45th FS, 15th FG, 7th Fighter Command, 20th AF, on Iwo Jima.

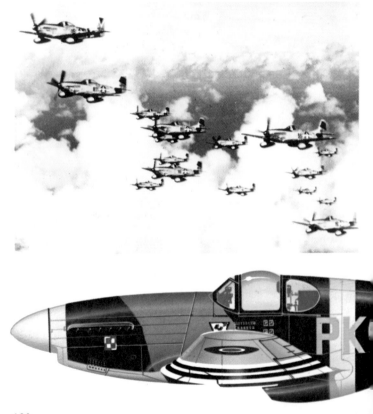

Above: Return of a P-51D of the 353rd Fighter Group, 8th AF, to Raydon, Suffolk.

Left: The Mustang III, with bulged Malcolm hood, of S/L Horbaczewski, CO of 315 Sqn at Brenzett. He once rescued a fellow-Pole from capture and flew back with him in the Mustang cockpit!

Northrop P-61 Black Widow
P-61A, B and C and F-15 (RF-61C) Reporter

Origin: Northrop Aircraft Inc, Hawthorne, California.
Type: (P-61) three-seat night fighter; (F-15) two-seat strategic reconnaissance.
Engines: Two Pratt & Whitney R-2800 Double Wasp 18-cylinder two-row radials; (P-61A) 2,000hp R-2800-10; (B) 2,000hp R-2800-65; (C and F-15) 2,800hp (wet rating) R-2800-73.
Dimensions: Span 66ft (20·12m); length (A) 48ft 11in (14·92m); (B, C) 49ft 7in (15·1m); (F-15) 50ft 3in (15·3m); height (typical) 14ft 8in (4·49m).
Weights: Empty (typical P-61) 24,000lb (10,886kg); (F-15) 22,000lb (9979kg); maximum loaded (A) 32,400lb (14,696kg); (B) 38,000lb (17,237kg); (C) 40,300lb (18,280kg); (F-15, clean) 28,000lb (12,700kg).
Performance: maximum speed (A, B) 366mph (590km/h); (C) 430mph (692km/h); (F-15) 440mph (708km/h); initial climb (A, B) 2,200ft (670m)/min; (C, F-15) 3,000ft (914m)/min; service ceiling (A, B) 33,000ft (10,060m); (C, F-15) 41,000ft (12,500m); range with maximum fuel (A) 500 miles; (B, C) 2,800 miles (4500km); (F.15) 4,000 miles (6440km).
Armament: Four Fixed 20mm M-2 cannon in belly, firing ahead (plus, in first 37 A, last 250 B and all C) electric dorsal turret with four 0·5in remotely controlled from front or rear sight station and fired by pilot; (B and C) underwing racks for 6,400lb load; (F-15A) no armament.
History: First flight (XP-61) 21 May 1942; service delivery (A) May 1944; first flight (F-15A) 1946.
User: USA (AAF).

Development: The first aircraft ever ordered to be designed explicitly as a night fighter, the XP-61 prototypes were ordered in January 1941 on the basis of combat reports from the early radar-equipped fighters of the RAF. A very big aircraft, the P-61 had the new SCR-720 AI radar in the nose, the armament being mounted well back above and below the rather lumpy nacelle housing pilot, radar operator and gunner with front and rear sighting stations. The broad wing had almost full-span double-slotted flaps, very small ailerons and lateral-control spoilers in an arrangement years ahead of its time. Black-painted (hence the name), the P-61A entered service with the 18th Fighter Group in the South Pacifice and soon gained successes there and in Europe. Buffet from the turret led to this soon being deleted, but the B and C had pylons for the very heavy load of four 250 gal tanks or 6,400lb (2900kg) bombs. Total production was 941, followed by 35 slim photo-reconnaissance versions. *continued* ▶

Below: Though late in reaching the war, the P-61 proved a tough and capable aircraft. This P-61A-5 was assigned in July 1944 to the 9th AF's 422nd NFS, based at Scorton, in North Yorkshire.

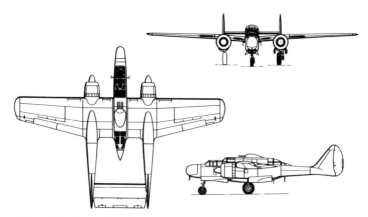

Above: Northrop P-61A with dorsal turret fitted.

Above: Despite its great size the P-61 had very good manoeuvrability, in part because of the patented spoiler-type lateral control and Deceleron aileron/airbrake surfaces. Most of the P-61s that reached Europe were engaged in night ground-attack missions; the P-61B and C could carry no less than 6,400lb of bombs.

Above: Most of the early production P-61As went to the 422nd NFS. This is 42-5578 pictured over West Germany late in the war. At this time the squadron had moved to Etain, in France.

Below: Another of the early P-61As of the 422nd, pictured at its dispersal at Scorton in the autumn of 1944, just before moving to France. The rival 425th NFS was then operating at Charmy Down.

Republic P-47 Thunderbolt
P-47B, C, D, M and N

Origin: Republic Aviation Corporation.
Type: Single-seat fighter; (D and N) fighter-bomber.
Engine: One Pratt & Whitney R-2800 Double Wasp 18-cylinder two-row radial; (B) 2,000hp R-2800-21; (C, most D) 2,300hp R-2800-59; (M, N) 2,800hp R-2800-57 or -77 (emergency wet rating).
Dimensions: Span 40ft 9¼in (12·4m); length (B) 34ft 10in; (C, D, M, N) 36ft 1¼in (11·03m); height (B) 12ft 8in; (C, D) 14ft 2in (4·3m); (M, N) 14ft 8in.
Weights: Empty (B) 9,010lb (4087kg); (D) 10,700lb (4853kg); maximum loaded (B) 12,700lb (5760kg); (C) 14,925lb; (D) 19,400lb (8800kg); (M) 14,700lb; (N) 21,200lb (9616kg).
Performance: Maximum speed (B) 412mph; (C) 433mph; (D) 428mph (690km/h); (M) 470mph; (N) 467mph (751km/h); initial climb (typical) 2,800ft (855m)/min; service ceiling (B) 38,000ft; (C-N) 42,000–43,000ft (13,000m); range on internal fuel (B) 575 miles; (D) 1,000 miles (1600km); ultimate range (drop tanks) (D) 1,900 miles (3060km); (N) 2,350 miles (3800km).
Armament: (Except M) eight 0·5in Colt-Browning M-2 in wings, each with 267, 350 or 425 rounds (M) six 0·5in; (D and N) three to five racks for external load of tanks, bombs or rockets to maximum of 2,500lb (1134kg).

**Below: This colourful
P-47D-25 belonged to the
352nd FS, 353rd FG, Raydon.**

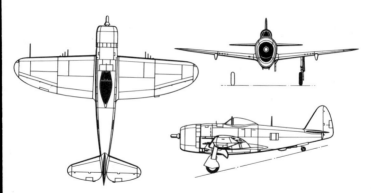

Above: Republic P-47D-25 prior to addition of dorsal fin.

History: First flight (XP-47B) 6 May 1941; production delivery (B) 18 March 1942; final delivery (N) September 1945.
Users: Australia, Brazil, France, Soviet Union, UK (RAF), USA (AAF).

Development: Before the United States entered World War II it was eagerly digesting the results of air combats in Europe and, in 1940, existing plans by Republic's chief designer Alexander Kartveli were urgently replaced by sketches for a much bigger fighter with the new R-2800 engine. ▶

Below: Despite their yellow engine cowls — later to denote the 361st Fighter Group of the 8th Air Force — these two early P-47Cs were photographed over Long Island in 1942 before any of this type were assigned to the 361st. Curiously, like the Typhoon the P-47 was thought to be readily mistaken for the Fw 190, and most early examples in the European theatre had white bands over the tail surfaces and white engine cowls to avoid confusion. Early models, prior to the bubble canopy, were called "razorbacks".

This appeared to be the only way to meet the Army Air Corps' new targets for fighter performance. Kartveli began by designing the best installation of the big engine and its turbocharger, placed under the rear fuselage. The air duct had to pass under the elliptical wing, and there were problems in achieving ground clearance for the big propeller (12ft diameter, even though it had the exceptional total of four blades) with landing gear able to retract inwards and still leave room in the wing for the formidable armament of eight 0·5in guns. After severe and protracted technical difficulties the P-47B was cleared for production in early 1942 and at the beginning of 1943 two fighter groups equipped with the giant new fighter (one the famed 56th, to become top scorers in Europe) joined the 8th AF in Britain to begin escorting B-17 and B-24 heavies. Their value was dramatically increased when they began to carry drop tanks and fly all the way to the target. The same capability turned the big and formidable fighter into a much-feared bomber and, with devastating firepower, vast numbers of P-47Ds strafed and bombed throughout the European and Pacific theatres until the end of World War II. Republic's output of D models (12,602) is the largest

Above: An early "razorback" P-47D, in D-Day markings and the checkered nose of the 78th FG based at Duxford.

total of one sub-type of any fighter in history, total production of the "Jug" amounting to 15,660. The lightweight M was too late for its role of chasing flying bombs but scored successes against the Me 262 and Ar 234 jets, while the long-range P-47N matched the M fuselage with a bigger wing for the Pacific war. There were numerous experimental versions, one of which reached 504mph. After World War II the "Jug" was popular with many air forces until well into the 1950s.

Below left: The name *Chunky* was particularly apt for this bombed and tanked P-47D-10; the popular name "Jug" was derived from Juggernaut.

Below: The P-47N's long-span wing with zero-length rocket launchers and extra fuel raised internal capacity to 594Imp gallons.

Vought V-166B F4U Corsair
F4U-1 to -7, F3A, FG, F2G and AU

Origin: Chance Vought Division of United Aircraft Corporation; also built by Brewster and Goodyear.

Type: Single-seat carrier-based fighter-bomber (sub-variants, see text).

Engine: (F4U-1) 2,000hp Pratt & Whitney R-2800-8(B) Double Wasp 18-cylinder two-row radial; (-1A) 2,250hp R-2800-8(W) with water injection; (-4) 2,450hp R-2800-18W with water-methanol; (-5) 2,850hp R-2800-32(E) with water-methanol; (F2G) 3,000hp P&W R-4360 Wasp Major 28-cylinder four-row radial.

Dimensions: Span 40ft 11¾in (12·48m), (British, 39ft 7in); length 33ft 8¼in (10·27m); (-1, -3) 33ft 4in; (-5N and -7) 34ft 6in; height 14ft 9¼in (4·49m); (-1, -2) 16ft 1in.

Weights: Empty (-1A) 8,873lb (4025kg); (-5, typical) 9,900lb (4490kg); maximum loaded (-1A) 14,000lb (6350kg); (-5) 15,079lb (6840kg); (AU-1) 19,398lb.

Performance: Maximum speed (-1A) 395mph (635km/h); (-5) 462mph (744km/h); initial climb (-1A) 2,890ft (880m)/min; (-5) 4,800ft (1463m)/min; service ceiling (-1A) 37,000ft (11,280m); (-5) 44,000ft (13,400m); range on internal fuel, typically 1,000 miles (1609km).

Armament: See "Development" text.

History: First flight (XF4U) 29 May 1940; (production -1) June 1942; combat delivery July 1942; final delivery (-7) December 1952.

Users: (Wartime) Mexico, New Zealand, UK (RN), USA (Navy, Marines).

Development: Designed by Rex Beisel and Igor Sikorsky, the inverted-gull-wing Corsair was one of the greatest combat aircraft in history. Planned to use the most powerful engine and biggest propeller ever fitted to a fighter, the prototype was the first US warplane to exceed 400mph and outperformed all other American aircraft. Originally fitted with two fuselage and two wing guns, it was replanned with six 0·5in Browning MG 53-2 in the folding outer wings, each with about 390 rounds. Action with land-based Marine squadrons began in the Solomons in February 1943; from then on the Corsair swiftly gained air supremacy over the previously un-troubled Japanese. The -1C had four 20mm cannon, and the -1D and most subsequent types carried a 160gal drop tank and two 1,000lb (907kg) ▶

Below: This F4U-1D was typical of the late-war production by Chance Vought and Goodyear. It is shown with rockets but no tanks in Marines livery.

Right: This F4U-1A, with hook removed for land-based operation, was one of 424 supplied in the final year of the war to the RNZAF. No 5315 was assigned to 18 Sqn, based at Bougainville from January 1945, and saw intensive combat duties throughout the Solomons and Guadalcanal.

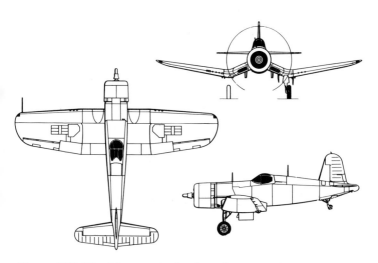

Above: F4U-1D with normal wingtip and armament.

Above: Taken in the spring of 1945, this photograph shows a Corsair (probably an F4U-1A) of the Marine Corps (probably VMF-124) making a carrier landing. A few units, such as VF-17 and VMF-214, gained widespread publicity, but the majority were seldom visited by official reporters.

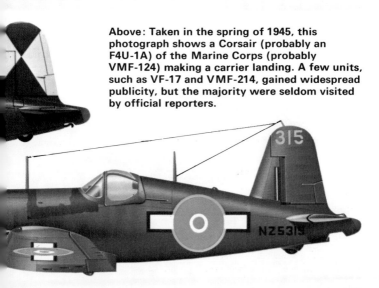

bombs or eight rockets. Many hundreds of P versions carried cameras, and N variants had an APS-4 or -6 radar in a wing pod for night interceptions. Brewster made 735 F3A, and Goodyear 4,008 FG versions, but only ten of the fearsome F2G. Fabric-skinned wings became metal in the post-war -5, most of which had cannon, while the 110 AU-1 attack bombers carried a 4,000lb load in Korea at speeds seldom exceeding 240mph! In December 1952 the last of 12,571 Corsairs came off the line after a longer production run (in terms of time) than any US fighter prior to the Phantom.

Above: An apparently new F4U-1, with revised canopy, flying in British waters in 1943. It bears no unit markings but is probably in Marine Corps hands, with the 1943 paint scheme of gloss/non-specular sea blue, intermediate blue and white.

Below: Running up on the Vought ramp at Stratford, JT531 was a Corsair II (F4U-1D) of the Fleet Air Arm. First model to operate from carriers, the Corsair II had clipped wings to fit below decks.

OTHER NATIONS

Of course, many important countries such as Argentina, Sweden and Switzerland did not officially participate in World War II and their aircraft are absent from this book. Other countries, such as Poland and the Netherlands, were overrun within weeks or days by the Nazi armies, and few of their aircraft survived to play any ongoing role. Australia, however, was a special case.

Geographically well separated from potential enemies, the Commonwealth of Australia had spent only token amounts on defence and had virtually no capability for manufacturing warplanes until after the start of World War II. But, partly through the initiative of Wing Commander Lawrence Wackett, who had formed Tugan Aircraft and then, in 1936, registered Commonwealth Aircraft Corporation, the germ of a planemaking industry did exist. This was strengthened by the decision in January 1939 to build the British Beaufort under Bristol licence, powered by locally made Twin Wasp engines.

These engines were the only ones available when, in January 1942, Australia found itself facing invasion by the all-conquering Japanese. Within weeks Wackett had completed the basic design of a tough but inevitably second-rate fighter, the Boomerang, to use the Twin Wasp. Like most things Australian, it had no frills but worked. To the end of the war Boomerangs were to be found "looking into the whites of the enemy's eyes",

This American-engined Dutch Fokker G.I was intended for Spain but was commandeered for home defence at the Fokker works. It flew a single mission on 13 May 1940.

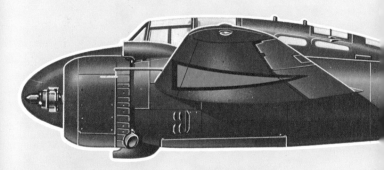

typically serving as a target marker for strikes by Hellcats, Corsairs or even large bombers.

In 1919 in Amsterdam Anthony Fokker got started as a planemaker by illegally tricking his former enemies, the Allies, into letting through trainloads of aircraft materials and parts. He became the most successful constructor in Western Europe, with both military and civil types. The D.XXI fighter was an effective intermediate design with an unbraced monoplane wing and variable-pitch propeller but old-fashioned structure and fixed landing gear. The small force was soon eliminated by the Luftwaffe. The big all-metal G.I created an international sensation when the prototype appeared at the Paris airshow in 1936; its firepower was exceptional, and matched by general size and power. On 10 May 1940, however, there were simply too few to make any difference.

Poland presented an even sorrier picture. In the mid-1930s its air force had been one of the strongest and best trained in Europe, and the large force of fighter regiments equipped with the P.11 would have deterred any aggressor. By 1939, however, they were out of date. There was, it is true, a successor, the PZL P.50 Jastrzab. Only one prototype was flying when the Germans invaded, and that was shot down by Polish AA gunners who thought it must be German.

Commonwealth Boomerang
CA-12 to CA-19 Boomerang
(data for CA-12)

Origin: Commonwealth Aircraft Corporation, Australia.
Type: Single-seat fighter.
Engine: 1,200hp Pratt & Whitney R-1830-S3C4G Twin Wasp 14-cylinder two-row radial.
Dimensions: Span 36ft 3in (11m); length 25ft 6in (7·77m); height 11ft 6in (3·5m).
Weights: Empty 5,450lb (2474kg); loaded 7,600lb (3450kg).
Performance: Maximum speed 296mph (474km/h); service ceiling 29,000ft (8845m); range at 190mph (304km/h) 930 miles (1490km).
Armament: Normally, two 20mm Hispano cannon and four 0·303in Browning machine guns in wings.
History: First flight 29 May 1942; first delivery August 1942; final deliveries, early 1944.
User: Australia.

Development: When Australia suddenly found itself in the front line, in December 1941, it had no modern fighters save a few Buffaloes supplied to the RAF in Singapore. To try to produce a stop-gap quickly the Commonwealth Aircraft Corporation at Fishermen's Bend, Melbourne, decided to design and build their own. But the design team, under Wing Commander Laurence J. Wackett, was severely restricted. The new fighter had to be based on the familiar North American trainer series, which since 1938 had served as the basis for the excellent Wirraway general-purpose combat machine and trainer, of which 755 were made by CAC by 1946. Moreover the only powerful engine available was the 1,200hp Twin Wasp, judged by 1942 to be much too low-powered for first-line fighters elsewhere. Despite these restrictions the resulting machine was tough, outstandingly manoeuvrable and by no means outclassed by the Japanese opposition. Wackett's team worked day and night to design the CA-12 in a matter of weeks and build and fly the prototype in a further 14 weeks. Testing and production went ahead together and, as there were no real snags, the first of 105 CA-12s were soon fighting in New Guinea. There followed 95 CA-13s with minor changes and 49 CA-19s, as well as a CA-14 with turbocharged engine and square tail. Boomerangs did not carry bombs but often marked targets for "heavies" and undertook close support with their guns.

Above right: Part of a formation of Boomerangs of No 5 Sqn, RAAF, operating from Bougainville, New Guinea, in 1944.

Below right: The second production CA-12, at roll-out.

Below: This Boomerang, actually the aircraft nearest the camera in the photograph above right, is a CA-13 incorporating numerous minor changes as the result of combat experience.

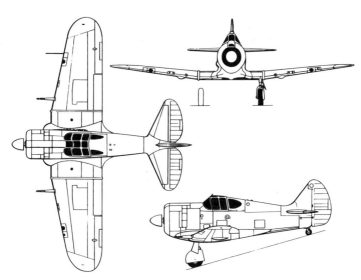

Above: Commonwealth CA-13 Boomerang (CA-12 and -19 similar).

Fokker D.XXI

D.XXI (D.21)

Origin: NV Fokker, Netherlands; licence-built by Valtion Lentokonetehdas, Finland; Haerens Flyvertroppernes Vaerkstader, Denmark; Spanish Republican Government plant.

Type: Single-seat fighter.

Engine: (Dutch) one 830hp Bristol Mercury VIII nine-cylinder radial; (Danish) 645hp Mercury VIS; (Finnish) 825hp Pratt & Whitney R-1535-SB4-G Twin Wasp Junior 14-cylinder two-row radial.

Dimensions: Span 36ft 1in (11m); length (Mercury) 26ft 11in (8·22m); (R-1535) 26ft 3in (8m); height 9ft 8in (2·94m).

Weights: Empty (Mercury) 3,180lb (1442kg); (R-1535) 3,380lb (1534kg); loaded (Mercury) 4,519lb (2050kg); (R-1535) 4,820lb (2186kg).

Performance: Maximum speed (Mercury VIII) 286mph (480km/h); (R-1535) 272mph (439km/h); climb to 9,842ft (3000m) 3·5min (Mercury); 4·5min (R-1535); service ceiling (Mercury) 36,090ft (11,000m); (R-1535) 32,000ft (9750m); range (Mercury) 590 miles (950km); (R-1353) 559 miles (900km).

Armament: (Dutch) four 7·9mm FN-Brownings, two in fuselage and two in wings; (Danish) two Madsen 7·9mm in wings and two Madsen 20mm cannon in underwing blisters; (Finnish) four 7·7mm machine guns in outer wings.

History: First flight, 27 March 1936; service delivery (Dutch) January 1938, (Finnish production) June 1938, (Danish production) 1939.

Users: Denmark, Finland, Netherlands.

Development: In the second half of the 1930s any sound warplane that was generally available could be sure of attracting widespread interest. The Fokker D.XXI came from a company with a great reputation all over the world, and though it was designed — by Ir. E. Schatzki, in 1935 — purely to meet the requirements of the Netherlands East Indies Army Air Service, it became the leading fighter of three major European nations and was planned as a standard type by a fourth. This was as well for Fokker, because the plans of the original customer were changed and a contract was never signed. Yet the little fighter was all one would expect: neat, tough and highly manoeuvrable, with good performance and heavy armament. It marked the transition between the fabric-covered biplane and the stressed-skin monoplane. The wing was wood, with bakelite/ply skin. The fuselage was welded steel tube, with detachable metal panels back to the cockpit and fabric on

Below: 26th of the 36 D.XXI fighters bought for the home LVA, assigned to the 2e Jachtvliegtuigafdeling at Amsterdam Schipol. Orange "neutrality" markings were adopted in October 1939.

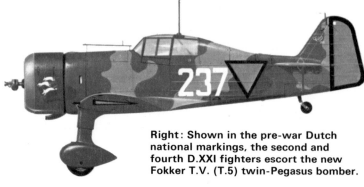

Right: Shown in the pre-war Dutch national markings, the second and fourth D.XXI fighters escort the new Fokker T.V. (T.5) twin-Pegasus bomber.

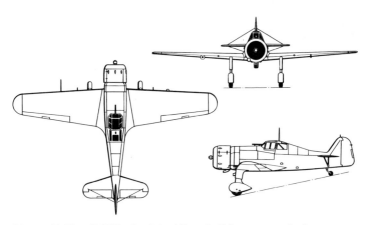

Above: Fokker D.XXI of original Dutch (Mercury engine) type.

the rear fuselage and tail. Landing gear was fixed. The prototype flew at Welschap on a Mercury VIS engine, and in May 1937 the home government ordered 36 with a more powerful Mercury, supplied from Bristol. There were many Fokker projects for developed D.XXIs with retractable landing gear and other engines, but the production aircraft was generally similar to the prototype. In the seventh (No 217) test pilot H. Leegstra set a Dutch height record at 37,250ft. Meanwhile production of a modified version was getting under way for Finland, which bought seven with a manufacturing licence. Denmark followed with an order for three and a manufacturing licence, and the fourth to adopt the D.XXI was Republican Spain. The latter set up a new plant and was about to start accepting deliveries when the area was overrun by Nationalist forces. The VL (Finnish state factory) delivered 38 in 1938–39 and all of them participated very successfully in air battles against the Soviet forces from the start of the Soviet invasion on 30 November 1939. The D.XXI was put into accelerated production, but as all the Finnish-built Mercuries were needed for Blenheims the Finnish D.XXI was redesigned to take the heavier but less powerful Twin Wasp Junior, 55 of this type being built (one having retractable landing gear). The Danish Royal Army Aircraft Factory gradually delivered ten with low-rated Mercury and two cannon, eight being taken over during the German invasion in March 1940. Finally, on 10 May 1940 the 29 combat-ready aircraft in Holland fought round the clock until their ammunition ran out on the third day.

Fokker G.I

G.Ia and G.Ib

Origin: NV Fokker, Netherlands.
Type: Three-seat (G.Ib, two-seat) heavy fighter and close-support.
Engines: (G.Ia) two 830hp Bristol Mercury VIII nine-cylinder radials; (G.Ib) two 750hp Pratt & Whitney R-1535-SB4-G Twin Wasp Junior 14-cylinder radials.
Dimensions: Span (G.Ia) 56ft 3¼in (17·2m); (G.Ib) 54ft 1½in (16·5m); length, (G.Ia) 37ft 8¾in (11·5m); (G.Ib) 33ft 9½in (10·3m); height 11ft 1¾in (3·4m).
Weights: Empty (G.Ia) 7,326lb (3323kg); (G.Ib) 6,930lb (3143kg); loaded, (G.Ia) 10,560lb (4790kg); (G.Ib) 10,520lb (4772kg).
Performance: Maximum speed (G.Ia) 295mph (475km/h); (G.Ib) 268mph (430km/h); time to climb to 19,680ft (6000m), (G.Ia) 8·9min; (G.Ib) 12·1min; service ceiling, (G.Ia) 30,500ft (9300m); (G.Ib) 28,535ft (8695m); range, (G.Ia) 945 miles (1520km); (G.Ib) 913 miles (1469km).
Armament: (G.Ia) row of eight 7·9mm FN-Browning machine guns fixed in nose, one similar gun manually aimed in tailcone; internal bomb bay for load of 880lb (400kg). (G.Ib) two 23mm Madsen cannon and two 7·9mm FN-Brownings in nose, otherwise same.
History: First flight, 16 March 1937; service delivery, May 1938.
Users: Denmark, Netherlands, Sweden.

Development: Appearance of the prototype G.I at the 1936 Paris Salon caused a sensation. The concept of a large twin-engined fighter was novel, and the devastating armament of the G.I caused it to be called "Le Faucheur" (the Grim Reaper). Nations practically queued to test-fly the Hispano-

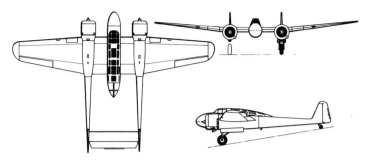

Above: Fokker G.I of original (Mercury engine G.Ia) type.

engined prototype and the first sale was 12 to Republican Spain in June 1937. Meanwhile the home LVA eventually signed for 36 of a much altered version with a third crew-member (radio operator) and Mercury engines in a larger airframe. Finland sought a licence, Sweden bought 18 and Denmark bought nine plus a licence. The Dutch placed an embargo on export of the Spanish aircraft, called G.Ib, and when Germany swept into Holland on 10 May 1940 these were still lined up at Schiphol. Guns were hastily taken from crashed or damaged aircraft and fitted to the Spanish machines which were thrown into the fight. The 23 combat-ready G.Ia fighters likewise fought until all were destroyed save one (in which, in 1942, two senior Fokker pilots escaped to England). There were several non-standard G.Is, including one with a ventral observation cupola. All surviving or unfinished aircraft were impressed into the Luftwaffe and used as combat trainers and tugs.

Left: This Twin Wasp Junior G.I (so-called "G.Ib") was one of those confiscated by the Dutch and parked at Schiphol on 10 May 1940. Hurriedly painted in LVA markings and number 346, it was assigned to 4 JaVA but on 13 May had brake failure and was captured intact by the Luftwaffe.

Below: The first production G.Ia (Mercuries) seen in May 1938.

PZL P.11

P.11a, 11b and 11c

Origin: Państwowe Zakłady Lotnicze, Poland.
Type: Single-seat fighter.
Engine: One Bristol-designed nine-cylinder radial; (11a) 500hp Skoda Mercury IVS2; (11b) 595hp IAR Gnome-Rhône K9 (Jupiter); (11c) 645hp PZL Mercury VIS2.
Dimensions: Span 35ft 2in (10·72m); length 24ft 9in or 24ft 9½in (7·55m); height 9ft 4in (2·85m).
Weights: Empty (11c) 2,524lb (1145kg); loaded 3,960lb (1795kg).
Performance: Maximum speed (11c) 242mph (390km/h); initial climb 2,625ft (800m)/min; service ceiling 36,090ft (11,000m); range (economic cruise, no combat) 503 miles (810km).
Armament: (11a) two 7·7mm (0·303in) Browning, each with 700 rounds, in sides of fuselage; (11c) two 7·7mm KM Wz 33 machine guns, each with 500 rounds, in sides of fuselage, and two more, each with 300 rounds, inside wing at junction of struts; provision for two 27lb (12·25kg) bombs.
History: First flight (P.11/I) August 1931; (production P.11a) June 1933.
Users: Bulgaria (P.24), Greece (P.24), Poland (P.11c), Romania (P.11b, P.24).

Development: Having hired brilliant young designer Zygmund Pulaski at its formation in 1928, the Polish PZL (National Aero Factory) set itself to building gull-winged monoplane fighters of outstanding quality. All the early production models were powered by Polish-built Jupiter engines, and large numbers of P.7a fighters formed the backbone of the young Polish Air Force. The P.11 was the natural successor, but when the prototype was about to fly Pulaski was killed in a crash and his place was taken by W. Jakimiuk (later designer for D. H. Canada and SNCASE). The first P.11 was powered by a Gnome-Rhône Jupiter and subsequent prototypes by a Mistral and Mercury from the same source, but after prolonged trials the P.11a went into production with the Polish-built Mercury IVS. In 1934 the fuselage was redesigned to improve pilot view by lowering the engine and raising the pilot (11c). A new tail and modified wings were introduced and provision was made for two wing guns and radio, but these were usually not available for fitting. The final production model was the export version of the 11a, the 11b, which was built in Romania as the IAR P.11f. Many

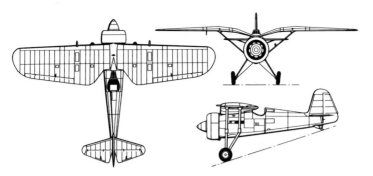

Above: PZL P.11c (showing two extra guns in the wings).

further developments were planned, but the main fighter force defending Poland in September 1939 comprised 12 squadrons of P.11c, most with only two guns and operating with no warning system in chaotic conditions. They nevertheless destroyed 126 Luftwaffe aircraft for the loss of 114 of their own number. Final PZL fighter was the P.24 family, of which there were many variants produced entirely for export. Most had a 970hp Gnome-Rhône 14N engine, and two cannon and two machine guns.

Above: P.11c fighters of the Dyon III/3, 3rd Air Regiment, pictured during the aviation parade at Warsaw in August 1936, when the Polish Army Air Force was one of the strongest and most modern in Europe. In the fighting of September 1939 Dyon III/3 distinguished itself as the highest-scoring of all the Polish fighter units.

Left: A PZL P.11c depicted in new condition and with the full planned armament of four KM Wz 33 machine guns, as fitted to only about one-third of the 175 aircraft of this type delivered for Polish use. Another fault was failure to procure radio sets for all but a small number of the fighters, though it had been intended that all should be so equipped. The P.11c was popularly called Jedenastka (the eleventh); this particular example served with 113 Sqn, 3rd Air Regiment.

GERMAN, ITALIAN AND JAPANESE
FIGHTERS
OF WORLD WAR II
Major Fighters and Attack Aircraft of the Axis Powers

Contents

Aircraft are arranged alphabetically by manufacturers' names, within national groups.

Introduction

This section describes the fighters of the Axis powers. To English-speaking readers this meant "enemy". The word Axis originally referred to the supposed "Berlin-Rome axis" following a pre-war treaty concluded between Hitler of Germany and Mussolini of Italy, but in 1942 the concept of the Axis was widened to include Japan.

Unquestionably, Nazi Germany was the technical leader. This is despite the fact that unfettered development of fighters was not possible in Germany until 1934, and also that, very remarkably, the mighty and swiftly growing Luftwaffe went to war in 1939 with only one type of single-engined fighter. This machine, the Messerschmitt Bf 109, was the very first fighter designed by Willy Messerschmitt, who had previously built sporting machines and small transports. When World War I ace Ernst Udet, soon to become the Luftwaffe's head of procurement, saw the prototype he exclaimed, "This machine will never make a fighter!" Not only did it make a very formidable fighter, but it was produced in larger numbers than any other single type of aircraft except the Soviet Il-2.

Messerschmitt also produced a big long-range twin, the Bf 110, but this fared badly against Hurricanes and Spitfires. Never envisaged as such at the time of its design, it later proved to be an outstanding radar-equipped night fighter, along with a much greater and more versatile aircraft, the Ju 88.

The Luftwaffe also recieved an outstanding fighter in the Focke-Wulf Fw 190. Small, chunky, all-electric, complex, heavy and amazingly tough, its original radial-engined version was superior in almost all respects except turn radius to the Spitfires of 1941, and for a while gave the RAF a hard time.

When Udet saw the first Bf 109 he was used to thinking in terms of biplanes with big wings, open cockpits and not much weight. Their pilots could crane their necks and look in all directions, and the aircraft could turn on the proverbial sixpence. The Luftwaffe soon learned to go the way of the 109, but in other countries the lesson took years longer. Italy, more than any other country, hung on to the agile biplane long after bitter experience had shown such machines to have little chance of winning. Even the Italian monoplanes stuck with engines of 840hp and an armament of two machine guns, until in late 1941 the first fighters began reaching squadrons with more powerful engines and cannon.

The Japanese, however went on fighting to the bitter end, long after it was abundantly clear that the war could have only one conclusion. Until 1940 Japan's Imperial Army and Navy had both clung to the belief that two machine guns were adequate armament for a fighter, though they had at least made the transition to the monoplane. By 1940, however, the Navy had begun actual combat operations with a fighter which, though still low-powered and fragile compared with those battling in Europe, was destined 18 months later to prove a terrible shock to the Allies. The A6M, better known as the "Zero", combined agility, good all-round performance, firepower and about double the combat radius anyone expected. Together with the weakly armed Ki-43 of the Army, The A6M virtually swept the Allies from the sky over a vast area of the globe.

It was not to last. Like Hitler's Luftwaffe, by 1944 the Japanese were still to a considerable degree flying upgraded versions of the aircraft with which they entered the war.

GERMANY

Naturally, Nazi Germany planned carefully for every eventuality, and where possible had more than one type of aircraft for each combat mission as well as new designs coming along as the next generation. And if ever a fighter had an inauspicious start it was the Messerschmitt Bf 109, first flown at the end of May 1935. Not only was Messerschmitt himself extremely unpopular with top-ranking Nazis, including the air minister, but even impartial experts such as Ernst Udet, head of procurement and one of the world's most famous fighter pilots, said the new 109 would 'never make a fighter'. It was perhaps too advanced in concept, with a long rakish fuselage, shallow enclosed cockpit and amazingly small wing (though liberally endowed with slats and flaps). Yet the 109, instead of being laughed off the scene as many had expected, was not merely the fighter the Luftwaffe selected but it was virtually the only Luftwaffe fighter from 1937 until 1942. Production rose year by year to the final collapse in 1945, and when the last one was built (in Spain, actually, as late as 1958) the total handsomely exceeded 30,000, surpassing that of all other aircraft outside the Soviet Union.

This is all the more remarkable when it is recalled that the only other day fighter worth mentioning, the Fw 190, which flew shortly before the war and began to reach the squadrons in 1941, was in almost all respects superior. Though markedly heavier it was at least as compact, had an incredible capability of carrying guns, bombs and other weapons, and suffered from none of the shortcomings in handling that would have made the mass-produced Bf 109G – the standard 109 from 1942 onward – quite

unacceptable to any Allied air force. Yet while the 190 swiftly became the No 1 tactical multirole attack aircraft, the 109 stayed the No 1 fighter; and in the hands of someone used to its tricky and often unpleasant characteristics it was deadly. Most of the top-scoring Luftwaffe pilots, with 250 to 352 kills each, flew the 109 throughout their careers.

The Luftwaffe, however, also used two quite different species of fighter in World War II in a way paralleled only by Britain. One was the radar-equipped night fighter and the other the jet. Though some 109s and 190s achieved a few night kills the most successful aircraft for bringing down heavy night bombers were all large twins, notably the Bf 110 and Ju 88. The 110 had been intended as a day *zerstörer* (destroyer) to sweep defending fighters out of the path of the Luftwaffe's bombers, but the RAF demonstrated its inability to survive against modern single-seaters. The even larger Ju 88 was designed as a bomber, but in fact by 1944 it had become one of the world's greatest night interceptors with a selection of sensors to help it find its prey, and devastating armament, including cannon firing upwards into the bomber's defenceless undersides.

By late 1944 not only was the twin-jet Me 262 coming into service in numbers but the Luftwaffe also used the highly unconventional Me 163 rocket-propelled interceptor which made up in rate of climb what it lacked in range and endurance. Surprisingly, both were beautiful to fly once in the air, but they suffered from various other problems that restricted their value, and they were too late to stave off defeat.

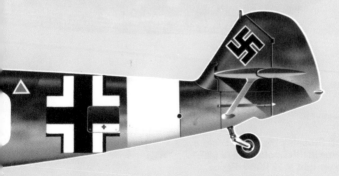

Arado Ar 68

Ar 68G

Origin: Arado Handelsgesellschaft, Warnemünde.
Type: Single-seat fighter.
Engine: 750hp BMW VI 12-cylinder vee liquid-cooled.
Dimensions: Span 36ft 0in (11m); length 31ft 2in (9·5m); height 10ft 10in (3·3m).
Weights: Empty 3,307lb (1500kg); loaded 4,410lb (2000kg).
Performance: Maximum speed 192mph (310km/h) at 13,125ft (4000m); service ceiling 24,280ft (7400m); range with service load 342 miles (550km).
Armament: Two 7·92mm MG 17 machine guns above engine; racks for six 110lb (50kg) bombs.
History: First flight November 1933; (Ar 68G) December 1935; termination of production, probably 1937.

Development: Forbidden to have a warlike air force by the Versailles Treaty, Germany produced no combat aircraft in the 1920s and early 1930s, though German design teams did produce important prototypes in Spain, Sweden and Switzerland. By the time the Nazi party seized power in 1933 there was a useful nucleus of talent and industrial strength and the Arado firm was, with Heinkel, charged with urgently building a first-line fighter for the new Luftwaffe. The result was the Ar 68V1 prototype, powered by the trusty BMW VI engine, rated at 660hp and constructed of welded steel tube and wood, with fabric covering except over the forward and upper fuselage. Like all Arado aircraft of the period it had a tailplane well behind

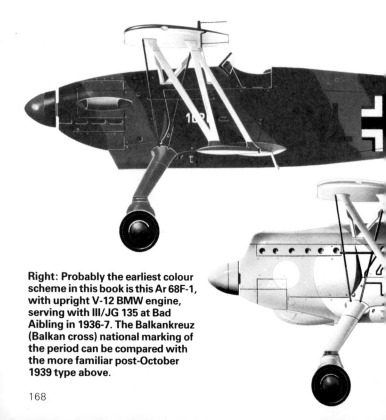

Right: Probably the earliest colour scheme in this book is this Ar 68F-1, with upright V-12 BMW engine, serving with III/JG 135 at Bad Aibling in 1936-7. The Balkankreuz (Balkan cross) national marking of the period can be compared with the more familiar post-October 1939 type above.

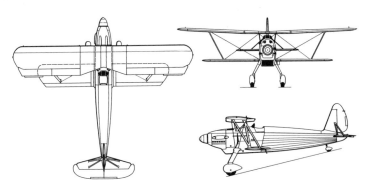

Above: Three-view of the Ar 68E with Jumo 210Da engine.

the fin and rudder, and the single-strut cantilever landing gear was distinctive. Two prototypes flew in 1934 with the 610hp Jumo 210 engine and this was selected for the production Ar 68E which entered service with the newly formed Luftwaffe in 1935. But the Ar 68F reverted to the BMW engine, uprated to 675hp, and the main production centred on the still more powerful Ar 68G. Despite good engines the Ar 68 was never an outstanding machine. It ran second in timing and performance to its great rival the He 51 and, apart from a few used as night fighters, had been relegated to training before World War II. One example of the Ar 68H, with BMW 132Dc radial and enclosed cockpit, was flown and a development, the Ar 197, would have been used aboard the carrier *Graf Zeppelin* had the vessel been commissioned.

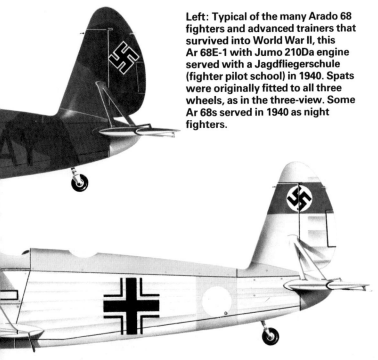

Left: Typical of the many Arado 68 fighters and advanced trainers that survived into World War II, this Ar 68E-1 with Jumo 210Da engine served with a Jagdfliegerschule (fighter pilot school) in 1940. Spats were originally fitted to all three wheels, as in the three-view. Some Ar 68s served in 1940 as night fighters.

Arado Ar 234 Blitz

Ar 234B-1 and B-2 Blitz

Origin: Arado Flugzeugwerke GmbH.

Type: Single-seat reconnaissance (B-1) or attack bomber (B-2).

Engines: Two 1,980lb (900kg) thrust Junkers Jumo 004B axial turbojets.

Dimensions: Span 46ft 3½in (14·2m); length 41ft 5½in (12·65m); height 14ft 1¼in (4·3m).

Weights: Empty 11,464lb (5200kg); loaded 18,541lb (8410kg); maximum with rocket takeoff boost 21,715lb (9850kg).

Performance: Maximum speed (clean) 461mph (742km/h); service ceiling 32,800ft (10,000m); range (clean) 1,013 miles (1630km), (with 3,300lb bomb load) 684 miles (1100km).

Armament: Two fixed MG 151 20mm cannon in rear fuselage, firing to rear and sighted by periscope; various combinations of bombs slung under fuselage and/or engines to maximum of 3,300lb (1500kg).

History: First flight (Ar 234V1) 15 June 1943, (Ar 234V9 with landing gear) March 1944, (Ar 234B-0 pre-production) 8 June 1944; operational delivery September 1944.

User: Germany (Luftwaffe).

Development: As the first jet reconnaissance bomber, the Ar 234 Blitz (meaning Lightning) spearheaded Germany's remarkably bold introduction of high-performance turbojet aircraft in 1944. Its design was begun under Walter Blume in 1941, after long studies in 1940 of an official specification for a jet-propelled reconnaissance aircraft with a range of 1,340 miles. The design was neat and simple, with two of the new axial engines slung under a high wing, and the single occupant in a pressurised cockpit forming the entire nose. But to achieve the required fuel capacity no wheels were fitted. When it flew on 15 June 1943 the first 234 took off from a three-wheel trolley and landed on retractable skids. After extensive trials with eight prototypes the ninth flew with conventional landing gear, leading through 20 pre-production models to the operational 234B-1, with ejection seat, autopilot and drop tanks under the engines. Main production centred on the 234B-2, made in many sub-variants, most of them able to carry a heavy bomb load. Service over the British Isles with the B-1 began in September 1944, followed by a growing force of B-2s which supported the Battle of the Bulge in the winter 1944–45. In March 1945 B-2s of III/KG76 repeatedly attacked the vital Remagen bridge across the Rhine with 2,205lb (1,000kg) bombs, causing its collapse. Though handicapped by fuel shortage these uninterceptable aircraft played a significant role on all European fronts in the closing months of the war, 210 being handed over excluding the many prototypes and later versions with four engines and an uncompleted example with a crescent-shaped wing.

Below: The Ar 234 was the only jet bomber to be operational in World War II, and though it did not affect the course of the war its pinpricks were usually unstoppable. This B-2/P Blitz served with 9/KG 76 operating from Achmer in February 1945. It is seen with 1,102-lb (SC500) bombs hung under the nacelles.

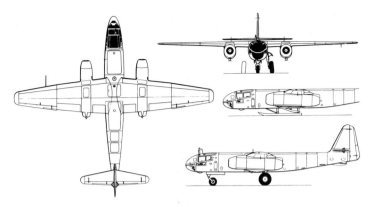

Above: Three-view of Ar 234B-2 (inset, Ar 234 V1 prototype).

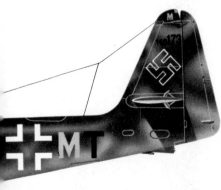

Above: First takeoff by the Ar 234 V9 (ninth prototype) at Alt Lönnewitz on 10 March 1944, with 66 Imp gal drop tanks. This was the first of the B-series, with landing gear; it also introduced pressurization and an ejection seat, one of the first on any production aircraft. This photograph was a frame from a ciné film in which it could be seen that the pale colour in the right jet nozzle was a sudden gout of flame!

Arado Ar 240

Ar prototypes ABC series and 440

Origin: Arado Flugzeugwerke GmbH.
Type: Zerstörer, heavy fighter, see text.
Engines: Two Daimler-Benz inverted-vee-12 liquid-cooled, see text.
Dimensions: Span (A-0) 43ft 9in (13·33m), (C-0) 54ft 5in (16·59m); length (A-0) 42ft 0¼in (12·81m); height 12ft 11½in (3·95m).
Weights: Empty (A-0) 13,669lb (6200kg), (C-0) 18,650lb (8460kg); maximum (A-0) 22,700lb (10,297kg), (C-0) 25,850lb (11,726kg).
Performance: Maximum speed (A-0) 384mph (618km/h), (C-0) 454mph (730km/h) with GM-1 boost at high alt.; max range (A-0) 1,242 miles (2000km).
Armament: (A-0) two fixed 7·92mm MG 17 and two remote-control barbettes each with two 7·92mm MG 81; (C-0) four fixed 20mm MG 151 and two barbettes each with two 13mm MG 131, plus external bomb load up to 3,968lb (1800kg).
History: First flight (V1) 10 May 1940, (A-0) October 1942, (C-0) March 1943, (440) early summer 1942.

Development: In 1938 Arado's technical director, Walter Blume, began studies which were intended to lead to an outstandingly advanced and formidable multi-role combat aircraft, but instead led to years of effort with little reward. Features of the E240 study included tandem seats in a pressurized cockpit, high-lift slats and flaps on a highly loaded wing, a unique

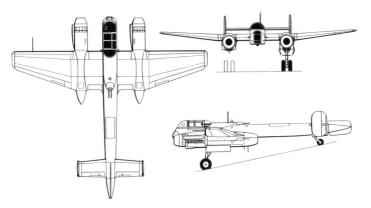

Above: Three-view of the Ar 240A-01 with ducted spinners.

dive brake doubling as the tailcone, and upper and lower rear gun barbettes sighted by the observer through an upper/lower magnifying periscope system. But from the start the Ar 240 was dogged by technical misfortune, the enduring problem being unacceptable flying characteristics (the V1 prototype was unstable about all three axes). Later aircraft switched from the 1,075hp DB 601 to the 1,750hp DB 603A, 1,475hp DB 605AM, 1,900hp DB 603G or BMW 801TJ radial.

Below: The Ar 240 V3 of spring 1941, with conventional spinners.

Bachem Ba 349 Natter

Ba 349 V1-V16, A and B series

Origin: Bachem-Werke GmbH, Waldsee.

Type: Part-expendable target-defence interceptor.

Engine: 4,410lb (2000kg) thrust Walter HWK 109-509C-1 bi-propellant rocket (vertical launch boosted by four 1,102lb (500kg) or two 2,205lb (1000kg) solid motors).

Dimensions: Span 11ft 9¾in (3·6m); length (A) 19ft 9in (6·02m); height (flying attitude) 7ft 4½in (2·25m).

Weights: Empty 1,940lb (880kg); loaded (with boost rockets) 4,920lb (2232kg).

Performance: Maximum speed (sea level) 497mph (800km/h), (at high altitude) 621mph (1000km/h); rate of climb 36,417ft (11,100m)/min; range after climb 20–30 miles (32–48km).

Armament: 24 Föhn 73mm spin-stabilized rockets, or 33 R4M 55mm spin-stabilized rockets, or (proposed) two 30mm MK 108 cannon each with 30 rounds.

Development: One of the most radical and desperate "fighters" ever built, the Natter (Viper) was born of necessity. In the summer of 1944 the mounting weight of daylight attacks by the US 8th Air Force called for unconventional defences, and the Luftwaffe picked a proposal by Dipl-Ing Erich Bachem for a manned interceptor which could be stationed in the path of hostile heavy bombers. As the American formations passed overhead the interceptor would be blasted vertically off the ground, thereafter climbing almost vertically on an internal rocket. Nearing the bombers, the pilot would sight on one and fire his battery of missiles. He would then use his remaining kinetic energy to climb higher than the bombers and swoop back for a ramming attack. Just before impact he was to trigger a mechanism to separate his seat (or front fuselage) and the rear portion with rocket motor.

Tests showed that no simple ejection system could be incorporated, and

Below: One of the Ba 349A Natters, armed with 24 Hs 217 Föhn (Storm) rockets exposed with the streamlined nosecap removed. The interceptor is strapped to its cradle on which it was then to be transported to the launch gantry on a special trailer for elevation to about 87°.

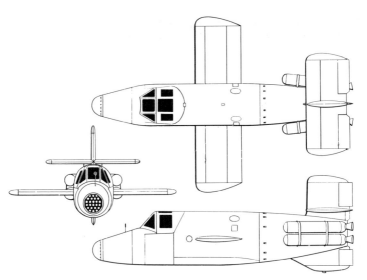

Above: Three-view of the Ba 349B (production aircraft).

the essence of the Natter was simplicity. The structure was wood, apart from the simple metal body with armoured cockpit. Eventually the ramming attack was abandoned, and the only parts saved were the pilot and rocket motor, for hopeful re-use. Following pilotless tests from the near-vertical ramp, and piloted gliding trials towed by an He 111 to about 18,000ft, the first manned shot was attempted on 28 February 1945. At about five seconds from lift-off the canopy came away (apparently hitting Oberleutnant Lothar Siebert) and the Natter curved over and crashed. By April 36 had flown, seven with pilots, but Allied troops overran the factory and launch site before any combat missions could take place.

Below: This almost complete Ba 349A was discovered by Allied troops in May 1945 strapped to its cradle and mounted on its towing trailer. The canopy is unlatched, and the jettisonable plastic nosecap is not fitted. On another trailer is one of the Schmidding solid-fuel takeoff rockets.

Blohm und Voss BV40

Bv40 V1 to V19 and BV 40A

Origin: Blohm und Voss (Abt. Flugzeugbau).
Type: Point-defence interceptor glider.
Dimensions: Span 25ft 11in (7·90m); length 18ft 8½in (5·70m); height 5ft 4¼in (1·66m).
Weights: Empty 1,844lb (836kg); maximum 2,094lb (950kg).
Performance: Maximum speed (Bf 109G tug) 344mph (553km/h), (109G towing two BV 40s) 315mph (507km/h); anticipated diving speed in free flight 560mph (900km/h); time to climb to 23,000ft (7000m), (one BV 40) 12 min, (two BV 40s) 16·8min.
Armament: Two 30mm MK 108 each with 35 rounds.
History: First flight, late May 1944.

Development: Desperate situations lead to desperate remedies, and often to genuine technical progress. This was certainly the case in the Luftwaffe's attempts to inflict heavier losses on the US 8th Air Force daylight bomber formations. One answer was the Ba 349, and an even stranger one was a glider, proposed by BV's technical director Richard Vogt. The reasoning was simple: the only way to reduce the chances of fighters being hit by the hail of fire from a B-17 formation was to reduce the frontal area, and the best way to do this was to eliminate the engine. Moreover, most of the BV 40 was planned for simple and cheap production on a vast scale by woodworkers, while the metal cockpit was to be protected by armour and thick glass representing more than one-quarter of the gross weight. Vogt hoped to use

Blohm und Voss BV 155

Me 155A and B, Bv 155 V1 to V3

Origin: Messerschmitt AG, later Blohm und Voss, Abt. Flugzeugbau.
Type: High-altitude interceptor.
Engine: (155B) DB 603A with TKL 15 turbocharger giving 1,450hp at 49,210ft (15,000m).
Dimensions: Span (B) 67ft 3in (20·5m); length 39ft 4½in (12·00m); height 9ft 9½in (2·98m).
Weights: (B) empty 10,734lb (4870kg); loaded (max armament) 13,263lb (6016kg).
Performance: (B) maximum speed 429mph (690km/h) at 52,493ft (16,000m); range at high alt, about 895 miles (1440km).

Development: Messerschmitt began the Me 155 as a derivative of the Bf 109 to operate from the resumed carrier *Graf Zeppelin*, but when this unhappy ship again fell from favour the 155 reappeared as a pinpoint bomber with 2,205lb (1000kg) bomb and finally in 1943 as a long-span interceptor to hit high-flying US bombers. In August 1943 work was passed from Messerschmitt (said to be overloaded) to Blohm und Voss, but the two firms disagreed violently on the design. The whole job eventually became the Bv 155, but had to be redesigned. The Bv 155 V1 flew on 1 September 1944 and a further redesign, the V2, in February 1945. With outstanding propulsion and aerodynamic features they would have been unmatched by Allied fighters at heights over 40,000ft, and were intended to have heavy groups of 15, 20 or 30mm cannon. At the final collapse work was well advanced on the V4 (C-series) with fuselage radiators.

Right: The BV 155 V3, still unfinished, at Farnborough in late 1945.

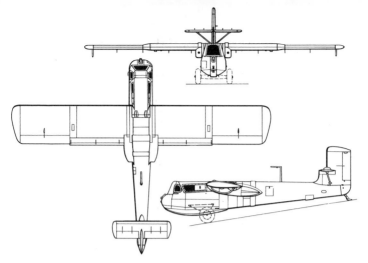

Above: Three-view of BV 40 V1, with jettisonable wheels shown.

one 30mm cannon and trail an explosive charge on a long wire for a second attacking pass, but the best answer was found to be two heavy guns to pump out the maximum firepower in the brief period available in a head-on attack. The whole programme was abandoned in the autumn of 1944 when the flight-test phase had been completed, with six of 19 prototypes, and studies were in hand for heavy bomb loads for release above bomber formations.

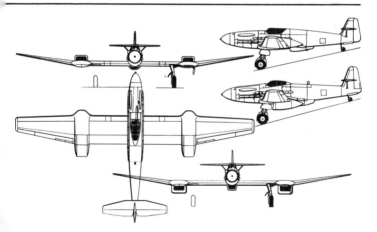

Above: Three-view of BV 155 V2 and V3 with (above) two views of V1.

Dornier Do 335 Pfeil

Do 335A-1 and A-6

Origin: Dornier-Werke GmbH.
Type: (A-1) single-seat fighter, (A-6) two-seat night fighter.
Engines: Two 1,900hp Daimler-Benz DB 603G 12-cylinder inverted-vee liquid-cooled, in push/pull arrangement.
Dimensions: Span 45ft 4in (13·8m); length 45ft 6in (13·87m); height 16ft 4in (4m).
Weights: Empty (A-1) 16,314lb (7400kg); (A-6) 16,975lb (7700kg); maximum loaded (both) 25,800lb (11,700kg).
Performance: Maximum speed (A-1) 413mph (665km/h) sustained; 477mph (765km/h) emergency boost (A-6 about 40mph slower in each case); initial climb (A-1) 4,600ft (1400m)/min; service ceiling (A-1) 37,400ft (11,410m); (A-6) 33,400ft (10,190m); maximum range (both) 1,280 miles (2050km) clean, up to 2,330 miles (3750km) with drop tank.
Armament: Typical A-1, one 30mm MK 103 cannon firing through front propeller hub and two 15mm MG 151/15 above nose; underwing racks for light stores and centreline rack for 1,100lb (500kg) bomb; A-6 did not carry bomb and usually had 15mm guns replaced by 20mm MG 151/20s.
History: First flight (Do 335V1) autumn 1943; (production A-1) late November 1944.
User: Germany (Luftwaffe).

Development: Dornier took out a patent in 1937 for an aircraft powered by two engines, one behind the other, in the fuselage, driving tractor and pusher propellers. In 1939–40 Schempp-Hirth built the Gö 9 research aircraft to test the concept of a rear propeller driven by an extension shaft and in 1941 work began on the Do 231 fighter-bomber. This was replaced by the Do 335 and by first flight Dornier had orders for 14 prototypes, ten preproduction A-0s, 11 production A-1s and three dual-control trainer A-10 and A-12 with stepped tandem cockpits. At high speed the 335 was prone to unpleasant porpoising and snaking, but production continued on the A-1, the A-4 reconnaissance batch and the A-6 with FuG 220 radar

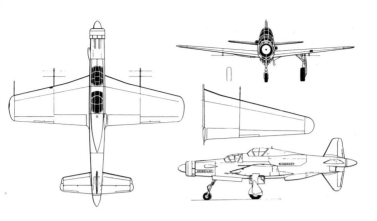

Above: Three-view of the Do 335A-6 two-seat night fighter with (inset) the long-span wing of B-8.

operated by a rear-seat observer. Though heavy, the 335 was strong and very fast and was notable in having the first production type of ejection seat (for obvious reasons). By VE-day about 90 aircraft had been rolled out, more than 60 flown and about 20 delivered to combat units. Work was also well advanced on a number of versions of the Do 335B heavy fighter, with added 30mm MK 108 cannon in the wings (some having two-stage engines and long-span wings), the Do 435 with various very powerful engines, and the twinned Do 635 with two Do 335 fuselages linked by a new parallel centre-section. The 635, which was being designed and produced by Junkers as the 8-635, would have weighed 72,000lb as a recon-naissance aircraft, and flown 4,050 miles cruising at 398mph. Pfeil means "arrow"

Below: The Do 335 V1 (first prototype), which flew on 26 October 1943. Pilots were enthusiastic, and 348mph (560km/h) was recorded with the front propeller feathered.

Focke-Wulf Fw 187 Falke

Fw 187 V1 to V6 and A0

Origin: Focke-Wulf Flugzeugbau GmbH.
Type: Zerstörer, heavy fighter.
Engines: Two Junkers Jumo 210 inverted-vee-12 liquid-cooled, (V1) 680hp 210Da, (most) 730hp 210Ga, (V6) 1,000hp DB 600A.
Dimensions: Span 50ft 2½in (15·30m); length 36ft 5½in (11·01m); height 12ft 7in (3·85m).
Weights: Empty (A-0) 8,157lb (3700kg); maximum 11,023lb (5000kg).
Performance: (A-0) Maximum speed 326mph (525km/h); initial climb, 3,445ft (1050m)/min; service ceiling 32,800ft (10,000m).
Armament: Four 7·92mm MG 17 and two 20mm MG FF.
History: First flight, early May 1937, (A-0) about February 1939.

Development: Though for various reasons it never went into production, Focke-Wulf's Fw 187 Falke (Falcon) was an extremely fine basis for development and, according to all accounts, could have led to an outstanding family of multi-role aircraft. The cramped single-seat V1 prototype was 50mph (80km/h) faster than the contemporary Bf 109B with two similar engines, despite the fact it weighed more than twice as much and had roughly double the range. The V3 was the first with a more spacious

Right: One of the 1940 propaganda photographs showing Fw 187A-0 zerstörers of the so-called Werkschutzstaffel Bremen, which was one of a number of locally raised units maintained and flown by manufacturer's personnel to defend aircraft factories. Only three such aircraft existed, but Goebbels' propaganda machine issued a stream of pictures to give the impression this was the Luftwaffe's new zerstörer (destroyer, ie heavy fighter).

Below: 'Zerstörer number 7' in the pseudo Luftwaffe long-range fighter staffel.

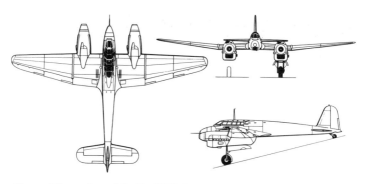

Above: Three-view of the Fw 187A-0.

tandem-seat cockpit, alongside which were the four MG 17s, the cannon being under the floor. The V6 reached 392mph (631km/h) on two DB 600A engines, faster than any other fighter in January 1939. Official interest in this promising fighter was slight, and only three A-0 pre-production Falkes were built, being used in combat by an Industrie-Schutzstaffel defending the company works at Bremen (Dipl-Ing Mehlhorn allegedly scored several kills). In the winter 1940–41 the trio were loaned to a Jagdstaffel in Norway, where they were said to be much preferred to the Bf 110; but when the RLM heard about it they were immediately recalled.

Focke-Wulf Fw 189 Uhu

Fw 189A-1, -2 and -3

Origin: Focke-Wulf Flugzeugbau GmbH; built under Focke-Wulf control by SNCASO, with outer wings from Breguet.

Type: Three-seat reconnaissance and close support.

Engines: Two 465hp Argus As 410A-1 12 cylinder inverted-vee air-cooled.

Dimensions: Span 60ft 4½in (18·4m); length 39ft 4½in (12m); height 10ft 2in (3·1m).

Weights: Empty 5,930lb (2690kg); loaded 8,708lb (3950kg).

Performance: Maximum speed 217mph (350km/h); climb to 13,120ft (4000m) in 8 min 20sec; service ceiling 23,950ft (7300m); range 416 miles (670km).

Armament: (A-2) one 7·92mm MG17 machine gun in each wing root, twin 7·92mm MG81 manually aimed in dorsal position and (usually) twin MG 81 in rear cone with limited field of fire; underwing racks for four 110lb (50kg) bombs.

History: First flight (Fw 189V1) July 1938; first delivery (pre-production Fw 189A-0) September 1940; final delivery August 1944.

User: Germany (Luftwaffe), Hungary, Slovakia.

Development: Today the diversity of aircraft layout makes us forget how odd this aircraft seemed. It looked strange to the customer also, but after outstandingly successful flight trials the 189 Uhu (Owl) was grudgingly bought in quantity as a standard reconnaissance aircraft. Though it flew in numbers well before the war — no two prototypes being alike — it was unknown by the Allies until it was disclosed in 1941 as "the Flying Eye" of the German armies. On the Eastern front it performed beyond all expectation, for it retained its superb handling (which made it far from a sitting duck to fighters) and also showed great toughness of structure and more than once returned to base with one tail shot off or removed by Soviet ramming attack. Attempts to produce special attack versions with small heavily armoured nacelles were not so successful, but 10 Fw 189B trainers were built with a conventional nacelle having side-by-side dual controls in a normal cockpit, with an observer above the trailing edge. The Fw 189A-3 was another dual-control version having the normal "glasshouse". Eventually the sole source became French factories with assembly at Bordeaux-Mérignac (today the Dassault Mirage plant), which halted as Allied armies approached. There were many different versions and several developments with more powerful engines, but the basic A-1, A-2 (better armament) and A-3 were the only types built in numbers, the total of these versions being 846.

Below: Though most Fw 189s served in the reconnaissance role this tough and manoeuvrable bird also flew close-support missions and with FuG 212 Lichtenstein C1 radar served as a night fighter. This particular machine, an A-1, served with 1(H)/32 at Petsamo (northern Finland) in December 1942.

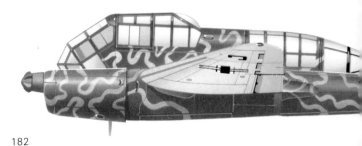

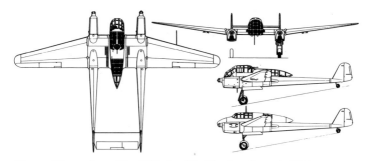

Above: Three-view of Fw 189A-2, with side view (lower) of B-0.

Below: Luftwaffe ground-recon trooper with an A-1 in USSR.

Focke-Wulf Fw 190 and Ta 152

Fw 190A series, D series, F series, G series and Ta 152

Origin: Focke-Wulf Flugzeugbau GmbH; extremely dispersed manufacture and assembly, and part-subcontracted to Brandt (SNCA du Centre), France; also built in France post-war.

Type: Single-seat fighter bomber.

Engine: (A-8, F-8) one 1,700hp (2,100hp emergency boost) BMW 801Dg 18-cylinder two-row radial; (D-9) one 1,776hp (2,240hp emergency boost) Junkers Jumo 213A-1 12-cylinder inverted-vee liquid-cooled; (Ta 152H-1) one 1,880hp (2,250hp) Jumo 213E-1.

Dimensions: Span 34ft 5½in (10·49m); (Ta 152H-1) 47ft 6¾in (14·5m); length (A-8, F-8) 29ft 0in (8·84m); (D-9) 33ft 5¼in (10·2m); (Ta 152H-1) 35ft 5½in (10·8m); height 13ft 0in (3·96m); (D-9) 11ft 0¼in (3·35m); (Ta 152H-1) 11ft 8in (3·55m).

Weights: Empty (A-8, F-8) 7,055lb (3200kg); (D-9) 7,720lb (3500kg); (Ta 152H-1) 7,940lb (3600kg); loaded (A-8, F-8) 10,800lb (4900kg); (D-9) 10,670lb (4840kg); (Ta 152H-1) 12,125lb (5500kg).

Performance: Maximum speed (with boost) (A-8, F-8) 408mph (653km/h); (D-9) 440mph (704km/h); (Ta 152H-1) 472mph (755km/h); initial climb (A-8, F-8) 2,350ft (720m)/min; (D-9, Ta 152) about 3,300ft (1000m)/min; service ceiling (A-8, F-8) 37,400ft (11,410m); (D-9) 32,810ft (10,000m); (Ta 152H-1) 49,215ft (15,000m); range on internal fuel (A-8, F-8 and D-9) about 560 miles (900km); (Ta 152H-1), 745 miles (1200km).

Armament: (A-8, F-8) two 13mm MG 131 above engine, two 20mm MG 151/20 in wing roots and two MG 151/20 or 30mm MK 108 in outer wings; (D-9) as above, or without outer MG 151/20s, with provision for 30mm MK 108 firing through propeller hub; (Ta 152H-1) one 30mm

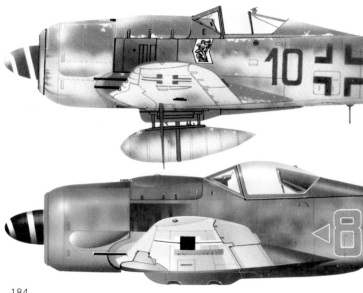

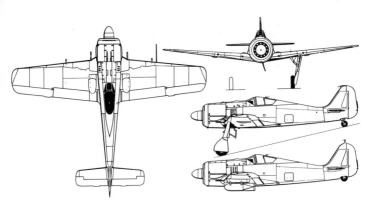

Above: Three-view of Fw 190A-3 with side view of A-4/U1.

MK 108 and two inboard MG 151/20 (sometimes outboard MG 151/20s as well); bomb load (A-8, D-9) one 1,100lb (500kg) on centreline; (F-8) one 3,968lb (1800kg) on centreline; (Ta 152H-1) (some reconnaissance H-models unarmed).

History: First flight (Fw 190V1) June 1, 1939, (production Fw 190A-1) September 1940, (Fw 190D) late 1942.

Users: Croatia, Germany (Luftwaffe), Slovakia, Turkey; post-war, Argentina, France (Armée de l'Air, Aéronavale).

Development: Though flown well before World War II this trim little fighter was unknown to the Allies and caused a nasty surprise when first met over France in early 1941. Indeed, it was so far superior to the bigger and more sluggish Spitfire V that for the first time the RAF felt not only outnumbered but beaten technically. In June 1942 an Fw 190A-3 landed by mistake in England, and the Focke-Wulf was discovered to be even better than expected. It was faster than any Allied fighter in service, had far heavier armament (at that time the standard was two 7·92mm MG 17s over ▶

Left: Built in greater numbers than any other version, the Fw 190A-8 was a versatile fighter and attack aircraft. It retained the MG 131 fuselage guns of the A-7, which caused the bulge ahead of the windscreen, and had the powerful armament of four MG 151 cannon in the wings. MW50 boosting was added to the engine. The aircraft shown served II/JG 11 at Darmstadt in early 1945, with yellow 'Eastern Front' theatre band.

Left: This F-8, serving with SG 4 at Köln-Wahn in December 1944, is typical of the chief family of close-support versions of the Fw 190 which from 1943 gradually equipped virtually all the Schlachtgruppen supporting the German ground forces. Most F-series had a belly rack for a 1,102-lb bomb, plus wing racks (not fitted here) for two 551lb. Note the bulged canopy.

the engine, two of the previously unknown Mauser cannon inboard and two 20mm MG FF outboard), was immensely strong, had excellent power of manoeuvre and good pilot view. It was also an extremely small target, much lighter than any Allied fighter and had a stable widetrack landing gear (unlike the Bf 109). Altogether it gave Allied pilots and designers an inferiority complex. Though it never supplanted the 109, it was subsequently made in a profusion of different versions by many factories.

The A series included many fighter and fighter bomber versions, some having not only the increasingly heavy internal armament but also two or four 20mm cannon or two 30mm in underwing fairings. Most had an emergency power boost system, using MW 50 (methanol/water) or GM-1 (nitrous oxide) injection, or both. Some carried torpedoes, others were two-seaters, and a few had autopilots for bad weather and night interceptions. The F series were close-support attack aircraft, some having the Panzerblitz array of R4M rockets for tank-busting (also lethal against heavy bombers). There were over 40 other special armaments, and some versions had armoured leading edges for ramming Allied bombers. The G was another important series of multi-role fighter/dive bombers, but by 1943 the main effort was devoted to what the RAF called the "long-nosed 190", the 190D. This went into production in the autumn of 1944, after much development, as the Fw 190D-9 ("Dora 9"). This was once more the fastest fighter in the sky and the later D-models were redesignated Ta 152 in honour of the director of Focke-Wulf's design team, Dipl Ing Kurt Tank. The early 152C ▶

Below: Fw 190G-3 long-range attack models over Romania in 1944.

Above: A row of Fw 190A-4 fighters with pilots at cockpit readiness, on a French airfield in 1943. This mottled camouflage was unusual on fighter 190s at this time, though it was seen on Jabo 190s bombing English coasts.

Below: This Fw 190A-5/U13 has been modified to F-8 standard with MG 131 fuselage guns and racks for a 1,102lb and two 551lb bombs.

Below: The very heavily armed Ta 152C-0/R11 (Ta 152C V7).

Above: Swinging the compass of the fifth Ta 152H at Cottbus.

series were outstandingly formidable, but the long-span H sacrificed guns for speed and height. Tank himself easily outpaced a flight of P-51D Mustangs which surprised him on a test flight; but only ten of the H sub-type had flown when the war ended. Altogether 20,051 Fw 190s were delivered, plus a small number of Ta 152s (67, excluding development aircraft). It is curious that the Bf 109, a much older and less attractive design with many shortcomings, should have been made in greater quantity and flown by nearly all the Luftwaffe's aces.

In 1945 the Fw 190A-5 was put into production at an underground plant in France managed by SNCASO. By 1946 a total of 64 had been delivered.

Focke-Wulf Ta 154
Ta 154 V1 to V15 and C series

Origin: Focke-Wulf Flugzeugbau GmbH, prototypes to V7 at Hanover—Langenhagen, V8–V15 (A-0 series) at Erfurt, production A-1 at Posen, Poland.
Type: Night and all-weather fighter.
Engines: Two Junkers Jumo inverted-vee-12 liquid-cooled, (V1, 2) 1,520hp 211N, (V3-V15, A-1) 1,750hp 213E, (C) 1,776hp 213A.
Dimensions: Span 52ft 6in (16·00m); length (with SN-2) 41ft $2\frac{3}{4}$in (12·56m); height (most) 11ft $9\frac{3}{4}$in (3·60m).
Weights: (A-1) Empty 14,122lb (6405kg); max loaded 21,050lb (9548kg).
Performance: Maximum speed (A-1) 404mph (650km/h); service ceiling 35,760ft (10,900m); range (two drop tanks) 1,156 miles (1850km).
Armament: (A-0, A-1) two 30mm MK 108 and two 20mm MG 151 in sides of fuselage.

Development: Hailed by the propaganda machine as "Germany's Mosquito", the wooden Ta 154 had an excellent performance and came near to being a major combat type. The Luftwaffe never considered defensive aircraft at all until 1941; then, for obvious reasons, in September 1942 the RLM issued a specification for a fighter to shoot down RAF heavy bombers at night. Tank had the Ta 154 V1 flying by 7 July 1943, and development generally went well, though the whole project posed inherently high risk in the use of wood for the structure of so advanced an aircraft. It was only the need to conserve light alloy, and the great success of the British Mosquito, that drove this policy relentlessly forward. By the summer of 1944 all 15 development aircraft had flown, most with C-1 or later SN-2 Lichten-stein radar, and A-1 production machines were coming off the line in Poland. The 154C was to follow, with two ejection seats under a sliding bubble canopy and Schräge Musik 30mm cannon, while the Ta 254 was a still later family. But on 28 June 1944 the second A-1 broke up in flight. It was found that, whereas the Tego-Film bonding used in earlier aircraft was satisfactory, the cold glue hastily brought in as adhesive after destruction

Above: Although described by Focke-Wulf as an Fw 190A-1, this is in fact a late A-0 fitted with MG FF outboard cannon like an A-1. This was the very first production version, in 1940.

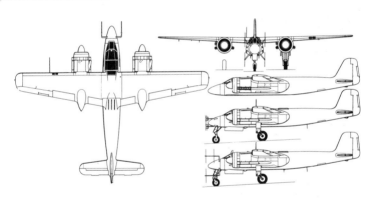

Above: Ta 154 V15, with side view of V1 (top) and V3 (centre).

by the RAF of the Tego-Film plant contained excess acid which ate away the wood. The 154 thus never got into service — not even six Pulk-Zerstörer conversions packed with explosives intended to break up US bomber formations.

Below: Third prototype, with Jumo 213s, radar and full armament.

Heinkel He 51

He 51A-1, B-2 and C-1

Origin: Ernst Heinkel AG; production see text.
Type: Single-seat fighter (B-2) reconnaissance seaplane; (C-1) land ground attack.
Engine: One 750hp BMW VI 7·3Z vee-12 water-cooled.
Dimensions: Span 36ft 1in (11m); length 27ft 6¾in (8·4m); (B-2) about 31ft; height 10ft 6in (3·2m); (B-2) about 11ft.
Weights: (A-1), empty 3,223lb (1462kg); loaded 4,189lb (1900kg).
Performance: Maximum speed (A-1) 205mph (330km/h); initial climb 1,969ft (600m)/min; service ceiling 24,610ft (7500m); range 242 miles (390km).
Armament: Standard, two 7·92mm Rheinmetall MG 17 synchronised above fuselage; (B-2) same plus underwing racks for up to six 22lb (10kg) bombs; (C-1) same plus underwing racks for four 110lb (50kg) bombs.
History: First flight (He 49a) November 1932; (He 49b) February 1933; (He 51A-0) May 1933; service delivery of A-1, July 1934.
Users: Germany, Spain.
Development: Gradually, as the likelihood of Allied legal action receded, Heinkel dared to build aircraft that openly contravened the Versailles Treaty. The most startling was the He 37, obviously a prototype fighter, which in 1928 achieved 194mph, or 20mph faster than the RAF Bulldog which was still a year away from service. Land and seaplane versions led to a succession of He 49 fighter prototypes in the 1930s and these in turn provided the basis for the refined He 51. After the Ar 65 this was the first fighter ordered into production by the Reichsluftfahrtministerium for the reborn Luftwaffe. Though the initial order for He 51A-1s was only 75, Heinkel was unused to such an order and many were built under licence by Ago, Erla, Arado and Fieseler — which were also fast tooling for their own designs. In March 1935 the Luftwaffe was publicly announced, and JG1 "Richthofen" fighter squadron was combat-ready at Döberitz with its new Heinkels. In November 1936, 36 He 51A-1s went to Spain with the Legion Kondor, giving a sufficiently good showing for the Nationalists to buy at least 30 from Heinkel. There followed a total of 50 of various He 51B seaplane versions, the 38 B-2s being for service aboard cruisers. The final batch comprised 79 C-1 ground attack fighters, of which 28 served in Spain. The He 51 was still in active service in September 1939, operating in the close-support role in Poland, and remained as an advanced trainer until 1943.

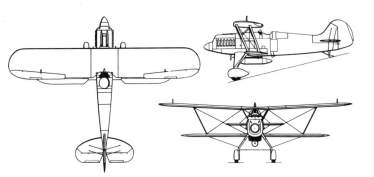

Above: Three-view of He 51C-1 (the B-1 was very similar).

Above: One of the surviving He 51B-1s photographed in about 1941 when it was serving as an advanced trainer at an A/B Schule, with drop tank to increase utilization. Guns were often fitted.

Left: After the start of World War II no He 51s were left in the front-line fighter role, though large numbers continued as advanced trainers and in utility roles. Most were assigned to the A/B schulen (pilot schools) or Jagdfliegerschulen (fighter-pilot schools) which were located all over German-occupied Europe. This He 51B was on the strength of A/B 123 at Agram (Zagreb, Yugoslavia) in the spring of 1942. By this time the spats over the main wheels had almost always been removed, though it was retained on the tailwheel. Colourful badges and emblems continued to be worn even in the training role, and often (as in this case) a theatre band was worn round the rear fuselage.

Heinkel He 100

He 100 V1 to V8 and 100D-1

Origin: Ernst Heinkel AG.
Type: Single-seat fighter.
Engine: 1,175hp Daimler-Benz DB 601 Aa inverted-vee-12 liquid-cooled.
Dimensions: Span 30ft 10¾in (9·41m); length 26ft 10¾in (8·195m); height 11ft 9¾in (3·60m).
Weights: (D-1) empty 3,990lb (1810kg); max loaded 5,512lb (2500kg).
Performance: (D-1) maximum speed 416mph (670km/h); service ceiling 36,090ft (11,000m); range 559 miles (900km).

Development: Undaunted by loss of the Luftwaffe's fighter orders to BFW with the 109, Heinkel proposed a much faster fighter, with structure completely different from the rather unimpressive He 112 to make it more efficient and much quicker and cheaper to build. The resulting Projekt 1035 was completed on 25 May 1937 and at the end of that year the now-informed RLM sanctioned a prototype and ten pre-production machines. Heinkel managed to secure the number "100" though this had been previously alotted to Fieseler. The first prototype flew on 22 January 1938, and was clearly outstandingly fast, being small and having a surface-evaporation cooling system instead of a draggy radiator. Though there were many problems, and Luftwaffe test pilots disliked the high wing loading, Udet himself flew the V2 to a new world 100km circuit record at 394·6mph (634·73km/h). On 30 March 1939 Hans Dieterle, flying the clipped-wing V3, took the world speed record at 463·92mph (746·6km/h). But the RLM saw no reason for mass production, and six prototypes were sold to the Soviet Union and three He 100D-0 to Japan, with armament of two MG 17

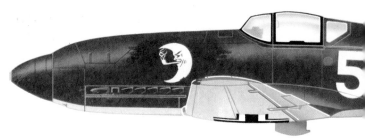

Below: One of the many photographs put out by the propaganda minister, Josef Goebbels, showing the 'He 113' in Luftwaffe use.

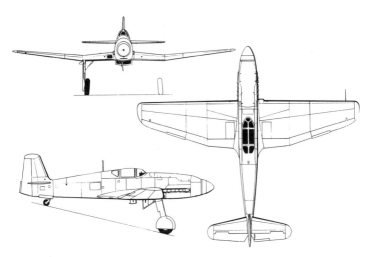

Above: Three-view of the Heinkel He 100D-1c.

and a 20mm MG/FF. The remaining 12 He 100D-1 fighters formed a Heinkel-Rostock defence unit, but in 1940 were publicised by Goebbels' propaganda machine in such a way as to convince Britain there was a fighter in large-scale service called the "He 113".

Left: Appearance of one of the dozen He 100D-1c pre-production fighters after it had been painted in completely fictitious 'unit markings' in 1940 for many widely published photographs describing the type as the non-existent 'He 113'. Of course, RAF pilots in late 1940 reported meeting He 113s over Germany! For sheer speed the He 100 had no rival in its day.

Below: This was one of the photographs issued to try to convince people the 'He 113' was a night fighter. Same aircraft shown above.

Heinkel He 112

He 112B-0 and B-1

Origin: Ernst Heinkel AG.
Type: Single-seat fighter and light ground attack.
Engine: One 680hp Junkers Jumo 210Ea inverted-vee-12 liquid-cooled.
Dimensions: (He 112) span 29ft 10¼in (9·1m); length 30ft 6in (9·3m); height 12ft 7½in (3·85m).
Weights: Empty 3,571lb (1620kg); loaded 4,960lb (2250kg).
Performance: Maximum speed 317mph (510km/h); initial climb 2,300ft (700m)/min; service ceiling 27,890ft (8500m); range 684 miles (1100km).
Armament: Two 20mm Oerlikon MG FF cannon in outer wings and two 7·92mm Rheinmetall MG 17 machine guns in sides of fuselage; underwing racks for six 22lb (10kg) fragmentation bombs.
History: First flight (He 112V-1) September 1935; (B-series production prototype) May 1937; final delivery (Romania) September 1939.

Development: One of the first requirements issued by the rapidly expanded RLM under the Nazis was a specification for a completely new monoplane fighter to replace the Ar 68 and He 51. Heinkel's team under the Gunthers used He 70 experience to create the shapely He 112, which was much smaller and of wholly light-alloy stressed skin construction. Powered by a British Kestrel, it was matched at Travemünde against the similarly powered Bf 109 prototype, as well as the "also rans", the Ar 80 and Fw 159. Though Heinkel's fighter was marginally slower, it had better field performance, much better pilot view (especially on the ground), a wide-track landing gear and considerably better manoeuvrability. Many, especially Heinkel, were amazed when the Messerschmitt design was chosen for the Luftwaffe,

Below: Six of the 30 Heinkel He 112B-0 fighters which were supplied to augment the fighter strength of the Luftwaffe during the 1938 Munich talks. A few weeks later they were exported.

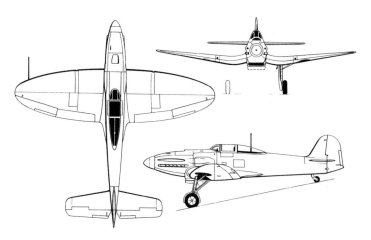

Above: Three-view of the He 112B-1 (700hp Jumo 210G).

though the He 112 was continued as an insurance. Nothing Heinkel could do with improved versions could shake the RLM's rejection, despite the delight of the RLM test pilots in flying them. Thirty He 112B-0 fighters were supplied to the Luftwaffe for evaluation, but 17 were promptly shipped to Spain (not as part of the Legion Kondor but flown by volunteer civilians). There they were judged superior to the Bf 109C, and 15 continued in Spanish service until after World War II. All but one of the other Luftwaffe machines were sold to the Japanese Navy, which disliked them intensely because of their high wing loading. Romania bought 13 B-0 and 11 B-1 fighters in 1939 and used them in the 1941 invasion of the Soviet Union.

Left: Though it was a shapely fighter, the He 112 had a shallow canopy and all-round visibility was not good. This aircraft was an He 112B-0 of III/JG 132 at Fürstenwalde in September 1938. The coolant radiator is shown fully extended (broken line in three-view).

Below: The civil-registered batch of 12 Heinkel He 112B-0 fighters lined up at Rostock-Marienehe before shipment to Japan in May 1938. The second batch was temporarily diverted to the Luftwaffe.

Heinkel He 162 Salamander

He 162A-2

Origin: Ernst Heinkel AG; first batch Vienna-Schwechat, production totally dispersed with underground assembly at Nordhausen (Mittelwerke), Bernberg (Junkers) and Rostock (Heinkel).

Type: Single-seat interceptor.

Engine: One 1,760lb (800kg) thrust BMW 003E-1 or E-2 Orkan single-shaft turbojet.

Dimensions: Span 23ft 7¾in (7·2m); length 29ft 8½in (9m); height 6ft 6½in (2–6m).

Weights: Empty 4,796lb (2180kg); loaded 5,940lb (2695kg).

Performance: Maximum speed 490mph (784km/h) at sea level, 522mph (835km/h) at 19,700ft (6000m); initial climb 4,200ft (1280m)/min; service ceiling 39,500ft (12,040m); range at full throttle 434 miles (695km) at altitude.

Armament: Early versions, two 30mm Rheinmetall MK 108 cannon with 50 rounds each; later production, two 20mm Mauser MG 151/20 with 120 rounds each.

History: First flight 6 December 1944; first delivery January 1945.

User: Germany (Luftwaffe).

Development: Popularly called "Volksjäger" (People's Fighter), this incredible aircraft left behind so many conflicting impressions it is hard to believe the whole programme was started and finished in little more than six months. To appreciate the almost impossible nature of the programme, Germany was being pounded to rubble by fleets of Allied bombers that darkened the sky, and the aircraft industry and the Luftwaffe's fuel supplies were inexorably running down. Experienced aircrew had nearly all been killed, materials were in critically short supply and time had to be measured

Below: This He 162A-2 was one of about 50 that reached Parchim by March 1945 for converting pilots of I/JG 1.

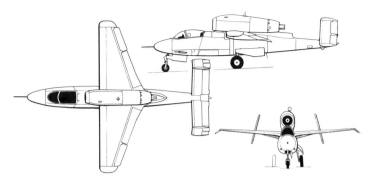

Above: Three-view of the mass-produced He 162A-2 Salamander.

not in months but in days. So on 8 September 1944 the RLM issued a specification calling for a 750km/h jet fighter to be regarded as a piece of consumer goods and to be ready by 1 January 1945. Huge numbers of workers were organised to build it even before it was designed and Hitler Youth were hastily trained in primary gliders before being strapped into the new jet. Heinkel, which had built the world's first turbojet aircraft (He 178, flown 27 August 1939) and the first jet fighter (He 280 twin-jet, flown on its jet engines 2 April 1941) won a hasty competition with a tiny wooden machine with its engine perched on top and blasting between twin fins. Drawings were ready on 30 October 1944. The prototype flew in 37 days and plans were made for production to rise rapidly to 4,000 per month. Despite extreme difficulties, 300 of various sub-types had been completed by VE-day, with 800 more on the assembly lines. I/JG1 was operational at Leck, though without fuel. Despite many bad characteristics the 162 was a fighter of a futuristic kind, created in quantity far quicker than modern aircraft are even drawn on paper.

Below: Some idea of what was accomplished in seven weeks is shown by this view of one of the many He 162A assembly shops, in this case a former salt mine at Tarthun. This remarkable fighter still looks modern today, but in fact it was much too advanced for Hitler Youth pilots.

Heinkel He 219 Uhu

He 219A-0 to A-7, B and C series

Origin: Ernst Heinkel AG.

Type: A series, two-seat night fighter.

Engines: Usually two 1,900hp Daimler-Benz DB 603G inverted-vee-12 liquid-cooled; other engines, see text.

Dimensions: (A-series) span 60ft 2in or 60ft 8in (18·5m); length (with aerials) 50ft 11¾in (15·54m); height 13ft 5½in (4·1m).

Weights: (A-7) empty 24,692lb (11,200kg); loaded 33,730lb (15,200kg).

Performance: (A-7) maximum speed 416mph (670km/h); initial climb 1,804ft (550m)/min; service ceiling 41,660ft (12,700m); range 1,243 miles (2000km).

Armament: Varied, see text.

History: First flight (219V-1) 15 November 1942; service delivery (prototypes) May 1943; (production 219A-1) November 1943.

User: Germany (Luftwaffe).

Development: Ernst Heinkel was the pioneer of gas-turbine jet aircraft, flying the He 178 on 27 August 1939 and the He 280 twin-jet fighter as a glider on 22 September 1940 and with its engines on 2 April 1941 (before the purely experimental Gloster E.28/39). But Heinkel was unable to build the extremely promising He 280 in quantity, which was fortunate for the Allies. He had no spare capacity for the He 219 either, which had excited little official interest when submitted as the P.1060 project in August 1940 as a high-speed fighter, bomber and torpedo carrier. It was only when RAF night attacks began to hurt, at the end of 1941, that he was asked to produce the 219 as a night fighter (Uhu meaning Owl). The He 219V-1, with 1,750hp DB 603AS and two MG 151/20 cannon, plus an MG 131 in the rear cockpit, was fast and extremely manoeuvrable and the test pilots at Rechlin were thrilled by it. Successive prototypes had much heavier armament and radar and 100 were ordered from five factories in Germany, Poland and Austria. The order was soon trebled and Luftwaffe enthusiasm was such that even the early prototypes were sent to Venlo, Holland, to form a special trials unit. The first six night sorties resulted in the claimed destruction of 20 RAF bombers, six of them the previously almost immune Mosquitoes! More ▶

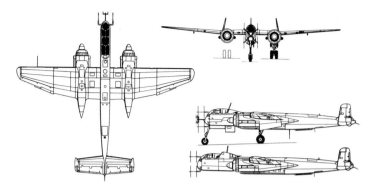

Above: Three-view of He 219A-5/R1; lower side view, the lengthened A-5/R4 with MG 131 in the rear cockpit for defence.

Above: An He 219A-5/R2 after capture of its airfield in 1945.

Below: The He 219A-7/R4 was one of the fastest and highest-flying versions, with ejection seats, but only four MG 151 forward-firing guns. Note the simplified late-war national marking.

Above: The He 219 V5 (fifth prototype) was the first to eliminate a previous unsightly step in the top of the fuselage.

than 15 different versions of the 219 then appeared, immediately proving outstandingly formidable. The A-2/R1 had 603As, two MG 151/20 in the wing roots and two or four in a belly tray and two 30mm MK 108 firing upward at 65° in a Schräge Musik (Jazz Music) installation for destroying bombers by formating below them. The A-7/R1 had MK 108s in the wing roots and two of these big guns and two MG 151/20 in the tray, plus the Schräge Musik with 100 rounds per gun (the most lethal of all). Some versions had three seats, long-span wing and DB 603L turbocharged engines, or Jumo 213s or even the 2,500hp Jumo 222 with six banks of four cylinders. The B and C families would have been enlarged multi-role versions with rear turrets. Total A-type production was only 268, the officials at one time ignoring Luftwaffe enthusiasm by ordering production to be stopped!

Above: The He 219C-2 Jagdbomber (fighter-bomber) would have had Jumo 222 engines and many other changes including a rear turret.

Below: This He 219A-5 appears to have a black-painted underside to its right wing; it carries both SN-2 and C-1 nose radars.

Heinkel He 280

He 280 V1 to V8

Origin: Ernst Heinkel AG.
Type: Single-seat fighter.
Engines: (Most) two 1,852lb (840kg) thrust Junkers Jumo 004A turbojets.
Dimensions: Span 39ft 4¼in (12·00m); length (most) 33ft 5½in (10·20m); height 10ft 5¾in (3·19m).
Weights: (V6) empty 7,386lb (3350kg); loaded 11,465lb (5200kg).
Performance: (V6) maximum speed 508mph (817km/h); range at height 382 miles (615km).

Development: A truly remarkable achievement, the He 280 was the world's first jet combat aircraft, the first twin-jet and the first jet to be other than a research aircraft. Yet it emerged at a time when the German leaders had a fixation on a brief Blitzkrieg victory, and showed no interest in jets or anything else that could not be used at once. The He 280 V1 was complete in September 1940 and flew as a glider on the 11th of that month behind an He 111. Fritz Schäfer then flew it on two 1,290lb (585kg) thrust HeS 8A centrifugal jets on 2 April 1941. Eventually eight of these attractive twin-finned machines were flown, but they came to nothing—despite Heinkel arranging a mock dogfight with an Fw 190 in early 1942 which the jet won easily. Intended armament was three 20mm MG 151; the proposed He 280B would have had six, plus 1,102lb (500kg) bomb load. Trials completed included twin Argus 014 duct propulsion, glider tests with no engine nacelles, and V-type butterfly tails.

Right: The first takeoff under power, on 2 April 1941. Prior to this date the only jet aircraft to have flown was the He 178.

Below: The first landing; the engine cowlings were left off to avoid build-up of dripping fuel, with consequent fire hazard.

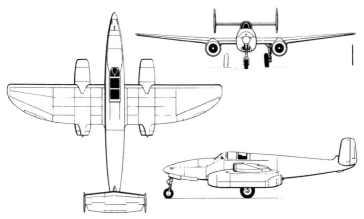

Above: Three-view of the He 280 V2, with Jumo 004 engines.

Henschel Hs 123

Hs 123A-1

Origin: Henschel Flugzeugwerke AG.
Type: Single-seat dive bomber and close-support.
Engine: One 880hp BMW 132 Dc nine-cylinder radial.
Dimensions: Span 34ft 5½in (10·5m); length 27ft 4in (8·3m) height 10ft 6½in (3·2m).
Weights: Empty 3,316lb (1504kg); loaded 4,888lb (2217kg).
Performance: Maximum speed 214mph (345km/h); initial climb 2,950ft (900m)/min; service ceiling 29,530 ft (9000m); range 530 miles (850km).
Armament: Two 7·92mm Rheinmetall MG 17 machine guns ahead of pilot; underwing racks for four 110lb (50kg) bombs, or clusters of anti-personnel bombs or two 20mm MG FF cannon.
History: First flight, spring 1935 (public display given 8 May); first delivery (Spain) December 1936; final delivery, October 1938.
User: Germany (Luftwaffe).

Development: Though representing a class of aircraft generally considered obsolete by the start of World War II, this trim little biplane was kept hard at work until 1942, achieving results which in retrospect seem almost unbelievable. The prototype needed extensive modification to produce the A-1 production version, which was tested in the Spanish Civil War. Contrary to the staff-college theories then adhered to by the newly formed Luftwaffe, the Henschels were able to give close support to ground troops of a most real and immediate kind, strafing and bombing with great accuracy despite the lack of any radio link or even an established system of operation. Eventually the Luftwaffe realised that the concept of a close-support aircraft was valid, and a few Henschels were allowed to operate in this role, but all the effort and money was put into the Ju 87, and the Hs 123 was phased out of production before World War II. Yet in the Polish campaign these aircraft proved unbelievably useful, having the ability to make pinpoint attacks with guns and bombs and, by virtue of careful setting of the propeller speed, to make a demoralising noise. Moreover, it established an extraordinary reputation for returning to base even after direct hits by AA shells. As a result, though the whole force was incessantly threatened with disbandment

Above right: An Hs 123A-1 pictured (possibly with Schlacht/LG 2) during the Blitzkrieg through the Low Countries in May 1940.

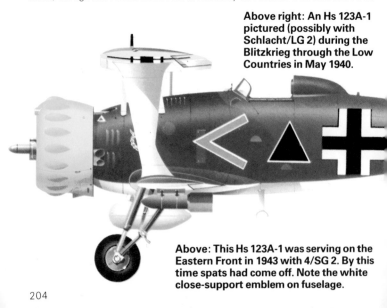

Above: This Hs 123A-1 was serving on the Eastern Front in 1943 with 4/SG 2. By this time spats had come off. Note the white close-support emblem on fuselage.

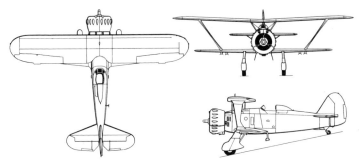

Above: Three-view of the Hs 123A-1.

or replacement by later types, the Hs 123 close-support unit II (Schlacht)/ LG2 was sent intact to the Balkans in April 1941 and thence to the USSR. Here the old biplanes fought around the clock, proving far better adapted to the conditions than more modern types and continuing in front-line operations until, by the end of 1944, there were no more left.

Right: A front-line photo taken deep in the USSR in 1942. The Polish campaign taught the Luftwaffe that close-support aircraft had to be clearly marked with large national insignia.

Henschel Hs 129

Hs 129A and B series

Origin: Henschel Flugzeugwerke AG.
Type: Single-seat close support and ground attack.
Engines: (B-series) two 690hp Gnome-Rhône 14M 04/05 14-cylinder two-row radials.
Dimensions: Span 46ft 7in (14·2m); length 31ft 11¾in (9·75m); height 10ft 8in (3·25m).
Weights: (Typical B-1) empty 8,940lb (4060kg); loaded 11,265lb (5110kg).
Performance: (Typical B-1) maximum speed 253mph (408km/h); initial climb 1,390ft (425m)/min; service ceiling 29,530ft (9000m); range 547 miles (880km).
Armament: See text.
History: First flight (Hs 129V-1) early 1939; service delivery (129A-0) early 1941; first flight (129B) October 1941; service delivery (129B) late 1942.
Users: Germany (Luftwaffe), Hungary, Romania.

Development: Though there were numerous types of specialised close support and ground attack aircraft in World War I, this category was virtually ignored until the Spanish Civil War showed, again, that it is one of the most important of all. In 1938 the RLM issued a specification for such an aircraft – the whole purpose of the Luftwaffe being to support the Wehrmacht in Blitzkrieg-type battles – to back up the purpose-designed Ju 87 dive bomber. Henschel's Dipl-Ing F. Nicholaus designed a trim machine somewhat resembling the twin-engined fighters of the period but with more armour and less-powerful engines (two 495hp Argus As 410A-1 air-cooled inverted-vee-12s). The solo pilot sat in the extreme nose behind a windscreen 3in thick, with armour surrounding the cockpit. The triangular-section fuselage housed self-sealing tanks, guns in the sloping sides and a hardpoint for a bomb underneath. Test pilots at Rechlin damned the A-0 pre-production batch as grossly underpowered, but these aircraft were used on the Eastern Front by the Romanian Air Force. The redesigned B-series used the vast

Below: This Hs 129B-2 was operating on the Russian Front with 4(Pz)/SchG 1 in 1942.

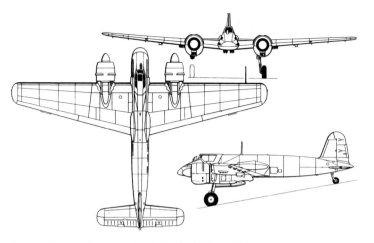

Above: Three-view of Hs 129B-1/R4 with bomb kit.

numbers of French 14M engines that were available and in production by the Vichy government for the Me 323. Altogether 841 B-series were built, and used with considerable effect on the Eastern Front but with less success in North Africa. The B-1/R1 had two 7·92mm MG 17 and two 20mm MG 151/20, plus two 110lb or 48 fragmentation bombs. The R2 had a 30mm MK 101 clipped underneath and was the first aircraft ever to use a 30mm gun in action. The R3 had a ventral box of four MG 17. The R4 carried up to 551lb of bombs. The R5 had a camera for vertical photography. The B-2 series changed the inbuilt MG 17s for MG 131s and other subtypes had many kinds of armament including the 37mm BK 3·7 and 75mm BK 7·5 with muzzle about eight feet ahead of the nose. The most novel armament, used against Russian armour with results that were often devastating, was a battery of six smooth-bore 75mm tubes firing recoilless shells down and to the rear with automatic triggering as the aircraft flew over metal objects.

Below: This Hs 129B-1 was one of the first of this type to reach the front line. Assigned to 8/Schlacht-geschwader 2 it was photographed near Tripoli in late 1942. It is being towed from each landing gear by a vehicle out of the picture, with a man steering the tailwheel. The lower half of each cowling is missing, no ventral gun is fitted and the ladder is out.

Henschel Hs 132

Hs 132 V1, V2 and A, B and C

Origin: Henschel Flugzeugwerke AG.
Type: Dive bomber.
Engine: 1,760lb (800kg) thrust BMW 003A-1 turbojet.
Dimensions: Span 23ft 7½in (7·20m); length 29ft 2½in (8·90m); height 9ft 10in (3·00m).
Weights: Empty, not known; loaded 7,496lb (3400kg).
Performance: Maximum speed (with bomb) 435mph (700km/h), (clean) 485mph (780km/h); range (with bomb, at 32,800ft, 10,000m) 696 miles (1120km).
Development: In 1937 the DVL research into dive bombing led to the Berlin-Charlottenberg B9 being built to study the advantages of the pilot lying prone, to better resist g forces. Extensive B9 testing throughout World War II showed how great the advantages were, and it was also clear that frontal area could be reduced. This led to the Henschel Hs 132 prone-pilot dive bomber, begun in early 1944. The 132A-series were to be dive bombers

---

Junkers Ju 87

Ju 87A, B and D series

Origin: Junkers Flugzeug und Motorenwerke AG; also built by Weser Flugzeugbau and components from SNCASO, France.
Type: Two-seat dive bomber and ground attack.
Engine: (Ju 87B-1) one 1,100hp Junkers Jumo 211Da 12-cylinder inverted-vee liquid-cooled; (Ju 87D-1, D-5) 1,300hp Jumo 211J.
Dimensions: Span (Ju 87B-1, D-1) 45ft 3¼in (13·8m); (D-5) 50ft 0½in (15·25m); length 36ft 5in (11·1m); height 12ft 9in (3·9m).
Weights: Empty (B-1, D-1) about 6,080lb (2750kg); loaded (B-1) 9,371lb (4250kg); (D-1) 12,600lb (5720kg); (D-5) 14,500lb (6585kg).
Performance: Maximum speed (B-1) 242mph (390km/h); (D-1) 255mph (408km/h); (D-5) 250mph (402km/h); service ceiling (B-1) 26,250ft (8000m); (D-1, D-5) 24,000ft (7320m); range with maximum bomb load (B-1) 373 miles (600km); (D-1, D-5) 620 miles (1000km). ***continued ▶***

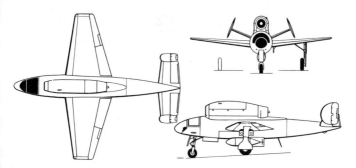

Above: Three-view of Hs 132A with 500kg bomb.

with 1,102lb (500kg) bomb but no guns. The 132B, with Jumo 004 engine, was to carry a similar bomb as well as two 20mm MG 151 cannon. It was believed Allied AA gunners would be unable to hit so small an aircraft diving at over 500mph. There were other projected versions, but the Soviet army occupied the factory just as the V1 was about to begin flight testing.

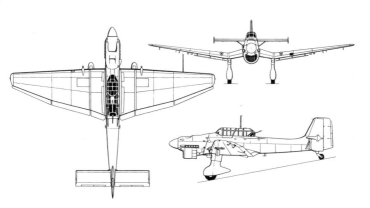

Above: Three-view of Ju 87B-2, without bombs.

Left: This Ju 87D-1/Trop was the aircraft of Oberstleutnant Walter Sigel, Geschwaderkommodore (wing commander) of Stukageschwader 3, at Derna, Libya, in June 1942. The much better shape of this later version can be seen by comparison with the three-view above. The aircraft is shown with a 500kg (1,102lb) bomb on the main crutch and twin MG 81 at the rear. The cylinder projecting horizontally ahead of the landing gear is a wind-driven siren.

Armament: (Ju 87B-1) two 7·92mm Rheinmetall MG 17 machine guns in wings, one 7·92mm MG 15 manually aimed in rear cockpit, one 1,102lb (500kg) bomb on centreline and four 110lb (50kg) on wing racks; (D-1, D-5) two MG 17 in wings, twin 7·92mm MG 81 machine guns manually aimed in rear cockpit, one bomb of 3,968lb (1800kg) on centreline; (D-7) two 20mm MG 151/20 cannon in wings; (Ju 87G-1) two 37mm BK (Flak 18, or Flak 36) cannon in underwing pods; (D-4) two underwing WB81 weapon containers each housing six MG 81 guns.

History: First flight (Ju 87V1) late 1935; (pre-production Ju 87A-0) November 1936; (Ju 87B-1) August 1938; (Ju 87D-1) 1940; termination of production 1944.

Users: Bulgaria, Croatia, Germany (Luftwaffe), Hungary, Italy, Romania, Slovakia.

Development: Until at least 1942 the Ju 87 "Stuka" enjoyed a reputation that struck terror into those on the ground beneath it. First flown with a British R-R Kestrel engine and twin fins in 1935, it entered production in 1937 as the Ju 87A with large trousered landing gear and full equipment for dive bombing, including a heavy bomb crutch that swung the missile well clear of the fuselage before release. The spatted Ju 87B was the first aircraft in production with the Jumo 211 engine, almost twice as powerful as the Jumo 210 of the Ju 87A, and it had an automatic device (almost an auto-pilot) to ensure proper pull-out from the steep dive, as well as red lines at 60°, 75° and 80° painted on the pilot's side window. Experience in Spain had shown that pilots could black-out and lose control in the pull-out. Later a whole formation of Ju 87Bs in Spain was late pulling out over misty ground and many hit the ground. In Poland and the Low Countries the Ju 87 was terribly effective and it repeated its success in Greece, Crete and parts of the Russian front. But in the Battle of Britain its casualty rate was such that it was soon withdrawn, thereafter to attack ships and troops in areas where the Axis still enjoyed some air superiority. In 1942–45 its main work was close support on the Eastern front, attacking armour with big guns (Ju 87G-1) and even being used as a transport and glider tug. Total production, all by Junkers, is believed to have been 5,709.

Though substantial numbers were built of the Ju 87A series with Jumo 210 engine, these were replaced in front-line units in 1939 by the more powerful B-series, serving thereafter until early 1943 as dive-bomber trainers. The Ju 87B was the first production application of the Jumo 211 engine, which by mid-1938 was available in improved Jumo 211Da form

Above: Flanked by a 500kg bomb, this Ju 87B-2 served with StG 77 in the Balkans and Crete, thence moving to the USSR.

rated at 1,200hp with direct fuel injection, making the engine insensitive to accelerations and flight attitudes. By the start of World War II all nine Stukagruppen had re-equipped with the Ju 87B-1, which was developed into sub-types with better radio, armour, skis, sand filters and many other improvements. Nevertheless the basic vulnerability of the Ju 87 had by this time resulted in a planned phase-out of production by 1940. Production was tapering off as the war started, but the shattering effect of the aircraft in ▶

Below: Distinguished by its two 66 Imp gal drop tanks under the outer wings, the Ju 87R family were essentially extended-range versions of the B-2. Usually restricted to a single 500kg bomb on the centreline, the R offered approximately twice the radius of action of the B-2, entering service in early 1940.

Poland caused its run-down to be postponed. In the campaign in the West in May 1940 the Stuka did even more to blast a path for the Wehrmacht, and not even its inability to survive over England was enough to stop it coming off the production line. In the spring of 1941 the greatly improved D-series thus entered production, with more power, greatly increased bomb load, extensive armour and many other changes. But the whole programme was totally unplanned. Output was always being tapered off, only to be suddenly boosted to meet urgent demands. Better aircraft kept failing to appear, Junkers themselves failed to produce the planned Ju 187, and output kept rising and falling until it at last ended in September 1944 when more than 5,700 had been delivered. Many of the final sub-types were of the G-series with tank-busting cannon, or dual-control H-series trainers. Most of the Stukas in action on the Eastern front after late 1942 had to be restricted (if possible) to night operations with large flame-damping exhaust pipes. Only a very few, flown by crews either deeply experienced or just joined, survived to VE-day. Various models served with the Slovakian, Romanian and Hungarian air forces and with the Regia Aeronautica (giving rise to the erroneous belief by the Allies it was built in Italy as the "Breda 201"), and among many special versions or modifications were fleet carrier-based models intended for *Graf Zeppelin,* glider tugs, large belly freight pods and passenger pods fitted above the wings.

Below: At the end of the war few Stukas were left in action, one of them being this Ju 87G-1 anti-tank aircraft on the Eastern Front. Unwieldy, it was very vulnerable to fighters.

Above: After Italy's entry to the war in June 1940 more than 200 Ju 87Bs were supplied to Italy's Regia Aeronautica. Britain believed there was an Italian-built 'Breda 201' version.

Junkers Ju 88

Many versions: data for Ju 88A-4, C-6, G-7, S-1

Origin: Junkers Flugzeug und Motorenwerke AG, dispersed among 14 plants with subcontract or assembly by ATG, Opel, Volkswagen and various French groups.

Type: Military aircraft designed as dive bomber but developed for level bombing, close support, night fighting, torpedo dropping, reconnaissance and as pilotless missile. Crew: two to six.

Engines: (A-4) two 1,340hp Junkers Jumo 211J 12-cylinder inverted-vee liquid-cooled; (C-6) same as A-4; (G-7) two 1,880hp Junkers Jumo 213E 12-cylinder inverted-vee liquid-cooled; (S-1) two 1,700hp BMW 801G 18-cylinder two-row radials.

Dimensions: Span 65ft 10½in (20·13m) (early versions 59ft 10¾in); length 47ft 2¼in (14·4m); (G-7, 54ft 1½in); height 15ft 11in (4·85m); (C-6) 16ft 7½in (5m).

Weights: Empty (A-4) 17,637lb (8000kg); (C-6b) 19,090lb (8660kg), (G-7b) 20,062lb (9100kg); (S-1) 18,300lb (8300kg); maximum loaded (A-4) 30,865lb (14,000kg); (C-6b) 27,500lb (12,485kg); (G-7b) 32,350lb (14,690kg); (S-1) 23,100lb (10,490kg).

Performance: Maximum speed (A-4) 269mph (433km/h); (C-6b) 300mph (480km/h); (G-7b) (no drop tank or flame-dampers) 402mph (643km/h); (S-1) 373mph (600km/h); initial climb (A-4) 1,312ft (400m)/ min; (C-6b) about 985ft (300m)/min; (G-7b) 1,640ft (500m)/min; (S-1) 1,804ft (550m)/min; service ceiling (A-4) 26,900ft (8200m); (C-6b) 32,480ft (9900m); (G-7b) 28,870ft (8800m); (S-1) 36,090ft (11,000m); range (A-4) 1,112 miles (1790km); (C-6b) 1,243 miles (2000km); (G-7b) 1,430 miles (2300km); (S-1) 1,243 miles (2000km).

Armament: (A-4) two 7.92mm MG 81 (or one MG 81 and one 13mm MG 131) firing forward, twin MG 81 or one MG 131 upper rear, one or two MG 81 at rear of ventral gondola and (later aircraft) two MG 81 at front of gondola; (C-6b) three 20mm MG FF and three MG 17 in nose and two 20mm MG 151/20 firing obliquely upward in Schräge Musik installation; (G-7b) four MG 151/20 (200 rounds each) firing forward from ventral

Below: Most Ju 88 night fighters had BMW 801 radial engines, but the G-7a of late 1944 had Jumo 213 engines. Note SN-2 nose radar.

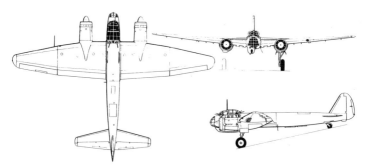

Above: Three-view of the first long-span version, the A-4.

fairing, two MG 151/20 in Schräge Musik installation (200 rounds each) and defensive MG 131 (500 rounds) swivelling in rear roof; (S-1) one MG 131 (500 rounds) swivelling in rear roof; bomb loads (A-4) 1,100lb (500kg) internal and four external racks rated at 2,200lb (1000kg) (inners) and 1,100lb (500kg) (outers) to maximum total bomb load of 6,614lb (3000kg); (C-6b and G-7b, nil); (S-1) up to 4,410lb (2000kg) on external racks.

History: First flight (Ju 88V1) 21 December 1936; (first Ju 88A-1) 7 September 1939; (first fighter, Ju 88C-0) July 1939; (Ju 88C-6) mid-1942; (first G-series) early 1944; (S series) late 1943; final deliveries, only as factories were overrun by Allies.

Users: Bulgaria (briefly), Finland, Germany (Luftwaffe), Hungary, Italy, Romania.

Development: Probably no other aircraft in history has been developed in so many quite different forms for so many purposes — except, perhaps, for the Mosquito. Flown long before World War II as a civil prototype, after a rapid design process led by two temporarily hired Americans well-versed in modern stressed-skin construction, the first 88s were transformed into the heavier, slower and more capacious A-1 bombers which were just entering service as World War II began. The formidable bomb load and generally good performance were offset by inadequate defensive armament, and in the A-4 the span was increased, the bomb load and gun power substantially augmented and a basis laid for diverse further development. Though it would be fair to describe practically all the subsequent versions as a hodge-podge of ▶

Above: Side views of the Ju 88G-7a night fighter (left) and Ju 88P-1 anti-tank aircraft with jettisonable 75mm gun (right).

lash-ups, the Ju 88 was structurally excellent, combined large internal fuel capacity with great load-carrying capability, and yet was never so degraded in performance as to become seriously vulnerable as were the Dornier and Heinkel bombers. Indeed, with the BMW radial and the Jumo 213 engines the later versions were almost as fast as the best contemporary fighters at all altitudes and could be aerobatted violently into the bargain. A basic design feature was that all the crew were huddled together, to improve combat morale; but in the Battle of Britain it was found this merely made it difficult to add proper defensive armament and in the later Ju 188 a much larger crew compartment was provided. Another distinctive feature was the large single struts of the main landing gear, sprung with stacks of chamfered rings of springy steel, and arranged to turn the big, soft-field wheels through 90° to lie flat in the rear of the nacelles. In 1940 to 1943 about 2,000 Ju 88 bombers were built each year, nearly all A-5 or A-4 versions. After splitting off completely new branches which led to the Ju 188 and 388, bomber development was directed to the streamlined S series of much higher performance, it having become accepted that the traditional Luftwaffe species of bomber was doomed if intercepted, no matter how many extra guns and crew it might carry. Indeed even the bomb and fuel loads were cut in most S sub-types, though the S-2 had fuel in the original bomb bay and

Junkers Ju 388J

Ju 388L-series, J-series and K-series

Origin: Junkers Flugzeug und Motorenwerke AG.
Type: (L) Recce, (J) night fighter, (K) bomber.
Engines: (Most) two 1,890hp BMW 801TJ 18-cyl two-row radials, (some) two 1,750hp Junkers Jumo 213E inverted-vee-12 liquid-cooled.
Dimensions: Span 72ft 2in (22.00m); length (L-1) 49ft 10½in (15.20m), (J-1) 53ft 5½in (16.29m) (58ft 1in with tail-warning radar); height 14ft 3in (4.35m).
Weights: Empty (L-1) 22,810lb (10,345kg), (J-1) 22,928lb (10,400kg); loaded (L-1, J-1) 32,350lb (14,675kg).
Performance: Maximum speed at altitude (L-1) 407mph (655km/h), (J-1) 362mph (582km/h); service ceiling (typical) 44,000ft (13,500m); range (L-1, internal fuel only) 1,838 miles (2950km).

Development: Originally the Ju 188S and T, these extremely important combat aircraft began as the Hubertus project in September 1943. The only type to reach the Luftwaffe in quantity was the L-1, built by ATG at Merseburg and Weser at Bremen. This was a pressurized three-seater, and like other versions had extremely highly rated turbocharged engines giving almost full power at around 35,000ft. None of the numerous K-series got into service, but the J-1 was so good a night and all-weather fighter it continued after the cancellation of all except "emergency fighter" programmes in July 1944. Most J-series did not have the twin-MG 131 tail barbette, but typical armament included two 30mm and two MG 151 firing ahead and two MG 151 in a Schräge Musik oblique installation in the rear fuselage. Nose radar included the FuG 218 Neptun with Morgenstern (Morning Star) aerial array mostly enclosed in a plywood nosecone.

Above: One of the first of nearly 15,000 Ju 88s was this long-span A-5 of 1939, seen with two external SC250 (551lb) bombs.

large bulged bomb stowage (which defeated the objective of reducing drag). Final bomber versions included the P series of big-gun anti-armour and close-support machines, the Nbwe with flame-throwers and recoilless rocket projectors, and a large family of Mistel composite-aircraft combinations, in which the Ju 88 lower portion was a pilotless missile steered by the fighter originally mounted on top. Altogether bomber, reconnaissance and related 88s totalled 10,774, while frantic construction of night fighter versions in 1944–45 brought the total to at least 14,980. The Ju 88 night fighters (especially the properly designed G-series) were extremely formidable, bristling with radar and weapons and being responsible for destroying more Allied night bombers than all other fighters combined.

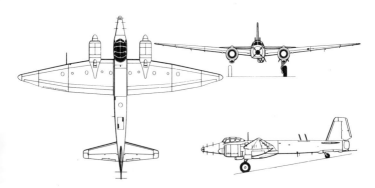

Above: Three-view of Ju 388J-1 with Neptun radar and oblique guns.

Below: The Ju 388 V2, prototype of the 388J Störtebeker (a legendary German pirate) night-fighter with SN-2 radar.

Messerschmitt Bf 109

Bf 109B, C, D, E, F, G, H and K series, S-99 and 199, Ha-1109 and -1112

Origin: Bayerische Flugzeugwerke, later (1938) renamed Messerschmitt AG; very widely subcontracted throughout German-controlled territory and built under licence by Dornier-Werke, Switzerland, and Hispano-Aviación, Spain (post-war, Avia, Czechoslovakia).

Type: Single-seat fighter (many, fighter bomber).

Engine: (B, C) one 635hp Junkers Jumo 210D inverted-vee-12 liquid-cooled; (D) 1,000hp Daimler-Benz DB 600Aa, same layout; (E) 1,100hp DB 601A, 1,200hp DB 601N or 1,300hp DB 601E; (F) DB 601E; (G) 1,475hp DB 605A-1, or other sub-type up to DB 605D rated 1,800hp with MW50 boost; (H-1) DB 601E; (K) usually 1,550hp DB 605ASCM/DCM rated 2,000hp with MW50 boost; (S-199) 1,350hp Jumo 211F; (HA-1109) 1,300hp Hispano-Suiza 12Z-89 upright vee-12 or (M1L) 1,400hp R-R Merlin 500-45.

Dimensions: Span (A to E) 32ft 4½in (9·87m); (others) 32ft 6½in (9·92m); length (B, C) 27ft 11in; (D, E, typical) 28ft 4in (8·64m); (F) 29ft 0½in; (G) 29ft 8in (9·04m); (K) 29ft 4in; (HA-1109-M1L) 29ft 11in; height (E) 7ft 5½in (2·28m); (others) 8ft 6in (2·59m).

Weights: Empty (B-1) 3,483lb; (E) 4,189lb (1900kg) to 4,421lb; (F) around 4,330lb; (G) 5,880lb (2667kg) to 6,180lb (2800kg); (K, typical) 6,000lb; maximum loaded (B-1) 4,850lb; (E) 5,523lb (2505kg) to 5,875lb (2665kg); (F-3) 6,054lb; (G) usually 7,496lb (3400kg); (K) usually 7,439lb (3375kg).

Performance: Maximum speed (B-1) 292mph; (D) 323mph; (E) 348--354 mph (560—570km/h); (F-3) 390mph; (G) 353 to 428mph (569—690km/h), (K-4) 452mph (729km/h); initial climb (B-1) 2,200ft/min; (E) 3,100 to 3,280ft (1000m)/min; (G) 2,700 to 4,000ft/min; (K-4) 4,823ft (1470m)/min; service ceiling (B-1) 26,575ft; (E) 34,450ft (10,500m) to 36,090ft (11,000m); (F, G) around 38,000ft (11,600m); (K-4) 41,000ft (12,500m); range on internal fuel (all) 365—460 miles (typically, 700km).

Right: The very first Bf 109 production variant was the B-1 which was delivered from February 1937, long before any production Hurricane or Spitfire. This example had the cropped spinner that became standard (the B-2 switched to the VDM-Hamilton variable-pitch propeller). This aircraft served with Luftkreiskommando II at Berlin in 1938.

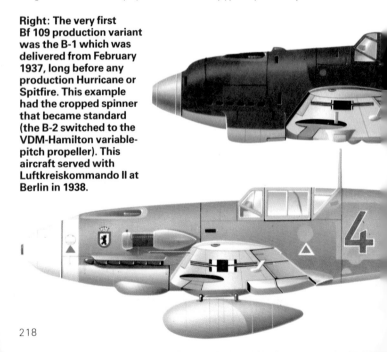

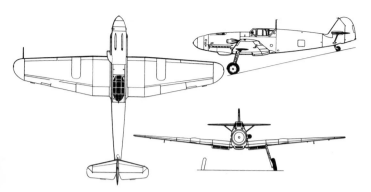

Above: Abandoned high-altitude variant, the Bf 109H of 1944.

Below: The original prototype, with British Kestrel engine.

Armament: (B) three 7·92mm Rheinmetall-Borsig MG 17 machine guns above engine and firing through propeller hub; (C) four MG 17, two above engine and two in wings, with fifth through propeller hub in C-2; (early E-1) four MG 17, plus four 50kg or one 250kg (551lb) bomb; (later E-1 and most other E) two MG 17 above engine, each with 1,000 rounds (or two ▶

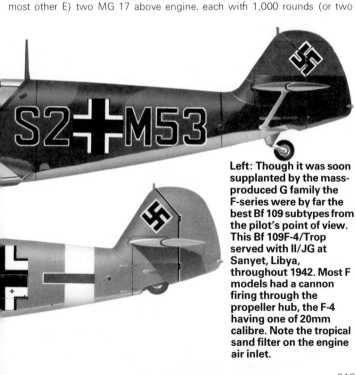

Left: Though it was soon supplanted by the mass-produced G family the F-series were by far the best Bf 109 subtypes from the pilot's point of view. This Bf 109F-4/Trop served with II/JG at Sanyet, Libya, throughout 1942. Most F models had a cannon firing through the propeller hub, the F-4 having one of 20mm calibre. Note the tropical sand filter on the engine air inlet.

Above: A frame from a propaganda film of 1941 showing two
Bf 109E-4/Trop fighters of I/JG 27 flying over Libya soon after the
formation of the Afrika Korps.

Below: One of the last of the E-series versions, this Bf 109E-7 was
photographed in 1942 flying with JG 5 on the Leningrad Front. Note the
pointed spinner and large air-inlet dust filter.

Above: These Bf 109G-6/R2 interceptors are equipped with the 210mm Wfr Gr 21 underwing mortars, firing large rockets. The weapon was a pulk-zerstörer (bomber-formation destroyer).

MG 17 with 500 rounds, plus 20mm MG FF firing through propeller hub) and two MG FF in wings, each with 60-round drum; (F-1) two MG 17 and one MG FF; (F-2) two 15mm MG 151 and one MG FF; (F-4) two MG 151, one MG FF and one 20mm MG 151 in fairing under each wing; (G-1) two MG 17 or 13mm MG 131 over engine and one MG 151; (G-6) one 30mm MK 108, two MG 131 above engine and two MG 151 under wings; (K-4) two MG 151 above engine and one MK 108 or 103; (K-6) two MG 131 above engine, one MK 103 or 108 and two MK 108 under wings; (S-199) two MG 131 above engine and two MG 151 under wings; (HA-1109 series) two wing machine guns or 20mm Hispano 404. Many German G and K carried two 210mm rocket tubes under wings or various bomb loads.

History: First flight (Bf 109 V-1) early September 1935; (production B-1) February 1937; (Bf 109E) January 1939; (Bf 109F prototype) July 1940; replacement in production by Bf 109G, May 1942.

Users: Bulgaria, Croatia, Finland, Germany (Luftwaffe), Hungary, Italy (ARSI), Japan, Jugoslavia, Romania, Slovakia, Slovak (CB Insurgent), Soviet Union (1940), Spain, Switzerland; (post-war) Czechoslovakia, Israel.

Development: During World War II the general public in the Allied nations at first regarded the Messerschmitt as an inferior weapon compared with the Spitfire and other Allied fighters. Only in the fullness of time was it possible to appreciate that the Bf 109 was one of the greatest combat aircraft in history. First flown in 1935, it was a major participant in the Spanish Civil War and a thoroughly proven combat aircraft by the time of Munich (September 1938). Early versions were the Bf 109B, C and D, all of ▶

221

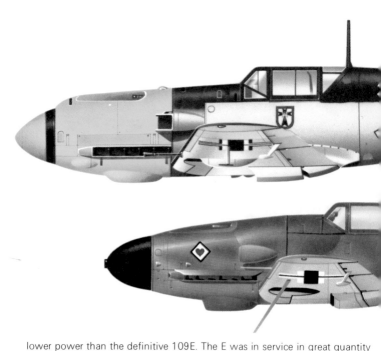

lower power than the definitive 109E. The E was in service in great quantity by the end of August 1939 when the invasion of Poland began. From then until 1941 it was by far the most important fighter in the Luftwaffe, and it was also supplied in quantity to numerous other countries (which are listed above). During the first year of World War II the "Emil", as the various E sub-types were called, made mincemeat of the many and varied types of fighter against which it was opposed, with the single exception of the Spitfire (which it greatly outnumbered). Its good points were small size, fast and cheap production, high acceleration, fast climb and dive, and good power of manoeuvre. Nearly all 109Es were also fitted with two or three 20mm cannon, with range and striking power greater than a battery of eight rifle-calibre guns. Drawbacks were the narrow landing gear, severe swing on take-off or landing, extremely poor lateral control at high speeds, and the fact that in combat the slats on the wings often opened in tight turns; while this prevented a stall, it snatched at the ailerons and threw the pilot off his aim. After 1942 the dominant version was the 109G ("Gustav") which made up over 70 per cent of the total received by the Luftwaffe. Though formidably armed and equipped, the vast swarms of "Gustavs" were nothing like such good machines as the lighter E and F, demanding constant pilot attention, constant high power settings, and having landing characteristics described as "malicious". Only a few of the extended-span high-altitude H-series were built, but from October 1944 the standard production series was the K with clear-view "Galland hood", revised wooden tail and minor structural changes. After World War II the Czech Avia firm found their Bf 109 plant intact and began building the S-99; running out of DB 605 engines they installed the slow-revving Jumo, producing the S-199 with even worse torque and swing than the German versions (pilots called it "Mezek" meaning mule), but in 1948 managed to sell some to Israel. The Spanish Hispano Aviación flew its first licence-built 1109 in March 1945 and in 1953 switched to the Merlin engine to produce the 1109-M1L Buchón (Pigeon). Several Hispano and Merlin versions were built in Spain, some being tandem-seat trainers. When the last HA-1112 flew out of Seville in late 1956 it closed out 21 years of manufacture of this classic fighter, during which total output approached 35,000.

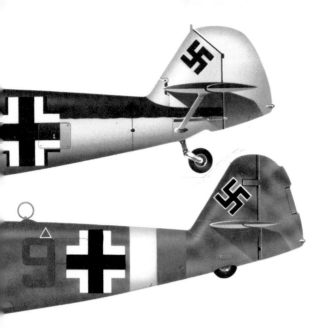

Top of page: Not all Emils (Bf 109E-series) had a blunt spinner (with or without cannon firing through the hub); this pointed-nose E-4 served with famed I/JG 1 at De Kooy, Holland, in 1941.

Above: One of the final versions was the 1944 K-series which usually had the so-called Galland hood and a new wooden tail. This aircraft was a K-4, serving with II/JG 77 at Hopsten.

Below: This Bf 109F-4 was photographed in early 1942 whilst serving with III/JG 26 (the staffel previously commanded by Adolf Galland who until late 1941 was geschwaderkommodore of the whole JG 26 wing). The F-series kept up the pressure on the RAF's Spitfires, which were inferior in climbing and diving but in general could turn more tightly if flown with determination.

Messerschmitt Bf 110

Bf 110B series to H series
(data for Bf 110C-4/B)

Origin: Bayerische Flugzeugwerke, after 1938 Messerschmitt AG; widely dispersed manufacture.

Type: Two-seat day and night fighter (also used on occasion for ground attack and reconnaissance).

Engines: Two 1,100hp Daimler-Benz DB 601A; (later C-4s) 1,200hp DB 601N 12-cylinder inverted-vee liquid-cooled; (G, H) two 1,475hp DB 605B, same layout.

Dimensions: Span 53ft 4¾in (16·25m); length 39ft 8½in (12·1m); height 11ft 6in (3·5m).

Weights: Empty 9,920lb (4500kg); loaded 15,430lb (7000kg).

Performance: Maximum speed 349mph (562km/h) at 22,966ft (7000m); climb to 18,045ft (5500m), 8 minutes; service ceiling 32,800ft (10,000m); range 528 miles (850km) at 304mph (490km/h) at 16,400ft (5000m).

Armament: Two 20mm Oerlikon MG FF cannon and four Rheinmetall 7·92mm MG 17 machine guns fixed firing forward in nose, one 7·92mm MG 15 manually aimed machine gun in rear cockpit; C-4/B also fitted with racks under centre section for four 551lb (250kg) bombs. (G-4 night fighter) two 30mm MK 108 and two 20mm MG 151 firing forward, and two MG 151 in Schräge Musik installation firing obliquely upwards (sometimes two 7·92mm MG 81 in rear cockpit).

History: First flight (Bf 110V1 prototype) 12 May 1936; (pre-production Bf 110C-0) February 1939; operational service with Bf 110C-1, April 1939; final run-down of production (Bf 110H-2 and H-4) February 1945.

User: Germany (Luftwaffe).

Development: As in five other countries at about the same time, the Reichsluftfahrtministerium decided in 1934 to issue a requirement for a new kind of fighter having two engines and exceptional range. Called a Zerstörer ▶

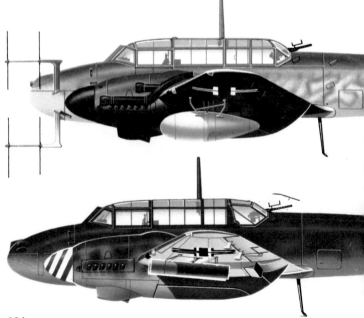

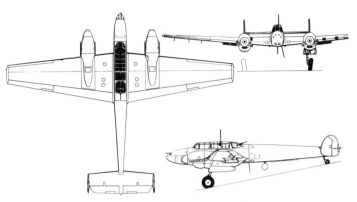

Above: Three-view of a Bf 110C-3 of early 1940.

Below: A frame from a propaganda film, this photograph shows a Bf 110D of 8/ZG 26 on escort duty from Sicily to Malta in 1942.

Left: Instead of being terminated in early 1941 production increased and by 1942 was becoming centred on night fighters. Typical of later DB 605-powered versions, this Bf 110G-4 served with 7/NJG 4 late in the war.

Left: This Bf 110G-2 served with 5/ZG 76 at Grossenhain in 1943–44. It had the larger fins, thick windscreen and other G features but was a day bomber destroyer with two Wfr Gr 21 210mm rockets under each wing.

Above: Splendid photograph of Bf 110D-1s of ZG 26 taken over the Libyan coast in 1941. The nearer aircraft wears the ZG 26 geschwader (wing) emblem and has red (8-staffel) spinners.

Below: This Bf 110C-4 of III/ZG 76 was also photographed in the Libyan desert in 1941, and has still to be painted in Sand Yellow (like the aircraft above) with white theatre band. *continued* ▶

(destroyer), it was to be as capable as small single-seaters of fighting other aircraft, possibly making up in firepower for any lack in manoeuvrability. Its dominant quality was to be range, to escort bombers on raids penetrating deep into enemy heartlands. Powered by two of the new DB 600 engines, the prototype reached 316mph, considered an excellent speed, but it was heavy on the controls and unimpressive in power of manoeuvre. Too late to be tested in the Spanish Civil War, the production Bf 110B-1, which was the first to carry the two cannon, was itself supplanted by the C-series with the later DB 601 engine with direct fuel injection and greater power at all heights. By the start of World War II the Luftwaffe had 195 Bf 110C fighters, and in the Polish campaign these were impressive, operating mainly in the close-support role but demolishing any aerial opposition they encountered. It was the same story in the Blitzkrieg war through the Low Countries and France, when 350 of the big twins were used. Only when faced with RAF Fighter Command in the Battle of Britain did the Bf 110 suddenly prove a disaster. It was simply no match for the Spitfire or even the Hurricane, and soon the Bf 109 was having to escort the escort fighters! But production of DB 605-powered versions, packed with radar and night-fighting equipment, was actually trebled in 1943 and sustained in 1944, these G and H models playing a major part in the night battles over the Reich in 1943–45.

Above: A rare photograph of the very first production version, the Bf 110A-01, at Augsburg-Haunstetten in August 1937. Powered by 680hp Jumo 210Da engines, it was slow and unimpressive.

Below: Carrying out an Rb 50/30 reconnaissance camera to a Bf 110C-5 in the Western (Libyan) desert. The 'cannon ports' are painted on.

Messerschmitt Me 210 and 410 Hornisse

Me 210A, B and C series, Me 410A and B series

Origin: Messerschmitt AG.

Type: Two-seat tactical aircraft for fighter, attack and reconnaissance duties with specialised variants.

Engines: (Me 210, usual for production versions) two 1,395hp Daimler-Benz DB 601F inverted-vee-12 liquid-cooled; (Me 410A series, usual for production versions) two 1,750hp DB 603A of same layout; (Me 410B series) two 1,900hp DB 603G.

Dimensions: Span (210) 53ft 7¼in, later 53ft 7¾in (16·4m); (410) 53ft 7¾in; length (without 50mm gun, radar or other long fitment) (210) 40ft 3in (12·22m); (410) 40ft 10in or 40ft 11½in (12·45m); height (both) 14ft 0½in (4·3m).

Weights: Empty (210A) about 12,000lb (5440kg); (410A-1) 13,560lb (6150kg); maximum loaded (210A-1) 17,857lb (8100kg); (410A-1) 23,483lb (10,650kg).

Performance: Maximum speed (both, clean) 385mph (620km/h); initial climb (both) 2,133ft (650m)/min; service ceiling (210A-1) 22,967ft (7000m); (410A-1) 32,800ft (10,000m); range with full bomb load (210A-1) 1,491 miles (2400km); (410A-1) 1,447 miles (2330km).

Armament: Varied, but basic aircraft invariably defended by two remotely-controlled powered barbettes on sides of fuselage each housing one 13mm MG 131 and, if bomber version, provided with internal weapon bay housing two 1,102lb (500kg) bombs; external racks on nearly all (210 and 410) for two 1,102lb stores (exceptionally, two 2,204lb). Normal fixed forward-firing armament of two 20mm MG 151/20 and two 7·92mm MG 17. Me 410 versions had many kinds of bomber-destroyer armament, as described in the text.

History: First flight (Me 210V-1) 2 September 1939; (pre-production 210A-0) April 1941; final delivery (210) April 1942; first flight (310) 11 September 1943; (410V-1) probably December 1942.

User: Germany (Luftwaffe).

Development: Planned in 1937 as a valuable and more versatile successor to the Bf 110 twin-engined escort fighter, the Me 210 was little more than a flop and made hardly any contribution to the German war effort. After

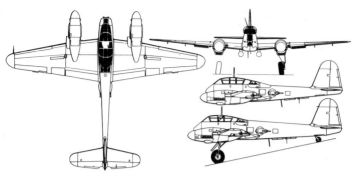

Above: Three-view of Me 210A-2 (upper side view, A-0).

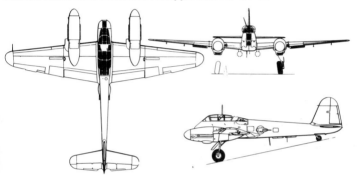

Above: Three-view of Me 410A-1 Hornisse.

severe flight instability and landing-gear problems some progress was made in 1941 towards producing an acceptable machine which could be put into production against the order for 1,000 placed "off the drawing board" in June 1939. Accidents were nevertheless frequent and manufacture was terminated at the 352nd aircraft. This major blow to the Luftwaffe and the company, which was reflected in an official demand for Willi Messerschmitt's resignation from the board, was partly salvaged by a further redesign and change to the DB 603 engine. The Me 310 was a high-

Below: This Me 410A-3 was captured by the RAF at Trapani (Sicily) in 1943; a deep-belly recon aircraft, it had served with 2(F)/122.

231

Top: Another Me 410A-3 of 2(F)/122 knocked out by the RAF in 1943, this one was shot down by fighters during the 8th Army's crossing of the Sangro river in Italy. Above: This view shows the deep fuselage of the Me 410A-3 reconnaissance version, which allowed for a proper camera installation in contrast to lash-ups used previously.

Right: Two of the last Me 210A-1s completed prior to cancellation in April 1942. Features included modified slotted wings, new rear fuselage and parallel-bar airbrakes.

altitude fighter-bomber with 58ft 9in wing and pressure cabin, but this was abandoned in favour of a less radical change designated 410. As with the 210, the reconnaissance 410s usually had cameras in the bomb bay and no MG 17s, while some attack or destroyer versions had four forward-firing MG 151 cannon, or two MG 151 and a 50mm BK 5 gun with 21 rounds. The Me 410A-2/U-2 was an important night fighter with SN-2 Lichtenstein radar and two MG 151 and two 30mm MK 108. Many of the 1,121 Me 410s carried Rüstsatz external packs housing two more MG 151, MK 108 or MK 103, and occasionally experienced pilots fitted as many as eight MG 151 all firing ahead. The 210mm rocket tube was a common fitment by 1944, some aircraft having a rotating pack of six tubes in the bomb bay.

233

Messerschmitt Me 163 Komet

Me 163B-1

Origin: Messerschmitt AG.
Type Single-seat interceptor.
Engine: One 3,750lb (1700kg) thrust Walter HWK 509A-2 bi-propellant rocket burning concentrated hydrogen peroxide (T-stoff) and hydrazine/methanol (C-stoff).
Dimensions: Span 30ft 7in (9·3m); length 18ft 8in (5·69m); height 9ft 0in (2·74m).
Weights: Empty 4,191lb (1905kg); loaded 9,042lb (4110kg).
Performance: Maximum speed 596mph (960km/h) at 32,800ft (10,000m); initial climb 16,400ft (5000m)/min; service ceiling 54,000ft (16,500m); range depended greatly on flight profile but under 100km (62 miles); endurance $2\frac{1}{2}$min from top of climb or eight min total.
Armament: Two 30mm MK 108 cannon in wing roots, each with 60 rounds.
History: First flight (Me 163V1) spring 1941 as glider, August 1941 under power; (Me 163B) August 1943; first operational unit (I/JG400) May 1944.
User: Germany (Luftwaffe).

Development: Of all aircraft engaged in World War II the Me 163 Komet (Comet) was the most radical and, indeed, futuristic. The concept of the short-endurance local-defence interceptor powered by a rocket engine was certainly valid and might have been more of a thorn in the Allies' side than it was. Even the dramatically unconventional form of the Me 163, with no horizontal tail and an incredibly short fuselage, did not lead to great

Top: Purging the steam-generation piping of a squadron aircraft (probably with JG 400).

Above: The first powered prototype was the Me 163A V1, which was flown as a glider in spring 1941, and with its rocket in August.

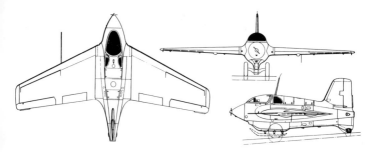

Above: Me 163B-1a showing takeoff trolley and landing skid.

difficulty; in fact, the production fighter was widely held to have the best and safest characteristics of any aircraft in the Luftwaffe. But the swift strides into uncharted technology were bold in the extreme. It was partly to save weight and drag that the tailless configuration was adopted, and partly because the moving spirit behind the project was at first Dr Alex Lippisch, who liked tailless designs. Choice of two rocket propellants that reacted violently when they came into contact solved the problem of ignition in the combustion chamber but added an extremely large element of danger. Moreover, the 163 had no landing gear, taking off from a jettisoned trolley and landing on a sprung skid, and the landing impact often sloshed residual propellants together causing a violent explosion. Many aircraft were lost this way, and the original test pilot, glider champion Heini Dittmar, was badly injured when the skid failed to extend. Nevertheless by 1944 these bat-like specks were swooping on US bomber formations with devastating effect. Numerous improved versions were flying at VE day, but only 370 Komets had seen service and these had suffered high attrition through accidents.

The roots of the project went back to the 1920s, with both Lippisch aerodynamics and the various rocket research projects that led to the Hellmuth Walter development of engines suitable for manned aircraft from 1936. It is worth emphasizing that nothing remotely like either the airframe or the engine was attempted in Britain, nor in any other country except the Soviet Union. The early aircraft research was centred at the DFS (German sailplane research institute), where the first tailless rocket aircraft was planned as the DFS 194. In March 1938 the design was complete, but in January 1939 it was transferred to Messerschmitt. Shortly after this the Walter R I-203 rocket flew (very badly) in the He 176 research aircraft. Results with this aircraft were poor, but when a similar motor was fitted to the DFS 194 tailless aircraft ▶

Below: An Me 163B-1a Komet of II/JG 400 based at Brandis. Many were mottled grey/grey-violet/ light blue.

the speed reached 342mph (550km/h) and climb was fantastic. Swiftly sanction for a rocket fighter was gained, and gliding trials with the Me 163 V1 began in the spring of 1941. Again the tailless machine floated like a bird (the main snag being that instead of landing where the pilot wanted, it kept floating) and in July–September 1941 Dittmar pushed the speed under rocket power higher and higher, far beyond the world speed record until, on 2 October 1941, he reached about 1004km/h (623·85mph), a speed measured by theodolites on the ground. At all times the flight characteristics of all 163 versions were exemplary, but there were countless snags and

Above: One of the very first of the true production Komets, this Me 163B-1a was assigned to Ekdo (Erprobungskommando) 16 at Zwischenahn experimental airfield in July 1944. This unit worked out the training and operational tactics and procedures for the 163.

Left: Most of the operational Komets were painted in one of the various late-war colour schemes similar to this Me 163B01a used by JG 400 at Brandis in early 1945. The nose windmill drove the electric generator.

catastrophes due to the dangerous propellants, the failure of hydraulics, the extreme difficulty of taking off exactly into wind on the unsprung dolly, and the equally rigorous constraints upon the pilot in landing. Everything had to be exactly right, because if the aircraft yawed, swung or ran too far on to rough ground, it would turn over and the propellants explode.

The final developments were the Me 163C, with fully retractable tail-wheel, long body of improved form, increased-span centre section and new motor with a small chamber to give 660lb (300kg) for cruising flight, and the derived Me 263.

Messerschmitt Me 262

Me 262A-1a Schwalbe, Me 262A-2 Sturmvogel, Me 262B-1a

Origin: Messerschmitt AG.
Type: (A-1a) single-seat fighter, (A-2a) single-seat bomber, (262B-1a) two-seat night fighter.
Engines: Two 1,980lb (900kg) thrust Junkers Jumo 004B single-shaft axial turbojets.
Dimensions: Span 40ft 11½in (12·5m); length 34ft 9½in (10·6m), (262B-1a, excluding radar aerials) 38ft 9in (11·8m); height 12ft 7in (3·8m).
Weights: Empty (A-1a, A-2a) 8,820lb (4000kg); (B-1a) 9,700lb (4400kg); loaded (A-1a, A-2a) 15,500lb (7045kg); (B-1a) 14,110lb (6400kg).
Performance: Maximum speed (A-1a) 540mph (870km/h); (A-2a, laden) 470mph (755km/h); (B-1a) 497mph (800km/h); initial climb (all) about 3,940ft (1200m)/min; service ceiling 37,565ft (11,500m); range on internal fuel, at altitude, about 650 miles (1050km).
Armament: (A-1a) four 30mm MK 108 cannon in nose, two with 100 rounds each, two with 80; (A-1a/U1) two 30mm MK 103, two MK 108 and two 20mm MG 151/20; (A-1b) as A-1a plus 24 spin-stabilised R4/M 50mm rockets; (B-1a) as A-1a; (B-2a) as A-1a plus two inclined MK 108 behind cockpit in Schräge Musik installation; (D) SG 500 Jagdfaust with 12 rifled mortar barrels inclined in nose; (E) 50mm MK 114 gun or 48 R4/M rockets; bomb load of two 1,100lb (500kg) bombs carried by A-2a.
History: First flight (262V1 on Jumo 210 piston engine) 4 April 1941; (262V3 on two Jumo 004-0 turbojets) 18 July 1942; (Me 262A-1a) 7 June 1944; first delivery (A-0 to Rechlin) May 1944; first experimental combat unit (EK 262) 30 June 1944; first regular squadron (8/ZG26) September 1944.
User: Germany (Luftwaffe).

continued ▶

Above: The Me 262A No 130 083 was redesignated V83 and test-flown with a 50mm BK 5 gun.

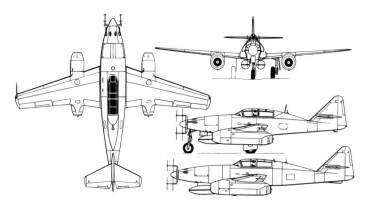

Above: Three-view of the first night-fighter version, the B-1a, rebuilt from the A-1a with SN-2 radar and a rear-seat radar operator, which was briefly operational against RAF Mosquito night intruders. Lower side view, the optimised Me 262B-2a.

Above: Starting engines of an Me 262A-1a of the Kommando Nowotny in late October 1944 (probably at Achmer).

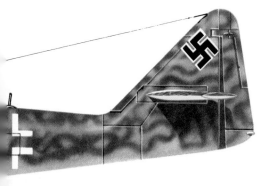

Left: One version of Me 262 to reach Luftwaffe was this Me 262A-1a/U3, an unarmed photo-reconnaissance conversion of the standard fighter which served with Einsatzkommando Braunegg in northern Italy in March 1945. Two oblique cameras (Rb 50/30s or a 20/30 and a 75/30) caused projecting bulges.

239

Above: This Me 262A-1a, Nr 110 025, was delivered to the first Me 262 combat unit, Kommando Nowotny, which became operational on 3 October 1944 (RAF 616 Sqn had Meteors in July).

Development: In the Me 262 the German aircraft industry created a potentially war-winning aircraft which could have restored to the Luftwaffe command of the skies over Germany. Compared with Allied fighters of its day, including the RAF Meteor I, which entered service a little earlier, it was much faster and packed a much heavier punch. Radar-equipped night fighter versions and sub-types designed to stand off from large bomber formations and blast them out of the sky were also developments against which the Allies had no answer. Yet for years the programme was held back by official disinterest, and by the personal insistence of Hitler that the world-beating jet should be used only as a bomber! It was in the autumn of 1938 that Messerschmitt was asked to study the design of a jet fighter, and the resulting Me 262 was remarkably unerring. First flown on a piston engine in the nose, it then flew on its twin turbojets and finally, in July 1943, the fifth development aircraft flew with a nosewheel. Despite numerous snags, production aircraft were being delivered in July 1944 and the rate of production was many times that of the British Meteor. On the other hand the German axial engines were unreliable and casualties due to engine failure, fires or break-up were heavy. The MK 108 gun was also prone to jam, and the landing gear to collapse. Yet the 262 was a beautiful machine to handle and, while Allied jets either never reached squadrons or never engaged enemy aircraft, the 100 or so Me 262s that flew on operations and had fuel available destroyed far more than 100 Allied bombers and fighters. Even more remarkable, by VE-day total deliveries of this formidable aircraft reached 1,433.

Below: An Me 262A-2a Sturmvogel bomber, with its two 500kg bombs in place. The first A-2a unit was III/KG 51, which became operational at Hopsten, near Rheine, on 5 October 1944.

Messerschmitt Me 263

Me 163D and 263A (Ju 248)

Origin: Messerschmitt AG; transferred to Junkers.
Type: Interceptor.
Engine: Walter HWK 109-509C-4 rocket with 3,750lb (1700kg) main chamber and 660lb (300kg) cruise chamber.
Dimensions: Span 31ft 2in (9·50m); length 25ft 10½in (7·88m); height 8ft 10¼in (2·70m).
Weights: Empty 4,640lb (2105kg); loaded 11,354lb (5150kg).
Performance: Maximum speed 620mph (1000km/h) at height; time to 49,213ft (15,000m) 3 min; max endurance, about 1hr including 15min under power.

Development: In retrospect the Me 163 need not have suffered from its most serious faults, and the 263 emerged on the Lippisch/Messerschmitt drawing boards in winter 1943—44 to rectify them. The new design had a larger and better-shaped body housing more propellants, a new engine with separate low-thrust cruise chamber for long endurance, and a proper landing gear. The 163D V1 was completed in spring 1944 but the RLM transferred the programme to Junkers to ease Messerschmitt's burdens. At Dessau Prof Hertel improved the 263A-1 into the Ju 248, with automatic slats, bubble hood and cut-down rear fuselage, larger flaps and other changes. Two 30mm

Messerschmitt Me 328

Me 328 V1, A-series and B-series

Origin: Messerschmitt AG; development and prototypes by DFS, and pre-production aircraft by Jacob Schweyer.
Type: See text.
Engines: See text.
Dimensions: Span (small) 20ft 11¾in (6·40m), (large) 27ft 10½in (8·50m); length (most) 22ft 4¾in (6·83m), (fuselage engines) 28ft 2½in (8·63m); height (on skid) (A) 6ft 10½in (2·10m), (B) 8ft 2½in (2·50m).
Weights: Empty (B-0, B-1) 3,400lb (1542kg); loaded (A-1) 4,850lb (2200kg), (A-2) 8,378lb (3800kg), (B-1) 5,953lb (2700kg), (B-2) 10,595lb (4730kg).
Performance: Maximum speed at low level (A-1) 469mph (755km/h), (A-2) 572mph (920km/h), (B-1) 423mph (680km/h), (B-2) 367mph (590km/h).

Development: This programme, extraordinary even for Nazi Germany, began in 1941 as a parasite fighter for launch from a bomber and subsequent retrieval. After widespread research and development the V1 glider began pick-a-back tests with Do 217 as carrier in autumn 1943. Powered tests began with two 660lb (300kg) thrust As 014 pulsejets on the rear fuselage, with severe problems. Then tests were made with two ducts under the wings, some being hung as far aft as possible because the intense noise damaged the wooden airframe. The A-1 fighter had two wing ducts and the A-2 four on the fuselage; respective armament was two MG 151 and two MK 103. The work then switched to assault (some expendable) with bomb loads up to 3,087lb (1400kg), the B-1 having wing engines and the B-2 bigger ducts of 880lb (400kg) each. Takeoff was by rocket trolley, cable winch and other means. Other versions were to be catapulted from U-boats.

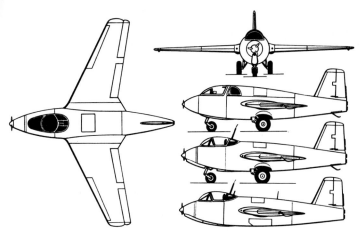

Above: Three-view of Me 263 VI (Ju 248) with upper side view as originally Me-built and lower view of proposed production 263A.

MK 108 were fitted in the wing roots. The RLM insisted on restoration of the Me 263A-1 designation, and hastened production, planning for the 5,511lb (2500kg) BMW 708 nitric-acid motor when ready, but in the chaos of late 1944 tooling was never finished, though a single Dessau-built 263A-1 flew as a glider in August 1944. It was briefly developed further by the Russians.

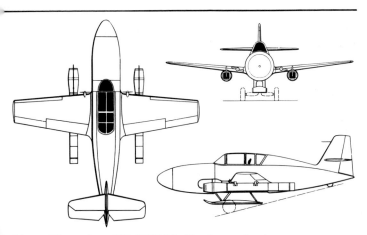

Above: Three-view of Me 328B-1 (with wing engines).
Below: One of the DFS-built towed prototypes, on skid gear.

ITALY

An observer of Italy in the 1930s would be bound to conclude that the nation was brilliant at advanced internal-combustion engines, had a flair for aircraft design and was outstanding in its aerobatic pilots. Coupled with its fascist government's top priority on military expansionism, and impressive displays of aerial power, Italy would have seemed a world leader in fighter aircraft. The exploits of the Aviazione Legionaria in the Spanish civil war reinforced this belief. Yet in World War II Italian air power, like Italian power on sea and land, was quickly regarded by Britain as a joke, a welcome light relief from the stern business of fighting Nazi Germany.

This was not due to individual lack of courage or skill on the part of Italian pilots but to many other factors of which a central one was the Italian aircraft themselves. Seeds of decline could have been discerned years earlier, in the dominant belief of the squadron pilots that manoeuvrability and pilot view mattered far more than performance or firepower, and in the abject failure of the procurement machine and industry to put sufficient effort behind the new generation of engines of much more than 1,000 horsepower. It was almost unbelievable that in June 1940, when Italy plucked up courage to join the struggle against what seemed to be enemies already defeated by Germany, virtually every one of its fighters had a Fiat A.74 engine, rated at a mere 840hp. No other major country was so crippled for lack of horsepower, and though Piaggio (for example) was flying engines of up to 1,700hp, not one got into service.

The inevitable result was a fighter force superbly equipped to

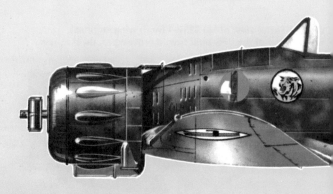

fight the battles of the pre-1937 era. The most numerous fighter was the C.R.42 biplane, a sheer delight to fly but hopelessly outclassed by Hurricanes and Spitfires. The other types available in quantity, the Fiat G.50 and Macchi C.200, were all-metal monoplanes but fitted with the same 840hp engine and same pair of 12·7mm (0·5in) machine guns. In a close dogfight fought only by ciné cameras they might have done well, but in actual warfare they were hacked out of the sky in droves.

The need for more horsepower and more firepower had been recognised well before the war, and the eventual answer was to import both from Germany. In 1939 Macchi arranged to import DB 601 engines and the first C.202 flew with such an engine in August 1940. Subsequently Fiat made the more powerful DB 605A under licence, while for firepower the extremely effective Mauser MG 151/20 cannon was adopted. The Italian industry thus had the ingredients for formidable fighters, and by all accounts the Fiat G.55, Macchi C.205 series and Reggiane Re 2005 were outstanding, with exceptional turn radius, adequate performance and considerable firepower.

In addition to these potentially staple types Italy also produced numerous other wartime fighters. Some were small and designed for economical mass production. Others were big twin-engined machines with devastating firepower, two quite dissimilar designs each having forward-firing armament of five MG 151! Another had a 1,700hp engine behind the pilot. But by 1943 Italy had lost both the capability and the will to fight, and hardly any of the good fighters were produced.

Fiat C.R.32

C.R.30, 32 and 32bis

Origin: Aeronautica d'Italia SA Fiat; built under licence by Hispano Aviaciòn, Spain.

Type: Single-seat fighter.

Engine: (C.R.30) one 600hp Fiat A.30 vee-12 water-cooled, (C.R.32) one 600hp Fiat A.30 RAbis.

Dimensions: Span (C.R.30) 34ft 5½in (10·45m); (C.R.32) 31ft 2in (9·5m); length (30) 25ft 8¼in (7·83m); (32) 24ft 5½in (7·45m); height (30) 8ft 7½in (2·62m); (32) 7ft 9in (2·4m).

Weights: Empty (both) about 3,100lb (1400kg); loaded (both) about 4,150lb (1900kg).

Performance: Maximum speed (30) 217mph (350km/h), (32) 233mph (375km/h); initial climb (both) 2,000ft (907m)/min; service ceiling (both) about 29,530ft (9000m); range (30) 528 miles (850km), (32) 466 miles (750km).

Armament: (C.R.30) two fixed Breda-SAFAT 7·7mm or 12·7mm machine guns above engine; (C.R.32) two 12·7mm; (C.R.32bis), two 12·7mm above engine and two 7·7mm above lower wings with provision for single 220lb (100kg) or two 110lb bombs.

History: First flight (C.R.30) 1932; (C.R.32) August 1933; final delivery, about October 1939.

Users: Argentina, China, Hungary, Italy (RA), Paraguay, Spain, Venezuela.

Development: In 1923 Ing Celestino Rosatelli supervised his first C.R. (Caccia Rosatelli) fighter. From it stemmed an unbroken line which reached its climax in the 1930s. The C.R.30 offered a considerable jump in performance, for it had much more power without increase in aircraft drag. The lusty Fiat vee-12 drove a metal propeller and was cooled by a prominent circular radiator in a duct in the chin position below the crankcase. The all-metal structure was notable for continuing the scheme of Warren (W-form) interplane bracing. The tail was also braced and the main gears had large wheel spats. The C.R.32 was a general refinement, built in larger numbers and forming the major part of the Regia Aeronautica fighter force in 1935–40. In August 1936 some were sent to form La Cucuracha squadron fighting for the Spanish Nationalist forces and this grew to become by far the largest of Franco's fighter units. Spain built many under licence as the Hispano HA-132-L Chirri, and more than 150 were exported by Fiat to China, Hungary and South American countries. The nimble little Fiats were compact, robust and highly manoeuvrable and gave impressive displays all over Europe in the hands of the Pattuglie Acrobatiche. Total Fiat output amounted to at least 1,212, the final 500 being mainly four-gun 32bis fighter-bombers and a few 32ter and 32quater versions with small modifications. The Regia Aeronautica did its best with the C.R.32 until 1942, finally using it for night tactical operations in Greece, Eritrea and Libya.

Above: This C.R.32 was used by J. G. Morato, an ace of the Spanish war.

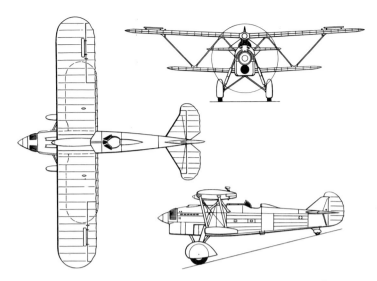

Above: Three-view of C.R.32 (32bis had guns above lower wings).

Immediately below: A C.R.32, photographed in the mid-1930s. By 1939 most had been camouflaged. Note "park bench" aileron balance visible above the upper wing.

Foot of page: The Pattuglie Acrobatiche team flew the C.R.32.

Fiat C.R.42 Falco

C.R.42, 42bis, 42ter, 42AS and 42N

Origin: Aeronautica d'Italia SA Fiat.
Type: Single-seat fighter.
Engine: One 840hp Fiat A.74 RC38 14-cylinder two-row radial.
Dimensions: Span 31ft 10in (9·7m); length 27ft 1¼in (8·25m); height 11ft 0in (3·35m).
Weights: Empty 3,790lb (1720kg); loaded 5,070lb (2300kg).
Performance: Maximum speed 267mph (430km/h); initial climb 2,400ft (732m)/min; service ceiling 34,450ft (10,500m); range 481 miles (775km).
Armament: (Early C.R.42) one 7·7mm and one 12·7mm Breda-SAFAT machine guns mounted above forward fuselage; (C.R.42bis) two 12·7mm; (C.R. 42ter) two 12·7mm and two more 12·7mm in fairings beneath lower wing; (C.R.42AS) two/four 12·7mm and underwing racks for two 220lb (100kg) bombs.
History: First flight (C.R.41) 1936; (C.R.42) January 1939; first service delivery, November 1939; termination of production, early 1942.
Users: Belgium, Finland, Hungary, Italy (RA), Sweden.

Development: In the mid-1930s the Fiat company made a firm move away from liquid-cooled vee engines and concentrated on air-cooled radials. Rosatelli prepared a fighter, the C.R.41, to take one of these, but only

Right: This C.R.42 served with the 95a Squadriglia, 18 Gruppo Caccia Terrestre, and in October 1940 was detached to Echeloo, Belgium, for missions against England. On 11 November it crossed the Suffolk coast, was intercepted and landed on the beach at Orford Ness. After testing as RAF BT 474 it was beautifully restored to its original condition at RAF St Athan and Biggin Hill.

Below: In front-line use on boggy ground many C.R.42s had their spats removed. This one in 1942 had its bomb racks loaded.

the prototype was built. Other nations were by this time (1936) giving up the open-cockpit, fabric-covered biplane in favour of the stressed-skin monoplane with retractable landing gear, but Rosatelli persisted with his C.R. family and developed the C.R.41 into the C.R.42. Though a robust, clean and very attractive design, it was really obsolete at the time of its first flight. Despite this – and perhaps confirming that Fiat knew the world market – the C.R.42 found ready acceptance. It went into large-scale production for the Regia Aeronautica and for Belgium (34, delivered January–May 1940), Hungary (at least 40, delivered December 1939–June 1940) and Sweden (72, delivered 1940–41). Total production, including the AS close support and N night fighter versions, amounted to 1,784. One group of 50 C.R.42bis provided the fighter element of the Corpo Aereo Italiano which operated from Belgium against England in October 1940–January 1941– with conspicuous lack of success. The rest persevered in the Mediterranean and North African areas, acting as both fighters and ground attack aircraft, a few being converted as dual trainers. One was built in 1940 as a twin-float seaplane and the final fling was a C.R.42B with 1,010hp DB 601A inverted-vee engine. The German power unit made it, at 323mph, the fastest biplane fighter but no production was attempted.

Below: Two C.R.42s of the 162a Squadriglia serving in North Africa. Its one asset was that it was a delight to fly.

Fiat G.50 Freccia

G.50, 50bis, 50ter and 55 Centauro

Origin: Aeronautica d'Italia SA Fiat; also built by CMASA.
Type: Single-seat fighter.
Engine: (G.50, G.50bis) one 840hp Fiat A.74 RC38 14-cylinder two-row radial; (G.50ter) 1,000hp A.76 RC40S; (G.55) 1,475hp Daimler-Benz DB 605A inverted-vee-12 liquid-cooled.
Dimensions: Span, (G.50) 36ft 0in (10·97m); (G.55) 38ft 10½in (11·85m); length, (G.50) 25ft 7in (7·79m); (G.55) 30ft 9in (9.37m); height (G.50) 9ft 8in (2·9m); (G.55) 10ft 3¼in (3·15m).
Weights: Empty (G.50) 4,188lb (1900kg); (G.55) 6,393lb (2900kg); loaded (G.50) 5,966lb (2706kg); (G.55) 8,179lb (3710kg).
Performance: Maximum speed (G.50) 293mph (471km/h); (G.55) 385mph (620km/h); initial climb (G.50) 2,400ft (731m)/min; (G.55) 3,300ft (1000m)/min; service ceiling (G.50) 32,810ft (10,000m); (G.55) 42,650ft (13,000m); range (G.50) 621 miles (1000km); (G.55) 994 miles (1600km).
Armament: (G.50, G.50bis) two 12·7mm Breda-SAFAT machine guns above front fuselage; (G.55/0) as above, plus one 20mm Mauser MG 151 cannon firing through propeller hub; (G.55/I) as G.55/0 plus two 20mm MG 151 in outer wings.
History: First flight 26 February 1937; (G.50bis) September 1940; (G.55) 30 April 1942.
Users: Finland, Italy (RA, CB, ARSI), Spain.

Development: In 1935 the issue of a specification for an all-metal monoplane fighter for the Regia Aeronautica attracted at least six competing designs. Though the Macchi 200 was ultimately to become dominant, the initial winner was the Fiat G.50, the first major design by Ing Giuseppe Gabrielli (hence the designation). Its flight trials went smoothly, an order was placed in September 1937 for 45 and deliveries began early in 1938. About a dozen of the first production G.50s were sent to reinforce the Aviazione Legionaria in Spain, where their good qualities of speed and ▶

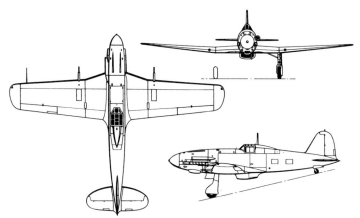

Above: Three-view of the G.55/1 with three cannon.

Below: One of the 12 G.50s from the original batch of 45 aircraft whch were sent in 1938 to the Gruppo Caccia Sperimentale in Spain. The markings are those applied in 1939, at 1° GCS based at Escalona.

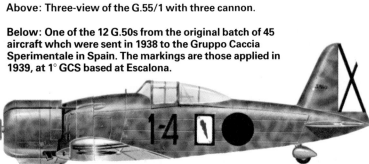

Below: M.M.5439, one of the last of the major production version, the G.50bis. This had an open-topped cockpit, broad but squat vertical tail, slotted flaps, landing gear by Magnaghi instead of Messier, and a fuel tank instead of an anti-personnel bomb bay.

Below: A swarm of Fiat G.50bis fighters serving with 51° Stormo of the Regia Aeronautica in 1941. They do not have white theatre bands and appear to be parked on a tiled apron.

Above: One of the few good photographs of a G.55, showing one of the first production machines in early 1943. It is probably fitted with a German-supplied DB 605 engine.

manoeuvrability were manifest. On the other hand pilots disliked having a sliding cockpit canopy, which was not easy to open quickly and interfered with vision, and in the next production batch of 200 an open cockpit was adopted. The poor armament was not changed, but fairings for the retracted wheels were added. Production from the CMASA plant at Marina di Pisa got under way in 1939, with deliveries replacing the C.R.32 in Regia Aeronautica fighter squadrons (not always to the pilots' delight), and a further 35 being flown to Finland in 1940 where they gave admirable service. The main production version was the G.50bis, with reprofiled fuselage giving improved pilot view, armour and self-sealing tanks. About 450 were built, mainly by CMASA. Other versions included the tandem-seat G.50B trainer, of which 139 were built; the G.50ter with more powerful engine; and prototypes of the G.50bis-A, with four 12·7mm guns and racks for two bombs, and of the DB 601A-powered G.50V.

By the time Italy entered the war in June 1940 it was obvious that the G.50 was becoming outclassed. Lack of engines of sufficient power was a major problem, but Fiat managed to obtain a Daimler-Benz DB 605A-1 from Germany and around this designed a splendid fighter with all-metal stressed-skin structure. The wing was especially efficient, and had left and right sections, each with two spars, joined on the centreline. The fuselage was well streamlined, and an enclosed cockpit was adopted without question. The prototype, called G.55 Centauro, was a vast improvement over various earlier Fiat fighters and projects using the DB 601 engine, and it flew on 30 April 1942. By January 1943 the production G.55/0 was on the line at Turin, and the 53° Stormo were delighted when they began to receive the new fighter in August 1943. Production was slow, because the Fiat RA.1050 RC58 Tifone (locally-built DB 605) was only trickling off the line, and only 105 were completed when the war ended.

Macchi M.C.200 Saetta

M.C.200 (Serie I-XXI) and M.C.201

Origin: Aeronautica Macchi.
Type: Single-seat day fighter.
Engine: One 870hp Fiat A74RC38 14-cylinder two-row radial.
Dimensions: Span 34ft 8½in (10·58m); length 26ft 10½in (8·2m); height 11ft 6in (3·38m).
Weights: (Typical) empty 4,188lb (1900kg); (prototype) 3,902lb; (final production Serie XXI) 4,451lb; loaded 5,182lb (2350kg); (prototype) 4,850lb; (Serie XXI) 5,598lb.
Performance: Maximum speed 312mph (501km/h); initial climb 3,215ft (980m)/min; service ceiling 29,200ft (8900m); range 354 miles (570km).
Armament: Two 12·7mm Breda-SAFAT machine guns firing above engine cowling; later-Serie aircraft also had two 7·7mm in wings; M.C.200 C.B. (caccia bombardiere) had underwing racks for two bombs of up to 352lb (160kg) each, or two 33gal drop tanks.
History: First flight 24 December 1937; service delivery October 1939; final delivery, about December 1944.
User: Italy.

Development: Mario Castoldi's design team at Aeronautica Macchi, at Varese in the north Italian lakeland, was the source of the best fighters used by the Regia Aeronautica in World War II. Castoldi's staff had earlier gained great experience with high-speed aircraft with their record-breaking Schneider seaplanes, but their first monoplane fighter, the C.200, bore little evidence of this. Though a reasonably attractive stressed-skin monoplane, it had an engine of low power and the performance was correspondingly modest. Moreover it never had anything that other countries would have regarded as proper armament, though the pilot did have the advantage of cockpit indicators showing the number of rounds of ammunition unfired.

Below: M.C.200 Saettas of the initial series, with fully enclosed cockpit, based near the maker's factory at Varese in 1940.

254

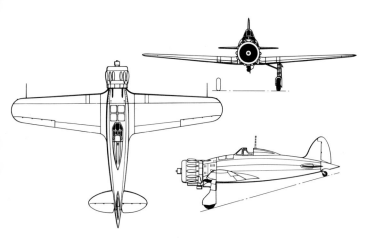

Above: Three-view of Macchi C.200 (late production serie).

Italian fighter pilots were by nature conservative; their protests caused the main production aircraft to have an open cockpit and fixed tailwheel, unlike the first batches, and combat equipment was simple in the extreme. Yet in combat with the lumbering Hurricane it proved effective, with outstanding dogfight performance and no vices. From late 1940 until Italy's surrender in September 1943 the C.200 saw more combat than any other Italian type, both around North Africa and Sicily and on the Eastern Front with the Corpo di Spedizone Italiano which claimed 88 Russian aircraft for the loss of 15 Saettas. The name Saetta, meaning lightning, refers to the lightning-bolts held by Jupiter, and is sometimes rendered as Arrow or Thunderbolt. ▶

Left: A Macchi C.200 (or M.C.200 for Mario Castoldi) of a late series in which the original sliding canopy had been replaced by a hinged hood open at the top. This one served the 90° Squadriglia, 10° Gruppo, 4° Stormo, based in Sicily in 1941. Its pilots had at first disliked the Macchi monoplanes which were instead (in 1939) first issued to the Ima Stormo.

Below: A late-series Saetta serving with the Regia Aeronautica in Italy in 1942, with (in the background) an IMAM Meridionali R.O.37 multi-role biplane, one of the most numerous types used by the Regia Aeronautica on every front during World War II.

Below: M.C.200 Saettas built by Macchi, SAI and Breda differed in many small respects, and most of the final batches had no cockpit canopy at all. There were many forms of carb-air inlet and oil cooler.

Below: This Saetta of the 373rd Squadriglia had the most common type of cockpit canopy with hinged side panels and open at the top.

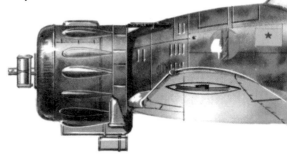

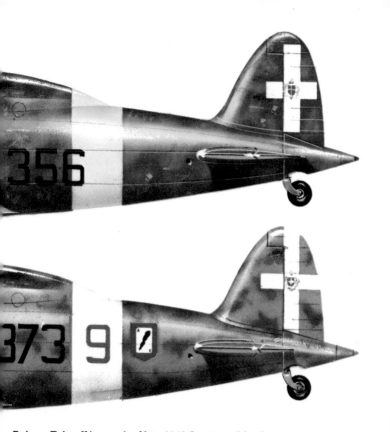

Below: Takeoff by a pair of late 1943 Saettas with wings similar to the M.C.202 with two wing machine guns.

Macchi C.202 and 205

C.202 Folgore (Lightning), C.205V Veltro (Greyhound) and C.205N Orione (Orion)

Origin: Aeronautica Macchi; production also by SAI Ambrosini and Breda.
Type: Single-seat fighter (some, fighter bomber).
Engine: (202) 1,175hp Alfa Romeo RA1000 RC41-I (DB 601A-1) inverted-vee-12; (205) 1,475hp Fiat RA1050 RC58 Tifone (Typhoon) (DB 605A-1).
Dimensions: Span 34ft 8½in (10·58m) (205N, 36ft 11in, 11·25m); length 29ft 0½in (8·85m) (205N, 31ft 4in, 9·55m); height 9ft 11½in (3·04m) (205N, 10ft 8in, 3·25m).
Weights: Empty (202) 5,181lb (2350kg), (205V) 5,691lb (2581kg), (205N-2) 6,082lb (2759kg); loaded (202) 6,636lb (3010kg), (205V) 7,514lb (3408kg), (205N-2) 8,364lb (3794kg).
Performance: Maximum speed (202) 370mph (595km/h), (205V) 399mph (642km/h), (205N-2) 389mph (626km/h); service ceiling (all) about 36,000ft (11,000m).
Armament: See text.
History: First flight (202) 10 August 1940; service delivery (202) July 1941; final delivery, early 1944.
User: Italy (RA, CB, ARSI).

Above: An M.C.202 Serie III. These were among the best fighters of the war, though available only in trivial numbers.

Above right: The prototype M.C.205V Veltro, first Italian fighter with the DB 605 engine, flown on 19 April 1942.

Right: Most of the handful of C.205V Veltro fighters served with the Aviazione Nazionale Repubblicana, the German puppet air force that continued to support the Axis after Italy's capitulation in October 1943. This Veltro is a Serie III aircraft with wing cannon serving instead with the Co-Belligerent air force.

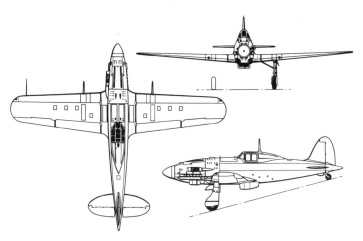

Above: Three-view of the Macchi C.205V Veltro.

Development: Essentially a re-engined Saetta, the MC202 was much more powerful and after quick and painless development went into production (first by Breda) in late 1940. Armament remained two 12·7mm Breda- ▶

SAFAT above the engine and two 7·7mm Breda-SAFAT in the wings, plus two bombs up to 353lb (160kg) or tanks. From the outset the cockpit was completely enclosed, opposition to this having finally withered. Up to Serie VIII many aircraft had no wing guns, while at least one Serie had two 20mm Mauser MG 151/20 in underwing fairings. About 1,500 were built by 1943, 392 by Macchi, achieving complete superiority over the Hurricane and P-40. The more powerful 205 flew on 19 April 1942, but pathetic industrial performance (on engine as well as airframe) limited output to 262. The 205 Serie III dropped the 7·7mm wing guns in favour of MG 151/20s. The 205N was a total structural redesign instead of a converted 200, the first flying on 1 November 1942 with one MG 151/20 and four 12·7mm, two in the wing roots. It was an outstanding machine, retaining all the agility of earlier Macchi fighters, and the 205N-2 added powerful armament with two more MG 151/20 instead of the wing-root 12·7mm. None reached service.

Below: Folgores taxiing out for takeoff in 1943 prior to the Italian capitulation. This was the most important Italian aircraft in 1943, over 1,000 serving on Italian and Eastern Fronts.

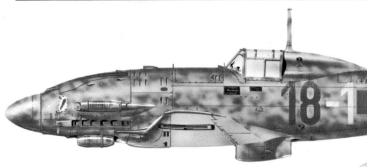

Above: One of the C.205V Serie III Veltro fighters serving in 1944 with the ARSI (Aviazione Repubblica Sociale Italiana) which operated as one of the German satellite air forces.

Above: Wartime colour photograph of a Macchi C.202 Folgore taxiing out along a newly prepared taxiway. A ground-crewman rides on each wing, standard practice with poor-vision fighters.

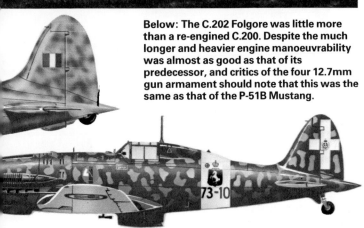

Below: The C.202 Folgore was little more than a re-engined C.200. Despite the much longer and heavier engine manoeuvrability was almost as good as that of its predecessor, and critics of the four 12.7mm gun armament should note that this was the same as that of the P-51B Mustang.

Reggiane Re 2000 series

Re 2000 Falco I (Falcon), 2001 Falco II, 2002 Ariete (Ram) and 2005 Sagittario (Archer)

Origin: Officine Meccaniche "Reggiane" SA; some Héjja built under licence by Mavag and Weiss Manfred, Hungary.
Type: Single-seat fighter.
Engine: (2000) one 1,025hp Piaggio P.XIbis RC40 14-cylinder two-row radial; (Héjja) 1,000hp WM K14; (2001) 1,175hp Alfa Romeo RA.1000 RC41 (DB 601) inverted-vee-12; (2002) 1,175hp Piaggio P.XIX RC45, (as P.XIbis); (2005) 1,475hp Fiat RA.1050 RC58 Tifone (Typhoon) (DB 605, as DB 601).
Dimensions: Span 36ft 1in (11m); length (2000) 26ft 2½in (7·95m); (2001–2) 26ft 10in; (2005) 28ft 7¾in; height (typical) 10ft 4in (3·15m).
Weight: Empty (2000) 4,200lb (1905kg); maximum loaded (2000) 5,722lb (2595kg); (2001) 7,231lb; (2002) 7,143lb; (2005) 7,848lb.
Performance: Maximum speed (2000–2) 329–337mph (say, 535km/h); (2005) 391mph (630km/h); initial climb (typical) 3,600ft (1100m)/min; service ceiling (2000) 36,745ft (11,200m); range (typical) 590 miles 950km).
Armament: See text.
History: First flight (2000) 1938; (2001) 1940; (2002) late 1941; (2005) September 1942. ***continued*** ▶

Right: This colourful fighter was a Héjja serving with Hungarian fighter squadron 1/1 on the Eastern Front in 1942. It was built in Italy in early 1940, but most Héjjas were constructed under licence in Hungary and were powered by a Wright R-1820 Cyclone or Manfred Weiss Gnome-Rhône K14 engine and had other detail differences.

Right: This Reggiane Re 2002 Ariete was one of a handful which reached the Regia Aeronautica prior to Italy's collapse in October 1943. So far as is known all went to the 5° Stormo da Assalto which was heavily engaged in Sicily and then southern Italy before being virtually eliminated. A handful also reached the 50° Stormo.

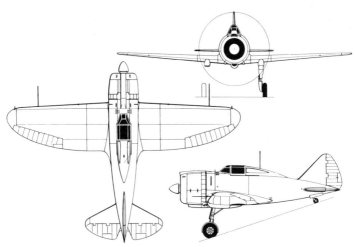

Above: Three-view of the Re 2000 Serie III.

Left: The 50° Stormo never became operational with the Re 2002 Ariete until after the capitulation in October 1943, and a handful of Arietes subsequently changed sides (as did this example) to fight with the Allied Co-Belligerent air force. This aircraft is depicted with an Italian 640kg (1,410lb) bomb, and tests were also made prior to the capitulation with a torpedo.

Users: (Re 2000) Hungary, Italy (Navy), Sweden; (2001) Italy (RA and ARSI); (2002) Germany (Luftwaffe), Italy (ARSI); (2005) Germany (Luftwaffe), Italy (ARSI).

Development: A subsidiary of Caproni, the Reggiane company copied the Seversky P-35 to produce the nimble but lightly built Re 2000. Extremely manoeuvrable, it had two 12·7mm Breda-SAFAT on the top decking and could carry a 441lb (200kg) bomb. Almost all the 170 built served non-Italian forces, Sweden using 60 (as the J 20) and Hungary about 100 (as the Héjja) on the Eastern front. Production of the 2001 reached 252, in four series with two 12·7mm either alone or augmented by two 7·7mm or (in 150 CN2 night fighters) 20mm wing guns, plus a 1,410lb (640kg) bomb. About 50 2002 were built and only 48 of the excellent 2005 with three 20mm and two 12·7mm.

Right: Only 252 Re 2001 Falco II fighters were completed, of which 150 were of the 2001 CN (Caccia Noce = night figher) version. The latter were painted black or blackish olive, but the Falco II shown here was a day fighter with the 362° Squadriglia, 22° Gruppo, Rome Capodichino, in May 1943. The 22° was named for ace Spauracchio.

Below: MM 494, the first prototype Re 2005 Sagittario, flown in September 1942. Only about 48 were delivered.

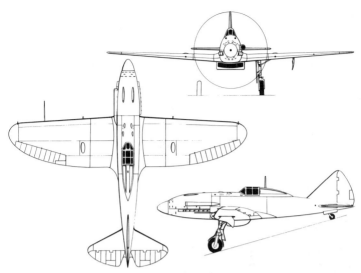

Above: Three-view of the Re 2005 Sagittario.

Left: It is claimed in Italian reports that, in mock dogfights against a Bf 109E in 1941 the Re 2000 Serie I was victorious in the hands of both Italian and German pilots. This fighter was however much too slow and weakly armed to be really effective.

Below: Reggiane Re 2001 CN night fighters, serving with the Regia Aeronautica before the armistice of September 1943.

JAPAN

As in the case of the Soviet Union, fighter development in Japan was almost completely unknown in Western countries at the time of Pearl Harbor in December 1941. For reasons never explained, the official belief in such places as London and Washington was that the Japanese could only make inferior copies of Western aircraft, and that their air force and navy was equipped almost entirely with biplanes with fixed landing gear – though there was abundant evidence to the contrary. The inevitable result was that when Allied pilots met Japanese fighters the latter were not merely a great and unpleasant shock but to some degree became regarded – on both sides – as almost invincible. Compared with the motley collection of second-rate Allied fighters, the Navy A6M and Army Ki-43 had adequate performance and just the essential superiority in manoeuvrability needed for victory, and especially in the case of the Navy fighter a range with drop tank greater than in any previous fighter enabled the Japanese to command the air at distances beyond anything Allied commanders had anticipated.

In fact the superiority of the Japanese fighters was only marginal, and magnified in practice by the immense psychological effect and the indifference of their opposition. In July 1942 an A6M was found almost undamaged but upside-down on an Aleutian island, and when it was dissected and test-flown in California it was found to be very far from invincible. In fact it was a typical 1937-style fighter, with only half the engine-power of the new crop of US fighters, and able to carry two wing cannon and a large quantity of fuel only by having a

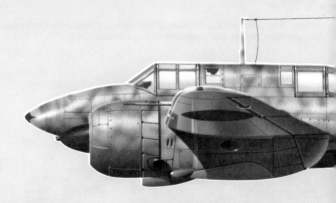

lightly built airframe and little protection It was clear that, as in Italy, a premium had been put on manoeuvrability at all costs.

Then the pendulum suddenly swung the other way; both Japanese Army and Navy staff officers and procurement officials decided their policy may have been mistaken and they bought fighters which sacrificed manoeuvrability and even pilot view to get more performance and firepower. Chief of this generation were the Army Ki-44 and Navy J2M, and the latter in particular was an outstanding fighter with excellent handling qualities. Like the Italians the Japanese seemed to have a knack for achieving good manoeuvrability with sweet handling, and in addition they had plenty of powerful engines including turbosupercharged types as good at high altitude as anything in the Allied nations. Yet the superior fighters suffered from delays and other problems, so that the ones the Allies met in numbers tended to be the same old A6M (Zero) and Ki-43 (Oscar).

One of the best Navy fighters was produced by the Kawanishi company by putting landing gear on a fighter seaplane; but it was complex and when a simplified model was developed and put into production on a gigantic scale the war was already nearly over. The Zero's direct replacement, the A7M, never did get into production. Radical new German-inspired jet and rocket fighters remained scarce prototypes without Germany's immense jet and rocket industrial background. Only one fighter introduced during World War II by Japan made any significant impact on the Allies, the Nakajima Ki-84 of the Army. And this, too, suffered from pinpricking snags that blunted its impact.

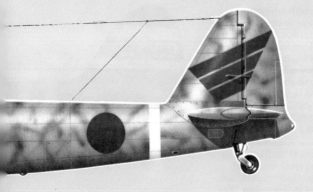

Aichi D3A "Val"

D3A1 and D3A2

Origin: Aichi Tokei Denki KK.
Type: Two-seat carrier dive bomber.
Engine: 1,075hp Mitsubishi Kinsei 44 14-cylinder radial (D3A2, 1,200hp Kinsei 54).
Dimensions: Span 47ft 1½in (14·365m); (D3A2) 47ft 8in (14·53m); length 33ft 5½in (10·2m); (D3A2) 33ft 7in (10·25m); height 11ft (3·35m); (D3A2 same).
Weights: Empty 5,309lb (2408kg); (D3A2) 5,772lb (2618kg); loaded 8,047lb (3650kg); (D3A2) 8,378lb (3800kg).
Performance: Maximum speed 242mph (389km/h); (D3A2) 281mph (450km/h); service ceiling 31,170ft (9500m); (D3A2) 35,700ft (10,880m); range with bomb 1,131 miles (1820km); (D3A2) 969 miles (1560km).
Armament: Two fixed 7·7mm guns in wings, one pivoted in rear cockpit; centreline bomb of 551lb (250kg), plus two bombs under wings each of 66lb (30kg); (D3A2: wing bombs 132lb, 60kg).
History: First flight August 1936; (D3A2) probably 1941; termination of production 1944.
User: Imperial Japanese Navy.

Development: In World War II the proper designations of Japanese aircraft were difficult to remember and often unknown to the Allies, so each major type was allotted a codename. Even today "Aichi D3A" may mean little to a grizzled veteran to whom the name "Val" will evoke memories of terrifying dive-bombing attacks. Aichi began this design for the Imperial Navy in 1936, its shape showing the influence of Heinkel who were secretly advising the Navy at that time. A total of 478 D3A1, also called Model 11 or Type 99, were built by August 1942, when production switched to the D3A2, Model 22. The D3A1 was the dive bomber that attacked Pearl Harbor on 7 December 1941. In April 1942 Aichis confirmed their bomb-hitting accuracy of 80–82% by sinking the British carrier *Hermes* and heavy cruisers *Cornwall* and *Dorsetshire*. They were extremely strong and manoeuvrable, and until 1943 were effective dogfighters after releasing their bombs. But loss of skilled pilots in great battles of 1943–44, especially

continued ▶

Right: Though inferior in several ways to the later and more numerous D3A2, it was the D3A1 that inflicted by far the gravest harm to the Allies. Skilfully flown by experienced crews, these aircraft devastated land targets and sank many ships including large surface combatants. Its design in the summer of 1936 was to some degree inspired by the Heinkel He 70, though the landing gear was fixed. The first production contract was placed in December 1939, and except for 201 of the later D3A2 model built by Showa at Tokyo all were made by Aichi at Nagoya.

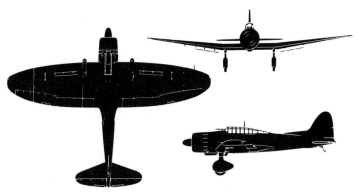

Above: Three-view of the cleaned-up Aichi D3A2.

Above; Takeoff of a D3A1 from a Japanese carrier on 7 December 1941, en route for Pearl Harbor and World War II.

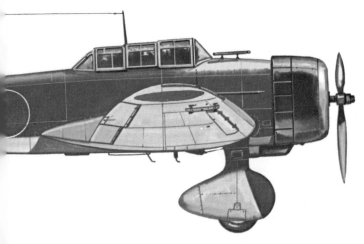

Above: A part of a scattered formation of the main production version, the D3A2 (Type 99 Model 22). Outward bound, these aircraft are carrying 250kg (551lb) bombs.

Right: In the final desperate months of the Pacific war hundreds of Japanese aircraft were used in one-way suicide missions. These D3A2s are leaving on such a mission from near Manila.

Midway and the Solomons, reduced bombing accuracy to 10% and the Aichis ceased to be the great threat they were in 1942. Production of the D3A2 was stopped in January 1944 at the 816th example of this cleaner and better-looking version. Some Aichis were converted as trainers or as overloaded Kamikaze aircraft. Nakajima developed a smaller version with retractable landing gear, the D3N1, but this was not adopted.

Aichi B7A Ryusei "Grace"

AM-23, 16-Shi Carrier Attack Bomber Ryusei (Shooting Star) (Allied code-name "Grace")

Origin: Aichi Kokuki KK; second-source production by Dai-Nijuichi Kaigun Kokusho (Sasebo Naval Air Arsenal).
Type: Two-seat carrier-based torpedo and dive bomber.
Engine: 1,825hp Nakajima NK9C Homare 12 18-cylinder radial.
Dimensions: Span 47ft 3in (14·40m); length 37ft 8½in (11·49m); height 13ft 4¼in (4·07m).
Weights: Empty 7,969lb (3614kg); loaded 12,568lb (5700kg).
Performance: Maximum speed 352mph (566km/h); service ceiling 29,365ft (8950m); range with full weapon load 1,150 miles (1850km); max range (overload) 1,889 miles (3040km).
Armament: Two 20mm Type 99 Model 2 in wings and single 7·92mm or 13mm gun aimed from rear cockpit; one 1,764lb (800kg) torpedo or similar weight of bombs.
History: First flight May 1942; service delivery May 1944; final delivery August 1945.
User: Japan (Imperial Navy).

Development: One of Japan's largest and most powerful carrier-based aircraft, the B7A was designed to a 1941 (16-Shi) specification for a fast and versatile aircraft to supplement and then replace the Nakajima B6N torpedo bomber and Yokosuka D4Y dive bomber. Though it did not carry

---

Kawanishi N1K1-J and 2-J Shiden "George"

N1K1-J and N1K2-J and variants

Origin: Kawanishi Kokuki KK; also built by Omura Kaigun Kokusho, Mitsubishi, Aichi, Showa and Dai-Juichi.
Type: Single-seat fighter.
Engine: One 1,990hp Nakajima Homare 21 18-cylinder two-row radial.
Dimensions: Span 39ft 3¼in (11·97m); length 29ft 1¾in (8·885m); (N1K2-J) 30ft 8¼in (9·35m); height 13ft 3¾in (4·058m); (N1K2-J) 13ft (3·96m).
Weights: Empty 6,387lb (2897kg); (N1K2-J) 6,299lb (2657kg); maximum loaded 9,526lb (4321kg); (N1K2-J) 10,714lb (4860kg).
Performance: Maximum speed 362mph (583km/h); (N1K2-J) 369mph (594km/h); initial climb (both) 3,300ft (1000m)/min; service ceiling 39,698ft (12,100m); (N1K2-J) 35,400ft (10,760m); range 989 miles (1430km); (N1K2-J) 1,069 miles (1720km).
Armament: Originally two 20mm in wings and two 7·7mm above fuselage; after 20 aircraft, two extra 20mm added in underwing blisters; (N1K1-Ja) as before without 7·7mm; N1K2-J, four 20mm in pairs inside wing, with more ammunition, plus two 550lb (250kg) bombs underwing or six rockets under fuselage; later prototypes, heavier armament.
History: First flight 24 July 1943; first flight (N1K2-J) 3 April 1944.
User: Japan (Imperial Navy).

Above: A rare photograph of a fully operational B7A, complete with torpedo, apparently about to depart on a combat mission. Every operational flight was from land airstrips.

any more weapons than its predecessors, the B7A1 prototype proved to be greatly superior in performance, with speed and manoeuvrability at least as good as an A6M "Zero". Unfortunately the troublesome engine delayed development until Japan had lost command of the air, and by the time deliveries took place the last carriers were being sunk and home industry bombed to a standstill (the destruction of the Aichi Funakata plant by a May 1945 earthquake did not help). Only 114 aircraft flew, nine being B7A1 prototypes and the rest B7A2 production machines used from land bases.

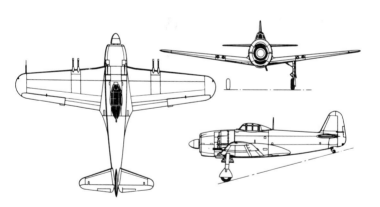

Above: three-view of N1K2-J Shiden-Kai.

Development: In September 1940 the JNAF issued a requirement for a high-speed seaplane naval fighter that did not need land airfields but could maintain air superiority during island invasions. The result was the formidable N1K1 Kyofu (mighty wind), produced by Kawanishi's Naruo plant and code-named "Rex" by the Allies. It was from this central-float seaplane that Kikuhara's team very quickly devised the N1K1-J landplane (Allied name: "George"). Though a hasty lash-up it was potentially one of the best of all Japanese fighters. Its manoeuvrability, boosted by automatic combat flaps worked by a manometer (mercury U-tube) that measured angle of attack, was almost unbelievable. Drawbacks were the engine, ▶

Above: The N1K2-J had 23,000 fewer parts than the complex original version, but it appeared too late to influence the war.

plagued with snags, the poor view with the mid wing and the complex and weak landing gear (legacy from the mid-wing float-plane and big four-blade propeller). Naruo therefore produced the N1K2-J with low wing, new tail and drastically simpler airframe that could be built in half the man-hours.

Kawasaki Ki-45 Toryu "Nick"
Ki-45 and 45A, Heavy Fighter Type 2, Kai B, C and D

Origin: Kawasaki Kokuki Kogyo.
Type: Originally long-range escort; later night fighter and attack.
Engines: Two 1,080hp Mitsubishi Ha-102 (Type 1) 14-cylinder two-row radials.
Dimensions: Span 49ft 3½in (15·02m); length (Kai C) 36ft 1in (11m); height 12ft 1½in (3·7m).
Weights: Empty (Kai A) 8,340lb (3790kg); (Kai C) 8,820lb (4000kg); loaded (all) 12,125lb (5500kg).
Performance: Maximum speed (all) 336mph (540km/h); initial climb 2,300ft (700m)/min; service ceiling 32,800ft (10,000m); range, widely conflicting reports, but best Japanese sources suggest 1,243 miles (2000km) with combat load for all versions.

continued ▶

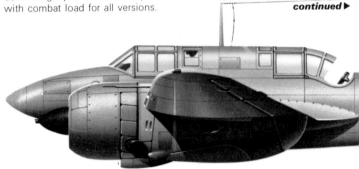

The unreliable engine still kept Shidens (the name meant violet lightning) mostly unserviceable, but they were potent and respected adversaries, encountered on all fronts from May 1944. Total production was 1,440. Huge production was planned from four companies and four Navy arsenals, but none produced more than ten aircraft, other than Kawanishi which delivered 543 1-Js and 362 2-Js from Naruo and 468 1-Js and 44 2-Js from Himeji. At Okinawa both versions were used in the Kamikaze role.

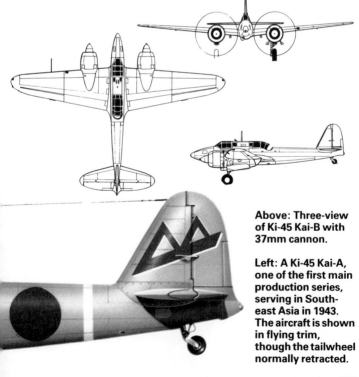

Above: Three-view of Ki-45 Kai-B with 37mm cannon.

Left: A Ki-45 Kai-A, one of the first main production series, serving in Southeast Asia in 1943. The aircraft is shown in flying trim, though the tailwheel normally retracted.

Armament: (Ki-45-I and Kai-A) two 12·7mm fixed in nose and two 7·7 mm manually aimed from rear cockpit; (Kai-B) same plus 37mm cannon in lower right forward fuselage (often with only one 12·7mm); (Kai-C) adapted for night fighting in May 1944, two 12·7mm installed at 30° between cockpits, with two 12·7mm and one 20mm or 37mm in nose; antiship versions, said to have carried 50mm or 75mm gun under nose, plus two 551lb (250kg) bombs under wings.

History: First flight (Ha-20 engine) January 1939; (Ha-25 engine) July 1940; (production Ki-45) September 1941.

User: Japan (Imperial Army).

Development: The first twin-engined fighter of the Imperial Japanese Army, the Ki-45 Toryu (dragon-slayer) was a long time in gestation. It was designed at Kawasaki's Gifu factory to meet a 1936 requirement issued in March 1937. Kawasaki had never used twin air-cooled engines and the

Top of page: Two pre-production development Ki-45s, probably photographed in 1942. Both differ from early production Ki-45s.

Nakajima Ha-20B was an undeveloped engine which misbehaved; pilots disliked the hand-cranked landing gear. After trying contraprops, the choice fell on the Navy Ha-25 Sakae engine, but this in turn was replaced by the Ha-102 soon after production began in 1941. The Akashi plant began to build the Ki-45 as a second source in late 1942, but combined output was only 1,698. Despite this modest total, and the fact that these aircraft were continually being modified, they were met on every Pacific front and known as "Nick". They were fairly fast and manoeuvrable but not really formidable until, on 27 May 1944, four Kai-B (modification B) made the first-ever suicide attack (on the north coast of New Guinea). By mid-1944 most Ki-45s had been modified to Kai-C configuration as night fighters, claiming seven victories over B-29s on the night of 15 June 1944. The two main Ki-45 bases at the close of the war were Hanoi and Anshan (Manchuria), from which aircraft made night interceptions and day Kamikaze attacks. The Ki-45 never operated in its design role of long-range escort.

Left: This colourful Ki-45 was a Hei (Kai-C) of the 53rd Sentai based at Matsudo, Chibà Prefecture. Assigned to the Shinten unit, its mission was interception of B-29s in mid-1945

Below: The first prototype differed markedly from later Ki-45s and, like the second, had elliptical wings and Ha-20b (Bristol Mercury) engines.

Kawasaki Ki-61 Hien "Tony"

Ki-61-I, II and III (Type 3 fighter) and Ki-100 (Type 5)

Origin: Kawasaki Kokuki Kogyo.

Type: Single-seat fighter.

Engine: (Ki-61-I) one 1,175hp Kawasaki Ha-40 inverted-vee 12 liquid-cooled; (Ki-61-II) one 1,450hp Kawasaki Ha-140 of same layout; (Ki-100) one 1,500hp Mitsubishi Ha-112-II 14-cylinder two-row radial.

Dimensions: Span 39ft 4½in (12m); length (-I) 29ft 4in (8·94m); (-II) 30ft 0½in (9·16m); (Ki-100) 28ft 11¼in (8·82m); height (all) 12ft 2in (3·7m).

Weights: Empty (-I) 5,798lb (2630kg); (-II) 6,294lb (2855kg); (Ki-100) 5,567lb (2525kg); loaded (-I) 7,650lb (3470kg); (-II) 8,433lb (3825kg); (Ki-100) 7,705lb (3495kg).

Performance: Maximum speed (-I) 348mph (560km/h); (-II) 379mph (610km/h); (Ki-100) 367mph (590km/h); initial climb (-I, -II) 2,200ft (675m)/min; (Ki-100) 3,280ft (1000m)/min; service ceiling (-I) 32,800ft (10,000m); (-II) 36,089ft (11,000m); (Ki-100) 37,729ft (11,500m); range (-I, -II) 990–1,100 miles (-I, 1800km, -II, 1600km); (Ki-100) 1,243 miles (2000km).

Armament: (Ki-61-Ia) two 20mm MG 151/20 in wings, two 7·7mm above engine; (-Id) same but wing guns 30mm; (-IIb) four 20mm Ho-5 in wings; (Ki-100) two Ho-5 in wings and two 12·7mm in fuselage, plus underwing racks for two 551lb (250kg) bombs.

History: First flight (Ki-60) March 1941; (Ki-61) December 1941; service delivery (Ki-61-I) August 1942; first flight (-II) August 1943; (Ki-100) 1 February 1945.

User: Japan (Imperial Army).

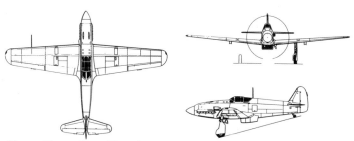

Above: Three-view of Ki-61 (interim aircraft with canopy having features of -I and -II and wing of -IIa).

Development: Kawasaki purchased a licence to build the German DB 601 engine in 1937 and the resulting revised and lightened engine emerged in 1940 as the Ha-40. Around this engine Kawasaki planned the Ki-60 and a lighter fighter designated Ki-61. Hien (the Japanese name meaning flying swallow). The latter was completed in December 1941 and flew well, reaching a speed of 368mph. During the first half of 1942 the prototype was extensively tested, performing very well against a captured P-40E and a Bf 109E sent to Japan by submarine. The submarine also brought 800 Mauser MG 151 cannon, and these were fitted to most early Ki-61s despite the unreliability of the supply of electrically fired ammunition. The Gifu plant delivered 2,654 (according to one authority, 2,750) Ki-61-I and -Ia, the latter being redesigned for easier servicing and increased manoeuvrability. They went into action around New Guinea in April 1943, were called "Tony" by the Allies, and were the only Japanese fighters with a liquid-cooled ▶

Below: One of the first Ki-61s, probably built about the time of Pearl Harbor, with Ha-40 engine and original style of canopy. It was evaluated successfully against many other fighters.

engine. They were constantly in air combat, later moving to the Philippines and finally back to Japan. By 1944 the Ki-61-II was trickling off the assembly line with an unreliable engine that could not meet production demands. The II had a bigger wing and new canopy, but was soon replaced by the IIa with the old, proven, wing. Only 374 of all -II versions were built, and in early 1945 one of 275 engineless airframes was fitted with the Ha-112 radial.

Kawasaki Ki-102 "Randy"
Ki-102a, b and c
(Allied code-name "Randy")

Origin: Kawasaki Kokuki Kogyo KK.
Type: Two-seat (a) high-altitude fighter, (b) ground-attack aircraft or (c) night fighter.
Engines: Two 1,500hp Mitsubishi Ha-112 14-cylinder radials, (a, c) Ha-112-II Ru with turbochargers.
Dimensions: Span (a, b) 51ft 1in (15·57m), (c) 56ft 6$\frac{1}{4}$in (17·23m); length (a, b) 37ft 6$\frac{3}{4}$in (11·45m), (c) 42ft 9$\frac{3}{4}$in (13·05m); height 12ft 1$\frac{3}{4}$in (3·70m).
Weights: Empty (a) 11,354lb (5150kg), (b) 10,913lb (4950kg), (c) 11,464lb (5200kg); loaded (a) 15,763lb (7150kg), (b) 16,094lb (7300kg), (c) 16,755lb (7600kg).
Performance: Maximum speed (a, b) 360mph (580km/h), (c) 373mph (600km/h); service ceiling (a) 42,650ft (13,000m), (b) 32,800ft (10,000m), (c) 44,295ft (13,500m); range (a, b) 1,243 miles (2000km), (c) 1,367 miles (2200km).
Armament: (a) one fixed 37mm Ho-203 in nose and two 20mm Ho-5 below, (b) one 57mm Ho-401 in nose, two Ho-5 below and manually aimed 12·7mm Ho-103 in rear cockpit, (c) two 30mm Ho-105 under fuselage and two 20mm Ho-5 mounted obliquely.
History: First flight March 1944; service delivery, about November 1944.
User: Japan (Imperial Army).

Development: In August 1942 the Ki-45 Toryu design team under

Left: Many Japanese fighters, of both the Imperial Army and Navy, were colourful. This Ki-61-IIb was assigned to the 244th Sentai of the 2nd Chutai, based in the Tokyo Defence Area in 1945 attempting to intercept high-flying B-29s and, at the end of the war, also having to tangle with the P-51D Mustang which was distinctly superior. The IIb(II Kai-B) did, however, have greater firepower with four Ho-5 cannon of 20mm calibre.

Despite the sudden lash-up conversion the result was a staggeringly fine fighter, easily the best ever produced in Japan. With desperate haste this conversion went into production as the Ki-100. One of the first Ki-100 units destroyed 14 Hellcats without loss to themselves in their first major battle over Okinawa and this easily flown and serviced machine fought supremely well against B-29s and Allied fighters to the end.

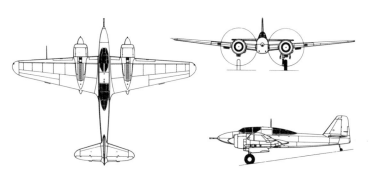

Above: Ki-102b with long-barrel 57mm and without D/F acorn.

Takeo Doi began work on a development designated Ki-96, three of these 3,000hp single-seat "heavy fighters" being built. In August 1943 approval was given for a further development with crew of two for use in the ground-attack role. Three prototypes and 20 pre-production Ki-102 were built, followed by 215 Ki-102b (Ki-102 Otsu) of which a few saw action in Okinawa. Some were used in the Igo-1-B air-to-ground missile programme. Two were rebuilt with pressure cabin as prototypes of the Ki-108, but the size of development task for this led to the Ki-102a being launched as a high-altitude fighter without pressure cabin. About 15 were delivered in July-August 1945 as the Ki-102 Ko. Right at the end of the war two Ki-102b were completely rebuilt as prototypes of the 102c night fighter with AI radar, greater span and length, new cockpit with rear-facing radar operator and different armament.

Left: An apparently standard Ki-102b after capture in 1945. In the nose is the muzzle of the short-barrel 57mm gun and a D/F loop acorn is visible above the mid-fuselage. Little known until after the war, Ki-102 was a useful type.

281

Mitsubishi A5M "Claude"

A5M1 to A5M4

Origin: Mitsubishi Jukogyo KK; also built by Dai-Nijuichi KK and KK Watanabe Tekkosho.

Type: Single-seat carrier-based fighter.

Engine: One Nakajima Kotobuki (Jupiter) nine-cylinder radial; (1) 585hp 2-Kai-I; (2) 610hp 2-Kai-3; (4) 710hp Kotobuki 41 or (A5M4 Model 34) 3-Kai.

Dimensions: Span (2) 35ft 6in, (4) 36ft 1in (11·0m); length (2) 25ft 7in; (4) 24ft 9½in (7·55m); height 10ft 6in (3·2m).

Weights: Empty (2, typical) 2,400lb (1090kg); (4) 2,681lb (1216kg); maximum loaded (2) 3,545lb (1608kg); (4) 3,763lb (1708kg).

Performance: Maximum speed (2) 265mph (426km/h); (4) 273mph (440km/h); initial climb (2) 2,215ft (675m)/min; (4) 2,790ft (850m)/min; service ceiling (typical, all) 32,800ft (10,000m); range (2) 460 miles (740km); (4, auxiliary tank) 746 miles (1200km).

Armament: (All) two 7·7mm Type 89 machine guns firing on each side of upper cylinder of engine; racks for two 66lb (30kg) bombs under outer wings.

History: First flight 4 February 1935; service delivery 1936; final delivery December 1939.

User: Japan (Imperial Navy).

Development: One of the neatest little warplanes of its day, the A5M was the chief fighter of the Imperial Japanese Navy throughout the Sino-Japanese war and was numerically the most important at the time of Pearl Harbor. It was built to meet a 1934 specification calling for a speed of 218mph and ability to reach 16,400ft in 6½ minutes, and beat these figures by a wide margin. Within days of first flight at Kagamigahara the Ka-14 prototype exceeded 279mph and reached 16,400ft in 5min 54sec, which the Japanese considered "far above the world level at that time". It was the Navy's first

Right: Two A5M2 fighters (they are probably 2a models) of a training unit photographed in the late 1930s. This model had a two-blade propeller but was otherwise very like the most important version, the long-range A5M4. The aircraft nearest the camera has had its rear spat sections removed.

Below: Probably photographed over China in about 1937, these appear to be of the original A5M1 version. Fuselage slogans were not uncommon.

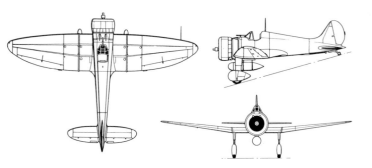

Above: Three-view of A5M4 with long-range tank.

monoplane fighter, and one of the first all-metal stressed-skin machines built in Japan. The production A5M1, called Type 96 or S-96 and later given the Allied code name "Claude", abandoned the prototype's inverted-gull wing, originally chosen to try to improve pilot view, and also switched to a direct drive engine. The elliptical wing had split flaps, manoeuvrablity was superb and from their first combat mission on 18 September 1937, with the 2nd Combined Air Flotilla based at Shanghai, they acquitted themselves very well. During the conflict with the Soviet Union along the Manchukuo-Mongolian border throughout 1939 the A5M proved the biggest menace to the Russian aircraft, having earlier, on 2 December 1937, destroyed no fewer than ten I-16Bs of the Chinese in one dogfight over Nanking. Such results completely overcame the Naval pilots' earlier distrust of so speedy a monoplane and when the final A5M4 model entered service it was very popular. Mitsubishi built "about 800" (one source states 782), while Kyushu Aircraft (Watanabe) and the Sasebo naval dockyard (D-N) made 200 more. The final version was the A5M4-K dual trainer produced by conversion of fighters in 1941.

Mitsubishi A6M Zero-Sen "Zeke"

A6M1 to A6M8c and Nakajima A6M2-N

Origin: Mitsubishi Jukogyo KK; also built by Nakajima Hikoki KK.
Type: Single-seat carrier-based fighter, (A6M2-N) float seaplane.
Engine: (A6M1) one 780hp Mitsubishi MK2 Zuisei 13 14-cylinder two-row radial: (M2) 925hp Nakajima NK1C Sakae 12 of same layout; (M3) 1,130hp Sakae 21; (M5) as M3 with individual exhaust stacks; (M6c) Sakae 31 with same rated power but water/methanol boost to 1,210hp for emergency; (M8c) 1,560hp Mitsubishi Kinsei 62 of same layout.
Dimensions: Span (1, 2) 39ft 4½in (12·0m); (remainder) 36ft 1in (11·0m); length (all landplanes) 29ft 9in (9·06m); (A6M2-N) 33ft 2¾in (10·13m); height (1, 2) 9ft 7in (2·92m); (all later landplanes) 9ft 8in (2·98m); (A6M2-N) 14ft 1¼in (4·3m).
Weights: Empty (2) 3,704lb (1680kg); (3) 3,984lb (1807kg); (5) typically 3,920lb (1778kg); (6c) 4,175lb (1894kg); (8c) 4,740lb (2150kg); (A6M2-N) 3,968lb (1800kg); maximum loaded (2) 5,313lb (2410kg); (3) 5,828lb (2644kg); (5c) 6,050lb (2733kg; 2952kg as overload); (6c) as 5c; (8c) 6,944lb (3149kg); (A6M2-N) 5,423lb (2460kg).
Performance: Maximum speed (2) 316mph (509km/h); (3) 336mph (541km/h); (5c, 6c) 354mph (570km/h); (8c) 360mph (580km/h); (A6M2-N) 273mph (440km/h); initial climb (1, 2, 3) 4,500ft (1370m)/min; (5, 6c) 3,150ft (960m)/min; (2-N) not known; service ceiling (1, 2) 33,790ft (10,300m); (3) 36,250ft (11,050m); (5c, 6c) 37,500ft (11,500m); (8c) 39,370ft (12,000m); (A6M2-N) 32,800ft (10,000m); range with drop tank (2) 1,940 miles (3110km); (5) 1,200 miles (1920km).
Armament: (1, 2, 3 and 2-N) two 20mm Type 99 cannon each with 60-round drum fixed in outer wings, two 7·7mm Type 97 machine guns each with 500 rounds above front fuselage, and wing racks for two 66lb (30kg) bombs; (5a) two 20mm Type 99 Mk 4 with belt of 85 rounds per gun, two 7·7mm in fuselage and wing racks for two 132lb (60kg) bombs; (5b) as 5a but one 7·7mm replaced by 12·7mm; (5c and all later versions) two 20mm Type 99 Mk 4 and two 13·2mm in wings, one 13·2mm (optional) in fuselage, plus wing racks for two 60kg.
History: First flight 1 April 1939; service delivery (A6M1) late July 1940; first flight (A6M2-N) December 1941; (A6M5) August 1943; (A6M2-K) January 1942.
User: Japan (Imperial Navy).

continued ▶

Right: One of the later versions of Japan's most important combat aircraft was the A6M5 Model 52, with stronger non-folding wings and various detail changes including ejector-stack exhausts. This example served with the Gensan Kokutai at Wonsan (Korea) in December 1944.

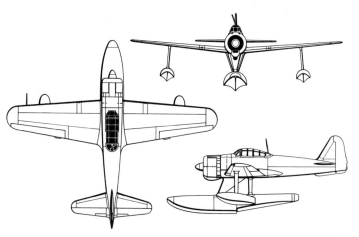

Above: Three-view of A6M2-N, by Nakajima.

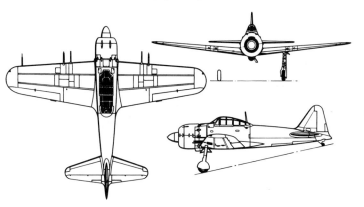

Above: Three-view of A6M5c, which introduced the final armament but was severely underpowered with unboosted engine.

Left: Painted sky grey overall, and with the markings of the *Hiryu* (aircraft carrier) group (2nd Koku Sentai) at the time of Pearl Harbor, this A6M2 was one of the first Japanese fighters to participate in World War II. It is almost beyond belief that the Allies had no knowledge of this fighter, used for years in China against US Army pilots and forming two-thirds of Navy seagoing fighter strength.

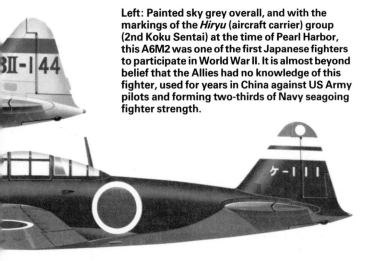

Development: The most famous of all Japanese combat aircraft possessed the unique distinction of being the first carrier-based fighter ever to out-perform corresponding land-based machines; it was also a singularly unpleasant shock to US and British staff which had apparently never studied the behaviour of this fighter in China or even discovered its existence. It was designed by Mitsubishi to meet the severe demands of the 1937 Navy carrier-based fighter specification, seeking a successor to the A5M. Demands included a speed of 500km/h (311mph) and armament of two cannon and two machine guns. Under team leader Jiro Horikoshi the new fighter took shape as a clean, efficient but lightly built aircraft with out-standing manoeuvrability. With a more powerful engine it was accepted for production as the A6M2, though as it was put into production in 1940, the Japanese year 5700, it became popularly the Zero-Sen (Type 00 fighter), and to millions of its enemies was simply the "Zero" (though the official Allied code name was "Zeke"). Before official trials were completed two squadrons with 15 aircraft were sent to China in July 1940 for trials under operational conditions. They eliminated all opposition, as forcefully reported to Washington by Gen Claire Chennault, commander of the Flying Tigers volunteer force (his warning was obviously filed before being read). More than 400 had been delivered by the time the A6M2 and clipped-wing M3 appeared at Pearl Harbor. During the subsequent year it seemed that thousands of these fighters were in use, their unrivalled manoeuvrability being matched by unparalleled range with a small engine, 156gal internal fuel and drop tanks. So completely did the A6M sweep away Allied air power that the Japanese nation came to believe it was invincible. After the Battle of Midway the Allies slowly gained the ascendancy, and the A6M found itself outclassed by the F4U and F6F. Mitsubishi urgently tried to devise improved versions and the A6M5 was built in quantities far ▶

Above: One of the best photographs of the Zero-Sen in service, this 1942 picture shows A6M3 Model 22 fighters, the first subtype to have the full wingspan restored with fixed rounded tips. These Zeros belonged to the 251st Kokutai and typified the long-range aircraft which during the Guadalcanal campaign operated up to 650 miles from their home bases.

Below: Nakajima developed the A6M2-N float seaplane version, and delivered the production batch of 327. They saw much action but were unable to win many combats against Allied fighters.

greater than any other Japanese combat aircraft. Improvements were mainly small and the combat-boosted Sakae 31 engine did not appear until the end of 1944. Only a few of the much more powerful A6M8c type were produced, the main reason for this change of engine being destruction of the Nakajima factory. The final model was the A6M7 Kamikaze version, though hundreds of Zeros of many sub-types were converted for suicide attacks. Total production amounted to 10,937, of which 6,217 were built by Nakajima which also designed and built 327 of the attractive A6M2-N single-float seaplane fighter version (code name "Rufe") which operated throughout the Pacific war. The A6M2-K was one of several dual trainer versions.

Right: Nearly all the identifiable Zeros in this photograph are of the A6M5 Model 52 version, the most numerous of all. The picture probably dates from 1943, when this once outstanding fighter was due to have been supplanted in production by the A7M Reppu. Complete failure to produce the new aircraft resulted in prolonged A6M5 production. The same thing happened to many front-line types for the Luftwaffe such as the Ju 87, He 111 and Bf 110.

Below: A frame from a propaganda ciné film taken on board the aircraft carrier *Hiryu* at the start of the Pearl Harbor raid just after dawn on 7 December 1941. The A6M2 in the foreground heads a close mass of B5N torpedo bombers. The ship had 18 of each type, as well as 18 D3As.

Mitsubishi J2M Raiden "Jack"

J2M1 to J2M7

Origin: Mitsubishi Jukogyo KK; also small number (J2M5) built by Koza Kaigun Kokusho.

Type: Single-seat Navy land-based interceptor.

Engine: Most versions, one 1,820hp Mitsubishi MK4R-A Kasei 23a 14-cylinder two-row radial; (J2M5) 1,820hp MK4U-A Kasei 26a.

Dimensions: Span 35ft 5¼in (10·8m); length (most) 31ft 9¾in (9·70m); (J2M5) 32ft 7¾in (9·95m); height (most) 12ft 6in (3·81m); (J2M5) 12ft 11¼in (3·94m).

Weights: Empty (2) 5,572lb (2527kg); (3) 5,675lb (2574kg); (5) 6,259lb (2839kg); normal loaded (2) 7,257lb (3300kg); (3) 7,573lb (3435kg); (5) 7,676lb (3482kg); max overload (2, 3) 8,700lb (3946kg).

Performance: Maximum speed (2) 371mph (596km/h); (3) 380mph (612km/h); (5) 382mph (615km/h); initial climb (2, 3) 3,610ft (1100m)/min; (5) 3,030ft (925m)/min; range (2, 3 at normal gross) 655 miles (1055km); (2, 3 overload) 1,580 miles (2520km); (5, normal gross with 30min reserve) 345 miles (555km).

Armament: See text.

History: First flight (prototype) 20 March 1942; service delivery (J2M2) December 1943; first flight (J2M5) May 1944.

User: Japan (Imperial Navy).

Development: Though designed by a team led by the legendary Jiro Horikoshi, creator of the Zero-Sen, this utterly different little interceptor did little to enhance reputations, though there was nothing fundamentally faulty in its conception. It broke totally new ground, partly in being an interceptor for the Navy (previously the preserve of the Army) and partly in the reversal of design parameters. Instead of concentrating on combat manoeuvrability at all costs the J1M was designed solely for speed and fast climb. Manoeuvrability and even handling took second place. Unusual features in the basic design included a tiny laminar-flow wing fitted with combat flaps, a finely streamlined engine with propeller extension shaft and fan cooling, a very shallow enclosed canopy and a surprising number of forged parts in the stressed-skin airframe. Powered by a 1,460hp Kasei, the prototype Mitsubishi M-20, named Raiden (Thunderbolt), gave a great deal of trouble and was almost redesigned to produce the J2M2 with different engine, much deeper canopy, multi-stack exhaust and new four-blade propeller. Even then the Raiden suffered endless snags and crashes,

Below: Representing a complete break with all previous tradition in Japanese fighter design, the J2M was tailored to performance rather than pilot view and manoeuvrability. This J2M3 Raiden 21a of the 302nd Kokutai had the heavy armament of four of the new fast-firing Type 99-II cannon. The planned output of 500 a month wasn't even approached.

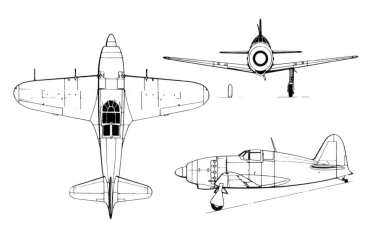

Above: Three-view of J2M3.

Above: One of the first J2M3 Raiden Type 21 fighters, the first model to have four cannon. At first the latter were all of the Type I variety but these were gradually replaced by Type II.

but eventually 155 J2M2 were delivered with two 20mm Type 99 and two 7·7mm above the fuselage. Production then switched to the J2M3 with machine guns removed and the wing fitted with two Type 99 and two fast-firing Type 99-II. The J2M3a had four Type 99-II. Fitted with bulged canopy these models became the J2M6 and 6a. A few high-flying J2M4 turbocharged versions were built, with six cannon, the two added guns being in the top fuselage decking. Best of all was the J2M5 with only two (wing) cannon but a far better engine, and it proved formidable against high-flying B-29s. After VJ-day, when only 480 of all models had been built by Mitsubishi (one month's planned output!), the Allies (who called this fighter "Jack") spoke in glowing terms of its performance and handling.

Mitsubishi Ki-15 "Babs"

Ki-15-I, Ki-15-II, C5M, Karigane

Origin: Mitsubishi Jukogyo KK.
Type: Two-seat light attack bomber.
Engine: (I) one 750hp Nakajima Ha-8 nine-cylinder radial; (II) one 800hp Mitsubishi A.14 (later named Kinsei) 14-cylinder two-row radial.
Dimensions: Span 39ft 4¾in (12·0m); length (I) 27ft 11in (8·50m); height 9ft 10in (3·0m).
Weights: Empty (I) 3,968lb (1800kg); maximum loaded (I) 5,070lb (2300kg); (II) 6,834lb (3100kg).
Performance: Maximum speed (I) 280mph (450km/h); (II) about 298mph (480km/h); initial climb (both) about 1,640ft (500m)/min; service ceiling (I) 28,220ft (8600m); range with bomb load (both) about 1,100 miles (1800km).
Armament: One 7·7mm Type 89 (not always fitted) fixed in outer wing firing forward, and one manually aimed from rear cockpit; bomb load of up to 551lb (250kg) in (I) or 1,100lb (500kg) in (II) carried externally.
History: First flight (Karigane prototype) May 1936; (Ki-15-I) probably late 1936.
User: Imperial Japanese Army.

Development: This trim little machine stemmed from a private venture by the giant Mitsubishi company, inspired by the emergence in the United States of modern stressed-skin monoplanes (particularly the Northrop A-17). With company funds, but sponsored by the Asahi (Rising Sun) newspaper, a prototype was built to demonstrate the ability of the fast-growing Japanese industry to build modern aircraft. It was a time of intense nationalism and the resulting machine, named Karigane (Wild Goose) by Mitsubishi, was individually christened "Kamikaze" (Divine Wind) and prepared as an instrument of national publicity. Its greatest achievement was a notably trouble-free flight of 9,900 miles from Tokyo to London in April 1937. Others were built for similar purposes (one being "Asakaze" (Morning Wind) of the Asahi Press) and as fast mailplanes, while in 1938 a small batch was built with the 550hp Kotobuki (licence-built Bristol Jupiter) replaced by the much more powerful A.14 engine. In 1937 construction began of 437 military Ki-15 series for the Army and these were soon one of the first really modern types to go into action in the Sino-Japanese war, which had simmered for years and finally broke out in 1937. The Ki-15 was used for level bombing, close support and photo-reconnaissance, but was replaced by the Ki-30 (p. 156). In 1939 the Imperial Navy began to receive 50 of two C5M versions with different engines. Allied code name was "Babs".

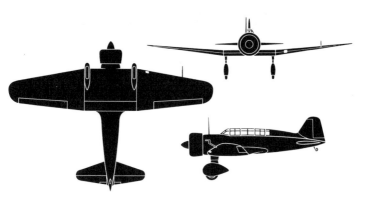

Above: Three-view of Mitsubishi Ki-15-I.

Above: Ki-15-I reconnaissance aircraft serving as pilot/observer trainers at the Kumagaya flying school (note badge on rudder).

Left: A Mitsubishi Ki-15-I of the 1st Chutai, 15th Hikosentai, of the Imperial Army. When the second Sino-Japanese war broke out in 1937 the Ki-15 was one of the first types to go into action. It had a speed higher than that of any Chinese aircraft except the Soviet-supplied I-16. It was a C5M2 of the Navy's 22nd Koku Sentai that, on 10 December 1941, spotted the warships HMS *Prince of Wales* and *Repulse;* a few hours later land-based bombers had sent both ships to the bottom.

293

Mitsubishi Ki-46 "Dinah"
Type 100 Models 1-4 (Ki-46-I to Ki-46-IVb)

Origin: Mitsubishi Jukogyo KK.
Type: Strategic reconnaissance (Ki-46-III-Kai, night fighter).
Engines: (I) two 870hp Mitsubishi Ha-26-I 14-cylinder two-row radials; (II) two 1,080hp Mitsubishi Ha-102 of same layout; (III) two 1,500hp Mitsubishi Ha-112-II of same layout; (IV) Ha-112-IIRu, same rated power but turbocharged.
Dimensions: Span 48ft 2¾in (14·7m); length (all except III-Kai) 36ft 1in (11·0m); (III-Kai) 37ft 8in (11·47m); height 12ft 8¾in (3·88m).
Weights: Empty (I) 7,450lb (3379kg); (II) 7,193lb (3263kg); (III) 8,446lb (3831kg); (IV) 8,840lb (4010kg); loaded (no overload permitted) (I) 10,630lb (4822kg); (II) 11,133lb (5050kg); (III) 12,620lb (5724kg); (IV) 13,007lb (5900kg); (III-Kai) 13,730lb (6227kg).
Performance: Maximum speed (I) 336mph (540km/h); (II) 375mph (604km/h); (III, III-Kai, IV) 391mph (630km/h); initial climb (I, II, III) about 1,970ft (600m)/min; (IV) 2,625ft (800m)/min; service ceiling (I, II, III) 34,500–36,000ft (10,500–11,000m); (IV) 38,000ft (11,500m); range (I) 1,305 miles (2100km); (II) 1,490 miles (2400km); (III) 2,485 miles (4000km); (III-Kai) 1,243 miles (2000km); (IV) not known, but at least 4000km.
Armament: (I, II) one 7·7mm manually aimed from rear cockpit; other types, none, except III-Kai, two 20mm Ho-5 cannon fixed in nose firing ahead and 37mm Ho-203 firing at elevation of 30° from top of fuselage.
History: First flight November 1939; (production II) March 1941; (III) December 1942; (III-Kai conversion) about September 1944.
User: Japan (Imperial Army).

Development: One of the most trouble-free and popular aircraft of the whole Pacific war, the Ki-46 "Shitei" (reconnaissance for HQ), code-named "Dinah" by the Allies, was one of only very few Japanese aircraft that could penetrate Allied airspace with some assurance it would survive. It was also almost the only machine with the proven ability to operate at the flight levels of the B-29. In the first year of its use, which extended to every part of the Japanese war throughout the Pacific and China, much trouble was experienced from sparking-plug erosion and crew anoxia, both rectified by improved design and greater oxygen storage. Allied radar forced the Ki-46 to fly even faster and higher, leading to the almost perfectly streamlined ▶

Right: Parachute -retarded bombs just miss three Ki-46-11 during an Allied attack on a Japanese airstrip in the South-west Pacific.

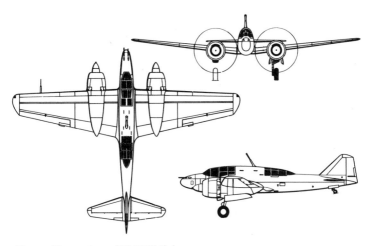

Above: Three-view of Ki-46-III-Kai.

Above: A Ki-46-II of the 18th Independent Reconnaissance Chutai (Dokuritsu Dai Shijugo Chutai).

Ki-46-III. These entered service in 1943, in which year many earlier versions were converted to Ki-46-II-Kai dual conversion trainers. Total production amounted to 1,742, all made by Mitsubishi at Nagoya and Toyama. Only four prototypes were finished of the turbocharged IVa, but many III models were hastily converted by the Army Tachikawa base into III-Kai night-fighters capable of intercepting B-29s. No radar was carried. At VJ-day Mitsubishi was trying to produce IIIc and IVb fighters and the IIIb ground-attack version.

Above: A Ki-46-III Kai of the 16th Dokuritsu Hikotai. Most of the
Ki-46-IIIs (in all 609 production aircraft were built of this model) were
unarmed reconnaissance machines with a distinctive streamlined shape
without a stepped windscreen. From this was derived the III Kai, also
called Army Type 100 Air Defence Fighter, with conventional windscreen
and a new nose housing two 20mm Ho-5 cannon; the upper mid-
fuselage fuel tank was removed and replaced by a 37mm Ho-203
cannon firing obliquely upward.

Nakajima B5N "Kate"
B5N1 and B5N2

Origin: Nakajima Hikoki KK; also built by Aichi Tokei Denki and Dai-Juichi Kaigun Kokusho (Hiro).

Type: (B5N1) three-seat carrier-based bomber; (2) torpedo bomber.

Engine: (B5N1 Model 11) one 770hp Nakajima Hikari 3 nine-cylinder radial; (B5N1 Model 12) 970 or 985hp Nakajima Sakae 11 14-cylinder two-row radial; (B5N2) 1,115hp Sakae 21.

Dimensions: Span 50ft 11in (15·52m); length (1) 33ft 11in; (2) 33ft 9½in (10·3m); height 12ft 1¾in (3·70m).

Weights: Empty (1) 4,645lb (2107kg); (2) 5,024lb (2279kg); normal loaded (1) 8,047lb (3650kg); (2) 8,378lb (3800kg); maximum loaded (2) 9,039lb (4100kg).

Performance: Maximum speed (1) 217mph (350km/h); (2) 235mph (378km/h); initial climb (both) 1,378ft (420m)/min; service ceiling (both) about 25,000ft (7640m); range (1) 683 miles (1100km); (2) normal gross, 609 miles (980km), overload (4100kg) 1,237 miles (1990km).

Armament: (1) one 7·7mm Type 89 manually aimed from rear cockpit; underwing racks for two 551lb (250kg) or six 132lb (60kg) bombs; (2) two 7·7mm manually aimed from rear cockpit; two 7·7mm fixed above forward fuselage; centreline rack for 1,764lb (800kg, 18in) torpedo or three 551lb bombs.

History: First flight January 1937; (production B5N1) later 1937; (B5N2) December 1939; final delivery, probably 1942.

User: Japan (Imperial Navy).

Development: Designed to meet a 1935 requirement, the B5N was

Below: Probably taken long before Pearl Harbor, this photograph shows early B5N1 attack aircraft, outstanding in their day.

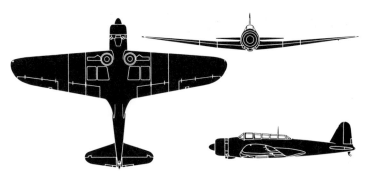

Above: Three-view of B5N1 Model 11.

judged ordinary and obsolescent in World War II, yet in its day it was advanced and bold. The Japanese keenly studied the stressed-skin aircraft of Northrop, Douglas and Clark, and swiftly copied new features. The B5N had not only a thoroughly modern structure but also variable-pitch propeller (not on RAF Hurricanes until mid-1940!), hydraulically retracting landing gear, Fowler flaps, NACA cowling, integral wing fuel tanks and, until judged troublesome, hydraulic wing-folding. The challenging specification demanded a speed of 330km/h (205mph), but the prototype beat this by 23mph. The B5N1 went into production in time to serve in the Sino-Japanese war; a few of the rival fixed-gear Mitsubishi B5M were bought as an insurance. By 1940 some attack B5N were converted into B5N1-K trainers, but 103 bombed at Pearl Harbor. In the same attack 40 of the new B5N2 torpedo bombers took part, at least half finding their mark. Subsequently the B5N2 played the chief role in sinking the US carriers *Yorktown*, *Lexington*, *Wasp* and *Hornet*. They soldiered on into 1944 alongside their replacement the B6N. Total production was 1,149, including 200 by Aichi and 280 by Hiro Arsenal. Their Allied name was "Kate".

Nakajima B6N Tenzan "Jill"

B6N1, B6N2

Origin: Nakajima Hikoki KK.
Type: Three-seat carrier-based torpedo bomber.
Engine: (B6N1) one 1,870hp Nakajima Mamori 11 14-cylinder two-row radial; (B6N2) 1,850hp Mitsubishi Kasei 25 of same layout.
Dimensions: Span 48ft 10¼in (14·894m); length 35ft 7½in (10·865m); height (1) 12ft 1¾in (3·7m); (2) 12ft 5½in (3·8m).
Weights: Empty 6,636lb (3010kg) (1, 2 almost identical); normal loaded 11,464lb (5200kg); maximum overload 12,456lb (5650kg).
Performance: Maximum speed (1) 289mph (465km/h); (2) 299mph (482km/h); initial climb (1) 1,720ft (525m)/min; (2) 1,885ft (575m)/min; service ceiling (1) 28,379ft (8650m); (2) 29,659ft (9040m); range (normal weight) (1) 907 miles (1460km); (2) 1,084 miles (1745km), (overload) (1) 2,312 miles (3720km); (2) 1,895 miles (3050km).
Armament: One 7·7mm Type 89 manually aimed from rear cockpit and one manually aimed by middle crew-member from rear ventral position, with fixed 7·7mm firing forward in left wing (often absent from B6N1); 1,764lb (800kg, 18in) torpedo carried offset to right of centreline, or six 220lb (100kg) bombs under fuselage.
History: First flight March 1942; service delivery (B6N1) early 1943; (B6N2) December 1943.
User: Japan (Imperial Navy).

Development: Named Tenzan (Heavenly Mountain) after a worshipped mountain in China, and code-named "Jill" by the Allies, the B6N was another conventional-looking aircraft which in fact was in many respects superior to the seemingly more advanced machines of the Allies (in this case the Grumman TBF and Fairey Barracuda). Designed as a replacement

Right: A dramatic photograph, of high quality, showing a B6N2 on fire after being hit by AA fire from USS *Yorktown* near Truk, in the Caroline Islands, on 29 April 1944. Torpedo still in place.

Below: A formation of B6N2s without torpedoes. They are probably painted dark green and pale grey, with black engine cowls. Note the stack of four exhaust pipes behind the engine.

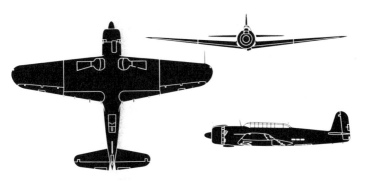

Above: Three-view of B6N2, without radar.

for B5N, Tenzan was slim and clean, with no internal weapon bay. The torpedo was offset, and to increase clearance on torpedo release the big oil cooler was offset in the other direction (to the left). The distinctive shape of the vertical tail was to minimise stowage length in the three-point attitude in carriers. Nakajima's big Mamori engine, driving a four-blade Hamilton-type propeller, suffered severe vibration and overheating, and though the B6N1 was kept in service it was replaced in production by the B6N2. The lower power of the proven Kasei was counteracted by the improved installation with less drag, and jet-thrust from the exhaust stubs. Tenzans went into action off Bougainville in the Marshalls campaign in June 1944. Subsequently they were heavily committed, many being later equipped with ASV radar for night attacks and ending in April-June 1945 with a hectic campaign of torpedo and suicide attacks off Okinawa and Kyushu. By this time the Imperial Navy had no operating carrier and hardly any skilled pilots.

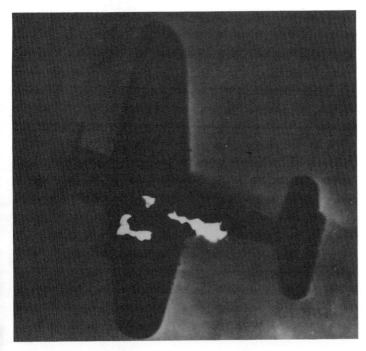

Nakajima J1N1 "Irving"

J1N1-C, J1N1-F, J1N1-S Gekko and J1N1-C-Kai

Origin: Nakajima Hikoki KK.

Type: (C, F) three-seat reconnaissance; (S, C-Kai) two-seat night fighter.

Engines: All operational versions, two 1,130hp Nakajima Sakae 21 14-cylinder two-row radials.

Dimensions: Span 55ft 8½in (16·98m); length (all, excluding nose guns or radar) 39ft 11½in (12·18m); height 14ft 11½in (4·562m).

Weights: Empty (C, S) 10,697lb (4852kg); loaded (C) 15,984lb (7250kg); (S) 15,212lb (6900kg); maximum overload (both) 16,594lb (7527kg).

Performance: Maximum speed (C, S) 315mph (507km/h); initial climb (C, S) 1,968ft (600m)/min; service ceiling 30,578ft (9320m); range (C, S, normal gross) 1,585 miles (2550km), (overload) 2,330 miles (3750km).

Armament: (J1N1-C) one 20mm Type 99 cannon and two 7·7mm Type 97 fixed in nose; (J1N1-S) four 20mm Type 99 Model 2 cannon fixed in rear cockpit, two firing obliquely upwards and two firing obliquely downwards; (J1N1-F) manual dorsal turret with single 20mm gun.

History: First flight May 1941; (production C) August 1942; service delivery (C) end of 1942; first flight (S) August 1943.

User: Japan (Imperial Navy).

Development: In 1938, before the Zero-Sen had flown, the Imperial Navy issued a specification for a twin-engined, long-range escort fighter, to reach a speed of 280 knots, and have a range of 1,300 nautical miles or 2,000 n.m. with extra fuel (the n.m. was the standard naval unit in Japan). Mitsubishi abandoned this project, but Nakajima's design team under K. Nakamura succeeded in producing a large prototype which proved to have remarkable manoeuvrability. Fitted with large fabric-covered ailerons, slotted flaps (opened 15° for combat) and leading-edge slats, it could dog-fight well with a Zero and the prototype was eventually developed to have

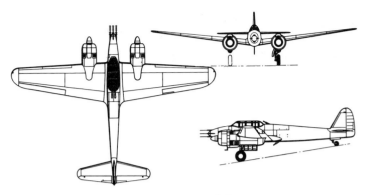

Above: Three-view of J1N1-S Gekko night fighter.

no flight limitations. But the Navy doubted the practicability of the complex scheme of two dorsal barbettes, each mounting two 7·7mm guns, remotely aimed in unison by the navigator. Eventually the Navy decided to buy the J1N1-C with these barbettes removed to serve as a three-seat photographic aircraft. (Some reports claim the failure as a fighter was due to lateral control problems, but Nakajima test pilots insist it was simply a matter of armament.) Soon after sorties began over the Solomons in the spring of 1943 the commander of the 251st Air Corps, Yasuna Kozono, hit on a way of intercepting Allied heavy night bombers. He had several aircraft modified as C-Kai night fighters with upper and lower pairs of oblique cannon. The armament proved effective, and most of the 477 J1N aircraft were built as J1N1-S Gekko (Moonlight) fighters with nose radar and a smoother cabin outline. They were good, robust aircraft, but unable to intercept the fast, high-flying B-29. Their Allied name was "Irving".

Below: The first prototype of the J1N1-C, the production version of the original reconnaissance aircraft.

Nakajima Ki-27 "Nate"

Ki-27a and -27b

Origin: Nakajima Hikoki KK; also built by Mansyu Hikoki Seizo KK.
Type: Single-seat interceptor fighter and light attack.
Engine: Prototype, one 650hp Nakajima Ha-1a (Jupiter-derived) nine-cylinder radial; 27a and 27b, one 710hp Ha-1b.
Dimensions: Span 37ft 0¾in (11·3m); length 24ft 8½in (7·53m); height 9ft 2¼in (2·8m).
Weights: Empty 2,403lb (1090kg); loaded 3,638lb (1650kg); (27b) up to 3,946lb.
Performance: Maximum speed 286mph (460km/h); initial climb 2,953ft (900m)/min; service ceiling, not recorded but about 34,400ft (10,500m); range 389 miles (625km).
Armament: Two 7·7mm Type 89 machine guns fixed in sides of fuselage, firing inside cowling; external racks for four 55lb (25kg) bombs.
History: First flight 15 October 1936; service delivery, early 1938; service delivery (Ki-27b) March 1939; final delivery July 1940.
User: Japan (Imperial Army) and Manchukuo.

Development: The Imperial Japanese Army's first low-wing monoplane fighter, the Ki-27 was in continuous production from 1937 to 1940 and was not only built in much larger quantities than other Japanese aircraft of its day but outnumbered almost every Japanese warplane of World War II. It was designed to meet a 1935 fighter requirement and competed against designs from Kawasaki and Mitsubishi. Though not the fastest, it was easily the most manoeuvrable; in fact it was probably the most manoeuvrable military aircraft of its day and possibly in all history, with plenty of engine power and (the Army having chosen the biggest of three possible sizes of wing) the extremely low loading of 17·9lb/ft². The loaded weight was roughly half that of contemporary Western fighters, and the penalty was paid in light construction and light armament. At the time Japanese pilots cared nothing for speed, fire-power or armour, but sacrificed everything for good visibility and manoeuvrability, and they resisted the introduction of later aircraft such as the Ki-43. Hundreds of Ki-27s fought Chinese and Soviet aircraft over Asia, scoring about 90 per cent of the claimed 1,252 Soviet aircraft (an exaggerated figure) shot down in 1939 after the Nomonhan Incident. Other Ki-27s served with the Manchurian air force, and at the time of Pearl Harbor they outnumbered all other Japanese fighters. Called "Nate" by the Allies, they continued in front-line use throughout the first year of the Pacific War. No fewer than 3,399 were built, 1,379 by the Manchurian (Mansyu Hikoki) company.

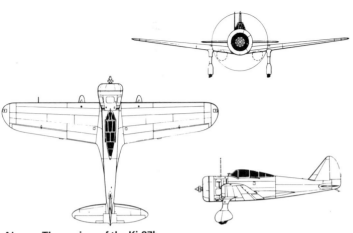

Above: Three-view of the Ki-27b.

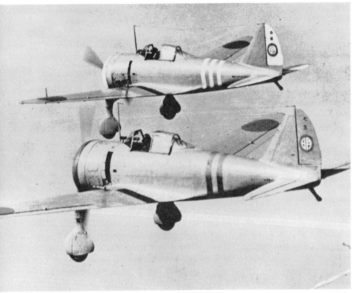

Above: The Nakajima Ki-27 appears to have been among the most manoeuvrable fighters of all time, though this quality was gained at the usual expense of light construction and light firepower. These Ki-27b fighters bear the badge of the Akeno fighter training school; most Army pilots in World War II trained on the Ki-27.

Left: This colourful Ki-27b served with the 1st Chutai of the 1st Hikosentai, numerically the preeminent flying unit of the Imperial Japanese Army. At the start of World War II this unit was still equipped with this nimble fighter, forming part of the 3rd Hikoshidan for operations against Malaya. In 1942 the Ki-27 was generally replaced by the same builder's Ki-43.

Nakajima Ki-43 Hayabusa "Oscar"

Ki-43-I to Ic, IIa and b, IIIa and b

Origin: Nakajima Hikoki KK; also built by Tachikawa Hikoki KK and Tachikawa Dai-Ichi Rikugun (Arsenal).

Type: Single-seat interceptor fighter (from IIa, fighter-bomber).

Engine: (Ki-43-I series) one 975hp Nakajima Ha-25 (Ha-35/12) Sakae 14-cylinder two-row radial; (II) 1,105hp Ha-115 Sakae; (III) 1,250hp Ha-112 (Ha-33/42) Kasei of same layout.

Dimensions: Span (I) 37ft 10½in; (IIa) 37ft 6¼in (11·437m); (IIb and subsequent) 35ft 6¾in (10·83m); length (I) 28ft 11¾in (8·82m); (II, III) 29ft 3¼in (8·92m); height (all) 10ft 8¾in (3·273m).

Weights: empty (I) 4,354lb (1975kg); normal loaded (I) 5,824lb (2642kg); (II series) 5,825–5,874lb (typically 2655kg); (III) 6,283lb (2850kg).

Performance: Maximum speed (I) 308mph; (II) 320mph (515km/h); (III) 363mph (585km/h); initial climb (typical II) 3,250ft (990m)/min; service ceiling (I) 38,500ft; (II, III) 36,800ft (11,215m); range (I) 746 miles (1200km); (II, III) internal fuel 1,060 miles (1700km), with two 45-gal drop tanks 1,864 miles (3000km).

Armament: (Ia) two 7·7mm Type 80 above engine; (Ib) one 12·7mm, one 7·7mm; (Ic) two 12·7mm; (all II series) two 12·7mm, each with 250 rounds, and wing racks for two 551lb (250kg) bombs; (IIIa) same; (IIIb) two 20mm Ho-5 cannon replacing 12·7mm in top decking, same bomb racks.

History: First flight January 1939; (production Ki-43-I) March 1941; (prototype IIa) February 1942; (prototype IIb) June 1942; (IIIa) December 1944.

Users: Japan (Imperial Army), Thailand; post-war, France (Indo-China) and Indonesia (against Dutch administration).

Development: Code-named "Oscar" by the Allies, the Ki-43 Hayabusa (Peregrine Falcon) was the most numerous of all Imperial Army warplanes and second only in numbers to the Zero-Sen. Compared with the famed Navy fighter it was smaller, lighter and much cheaper to produce. It was cast in the traditional Army mould in which everything was sacrificed for manoeuvrability, though the first prototype (designed by Hideo Itokawa to meet a 1938 Army contract which was simply awarded to Nakajima, without any industrial competition) was very heavy on the controls and disappointing. One prototype was even given fixed landing gear to save weight, but after many changes, and especially after adding a "combat manoeuvre flap" under the wings, the Ki-43 was turned into a dogfighter that could out-manoeuvre every aircraft ever ranged against it. After a few had carelessly got in the way of Allied fighters the more powerful II appeared with some

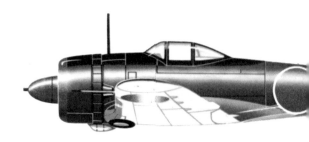

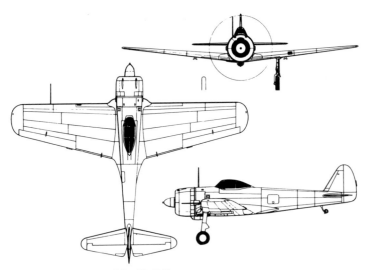

Above: Three-view of the Ki-43-IIa.

armour, self-sealing tanks and slightly reduced span. The mass-produced clipped-wing IIb followed, serving in every Japanese battle. To the end, this nimble fighter remained totally deficient in firepower (except for the few examples of the IIIb at the end of the war), and owing to its very light structure often disintegrated when hit by 0·5in fire. On the other hand, most of Japan's Army aces gained nearly all their scores on this popular little fighter. It was kept in production long after it was obsolete, 5,919 being delivered, including 2,629 by Tachikawa and 49 by the 1st Arsenal.

Above: A puzzling photograph showing what appears to be a Ki-43-Ib being either washed down or (unlikely) refuelled from a bucket. The fighter in the background is a Ki-44 on a trestle with work being done under the tail. Hundreds of Japanese combat aircraft were captured in 1945 but today survivors are pathetically few. There are only three reasonably complete Ki-43s and no Ki-44, and like many surviving World War II aircraft they are not quite authentic, having modern parts added.

Nakajima Ki-44 Shoki "Tojo"

Ki-44-Ia, b and c, IIa, b and c and III

Origin: Nakajima Hikoki KK.

Type: Single-seat interceptor fighter and (II onwards) fighter-bomber.

Engine: (Ia) one 1,260hp Nakajima Ha-41 14-cylinder two-row radial; (Ib and all subsequent) 1,520hp Nakajima Ha-109 of same layout.

Dimensions: Span 31ft (9·448m); length 28ft 8½in (8·75m); height 10ft 8in (3·248m).

Weights: Empty (Ia) 3,968lb (1800kg); (II, typical) 4,643lb (2106kg); normal loaded (no overload permitted) (Ia) 5,622lb (2550kg); (IIc) 6,107lb (2770kg); (III) 5,357lb (2430kg).

Performance: Maximum speed (Ia) 360mph (579km/h); (IIc) 376mph (605km/h); initial climb (IIc) 3,940ft (1200m)/min; service ceiling (IIc) 36,745ft (11,200m); range on internal fuel (typical) 560 miles (900km) (endurance, 2hr 20min).

Armament: (Ia) two 12·7mm Type I in wings and two 7·7mm Type 89 in fuselage; (Ib, IIa, IIb) four 12·7mm Type I, two in fuselage and two in wings, with (II series) wing racks for two 220lb (100kg) bombs; (IIc) two 12·7mm in fuselage, two 40mm Ho-301 low-velocity cannon; (III) two 12·7mm in fuselage, two 20mm Ho-5 cannon in wings.

History: First flight (first of ten prototypes) August 1940; (production Ki-44-Ia) May 1942; (Ib, Ic) 1943; (IIb) December 1943.

User: Japan (Imperial Army).

Development: Marking a complete break with the traditional emphasis on manoeuvrability, the Ki-44 (code-named "Tojo" by the Allies) contrasted with the Ki-43 as did the J2M with the Zero-Sen. Suddenly the need was for greater speed and climb, even at the expense of poorer manoeuvrability and faster landing. In late 1940 a Ki-44 was tested against a Kawasaki Ki-60 and an imported Bf 109E, outflying both; but production was delayed until mid-1942 by the priority accorded the old Ki-43. Pilots did not like the speedy small-winged fighter, with poor view on take-off and such poor control that flick rolls and many other manoeuvres were

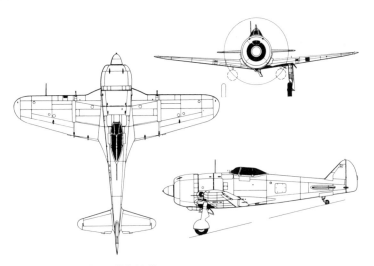

Above: Three-view of Ki-44-IIb.

banned. But gradually the fact that the Ki-44 could climb and dive as well as its enemies brought some measure of popularity, even though many inexperienced pilots were killed in accidents. Most Shokis (Demons) were -II series with retractable tailwheel and other changes, including a glazed teardrop canopy. The heavy cannon of the -IIc, firing caseless ammunition at 400 rounds per minute, were effective against Allied bombers. Probably the most successful mission ever flown in defending Japan was that of 19 February 1945 when a small force of Ki-44 (probably -IIc) climbed up to 120 B-29s and destroyed ten, two reportedly by suicide collisions. Total production was 1,233, including a few of the lightened -III series.

Below: A rare sub-type, the Ki-44-Ic, probably delivered about a year after Pearl Harbor. This model was basically a Ib with wheel-well doors repositioned on the fuselage instead of the legs.

Nakajima Ki-84 Hayate "Frank"

Ki-84-I to Ic, and many projects

Origin: Nakajima Hikoki KK; also built by Mansyu Hikoki Seizo KK and (three Ki-106) Tachikawa Hikoki KK.
Type: Single-seat fighter-bomber.
Engine: In all production models, one 1,900hp Nakajima Homare Ha-45 Model 11 18-cylinder two-row radial.
Dimensions: Span 36ft 10½in (11·238m); length 32ft 6½in (9·92m); height 11ft 1¼in (3·385m).
Weights: Empty 5,864lb (2680kg); normal loaded 8,267lb (3750kg); maximum overload (seldom authorised) 9,150lb (4150kg).
Performance: Maximum speed 388mph (624km/h); initial climb 3,600ft (1100m)/min; service ceiling 34,450ft (10,500m); range on internal fuel 1,025 miles (1650km); range with 98-gal drop tanks, 1,815 miles (2920km).
Armament: (Ia) two 20mm Ho-5 in wings, each with 150 rounds, and two 12·7mm Type 103 in top of fuselage with 350 rounds; (Ib) four 20mm, each with 150 rounds, two in wings and two in fuselage; (Ic) two 20mm in fuselage and two 30mm Ho-105 cannon in wings; (all operational models) two racks under outer wings for tanks or bombs up to 551lb (250kg) each.
History: First flight March 1943; (production Ia) August 1943; service delivery April 1944.
User: Japan (Imperial Army).

Development: Code-named "Frank" by the Allies, the Ki-84 of the Imperial Army was generally regarded as the best Japanese fighter of World War II. Yet it was not without its problems. Part of its fine all-round performance stemmed from the extremely advanced direct-injection engine, the first Army version of the Navy NK9A; yet this engine gave constant trouble and needed skilled maintenance. T. Koyama designed the Ki-84 to greater strength factors than any earlier Japanese warplane, yet poor heat-treatment of the high-strength steel meant that landing gears often simply snapped. Progressive deterioration in quality control meant that pilots never knew how particular aircraft would perform, whether the brakes would work or whether, in trying to intercept B-29s over Japan, they would even ▶

Above: Most Japanese fighters were camouflaged in overall dark green (as at right) or in mottled shades, but this attractive Ki-84-Ia painted pale grey served with HQ Chutai, 29th Sentai, on Taiwan (Formosa) in the summer of 1945.

Right: Another Ki-84-Ia series, this Hayate was on the strength of the 58th Shimbu-Tai in the home defence of Japan at the end of the war.

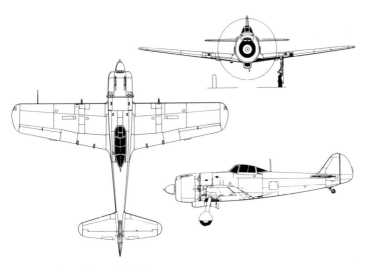

Above: Three-view of Ki-84-Ia.

Above: A shotai (section of three aircraft) from the 52nd Sentai photographed in late 1944 when about to leave on a long-range attack mission. Each carries one drop tank and one bomb, a tricky combination which inevitably means lateral-control problems as fuel is consumed. The usual size of bomb was 250kg (551lb).

Above: Another Ki-84-la serving in the southwest Pacific in 1944, in this case with the 11th Sentai. A detail visible in this picture is that the 'butterfly' combat flaps are lowered.

be able to climb high enough. Despite this, the Ki-84 was potentially superb, a captured -la out-climbing and outmanoeuvring a P-51H and P-47N! First batches went to China, where the 22nd Sentai flew rings round Gen Chennault's 14th Air Force. The unit then moved to the Philippines, where the rot set in, with accidents, shortages and extremely poor serviceability. Frequent bombing of the Musashi engine factory and extreme need to conserve raw material led to various projects and prototypes made of wood (Ki-84-II series and Ki-106) or steel (Ki-113) and advanced models with the 2,000hp Ha-45ru turbo charged engine, Ha-45/44 with two-stage three-speed blower and 2,500hp Ha-44/13. Total production of the Hayate (Hurricane) was 3,514 (2,689 at Ohta, 727 at Utsonomiya and 95 in Manchuria by Mansyu, which also flew the Ki-116 with smaller Ha-112 engine) and three at Tachikawa.

Above and right: Two more attractively painted Ki-84-la fighters which saw action in the Pacific campaigns. Above, with the 1st Chutai, 47th Sentai, based at Narumatsu; right, with the 1st Chutai, 73rd Senai, Philippines, December 1944. Combat victories were not painted on aircraft.

Above: An early Ki-84-la Hayate. The long landing gears were prone to structural failure, as a result of faulty heat-treatment of the steel legs, and the complex and closely cowled engine gave prolonged trouble; so did the hydraulics.

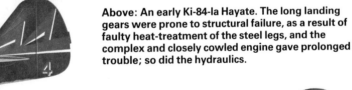

Yokosuka D4Y Suisei "Judy"
D4Y1 and 1-C, D4Y2, 2-C and 2-S, D4Y3 and D4Y4

Origin: Dai-Ichi Kaigun Koku Gijitsusho, Yokosuka; production aircraft built by Aichi Kokuki KK and Dai-Juichi Kaigun Kokusho.

Type: Two-seat carrier dive bomber; (1-C, 2-C, reconnaissance; 2-S night fighter; D4Y4, single-seat Kamikaze).

Engines: (1) one 1,200hp Aichi Atsuta 21 inverted-vee-12 liquid-cooled (Daimler-Benz 601); (2) 1,400hp Atsuta 32; (3, 4) 1,560hp Mitsubishi Kinsei 62 14-cylinder two-row radial).

Dimensions: Span (1, 2) 37ft 8½in (11·493m); (3, 4) 37ft 9in (11·50m); length (all, despite engine change) 33ft 6½in (10·22m); height (1, 2) 12ft 1in (3·67m); (3, 4) 12ft 3¼in (3·74m).

Weights: Empty (1) 5,650lb (2565kg); (2) 5,840lb (2635kg); (3) 5,512lb (2501kg); (4) variable; maximum loaded (1) 9,615lb (4361kg); (2) 9,957lb (4353kg); (3) 10,267lb (4657kg); (4) 10,434lb (4733kg).

Performance: Maximum speed (1) 339mph (546km/h); (2) 360mph (580km/h); (3) 356mph (574km/h); initial climb (1) 1,970ft (600m)/min; (others) 2,700ft (820m)/min; service ceiling (typical) 34,500ft (10,500m); range (2) 749 miles (1205km); (3) 945 miles (1520km).

Armament: Normally, two 7·7mm Type 97 fixed above engine, one 7·7mm manually aimed from rear cockpit; internal bomb bay for single 551lb (250kg) bomb, plus one 66lb (30kg) bomb under each wing; (4) see text.

History: First flight November 1940; (production D4Y1) May 1941; service delivery, late' 1941.

User: Japan (Imperial Navy).

Development: Designed to a challenging specification of the Imperial Japanese Navy of 1937, which called for a long-range two-seat dive bomber as fast as the "Zero" fighter, the D4Y was one of the very few Japanese aircraft to go into production with a liquid-cooled engine. The supposed lower drag of such an engine had been one of the factors in meeting the requirement, but the Japanese version of the DB 601 had an unhappy history in carrier service. The first D4Y versions in combat were 1-C reconnaissance aircraft flying from the carrier *Soryu* during the Battle

Below: A D4Y3 Suisei Model 33, with two 72.6 Imp gal drop tanks. By the time this radial-engined model was delivered nearly all Suiseis had to be assigned to land-based units.

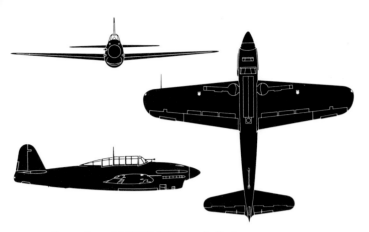

Above: Three-view of D4Y1 (D4Y2 very similar).

of Midway in June 1942. The carrier was sunk in that encounter, and soon most D4Y were being operated by unskilled crews from island airstrips. In 1943 the main problems with the aircraft — named Suisei (Comet), and called "Judy" by the Allies — were solved by switching to the smooth and reliable radial engine. During the final year of the war the D4Y4 appeared as a single-seat suicide attacker carrying 1,764lb (800kg) of explosives, while some dozens of Atsuta-engined examples were turned into 2-S night fighters with one or two 20mm cannon fixed obliquely behind the rear cockpit. Total production was 2,038.

Below: The US Navy identified this suicide attacker as a D4Y4, the specially converted single-seat D4Y version (though it seems to have fixed landing gears). It hit the cruiser *Columbia* at Lingayen Gulf on 6 January 1945, causing much damage.

Yokosuka MXY-7 Ohka "Baka

MXY-7 Model 11 and Model 22

Origin: Dai-Ichi Kaigun Koku Gijitsusho, Yokosuka; 600 Model 11 built by Dai-Ichi Kaigun Kokusho.

Type: Single-seat piloted missile for surface attack.

Engine: (11) one three-barrel Type 4 Model 20 rocket motor with sea-level thrust of 1,764lb (800kg); (22) TSU-11 jet engine, with piston-engined compressor, rated at 441lb (200kg) thrust.

Dimensions: Span (11) 16ft 4¾in (5m); (22) 13ft 6¼in (4·12m); length (11) 19ft 10¾in (6·07m); (22) 22ft 6¾in (6·88m); height (both) about 3ft 11¼in (1·20m).

Weights: Empty (no warhead) (11) 970lb (440kg); (22) 1,202lb (545kg); loaded (11) 4,718lb (2140kg); (22) 3,200lb (1450kg).

Performance: Maximum speed on level (11) 534mph (860km/h); (22) about 300mph (480km/h); final dive speed (both) 621mph (1000km/h); climb and ceiling, normally launched at about 27,000ft (8200m); range (11) 55 miles (88km).

Armament: (11) warhead containing 2,645lb (1200kg) of tri-nitroaminol; (22) warhead weight 1,323lb (600kg).

History: Start of design August 1944; start of quantity production (11) September 1944; service delivery, early October 1944.

User: Japan (Imperial Navy).

Development: Having accepted the principle of the Kamikaze suicide attack, the Imperial Navy was only logical in designing an aircraft for this duty instead of using inefficient and more vulnerable conventional machines having less devastating effect. Built partly of wood, Model 11 was carried

Below: a genuine operational Model 11, complete with warhead and motor, found abandoned (probably on Okinawa). All Ohka variants carried a cherry blossom motif on the side of the fuselage (here partly obscured by the joint strap). What appears to be a pitot head above the fuselage is probably not part of the aircraft.

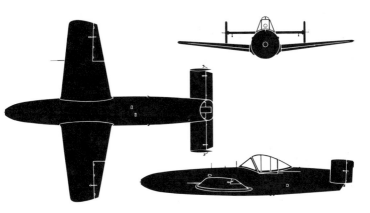

Above: Three-view of MXY-7 Model 11.

aloft by a G4M ("Betty"), without bomb doors and specially modified for the task, and released about 50 miles from the target. The pilot then held a fast glide at about 290mph (466km/h), electrically igniting the rocket while pushing over into a steep final dive for the last 30 seconds of trajectory. Though nearly all these missiles failed to reach their objectives, the few that did wrought fearful havoc. Ohka (Cherry Blossom) was called "Baka" (Japanese for "fool") by the Allies, which was not very appropriate. Several manufacturers delivered 755, and 45 unpowered K-1 versions were delivered for training. The Model 22, of which some 50 were delivered, was underpowered. Not completed by VJ-day, the Model 33 would have had the Ne-20 turbojet; Models 43A and 43B were for launching from submarines and land catapults, respectively, but these too failed to see service.

Below: A fully operational Ohka Model 11 found on Yontan airfield, Okinawa, an island infested with these missiles. The three nozzles of the solid-propellant rocket motor can be seen, as can the serial number 1022 on one rudder and the rear fuselage. The aircraft in the background appears to be an Army Ki-61 fighter.

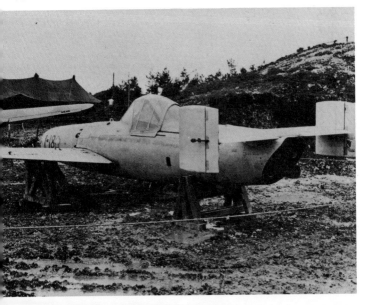

Yokosuka P1Y1 Ginga "Frances"
P1Y1 Model 11, P1Y1-S, P1Y2 and 2-S

Origin: Design by Dai-Ichi Kaigun Koku Gijitsusho, but all construction by Nakajima Hikoki KK and Kawanishi Kokuki KK.

Type: Three-seat multi-role attack bomber; -S, two-seat night fighter.

Engines: (1) two 1,820hp Nakajima Ho-21 Homare 11 18-cylinder two-row radials; (2) 1,825hp Mitsubishi Kasei 25 14-cylinder two-row radials.

Dimensions: Span 65ft 7½in (20m); length 49ft 2½in (15m); height 14ft 1¼in (4·30m)

Weights: Empty (1) 14,748lb (6690kg); normal loaded (1) 23,148lb (10,500kg); maximum loaded (1) 29,762lb (13,500kg).

Performance: Maximum speed (1) 345mph (556km/h); (2) 354mph (570km/h); initial climb (1) 2,100ft (650m)/min; service ceiling 33,530ft (10,220m); range (1) 2,728 miles (4390km).

Armament: (1 and 2) one 20mm Type 99-II cannon manually aimed from nose, one 20mm or 12·7mm manually aimed from rear cockpit (a few aircraft had dorsal turret with two 20mm or 12·7mm); internal bay for two 551lb (250kg) bombs, plus small bombs beneath outer wings; as alternative, one 1,764lb (800kg) or 1,874lb (850kg) torpedo externally, or two 1,102lb (500kg) bombs inboard of engines; (1-S, 2-S) two 20mm fixed firing obliquely upward in centre fuselage, plus single 20mm aimed from rear cockpit, or powered dorsal turret with two 20mm.

History: First flight (Y-20 prototype) early 1943; (production P1Y1) August 1943; (prototype P1Y2-S) June 1944.

User: Japan (Imperial Navy).

Development: Similar to late-model Ju 88 aircraft in size, power and

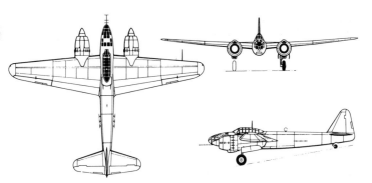

Above: Three-view of late-model P1Y1 with ASV search radar.

capability, this fine-looking aircraft was one of the best designed in Japan during World War II. The 1940 Navy specification called for a land-based aircraft capable of level and dive bombing, but by the time production began at the Nakajima factories at Koizumi and Fukushima it had already become a torpedo bomber, and it was to do much more before its brief career was over. At sea level it could outrun many Allied fighters and it was manoeuvrable and well protected; yet it carried 1,290gal of fuel and had greater range than any other aircraft in its class. Called Ginga (Milky Way), and christened "Frances" by the Allies, this machine would have been a menace had it not been crippled by lack of skilled crews, lack of fuel and lack of spares. Nevertheless Nakajima built 1,002, of which some were used as suicide aircraft while a few were converted into the P1Y1-S night fighter. Kawanishi had meanwhile developed a completely new version, the Kasei-engined P1Y2, and delivered 96 P1Y2-S night fighters called Kyokko (Aurora), which saw little action.

Left: This appears to be one of the unpainted P1Y1 development prototypes; it almost certainly has a retractable tailwheel, a sure means of identifying pre-production machines, and subsequent aircraft were invariably fully painted. An outstanding aircraft in almost all respects, the P1Y1 was used for numerous trials and research programmes including tests of radars, weapons and the first small Japanese turbojet. One model was to have been armed with 16 forward-firing 20mm cannon.

Below: A dramatic photograph showing a P1Y1 making a suicide attack on an American warship (whose AA fire is visible) while pursued by an F4U Corsair which has hit the left engine.

SECTION III

BOMBERS
OF WORLD WAR II

Contents

Aircraft are arranged in alphabetical order of manufacturers' names, followed by the countries of origin.

Introduction

Nearly all the bombers of World War II were of types first flown back in the 1930s, and many had seen action in Spain and other wars of the period. Yet nearly all were monoplanes of all-metal stressed skin construction, notable exceptions being the mixed metal/wood/fabric Italian bombers, and the fabric-covered "geodetic" Wellington.

In Spain the new crop of German bombers, such as the Do 17 and He 111, proved very effective when defended by three hand-aimed rifle-calibre machine guns, but this was woefully inadequate over Britian. More guns were hastily added in an ill-planned way, but, though German guns were outstanding, the Germans completely failed to get a really good heavy bomber into service and the poor old He 111 soldiered on to the end. By 1945 something approaching 7,000 of these broad-winged machines had been built — well liked, but totally outclassed and unable to sustain the once-victorious Blitzkrieg.

Its equally successful partner in 1939 had been the Ju 87 "Stuka" dive bomber, and by 1945 this too was reduced to skulking about wherever Allied fighters were unlikely to appear. It is described elsewhere in this book, together with the Ju 88, a valuable and versatile aircraft which, despite having first flown in 1936, went from strength to strength as the war progressed. In this it contrasted sharply with the He 177, which at the start of the war was confidently regarded as the Luftwaffe's future heavy bomber. It proved unreliable and dangerous, and throughout the war the Luftwaffe lacked a good "heavy" and failed in many attempts to create one.

Germany's neighbour, France, had an unbroken history of large bomber forces. When war broke out there were probably more bombers in the Armée de l'Air than in any other air force, but most were sadly out of date. Newest of the heavies, the

Farman F.222, was typical of the technology of 1930. Large numbers of various Blochs and Amiots were likewise outdated and vulnerable, though the sleek Amiot 350 series were just coming into service, as was the outstanding LeO 45. To try to make good the lack of modern bombers, large orders were placed for the American Douglas DB-7 and Martin 167; but, like the host of new French bombers, these were simply too late to have much effect in May 1940.

Despite a belief in "disarmament", Britain just managed from 1935 onwards to find enough money to expand and upgrade the Royal Air Force. In the final years of peace 1,000 Battles and 1,000 Blenheims were delivered. These were a far cry from the era of fabric-covered biplanes, but when faced by Bf 109Es and modern flak they were shot down in droves, killing many of the nation's experienced aircrew. Gradually the emphasis swung towards strategic operations at night, initially with the Wellington, Whitley and Hampden. From 1941 the Whitley was switched to Coastal Command and glider towing, and the Hampden to minelaying, but the "Wimpey" — as the Wellington was called, from Popeye's friend J. Wellington Wimpey — became Britains most numerous bomber with 11,461 built.

Lord Trenchard and others had imbued the RAF with the belief that strategic bombing could be decisive in any protracted war, and this belief was given tangible form in the decision in 1936 to order large heavy bombers. The war-winner was expected to be the mighty Short Stirling, but — in part because of a customer requirement that the wing span should pass through a 100ft (30m) hangar door opening — this aircraft had an effective combat altitude that put it amidst all the worst of the heavy flak over Hitler's Europe. Another

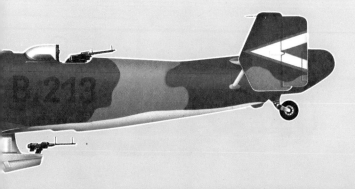

specification, P.13/36, called for big bombers powered by twin Vulture engines. Handley Page changed their design to have four Merlins, and it became the Halifax. A great aircraft, it became even better with more span, a new tail and Hercules engines. The other P.13/36 aircraft, the Avro Manchester, went into service with Vultures. These gave much trouble, and eventually Avro followed HP's lead and switched to four Merlins, on a longer-span wing. The resulting Lancaster was the king of Bomber Command, and devastated Germany. One can argue indefinitely about just how far this won the war.

In the USA, only the Army had aircraft that could be called bombers. Vast numbers were made of some excellent twins, such as the A-20, B-25, B-26 and above all the A-26 (which, restyled B-26, was to serve for 30 years and play a big role in Vietnam!). But despite a parsimonious Congress the Air Corps managed gradually to build up a fleet of B-17s which combined unprecedented operating height, unprecedented defensive firepower, and unprecedented navigational and bombing accuracy. Together with the B-24 these aircraft equipped the Bomb Groups of the mighty 8th Air Force which not only really hurt Hitler's war machine with precision attacks but also gradually, and at grievous loss, sapped at the vitals of the once mighty Luftwaffe until it could no longer even control the daytime sky over the heart of Germany.

While the mighty heavy bomber force was being built up, Boeing was developing the most advanced bomber of the war, the B-29. In such features as the wing loading (more than double that of most of its contemporaries), wing skin thickness, engine turbosupercharge, cabin pressurization, remotely controlled turrets housing heavy machine guns and cannon, and fuel capacity, it set standards never before even

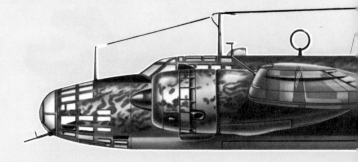

approached. The result was a mighty trucking system that could take the war to Japan from islands over 1,500 miles (2,410km) distant, or from India and China, finally coming over the target at well over 30,000ft (9,140m). The B-29 alone brought utter devastation to Japan's cities, one fire raid on Tokyo causing more casualties than any nation has suffered in one day at any time before or since. Two nuclear bombs dropped by B-29s brought the war to a speedy conclusion, sparing humanity the carnage of a direct invasion over the Japanese beaches.

This important section also includes bombers from Italy, Japan, the Soviet Union, the Netherlands and Poland. These were invariably flown with skill and sustained courage, but usually with only a small impact on the fortunes of the war.

In the West not much has been written about the long strategic missions of the Il-4s or the tremendous work done by 11,427 Pe-2s in support of the gigantic ground forces along the 3,000 miles (4,800km) of the Eastern Front. This was a harsh theatre, where bomber bases had no runways (unless they were made from hastily laid irregular wooden boards) and certainly no hangars or any kind of permanent building. Things were not much more luxurious in the Pacific, where bombers played a very significant role in allowing the Japanese armies to sweep over a greater area of our planet in six months than any previous nation had controlled before. But two years later the same armies, or their replacements, were in desperate retreat. The proud Imperial Army and Navy air forces were reduced to suicide missions, often with heavy bombs strapped to aircraft not previously considered as bombers.

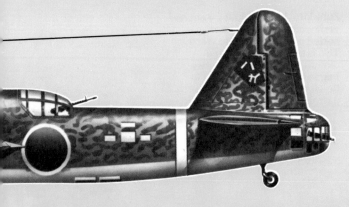

Armstrong Whitworth A.W.38 Whitley

Whitley I to VIII (data for V)

Origin: Sir W. G. Armstrong Whitworth Aircraft.
Type: Five-seat heavy bomber.
Engines: Two 1,145hp Rolls-Royce Merlin X vee-12 liquid-cooled.
Dimensions: Span 84ft 0in (25·6m); length 70ft 6in (21·5m); height 15ft 0in (4·57m).
Weights: Empty 19,330lb (8768kg); maximum 33,500lb (15,196kg).
Performance: Maximum speed 222mph (357km/h); cruising speed, about 185mph (297km/h); initial climb 800ft (244m)/min; service ceiling from 17,600–21,000ft (5400–6400m); range with maximum bomb load 470 miles (756km); range with 3,000lb (1361kg) bombs 1,650 miles (2650km).
Armament: One 0·303 in Vickers K in nose turret; four 0·303 in Brownings in tail turret; up to 7,000lb (3175kg) bombs in cells in fuselage and inner wings.
History: First flight (prototype) 17 March 1936; first delivery (Mk I) January 1937; first flight (Mk V) December 1938; first delivery (Mk V) August 1939; production termination June 1943.
User: UK (RAF, BOAC).

Development: Designed to Specification B.3/34, this heavy bomber was at least an all-metal monoplane with retractable landing gear, but the original Mk I was still primitive. Its thick wing, which in the first batch had no dihedral, was set at a marked positive incidence, so that at normal cruising speeds the long slab-sided Whitley flew in a characteristic nose-down attitude. Powered by 795hp Armstrong Siddeley Tiger IX radials, the Mk I was soon replaced by the Mk II, and then by the III with the 920hp

Fully kitted-up, a Whitley V aircrew wait while a last-minute snag is sorted out early in World War II. This is a Bomber Command aircraft; from 1941 the Whitley began to be more important in Coastal Command flying ocean patrols.

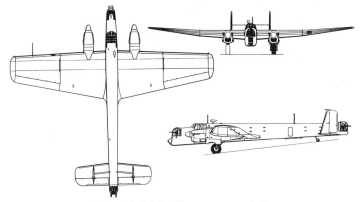

Above: Typical Whitley V with landing gear extended.

Tiger VIII. In 1938 production switched to the greatly improved Mk IV, with Merlin engines and a power-driven rear turret mounting four machine guns. The Mk IVA had a more powerful Merlin, and this was retained in the Mk V which was 15in longer and had straight-edged fins. AWA made 1,466 Whitley Vs, the last in June 1943, and also delivered 146 longer-range GR.VIII patrol aircraft with ASV radar for Coastal Command. Whitleys bore the brunt of long leaflet raids, starting on the first night of the war. On 19 March 1940 Whitleys dropped the first bombs to fall on Germany since 1918, and during the next two years these tough and capable aircraft made missions as far as Turin and Pilsen, often in terrible conditions, highlighting deficiencies in navigation and equipment the hard way. Coastal's first U-boat kill was U-206, sunk by a Whitley VII in November 1941. From 1942 the Whitley served mainly as a trainer for paratroops, as a glider tug and with 100 Group as a carrier of experimental or special-purpose radars and countermeasures. Total production was 1,737.

Left: This Whitley V served in the early part of the war with 102 Sqn. It took part in many leaflet raids, minelaying sorties and early missions to bomb targets in Germany and northern Italy.

Avro 679 Manchester

679 Manchester I and IA

Origin: A. V. Roe Ltd, Chadderton.
Type: Heavy bomber.
Engines: Two Rolls-Royce Vulture I 24-cylinder X-form, rated at 1,760hp but in fact derated to 1,480–1,500hp.
Dimensions: Span 90ft 1in (27·46m); length 70ft 0in (21·34m); height 19ft 6in (5·94m).
Weights: Empty 31,200lb (14,152kg); maximum 56,000lb but in fact never authorised above 50,000lb (22,680kg).
Performance: Maximum speed (typical) 250mph (402km/h); service ceiling (42,000lb) 19,500ft (5852m); range with maximum bomb load 1,200 miles (1930km).
Armament: Eight 0·303in Browning in power turrets in nose (2), mid-upper (2) and tail (4); internal fuselage bay accommodating bomb load up to 10,350lb (4695kg).
History: First flight 25 July 1939; service delivery November 1940; withdrawal from production November 1941.
User: UK (RAF).

Development: Rolls-Royce's decision in 1935 to produce a very powerful engine by fitting two sets of Peregrine cylinder-blocks to one crankcase (the lower pair being inverted, to give an X arrangement) prompted the Air Ministry to issue specification P.13/36 for a twin-engined heavy bomber of unprecedented capability. Handley Page changed to four Merlins (see Halifax) but Avro produced the Manchester with the Vulture engine. In most respects it was the best of all the new heavy bombers, but the engine was grossly down on power, and had to be derated further because of extreme unreliability. Originally the Manchester had two fins; in the production Mk I a fixed central fin was added, and the bulk of the 209 delivered had two larger fins (no central fin) and were designated IA. So hopeless was the engine situation that the plans to build Manchesters at Armstrong Whitworth and Fairey were cancelled, and Metropolitan-Vickers stopped at No 32. Avro went on until the vastly superior Lancaster could take over, the first batches of Lancasters having Manchester fuselages with a row of small windows along each side.

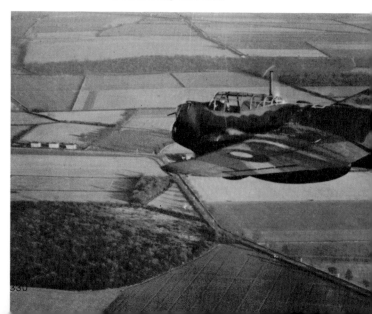

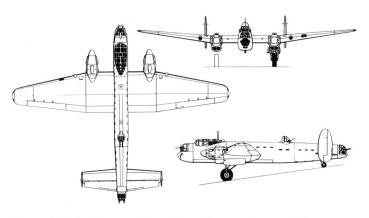

Above: Mk 1A with two enlarged fins on increased-span tailplane.

Above: L7516, "S-Sugar" of 207 Sqn, the first unit to receive the Manchester in November 1940. This aircraft was a Mk IA.

Below: L7284 was the ninth production Manchester I, the original model with a central fin. It was photographed in 1940 soon after delivery to 207 Sqn. Later, fuselage sides were black (above).

Avro 683 Lancaster
683 Lancaster I to MR.7 (data for I)

Origin: A. V. Roe Ltd; also Armstrong Whitworth, Austin Motors, Metropolitan-Vickers and Vickers-Armstrongs, UK, and Victory Aircraft, Canada.
Type: Seven-seat heavy bomber.
Engines: Four 1,460hp Rolls-Royce or Packard Merlin 20 or 22 (Mk II only: four 1,650hp Bristol Hercules VI, 14 cylinder two-row, sleeve-valve radials).
Dimensions: Span 102ft 0in (31·1m); length 69ft 4in (21·1m); height 19ft 7in (5·97m).
Weights: Empty 36,900lb (16,705kg); loaded 68,000lb (30,800kg); overload with 22,000lb bomb 70,000lb (31,750kg).
Performance: Maximum speed 287mph (462km/h) at 11,500ft (3500m); cruising speed 210mph (338km/h); climb at maximum weight to 20,000ft (6095m) 41 minutes; service ceiling 24,500ft (7467m); range with 14,000lb (6350kg) bombs 1,660 miles (2675km).
Armament: Nose and dorsal turrets (Mk II also ventral) with two 0·303in Brownings (some, including Mk VII, had Martin dorsal turret with two 0·5in), tail turret with four 0·303 in Brownings, 33ft 0in (10·06m) bomb bay carrying normal load of 14,000lb (6350kg) or 22,000lb (9979kg) bomb with modification.
History: First flight 9 January 1941; service delivery (for test and training) September 1941; last delivery from new 2 February 1946.
Users: Australia, Canada, New Zealand, Poland, UK (RAF, BOAC).

Development: Undoubtedly one of the major influences on World War II, and one of the greatest aircraft of history, the "Lanc" came about because of the failure of its predecessor. In September 1936 the Air Staff issued specification P.13/36 for a twin-engined bomber of exceptional size and capability to be powered by two of the very powerful engines then under development: the Rolls-Royce Vulture 24-cylinder X engine was preferred. Handley Page switched to four Merlins with the Halifax, but A. V. Roe adhered to the big-twin formula and the first Type 679 Manchester flew on 25 July 1939. Altogether 209 Manchesters were delivered by November 1941, but the type was plagued by the poor performance and unreliability of its engine. Though it equipped eight Bomber Command squadrons, and parts of two others plus a flight in Coastal Command, the Manchester was withdrawn from service in June 1942 and survivors were scrapped.

Nevertheless the basic Manchester was clearly outstandingly good, and in 1940 the decision was taken to build a longer-span version with four Merlin engines. The first Lancaster (BT 308) flew as the Manchester III at the beginning of 1941. So outstanding was its performance that it went ▶

Below: The famous Lancaster S-Sugar now preserved in the RAF Museum at Hendon. A B.I that served with 467 Sqn, from Waddington, it completed 137 missions, thought to be a record. Unfortunately the true leader, with 140 missions, was scrapped.

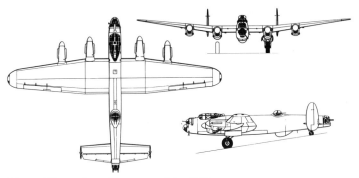

Above: Three-view of Lancaster B.I or B.III.

Below: Lancasters bombing through cloud. Bomber Command perfected many advanced methods of radio and radar navigation, target marking and blind bombing, as well as more than 17 types of ECM (electronic countermeasures) and spoofing or decoys.

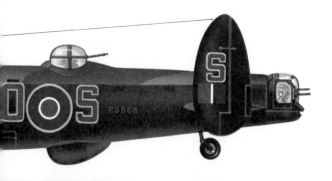

into immediate large-scale production, and Manchesters already on the line from L7527 onwards were completed as Lancasters (distinguished from later aircraft by their row of rectangular windows in the rear fuselage). Deliveries began in early 1942 to 44 Sqn at Waddington, and on 17 April 1942 a mixed force of 44 and 97 Sqns made a rather foolhardy daylight raid against the MAN plant at Augsburg, whereupon the new bomber's existence was revealed.

From then until the end of World War II Lancasters made 156,000 sorties in Europe and dropped 608,612 long tons of bombs. Total production, including 430 in Canada by Victory Aircraft, was 7,377. Of these 3,425

were Mk I and 3,039 the Mk III with US Packard-built engines. A batch of 300 was built as Mk IIs with the more powerful Bristol Hercules radial, some with bulged bomb bays and a ventral turret. The Mk I (Special) was equipped to carry the 12,000lb (5443kg) light-case bomb and the 12,000lb and 22,000lb (9979kg) Earthquake bombs, the H_2S radar blister under the rear fuselage being removed. The Mk I (FE) was equipped for Far East ▶

Below: The first unit to convert to the Lancaster was No 44 (Rhodesia) Sqn, previously equipped with Hampdens. This fine photograph of some of 44's Lancs was taken later in 1942.

operations with Tiger Force. The aircraft of 617 (Dambusters) Sqn were equipped to spin and release the Wallis skipping drum bomb. The Mk VI had high-altitude Merlins and four-blade propellers and with turrets removed served 635 Sqn and 100 Grp as a countermeasure and radar spoof carrier. Other marks served as photo-reconnaissance and maritime reconnaissance and air/sea rescue aircraft, the last MR.7 leaving RAF front-line service in February 1954.

Lancasters took part in every major night attack on Germany. They soon showed their superiority by dropping 132 long tons of bombs for each aircraft lost, compared with 56 (later 86) for the Halifax and 41 for the Stirling. They carried a heavier load of bigger bombs than any other aircraft in the European theatre. The 12,000lb AP bomb was used to sink the *Tirpitz*, and the 22,000lb weapon finally shook down the stubborn viaduct at Bielefeld in March 1945. Around Caen, Lancasters were used en masse in the battlefield close-support role, and they finished the war dropping supplies to starving Europeans and ferrying home former prisoners of war.

Right: The last of a dozen thousand-pounders is winched up into the capacious bay of a Lancaster. Behind the armourer, who is stripped to the waist, can be seen the black bulge housing the H₂S radar which Luftwaffe night fighters found a useful beacon.

Below: An inspiring sight to anyone who remembers those great days – the final assembly line at A. V. Roe's Woodford plant in 1943 (Mk is with serials in the batch JA672-JB748).

Bloch 174

174 A3, 175 B3 and T

Origin: SNCASO.

Type: Three-seat reconnaissance, target marker and light bomber.

Engines: Two 1,140hp Gnome-Rhône 14N 14-cylinder radials.

Dimensions: Span 58ft 9½in (17·9m); length 40ft 1½in (12·23m); height 11ft 7¾in (3·59m).

Weights: Empty 12,346lb (5600kg); maximum 15,784lb (7160kg).

Performance: Maximum speed 329mph (529km/h) at 17,060ft (5200m); cruising speed 248mph (400km/h); climb to 26,250ft (8000m) 11min; service ceiling 36,090ft (11,000m); maximum range with 880lb (400kg) bomb load 800 miles (1,450km).

Armament: Two 7·5mm MAC 1934 fixed in wings, three fixed at different angles below and to the rear, and two manually aimed from rear cockpit; internal bay for eight 110lb (50kg) bombs, wing racks for light bombs or flares (175, three 441lb or equivalent).

History: First flight (170-01) 15 February 1938; (174-01) 5 January 1939; (first production 174 A3) 5 November 1939; first delivery to combat unit (GR II/33) 19 March 1940.

Users: France (Armée de l'Air, Aéronavale, Vichy AF), Germany (Luftwaffe).

Development: Under chief designer Henri Deplante the Bloch 170 was planned as a bomber and army co-operation machine in 1936–37. As a result of indecision by the Armée de l'Air this took three years to evolve into the Bloch 174 A3 reconnaissance and target-marking aircraft, with secondary capability as a bomber. By the time production of the 174 stopped in May 1940 a total of 50 had been delivered. The first sortie was flown in March 1940 by the famed Capitaine Antoine de Saint-Exupéry. As it had an insignificant bomb load the 174 made little impact on the Blitzkrieg – it was only in 1942, in Tunisia, that the survivors were fitted to conduct shallow dive-bombing with bombs of up to 500kg (1,102lb) – but the performance and handling were so outstanding and made such a difference to the casualty-rate among squadrons equipped with the type, that the Bloch 175 was hurriedly planned as a purpose-designed bomber. Altogether 25 Bloch 175 B3s were completed before France collapsed, with more than 200 on the production line, and had France been able to resist longer the 175 would have been a potent weapon. A few 174 and 175 aircraft saw service with the Luftwaffe, but most served Vichy France in North Africa and many survived the war. Indeed the torpedo-carrying 175T remained in production for the Aéronavale until 1950.

Below: A Bloch 174 A3 serving with GR II/33 of the Vichy forces based at Tunis El Aouina in 1941-42. Some of these aircraft had engine cowlings painted in yellow/red stripes in common with many other aircraft of the Vichy forces, including US-supplied types.

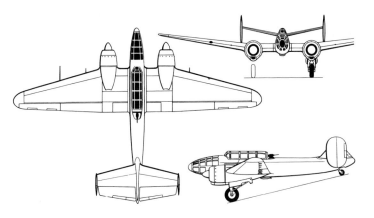

Above: Three-view of Bloch 174A3.

Above: The Bloch 174 A3 was an outstanding multi-role aircraft and, had it not been for the disastrous and defeatist political and industrial environment into which it was born, it might have made a major contribution to Allied victory. As it was, not one reached the Armée de l'Air until 19 March 1940, and the first operational sortie took place ten days later. Barely a year later the chief contribution of this machine was to provide a fully developed engine for the German Messerschmitt Me 323 Gigant cargo transport, some of which actually flew with engines, cowlings and propellers taken from Bloch 175s already completed.

Boeing B-17 Fortress

Model 299, Y1B-17 and B-17 to B-17G (basic data for G)

Origin: Boeing Airplane Company, Seattle; also built by Vega Aircraft Corporation, Burbank, and Douglas Aircraft Company, Tulsa.

Type: High-altitude bomber, with crew of six to ten.

Engines: Four 1,200hp Wright R-1820-97 (B-17C to E, R-1820-65) Cyclone nine-cylinder radials with exhaust-driven turbochargers.

Dimensions: Span 103ft 9in (31·6m): length 74ft 9in (22·8m); (B-17B, C, D) 67ft 11in; (B-17E) 73ft 10in; height 19ft 1in (5·8m); (B-17B, C, D) 15ft 5in.

Weights: Empty 32,720–35,800lb (14,855–16,200kg); (B-17B, C, D) typically 31,150lb; maximum loaded 65,600lb (29,700kg) (B-17B, C, D) 44,200–46,650lb; (B-17E) 53,000lb.

Performance: Maximum speed 287mph (462km/h); (B-17C, D) 323mph; (B-17E) 317mph; cruising speed 182mph (293km/h); (B-17C, D) 250mph; (B-17E) 210mph; service ceiling 35,000ft (10,670m); range 1,100 miles (1,760km) with maximum bomb load (other versions up to 3,160 miles with reduced weapon load).

Armament: Twin 0·5in Brownings in chin, dorsal, ball and tail turrets, plus two in nose sockets, one in radio compartment and one in each waist position. Normal internal bomb load 6,000lb (2724kg), but maximum 12,800lb (5800kg).

History: First flight (299) 28 July 1935; (Y1B-17) January 1937; first delivery (B-17B) June 1939; final delivery April 1945.

Users: UK (RAF), US (AAC/AAF, Navy).

Development: In May 1934 the US Army Air Corps issued a specification for a multi-engined anti-shipping bomber to defend the nation against enemy fleets. The answer was expected to be similar to the Martin B-10, but Boeing proposed four engines in order to carry the same bomb load faster and higher. It was a huge financial risk for the Seattle company but the resulting Model 299 was a giant among combat aircraft, with four 750hp Pratt & Whitney Hornet engines, a crew of eight and stowage for eight 600lb (272kg) bombs internally.

The service-test batch of 13 Y1B-17 adopted the Wright Cyclone engine, later versions all being turbocharged for good high-altitude performance. The production B-17B introduced a new nose and bigger rudder and flaps,

continued ▶

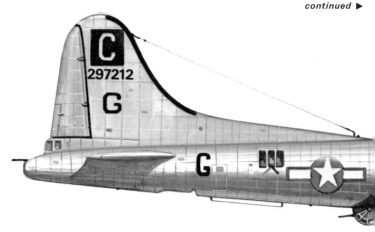

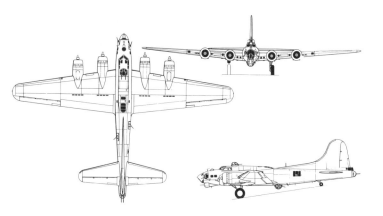

Above: Three-view of B-17G.

Above: The RAF used hundreds of Fortress IIs (B-17F) and IIIs (B-17G), the former mainly with Coastal Command with which this example was serving in 1943. The Fortress IIIs included black-painted 'specials' used by the secret 100 Group on bomber support.

Below: This B-17G-25 served in 1944 with the US 8th Army Air Force's 96th Bomb Group at Snetterton Heath. Though a much older design than the B-24 the B-17 predominated in Europe.

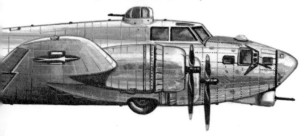

though the wing loading was conservative and an enduring characteristic of every "Fort" was sedate flying.

With the B-17C came a ventral bathtub, flush side guns, armour and self-sealing tanks. In return for combat data 20 were supplied to the RAF, which used them on a few high-altitude daylight raids with 90 Sqn of Bomber Command. It was found that the Norden sight tended to malfunction, the Browning guns to freeze at the high altitude and German fighters to attack from astern in a defensive blind spot. While surviving Fortress Is operated with Coastal and Middle East forces, the improved B-17D joined the US Army and bore the brunt of early fighting in the Pacific. But extensive combat experience led to the redesigned B-17E, with powered dorsal, ventral (ball) and tail turrets, a huge fin for high-altitude bombing accuracy and much more armour and equipment. This went into mass production by Boeing, Lockheed-Vega and Douglas-Tulsa. It was the first weapon of the US 8th Bomber Command in England and on 17 August 1942 began three gruelling years of day strategic bombing in Europe.

Soon the E gave way to the B-17F, of which 3,405 were built, with many detail improvements, including a long Plexiglas nose, paddle-blade propellers and provision for underwing racks. At the end of 1942 came the final

Below: A small portion of an 8th AF B-17G formation (from the 381st Bomb Group) with a P-51B escort fighter just beyond.

Above: Almost certainly taken in 1943, this photograph shows a B-17F in full battle trim, and was taken from the left waist gun position of another. Note olive-drab paint scheme.

bomber model, the B-17G, with chin turret and flush staggered waist guns. A total of 8,680 G models were made, Boeing's Seattle plant alone turning out 16 a day, and the total B-17 run amounted to 12,731. A few B-17Fs were converted to XB-40s, carrying extra defensive guns to help protect the main Bomb Groups, while at least 25 were turned into BQ-7 Aphrodite radio-controlled missiles loaded with 12,000lb of high explosive for use against U-boat shelters. Many F and G models were fitted with H_2X radar with the scanner retracting into the nose or rear fuselage, while other versions included the F-9 reconnaissance, XC-108 executive transport, CB-17 utility transport, PB-1W radar early-warning, PB-1G lifeboat-carrying air/sea rescue and QB-17 target drone. After the war came other photo, training, drone-director, search/rescue and research versions, including many used as engine and equipment testbeds. In 1970, 25 years after first flight, one of many civil Forts used for agricultural or forest-fire protection was re-engined with Dart turboprops!

Below: "Stop" waves a ground-crewman to the skipper of a red-tailed G-model on the green grass of a British base.

Boeing B-29 Superfortress
Model 345, B-29 to -29C

Origin: Boeing Airplane Company, Seattle, Renton and Wichita; also built by Bell Aircraft, Marietta, and Glenn L. Martin Company, Omaha.
Type: High-altitude heavy bomber, with crew of 10–14.
Engines: Four 2,200hp Wright R-3350-23 Duplex Cyclone 18-cylinder radials each with two exhaust-driven turbochargers.
Dimensions: Span 141ft 3in (43·05m); length 99ft (30·2m); height 27ft 9in (8·46m).
Weights: Empty 74,500lb (33,795kg); loaded 135,000lb (61,240kg).
Performance: Maximum speed 357mph (575km/h) at 30,000ft (9144m); cruising speed 290mph (467km/h); climb to 25,000ft (7620m) in 43min; service ceiling 36,000ft (10,973m); range with 10,000lb (4540kg) bombs 3,250miles (5230km).
Armament: Four GE twin-0·50in turrets above and below, sighted from nose or three waist sighting stations; Bell tail turret, with own gunner, with one 20mm cannon and twin 0·50in; internal bomb load up to 20,000lb (9072kg). Carried first two nuclear bombs. With modification, carried two 22,000lb British bombs externally under inner wings.
History: First flight 21 September 1942; (pre-production YB-29) 26 June 1943); squadron delivery July 1943; first combat mission 5 June 1944; last delivery May 1946.
User: US (AAF, Navy).

Development and mass production of the B-29, the Boeing Model 345, was one of the biggest tasks in the history of aviation. It began with a March 1938 study for a new bomber with pressurised cabin and tricycle landing gear. This evolved into the 345 and in August 1940 money was voted for two prototypes. In January 1942 the Army Air Force ordered 14 YB-29s and 500 production aircraft. By February, while Boeing engineers worked night and day on the huge technical problems, a production organisation was set up involving Boeing, Bell, North American and Fisher (General Motors). Martin came in later and, by VJ-day more than 3,000 Superforts

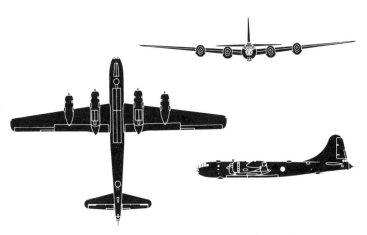

Above: Three-view of B-29 (two-gun forward dorsal turret).

had been delivered. This was a fantastic achievement because each represented five or six times the technical effort of any earlier bomber. In engine power, gross weight, wing loading, pressurisation, armament, airborne systems and even basic structure the B-29 set a wholly new standard. First combat mission was flown by the 58th Bomb Wing on 5 June 1944, and by 1945 20 groups from the Marianas were sending 500 B-29s at a time to flatten and burn Japan's cities. (Three aircraft made emergency landings in Soviet territory, and Tupolev's design bureau put the design into production as the Tu-4 bomber and Tu-70 transport.) The -29C had all guns except those in the tail removed, increasing speed and altitude. After the war there were 19 variants of B-29, not including the Washington B.I supplied to help the RAF in 1950–58.

Below: Two of the first production B-29s, painted olive drab on upper and side surfaces. All subsequent B-29s were delivered unpainted. It was a B-29, "Enola Gay", that dropped the first atomic bomb, on Hiroshima.

Bristol Type 152 Beaufort
Beaufort I to VIII

Origin: Bristol Aeroplane Company; also made by Department of Aircraft Production, Fishermen's Bend, Australia.

Type: Four-seat torpedo bomber.

Engines: Two 1,130hp Bristol Taurus VI 14-cylinder sleeve-valve radials (most other marks, two 1,200hp Pratt & Whitney Twin Wasp).

Dimensions: Span 57ft 10in (17·63m); length 44ft 2in (13·46m); height 14ft 3in (4·34m).

Weights: Empty 13,107lb (5945kg); loaded 21,230lb (9629kg).

Performance: Maximum speed 260mph (418km/h) clean, 225mph (362km/h) with torpedo; service ceiling 16,500ft (5030m); range 1,600 miles (2575km).

Armament: Various, but typically two 0·303in Vickers K in dorsal turret and one fixed forward-firing in left wing, plus one 0·303in Browning in remote-control chin blister. Alternatively four 0·303in Brownings in wing, two Brownings manually aimed from beam windows and (Mk II) twin Brownings in dorsal turret (final 140 Australian Mk VIII, two 0·50in Brownings in dorsal turret). One 18in torpedo semi-external to left of centreline or bomb load of 2,000lb (907kg).

History: First flight 15 October 1938; first delivery October 1939; first flight of Australian aircraft (Mk V) August 1941; last delivery (Australia) August 1944.

Users: Australia, Turkey, UK.

Development: Derived from the Blenheim, the torpedo-carrying Beaufort was inevitably heavier because the Air Staff demanded a crew of four. Performance on Mercury engines was inadequate and, after studying an installation of the sleeve-valve Perseus, the choice fell on the Taurus, an extremely neat two-row engine only 46in in diameter. A clever installation was schemed for this but it overheated and various engine troubles held the programme back in the early days, but 22 and 42 Sqns of Coastal Command were fully operational by August 1940. As well as laying hundreds of mines they bombed the battlecruiser *Scharnhorst*, torpedoed the *Gneisenau* and sank numerous smaller ships. In 1939 plans were laid for Beaufort production in Australia and, because of the difficulty of supplying engines from Britain, the Australian Mks V-VIII had Twin Wasp engines, most of them made in Australia. A large batch of British Beauforts (Mk II) had this engine, but a Merlin-Beaufort was abandoned and from No 165 the Mk II reverted to later models of Taurus. The total built was 2,080, including 700 built in Australia for duty in the Southwest Pacific. Australian models had a bigger fin and progressed through four series with different equipment, ending with transport and trainer versions. The finest RAAF missions were against Japanese fleets at Normanby Island, in the Timor Sea and around New Guinea and the Solomons.

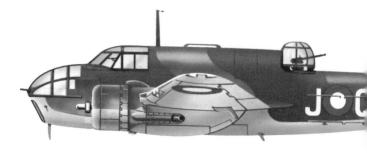

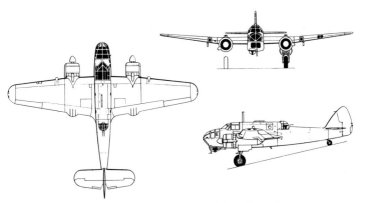

Above: Three-view of Beaufort I Series II with trailing edge extensions and rearward-firing barbette under the nose.

Below: One of the first Beaufort Is to go into operational service was this machine from 42 Sqn, RAF Coastal Command. By 1942 such aircraft had been repainted in the deep sea grey and white colour scheme, while many Beauforts had been sent to the Mediterranean and other overseas theatres. Another change was the addition of semicircular trailing-edge plates as shown in the three-view above.

Left: Australia's biggest wartime production programme of combat aircraft concerned the Beaufort, though in versions slightly different from those built in Britain. All were powered by Pratt & Whitney Twin Wasp engines, and the vast majority were Beaufort VIIIs, one of which is depicted here serving with (probably) 86 Sqn of the RAAF. Features included an improved turret, larger fin and rudder and ASV radar.

continued ▶

Little colour photography was possible in Britain during World War II because such film was virtually unobtainable. This shot shows Beaufort Is of 217 Sqn armed with torpedoes, in 1940 markings. Later, Coastal Command aircraft were grey/white.

Parked in one of the blast pens built at Luqa airport from the bombed buildings of Malta, this Beaufort is a Twin Wasp-powered Mk II. It is probably serving with RAF No 86 Sqn, which took over in Malta when 217 Sqn was posted to Burma.

Bristol Type 142 Blenheim

Types 142 M, 149 and 160 Blenheim/Bisley/ Bolingbroke (data for Blenheim IVL)

Origin: Bristol Aeroplane Company; also made by A. V. Roe, Rootes Securities and Canadian Vickers Ltd.

Type: Three-seat light bomber (IF, IVF, fighter versions).

Engines: Two 920hp Bristol Mercury XV (I, Bolingbroke I, II, 840hp Mercury VIII; Bolingbroke IV series, 750–920hp Twin Wasp Junior, Cyclone or Mercury XX; Blenheim V, 950hp Mercury XXX).

Dimensions: Span 56ft 4in (17·17m) (V, 56ft 1in); length 42ft 9in (13m) (I, 39ft 9in; Bolingbroke III, 46ft 3in; V, 43ft 11in); height 12ft 10in (3·91m) (Bolingbroke III, 18ft).

Weights: Empty 9,790lb (4441kg) (I, Bolingbroke III, 8,700lb; V, 11,000lb); loaded 14,400lb (6531kg) (I, 12,250lb; Bolingbrokes 13,400lb; V, 17,000lb).

Performance: Maximum speed 266mph (428km/h); (I) 285mph; (early IV) 295mph; (Bolingbrokes and V) 245–260mph; initial climb 1,500ft (457m)/min (others similar); service ceiling 31,500ft (9600m) (others similar except Bolingbroke III, 26,000ft); range 1,950 miles (3138km); (I) 1,125 miles; (Bolingbrokes) 1,800 miles; (V) 1,600 miles.

Armament: One 0·303in Vickers K in nose, two 0·303in Brownings in FN.54 chin turret and two 0·303in Brownings in dorsal turret; (I) single fixed Browning and single Vickers K in dorsal turret; (IF, IVF) four fixed Brownings under fuselage; bomb load 1,000lb (454kg) internal (non-standard aircraft had underwing 500lb racks).

History: First flight (Type 142) 12 April 1935; (142M Blenheim I) 25 June 1936; service delivery November 1936; termination of production (VD) June 1943; withdrawal from service (Finland) 1956.

Users: Canada, Finland, France, Greece, Jugoslavia, Lithuania, Portugal, Romania, Turkey, UK (RAF).

Development: It was the newspaper magnate Lord Rothermere who asked the Bristol company to build him a fast executive aircraft to carry a pilot and six passengers at 240mph, appreciably faster than any RAF fighter in 1934. The result was the Type 142, the first modern stressed-skin monoplane in Britain with retractable landing gear, flaps and, after a wait, imported American variable-pitch propellers. Its performance staggered even the designer, Barnwell, for on Air Ministry test it reached 307mph. The inevitable result was the Blenheim bomber, to produce which Barnwell designed a new fuselage with mid-wing and bomb bay beneath it. Pilot and nav/bomb-aimer sat in the neat glazed nose, and a part-retractable dorsal turret was added behind the wing. The Blenheim I was ordered in what were huge quantities to a company almost devoid of work. Ultimately 1,134 were built, many of which made gallant bombing raids early in the war and were then converted to IF fighter configuration (some having the AI Mk III, the first operational fighter radar in the world). The fast new bomber excited ▶

Right: L8609 was one of the Blenheim 1 bombers built in 1937–38 by Roots Securities at the giant new Shadow Factory at Speke, Liverpool. It survived the hectic campaign of 1939–40, when the Blenheim was possibly the busiest type in the RAF, and is shown as it was late in that year serving with 60 Sqn at Lahore, India.

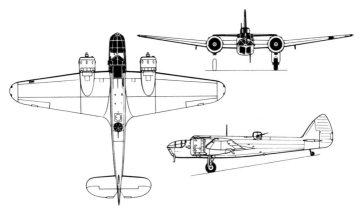

Above: Mk IV as originally delivered without under-nose gun.

Above: Almost certainly taken at Northolt shortly after the start of World War II, this line up of 604 (County of Middlesex) Sqn shows the Mk IF fighter. Soon this acquired the world's first airborne radar and operated mainly by night.

intense foreign interest and many were exported to Finland, Turkey, Jugoslavia, Lithuania, Romania and Greece. To provide a nav/bomb-aimer station ahead of the pilot the nose was then lengthened 3ft and this type was named Bolingbroke, a name retained for all the variety of Blenheims built in Canada (the Bolingbroke Mk III being a twin-float seaplane). A revised asymmetric nose was adopted for production in the speedy Mk IV, which later acquired a fighter gun pack (IVF) or a manual rear-firing chin gun (IVL), finally having a two-gun chin turret. Made by Bristol, Avro and Rootes, like the Mk I, the IV was the main combat version with the RAF, 3,297 being delivered and making many daylight missions in many theatres. The heavily armed and armoured two-seat Bisley attack aircraft did not go into production, but the three-seat equivalent did, as the Blenheim Mk V. Heavy and underpowered, the 902 VDs served in North Africa and the Far East.

Right: Blenheim IV bombers of No 139 Sqn, RAF, painted as they were at the time of the outbreak of war. On 3 September 1939, two hours after the start of hostilities, a 139 Sqn Blenheim was the first Allied aircraft to cross the German frontier.

Below: a rare colour photograph showing aircrew and ground crew of a Blenheim IV in 1941, probably about to go on one of the dangerous 'daylight sweeps' over occupied Europe. Note the asymmetric nose added to provide room for the navigator.

Cant Z.1007 Alcione

Z.1007, 1007 bis and 1018

Origin: CRDA "Cant".
Type: Four/five-seat medium bomber.
Engines: Three 1,000hp Piaggio P.Xlbis RC40 14-cylinder two-row radials.
Dimensions: Span 81ft 4in (24·8m); length 60ft 4in (18·4m); height 17ft 1½in (5·22m).
Weights: Empty 19,000lb (8630kg); loaded 28,260–30,029lb (12,840–13,620kg).
Performance: Maximum speed 280mph (448km/h); initial climb 1,550ft (472m)/min; service, ceiling 26,500ft (8100m); range 800 miles (1280km) with maximum bombs, 3,100 miles (4989km) with maximum fuel.
Armament: (First 25) four 7·7mm Breda-SAFAT machine guns in dorsal turret, two beam hatches and ventral position; (remainder) as before except dorsal and ventral guns 12·7mm Breda-SAFAT; internal bomb capacity 4,410lb (2000kg); alternatively two 1,000lb (454kg) torpedoes and four bombs up to 551lb (250kg) each on underwing racks.
History: First flight May 1937; (first production aircraft) 1939; entry to service 1939.
User: Italy (RA, CB, ARSI).

continued ▶

Below: A priceless colour photograph showing twin-finned Z.1007bis bombers on a bleak airfield which may be in Sicily (it looks like North Africa but only one squadriglia briefly operated in that theatre). Single- and twin-finned Alciones operated together, and there was no distinguishing designation.

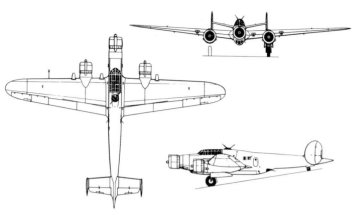

Above: Three-view of typical Z.1007bis (twin-finned version).

Below: Again it is the twin-finned model that forms the subject of this painting, the unit being the 230a Squadriglia, 950 Gruppo. Despite its wooden construction this bomber stood up well to the heat of Libya and the bitter cold of the Russian front.

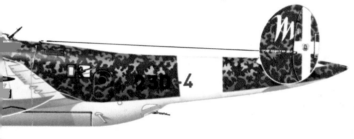

Development: A famous Italian naval yard, the Cantieri Monfalcone (Trieste), entered the aircraft construction business in 1923, forming a subsidiary called Cantieri Riuniti dell' Adriatico (always shortened to Cant). Their first products were seaplanes and flying boats and the most important of these was the three-engined Z.506B Airone (Heron) twin-float seaplane used in large numbers in World War II. Designer Filippo Zappata then produced a landplane bomber version, powered by three 840hp Isotta-Fraschini Asso inverted-vee liquid-cooled engines. Like the seaplane this new bomber, the Z.1007, was built entirely of wood. It received a generally favourable report from the Regia Aeronautica's test pilots and after modifications went into production, two other firms — Meridionali and Piaggio — later being brought in to increase rate of output. Nearly all the several hundred production Alciones (Kingfishers) were powered by the Piaggio radial engine, and this version, the Z.1007 bis, also had a longer fuselage, bigger wings and stronger landing gear. Almost half also had twin tail fins. Though easy meat for RAF fighters, Alciones were bravely operated throughout the Mediterranean, and many even served on the Russian front. Various developments culminated in the excellent twin-engined Z.1018 Leone (Lion), with metal airframe and 1,350hp engines, but few of these had been delivered when Italy surrendered in 1943.

Right: Single-finned Alciones of the 230a Squadriglia in quite tight formation at low level over cultivated but otherwise featureless terrain. The photograph is dated 1940, a year in which fewer than 90 of this type had been delivered.

Caproni Ca 133
Ca 101, 111 and 133 (data for 133)

Origin: Società Italiana Caproni.
Type: Colonial bomber and transport.
Engines: Three 450/460hp Piaggio P.VII RC14 Stella seven-cylinder radials.
Dimensions: Span 69ft 8in (21·3m); length 50ft 4¾in (15·35m); height 13ft 1in (4m).
Weights: Empty 8,598lb (3900kg); loaded 14,330lb (6500kg).
Performance: Maximum speed 174mph (280km/h); initial climb 940ft (286m)/min; service ceiling 21,325ft (6500m); range 839 miles (1350km).
Armament: One or two 7·7mm or one 12·7mm machine gun on pivoted mounting in roof at trailing edge of wing; one machine gun in sliding hatchway in floor of rear fuselage; often one 7·7mm on each side in aft window-openings; bomb load (up to 2,200lb, 1000kg) carried in internal bay and on external racks under fuselage.
History: First flight (Ca 101) 1932; (Ca 111) 1933; (Ca 133) 1935; end of production, prior to 1938.
Users: Austria, Hungary, Italy (RA).

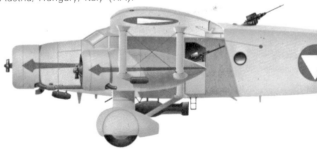

Development: As Mussolini restored "the lost colonies" and Italy forcibly built up an overseas empire, so did the need arise for "colonial" type aircraft similar to the British Wapiti and Vincent. Caproni produced the Ca 101 to meet this need, at least 200 being delivered in the early 1930s to serve as bomber, troop carrier, reconnaissance and ground attack machines and, most of all, to supply forward troops with urgent stores. Powered by three 235hp Alfa Romeo engines, it was made of robust welded steel tube with fabric covering. The Ca 111, powered by a single 950hp Isotta-Fraschini engine, gave even better service and survived the Albanian and Ethiopian campaigns to operate against Jugoslav partisans in World War II. The Ca 133 was the most important of all and many hundreds were built. When Italy entered the war in 1940 it equipped 14 Squadriglie di Bombardimento Terrestri (bomber squadrons), nearly all in East or North Africa. Though scorned by the RAF and easy meat on the ground or in the air, these versatile STOL machines worked hard and well and finished up as ambulances and transports in Libya, on the Russian Front and in Italy (on both sides after the 1943 surrender).

Left: A fully armed Ca 133 of Fliegerregiment 2 of the Austrian Air Force, one of several export customers. In the 1930s these versatile machines gave excellent service, but by the time Italy entered World War II they were outclassed. Their crews called them Vacca (cow) or Caprona (she-goat), which was a play on the name of the manufacturer. Two advanced models, the Ca 142 and 148, did not go into production.

Caproni Ca 135

Ca 135 and 135bis (data for 135bis)

Origin: Società Italiana Caproni.
Type: Five-seat medium bomber.
Engines: Two 1,000hp Piaggio P.XIbis RC40 14-cylinder two-row radials.
Dimensions: Span 61ft 8in (18·75m); length 47ft 1in (14·4m); height 11ft 2in (3·4m).
Weights: Empty 9,921lb (4500kg); loaded 18,740lb (8500kg).
Performance: Maximum speed 273mph (440km/h); initial climb 1,435ft (437m)/min; service ceiling 22,966ft (7000m); range with bomb load 746 miles (1200km).
Armament: Three Breda-SAFAT turrets, each mounting one 12·7mm or two 7·7mm guns, in nose, dorsal and ventral positions (dorsal and ventral retractable); bomb cells in fuselage and inner wings for up to 3,527lb (1600kg) weapon load.
History: First flight (135) 1 April 1935; (135bis) about November 1937.
Users: Hungary, Italy (RA).

Caproni Ca 309-316

Ca 309 Ghibli (Desert Wind), 310 Libeccio (Southwest Wind), 311 and 311M, 312 and variants, 313, 314 and variants and 316

Origin: Cantieri Aeronautici Bergamaschi; production by various other Caproni companies, mainly at Castellamare and Taliedo.
Type: (309) colonial utility, (310) utility transport, (311) light bomber, (312) bomber and torpedo (312bis, 312IS, seaplanes), (313) bomber/torpedo bomber, (314) coastal patrol torpedo bomber, (316) catapult reconnaissance seaplane.
Engines: (309) two 185hp Alfa Romeo A.115 six-in-line; (310, 316) two 470hp Piaggio P.VII C.16 seven-cylinder radials; (311, 312) two

continued ▶

Development: When the great Caproni combine took on Breda's designer Cesare Pallavicino it embarked on a series of modern aircraft of higher performance. The most important appeared to be the Ca 135 medium bomber, designed in the summer of 1934 to meet a Regia Aeronautica specification. A curious blend of wooden wings, light-alloy monocoque forward fuselage and steel tube plus fabric rear fuselage and tail, the prototype had two 800hp Isotta-Fraschini Asso engines but no guns. After over a year of testing the government ordered 14 as the Tipo Spagna to serve in the Spanish civil war. Peru bought six Tipo Peru, eventually purchasing 32. Yet the Ca 135 was not as good as the S.M.79 and Z.1007 by rival makers and the Regia Aeronautica kept delaying a decision. More powerful Fiat A.80 RC41 radials improved behaviour but at the expense of reliability and a good 135 did not appear until the Milan Aero Show in October 1937, when the Piaggio-engined 135bis was displayed. Though never adopted by the Regia Aeronautica it was frequently identified as having been used against Malta, Jugoslavia and Greece! The real raiders in these cases were probably BR.20s, but the 135 bis did find a customer: the Hungarian Air Force. Several hundred were operated by that service whilst attached to Luftflotte IV in the campaign on the Eastern Front in 1941–43.

Left: One of the colourful Ca 135bis bombers operated on the Eastern Front by the Hungarian Air Force (note tactical theatre marking of yellow bands). This example belonged to 4/III Bomb Group, but few of the Capronis lasted even until the end of 1942, and they were progressively replaced by superior German aircraft such as the Ju 88.

Above: The Ca 310 Libeccio was the first of the family to have retractable landing gear. This example is a civil-registered aircraft, probably used as a six-seat colonial transport, but most had a bomb-aimer's position in the nose and three machine guns, two fixed in the wing roots and one in the retractable turret.

Left: This Ca 310 is one of the armed multi-role models, and it was one of a batch sold in 1939 to the Norwegian army flying service (Haerens Flyvevàben). It was based at Sola airfield, Stavanger, where it was probably knocked out on 9 April 1940. The Ca 310 lacked the range to escape to Britain.

The Ca 314 was one of the most powerful and most important of the entire family. The fully glazed interior was similar to that of the Anson, but the Italian machine was much more powerful and this version could carry a torpedo.

650hp Piaggio P.XVI RC35 nine-cylinder radials; (313, 314) two 650hp Isotta-Fraschini Delta RC35 inverted-vee-12.

Dimensions: Span (309-312) 53ft 1¾in (16·20m), (313) 52ft 10½in (16·11m), (314) 54ft 7½in (16·65m), (316) 52ft 2in (15·90m); length (309) 43ft 7½in (13·30m), (311, 313, 314) 38ft 8in (11·79m), (310, 312) 40ft 0½in (12·20m), (316) 42ft 3in (12·88m); height 10ft 8in to 13ft 3in (floatplanes about 16ft 9in) (3·26 to 4·04m, floatplanes 5·10m).

Weights: Empty (309) 3,850lb (1746kg), (others) about 7,050lb (3200kg); loaded (309) 6,067lb (2750kg), (others) 10,252–13,580lb (4650–6160kg).

Performance: Maximum speed (309) 158mph (254km/h), (others) 227–271mph (365–435km/h) except 316 only 204mph (328km/h).

Armament: See text.

History: First flight (309) 1936; main production 1938–42.

Users: Italy (civil, RA, CB, ARSI, post-war AF), Germany (Luftwaffe), Croatia, Hungary, Jugoslavia, Norway, Spain, Sweden.

Development: This diverse family had wooden wings, and fuselages of welded steel tube covered with fabric. The Ghibli was a light multi-role machine for African use, with radio, cameras, light bomb racks and two machine guns (one fixed, one in a dorsal position). The more powerful examples carried up to five 12·7mm and three 7·7mm guns with bomb/torpedo loads up to 1,764lb (800kg). Total production of all models was about 2,400.

Below: The Ca 311 and (shown here) 312 had a streamlined nose with no stepped windscreen. The radial engines were similar in power to the aircooled inverted V-12s of the Ca 314 above.

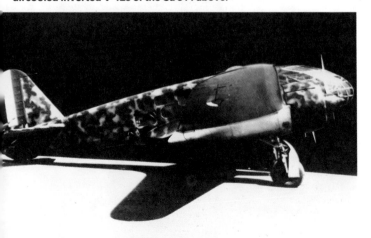

Consolidated Vultee Model 32 B-24 Liberator

For variants, see text
(data for B-24J Liberator B.VI)

Origin: Consolidated Vultee Aircraft Corporation; also built by Douglas, Ford and North American Aviation.

Type: Long-range bomber with normal crew of ten.

Engines: Four 1,200hp Pratt & Whitney R-1830-65 Twin Wasp 14-cylinder two-row radials.

Dimensions: Span 110ft 0in (33·5m); length 67ft 2in (20·47m); height 18ft 0in (5·49m).

Weights: Empty 37,000lb (16,783kg); loaded 65,000lb (29,484kg).

Performance: Maximum speed 290mph (467km/h); initial climb 900ft (274m)/min; service ceiling 28,000ft (8534m); range at 190mph (306km/h) with 5,000lb (2268kg) bomb load 2,200 miles (3540km).

Armament: Ten 0·50in Brownings arranged in four electrically operated turrets (Consolidated or Emerson in nose, Martin dorsal, Briggs-Sperry retractable ventral "ball" and Consolidated or Motor Products tail) with two guns each plus two singles in manual waist positions; two bomb bays with roll-up doors with vertical racks on each side of central catwalk for up to 8,000lb (3629kg); two 4,000lb (1814kg) bombs could be hung externally on inner-wing racks instead of internal load.

History: First flight (XB-24) 29 December 1939; first delivery (LB-30A) March 1941; first combat service (Liberator I) June 1941; first combat service with US Army (B-24C) November 1941; termination of production 31 May 1945; withdrawal from service (various smaller air forces) 1955–56.

Users: Australia, Brazil, Canada, China, Czechoslovakia, France, India, Italy (CB), New Zealand, Portugal, South Africa, Soviet Union, Turkey, UK (RAF, BOAC), US (AAF, Navy, Marines); other countries post-war.

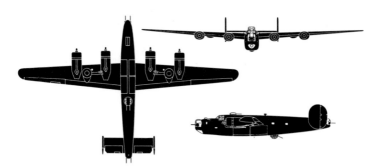

Above; Three-view of B-24H (B-24J similar except front turret).

Development: This distinctive aircraft was one of the most important in the history of aviation. Conceived five years after the B-17 it did not, in fact, notably improve on the older bomber's performance and in respect of engine-out performance and general stability and control it was inferior, being a handful for the average pilot. It was also by far the most complicated and expensive combat aircraft the world had seen — though in this it merely showed the way things were going to be in future. Yet it was built in bigger numbers than any other American aircraft in history, in more versions for more purposes than any other aircraft in history, and served on every front in World War II and with 15 Allied nations. In terms of industrial effort it transcended anything seen previously in any sphere of endeavour.

It had a curious layout, dictated by the slender Davis wing placed above the tall bomb bays. This wing was efficient in cruising flight, which combined with great fuel capacity to give the "Lib" longer range than any other landplane of its day. But it meant that the main gears were long, and they were retracted outwards by electric motors, nearly everything on board being electric. Early versions supplied to the RAF were judged not combat-ready, and they began the Atlantic Return Ferry Service as LB-30A transports. Better defences led to the RAF Liberator I, used by Coastal Command with ►

Left: Though the B-17 Fortress was the more important USAAF bomber in the European theatre, the B-24 was made in much greater numbers and saw action on every Allied front, and with many air forces. This Liberator B.VI operated with 356 Sqn RAF from Salbani, India.

Below: One of the dramatic pictures taken on the raid on the Ploesti (Romania) refinery on 31 May 1944.

ASV radar and a battery of fixed 20mm cannon. The RAF Liberator II (B-24C) introduced power turrets and served as a bomber in the Middle East. The first mass-produced version was the B-24D, with turbocharged engines in oval cowls, more fuel and armament and many detail changes; 2,738 served US Bomb Groups in Europe and the Pacific, and RAF Coastal Command closed the mid-Atlantic gap, previously beyond aircraft range, where U-boat packs lurked.

Biggest production of all centred on the B-24G, H and J (Navy PB4Y and RAF B.VI and GR.VI), of which 10,208 were built. These all had four turrets, and were made by Convair, North American, Ford and Douglas. Other variants included the L and M with different tail turrets, the N with single fin, the luridly painted CB-24 lead ships, the TB-24 trainer, F-7 photo-reconnaissance, C-109 fuel tanker and QB-24 drone. There was also a complete family of Liberator Transport versions, known as C-87 Liberator Express to the Army, RY-3 to the Navy and C.VII and C.IX to the RAF, many having the huge single fin also seen on the PB4Y-2 Privateer. Excluding one-offs such as the redesigned R2Y transport and 1,800 equivalent aircraft delivered as spares, total production of all versions was a staggering 19,203. Their achievements were in proportion.

Consolidated Vultee Model 33 B-32 Dominator
XB-32, B-32 and TB-32

Origin: Consolidated Vultee Aircraft Corporation (Convair), Fort Worth, Texas; second-source production by Convair, San Diego.
Type: Long-range strategic bomber; (TB) crew trainer.
Engines: Four 2,300hp Wright R-3350-23 Duplex Cyclone 18-cylinder radials.
Dimensions: Span 135ft 0in (41·15m); length 83ft 1in (25·33m); height 32ft 9in (9·98m).
Weights: Empty 60,272lb (27,340kg); loaded 111,500lb (50,576kg); maximum 120,000lb (54,432kg).
Performance: Maximum speed 365mph (587km/h); service ceiling at normal loaded weight 35,000ft (10,670m); range (max bomb load) 800 miles (1287km), (max fuel) 3,800 miles (6115km).
Armament: (XB) two 20mm and 14 0·50in guns in seven remote-controlled turrets; (B) ten 0·50in in nose, two dorsal, ventral and tail turrets; max bomb load 20,000lb (9072kg) in tandem fuselage bays.
History: First flight (XB) 7 September 1942; service delivery (B) 1 November 1944.
User: USA (AAF).

Development: Ordered in September 1940, a month after the XB-29, the XB-32 was designed to the same Hemisphere Defense Weapon specification and followed similar advanced principles with pressurized cabins and remote-controlled turrets. Obviously related to the smaller B-24, the XB-32 had a slender wing passing above the capacious bomb bays, but the twin-wheel main gears folded into the large inner nacelles. There was a smoothly streamlined nose, like the XB-29, and twin fins. The second aircraft introduced a stepped pilot windscreen and the third a vast single fin like the final B-24 versions. Eventually the heavy and complex armament system was scrapped and replaced by simpler manned turrets, while in late 1943 the decision was taken to eliminate the troublesome pressurization and operate at 30,000ft or below. The B-32 was late and disappointing, though still a great performer. Large orders were placed at Fort Worth and

Above: To assist the gigantic formations of the 8th Air Force to form up, each Bomb Group had a distinctively painted lead ship. This spotted B-24H belonged to the 458th BG, based at Horsham St Faith, Norwich.

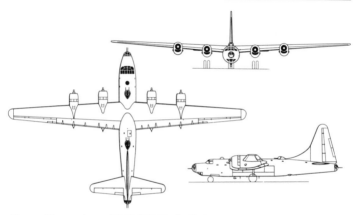

Above: Three-view of B-32 (TB-32 similar).

San Diego, but only 115 had been delivered by VJ-day and a single squadron in the Marianas made two combat missions.

Below: One of the production B-32 Dominators, with full armament. Few of these bombers saw active service.

Dornier Do 17

Do 17E, F, P, U and Z and Do 215

Origin: Dornier-Werke GmbH.
Type: (E, F, P) three-seat bomber (F = recon); (U) five-seat pathfinder; (Z, 215) four-seat bomber/recon.
Engines: (E, F) two 750hp BMW VI 7, 3 water-cooled vee-12; (P) two 865hp BMW 132N nine-cylinder radials; (Do 215B-1) two 1,075hp Daimler-Benz DB 601A 12-cylinder inverted-vee liquid-cooled.
Dimensions: (Both) span 59ft 0½in (18m); length 51ft 9½in (15·79m); height 14ft 11½in (4·56m).
Weights: Empty (Do 17Z-2) 11,484lb (5210kg); (Do 215B-1) 12,730lb (5775kg); loaded (both) 19,841lb (9000kg).
Performance: Maximum speed (Do 17Z-2) 263mph (425km/h); (Do 215B-1) 280mph (450km/h); service ceiling (Do 17Z-2) 26,740ft (8150m); (Do 215B-1) 31,170ft (9500m); range with half bomb load (Do 17Z-2) 721 miles (1160km); (Do 215B-1) 932 miles (1500km).
Armament: Normally six 7·92mm Rheinmetall MG 15 machine guns, one fixed in nose, remainder on manually aimed mounts in front windscreen, two beam windows, and above and below at rear; internal bomb load up to 2205lb (1000kg).
History: First flight (civil prototype) 23 November 1934; (Do 17Z-2) early 1939; (Do 215V1 prototype) late 1938; first delivery (Do 17Z-1) January 1939, (Do 215A-1) December 1939; termination of production (Do 17Z series) July 1940, (Do 215 series) January 1941.
Users: Croatia (puppet of Germany), Finland, Germany (Luftwaffe), Jugoslavia and Spain.

Development: Dornier designed the Do 17 as a fast passenger airliner, but made it so slim (early models got the nickname "Flying Pencil") that Lufthansa deemed it unacceptable for fare-paying customers. By chance ►

Below: It is easy to see from this photograph why early versions of the Do 17 were called 'flying pencils'. This is a Do 17P-1, resembling the E and F (drawings, upper right) but with 865hp BMW 132N radials. It equipped 22 reconnaissance squadrons in 1939.

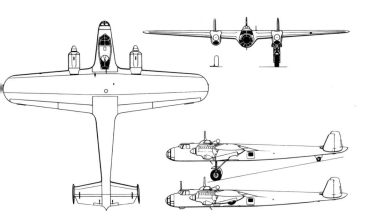

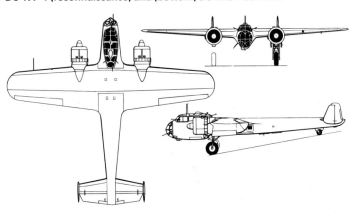

Above: Three-view of the first major Luftwaffe versions, the Do 17F-1 (reconnaissance) and (bottom) Do 17E-1 bomber.

Above: Three-view of the Do 17Z-2.

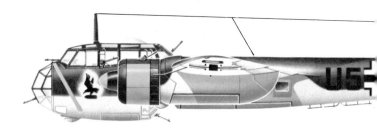

an Air Ministry officer test-flew a prototype and was so impressed he suggested it could form the basis of a bomber. By the end of 1935 the Do 17E and F were on order from three large factories, and with the more powerful P formed the basis of tactical bomber strength in the late 1930s. In 1938 Dornier produced a new and much more capacious nose housing four men and with a gun firing below to the rear. This led to the main wartime model, the Z, and 215.

Considerably heavier, the Do 17Z, powered by the Bramo radial, was at first underpowered and full bomb load had to await the more powerful Fafnir 323P of the 17Z-2. Between late 1939 and the summer of 1940 about 535 Do 17Z series bomber and reconnaissance machines were delivered and, though they suffered high attrition over Britain, they did much

Left: Most important of all Do 17 and 215 variants was the Do 17Z-2, the more powerful version of the new 1939 series with enlarged crew compartment rather like that of the larger and more capable Ju 88. This Z-2 belonged to III/KG 2, one of the crack Luftwaffe bomber units in the first two years of war. By the end of 1941 KG 2 had re-equipped with the Do 217E.

effective work and were the most popular and reliable of all Luftwaffe bombers of the early Blitzkrieg period. The Do 215 was the Do 17Z renumbered as an export version, with the more powerful DB 601 engine. The Do 215A-1 for Sweden became the Do 215B-0 and B-1 for the Luftwaffe and altogether 101 were put into service for bomber and reconnaissance roles; 12 were converted as Do 215B-5 night intruders, with a "solid" nose carrying two cannon and four machine guns, and operated by night over Britain before transfer to Sicily in October 1941.

Below: Pumping hot air into a Do 17Z-2 of III/KG 3 in bitter weather on the Eastern Front about six months after the invasion of the Soviet Union. All were replaced by the end of 1942.

Dornier Do 217

Do 217E-2, K-2, M-1, J-2/N-2, P-1

Origin: Dornier-Werke GmbH.
Type: (E, K, M) four-seat bomber; (J, N) three-seat night fighter; (P) four-seat high-altitude reconnaissance.
Engines: (E-2, J-2) two 1,580hp BMW 801A or 801M 18-cylinder two-row radials; (K-2) two 1,700hp BMW 801D; (M-1, N-2) two 1,750hp Daimler-Benz DB 603A 12-cylinder inverted-vee liquid-cooled; (P-1) two 1,860hp DB 603B supercharged by DB 605T in the fuselage.
Dimensions: Span 62ft 4in (19m); (K-2) 81ft 4½in (24·8m); (P-1) 80ft 4in (24·4m); length 56ft 9¼in (17·3m); (E-2 with early dive brakes) 60ft 10½in (18·5m); (K-2 and M-1) 55ft 9in (17m); (J and N) 58ft 9in (17·9); (P) 58ft 11in (17·95m); height 16ft 5in (5m) (all versions same within 2in).
Weights: Empty (E-2) 19,522lb (8850kg); (M-1) 19,985 (9000kg); (K-2, J and N) all about 21,000lb (9450kg); (P) about 23,000lb (10,350kg); loaded (E-2) 33,070lb (15,000kg); (K-2, M-1) 36,817lb (16,570kg); (J and N) 30,203lb (13,590kg); (P) 35,200lb (15,840kg).
Performance: Maximum speed (E-2) 320mph (515km/h); (K-2) 333mph (533km/h); (M-1) 348mph (557km/h); (J and N) about 311mph (498km/h); (P) 488mph (781km/h); service ceiling (E-2) 24,610ft (7500m); (K-2) 29,530ft (9000m); (M-1) 24,140ft (7358m); (J and N) 27,560ft (8400m); (P) 53,000ft (16,154m); range with full bomb load, about 1,300 miles (2100km) for all versions.

Right: This Do 217E-2 R19 served with 9/KG 2 based at Gilze-Rijen on night missions against England in 1941-43. The designation suffix R19 denoted the fitting of MG 81Z, twin MG 81 guns in the tailcone.

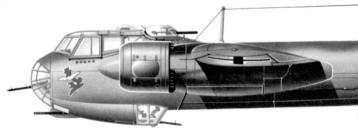

Right: A Do 217E-5 of 6/KG 100 based at Istres, near Marseilles. This was one of the first aircraft to use the Hs 293 radio-guided missile in action.

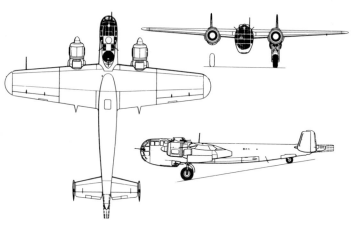

Above: The Do 217K-1 with new cockpit but original wing.

Armament: (E-2) one fixed 15mm MG 151/15 in nose, one 13mm MG 131 in dorsal turret, one MG 131 manually aimed at lower rear, and three 7·92mm MG 15 manually aimed in nose and beam windows; maximum bomb load 8818lb (4000kg), including 3307lb (1500kg) external; (K-2) defensive armament similar to E-2, plus battery of four 7·92mm MG 81 fixed rearward-firing in tail and optional pair fixed rearward-firing in nacelles (all sighted and fired by pilot), and offensive load of two FX 1400 ▶

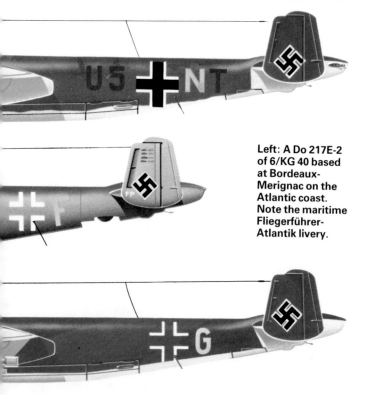

Left: A Do 217E-2 of 6/KG 40 based at Bordeaux-Merignac on the Atlantic coast. Note the maritime Fliegerführer-Atlantik livery.

radio-controlled glide bombs and/or (K-3 version) two Hs 293 air-to-surface rocket guided missiles; (M-1) as E-2 except MG 15s replaced by larger number of MG 81; (J-2 and N-2) typically four 20mm MG FF cannon and four 7·92mm MG 17 in nose plus MG 131 for lower rear defence (N-2 often had later guns such as MG 151/20 in nose and MG 151/20 or MK 108 30mm in Schräge Musik upward-firing installation); (P) three pairs of MG 81 for defence, and two 1102lb bombs on underwing racks.

History: First flight (Do 217V1) August 1938; (pre-production Do 217A-0) October or November 1939; first delivery of E series, late 1940; termination of production, late 1943.

Users: Germany (Luftwaffe), (217 J) Italy (RA).

Development: Superficially a scaled-up Do 215, powered at first by the same DB 601 engines, the 217 was actually considerably larger and totally different in detail design. Much of Dornier's efforts in 1938–40 were devoted to finding more powerful engines and improving the flying qualities, and when the BMW 801 radial was available the 217 really got into its stride and carried a heavier bomb load than any other Luftwaffe bomber of the time. Early E models, used from late 1940, had no dorsal turret and featured a

Above: Heaviest of all the regular Do 217 bomber versions was the 217K-2. Major structural stiffening and other changes allowed the wing span to be extended to 81ft 4½in and enabled takeoffs to be made with additional fuel as well as two of the monster Fritz-X radio-controlled bombs which weighed 3,454lb each. This aircraft, Werk-Nr 4572, was the first of the K-2 series.

very long extension of the rear fuselage which opened into an unusual dive brake. This was soon abandoned, but the 217 blossomed out into a prolific family which soon included the 217J night fighter, often produced by converting E-type bombers, and the N which was likewise produced by converting the liquid-cooled M. Several series carried large air-to-surface missiles steered by radio command from a special crew station in the bomber. Long-span K-2s of III/KG 100 scored many successes with their formidable missiles in the Mediterranean, their biggest bag being the Italian capital ship *Roma* as she steamed to the Allies after Italy's capitulation. The pressurised high-altitude P series had fantastic performance that would have put them out of reach of any Allied fighters had they been put into service in time. From 1943, Dornier devoted more effort to the technically difficult Do 317, which never went into service.

Left: In the foreground is a Do 217N-1 night fighter, with DB 603A liquid-cooled engines, FuG 202 Lichtenstein BC radar and heavy cannon armament. The subsequent N-2 version discarded the turret. In the background is an experimental prototype in the E-series.

Below: Still in factory code letters, this was the sixth of the pre-production batch of Do 217E-0 bombers of September/October 1940.

Douglas A-26 Invader

A-26 (later B-26) and JD-1 Invader; rebuilt as B-26K, redesignated A-26A

Origin: Douglas Aircraft Company; (post-war B-26K) On Mark Engineering.
Type: Three-seat attack bomber; FA-26 reconnaissance, JD target tug.
Engines: Two 2,000hp Pratt & Whitney R-2800-27, -71 or -79 Double Wasp 18-cylinder two-row radials; On Mark B-26K, 2,500hp R-2800-103W.
Dimensions: Span 70ft (21·34m) (B-26K, 75ft, 22·86m, over tip tanks); length 50ft (15·24m); height 18ft 6in (5·64m).
Weights: Empty, typically 22,370lb (10,145kg); loaded, originally 27,000lb (12,247kg) with 32,000lb (14,515kg) maximum overload, later increased to 35,000lb (15,876kg) with 38,500lb (17,460kg) maximum overload.
Performance: Maximum speed 355mph (571km/h); initial climb 2,000ft (610m)/min; service ceiling 22,100ft (6736m); range with maximum bomb load 1,400 miles (2253km).
Armament: (A-26B) ten 0·5in Brownings, six fixed in nose and two each in dorsal and ventral turrets; internal bomb load of 4,000lb (1814kg), later supplemented by underwing load of up to 2,000lb (907kg); (A-26C) similar but only two 0·5in in nose; (B-26K, A-26A) various nose configurations with up to eight 0·5in or four 20mm, plus six 0·30in guns in wings and total ordnance load of 8,000lb (3629kg) in bomb bay and on eight outerwing pylons.
History: First flight (XA-26) 10 July 1942; service delivery December 1943; final delivery 2 January 1946; first flight of B-26K, February 1963.
Users: US (AAF, Navy).

Development: The Douglas Invader has a unique history. It was one of very few aircraft to be entirely conceived, designed, developed, produced in quantity and used in large numbers all during World War II. The whole programme was terminated after VJ-Day and anyone might have judged the aircraft finished. With new jets under development, Douglas made no effort to retain any design team on Invader development, neither did the Army Air Force show any interest. Yet this aircraft proved to be of vital importance in the Korean war and again in Vietnam and, by 1963, was urgently being manufactured for arduous front-line service. Some were in combat units 33 years after they were first delivered, a record no other kind of aircraft can equal. The design was prepared by Ed Heinemann at El Segundo as a natural successor to the DB-7 family, using the powerful new R-2800 engine. The Army Air Corps ordered three prototypes in May 1941, one with 75mm gun, one with four 20mm forward-firing cannon

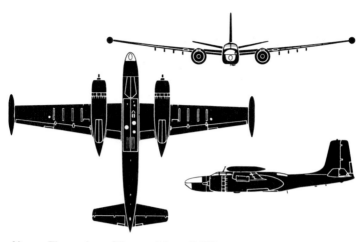

Above: Three-view of the much later B-26K.

and four 0·5in guns in an upper turret, with radar nose, and the third as an attack bomber with optical sighting station in the nose and two defensive turrets. In the event it was the bomber that was bought first, designated A-26B. Much faster than other tactical bombers with the exception of the Mosquito, it was 700lb lighter than estimate, and capable of carrying twice the specified bomb load. It was the first bomber to use a NACA laminar-flow airfoil, double-slotted flaps and remote-control turrets (also a feature of the B-29). Combat missions with the 9th AF began on 19 November 1944 and these aircraft dropped over 18,000 tons of bombs on European targets. A total of 1,355 A-26Bs were delivered, the last 535 having -79 engines boosted by water injection. The A-26C, in service in January 1945, had a transparent nose, lead-ship navigational equipment and was often fitted with H_2S panoramic radar; production of this model was 1,091. In 1948 the B-26 Marauder was retired from service and the Invaders were redesignated B-26. Over 450 were used in Korea, and in Vietnam these fine aircraft were one of the most favoured platforms for night attack on the Ho Chi Minh trail and in other interdiction areas. Though top speed was depressed to about 350mph, the A-26A (as the rebuilt B-26K was called) could carry up to 11,000lb (4990kg) of armament and deliver it accurately and, with 2 hr over target, over a wide radius. In 1977 six air forces retained Invader squadrons.

Below: Most of the Invaders used in World War II were 'solid-nosed' A-26bs. All ten heavy machine guns could fire ahead.

Douglas DB-7 family
A-20, Boston, Havoc

A-20, Boston, Havoc, BD-2, F-3 and P-70

Origin: Douglas Aircraft Company; (Boston IIIA, Boeing Airplane Company).

Type: Two-seat fighter and intruder, three-seat bomber or two-seat reconnaissance aircraft.

Engines: Early DB-7 versions (Boston I, II, Havoc II) two 1,200hp Pratt & Whitney R-1830-S3C4-G Twin Wasp 14-cylinder two-row radials; all later versions, two 1,500, 1,600 or 1,700hp Wright GR-2600-A5B, -11, -23 or -29 Double Cyclone 14-cylinder two-row radials.

Dimensions: Span 61ft 4in (18·69m); length varied from 45ft 11in to 48ft 10in (A-20G, 48ft 4in, 14·74m); height 17ft 7in (5·36m).

Weights: Early Boston/Havoc, typically empty 11,400lb (5171kg), loaded 16,700lb (7574kg); (A-20G, typical of main production) empty 12,950lb (5874kg), loaded 27,200lb (12,340kg).

Performance: Maximum speed, slowest early versions 295mph (475km/h); fastest versions 351mph (565km/h); (A-20G) 342mph (549km/h); initial climb 1,200–2,000ft (366–610m)/min; service ceiling typically 25,300ft (7720m); range with maximum weapon load typically 1,000 miles (1,610km).

Armament: (Havoc I), eight 0·303in Brownings in nose, one 0·303in Vickers K manually aimed in rear cockpit; (Havoc II) twelve 0·303in in nose, (Havoc intruder), four 0·303in in nose, one Vickers K, and 1,000lb (454kg) bomb load; (A-20B) two fixed 0·5in Brownings on sides of nose, one 0·5in manually aimed dorsal, one 0·30in manually aimed ventral, 2,000lb (907kg) bomb load; (Boston III bomber) four fixed 0·303in on sides of nose, twin manually aimed 0·303in dorsal, twin manually aimed 0·303in ventral, 2,000lb (907kg) bomb load; (Boston III intruder) belly tray of four 20mm Hispano cannon, 2,000lb (907kg) bomb load; (A-20G) four 20mm and two 0·5in or six 0·5in in nose, dorsal turret with two 0·5in, manually aimed 0·5in ventral, 4,000lb (1814kg) bomb load. Many other schemes, early A-20s having fixed rearward firing 0·30in in each nacelle.

History: First flight (Douglas 7B) 26 October 1938; (production DB-7) 17 August 1939; service delivery (France) 2 January 1940; termination of production September 1944.

Users: Australia, Brazil, Canada, France, Netherlands, New Zealand, South Africa, Soviet Union, UK (RAF), US (AAC/AAF, Navy).

Development: Designed by Jack Northrop and Ed Heinemann, the DB-7 family was one of the great combat aircraft of all time. Originally planned to meet a US Army Air Corps attack specification of 1938, it was dramatically altered and given more powerful Twin Wasp engines and a nosewheel-type landing gear (for the first time in a military aircraft). In February 1939 the French government ordered 100 of a further modified type, with deeper but narrower fuselage and other gross changes. This model, the DB-7, went into production at El Segundo and Santa Monica,

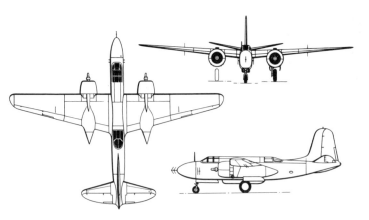

Above: Three-view of P-70 with four M-2 cannon and AI.IV radar.

with 1,764lb (800kg) bomb load and armament of six 7·5mm MAC 1934 machine guns. Delivery took place via Casablanca and about 100 reached the Armée de l'Air, beginning operations on 31 May 1940. Much faster than other bombers, the DB-7 was judged "hot", because it was a modern aircraft in an environment of small unpaved airfields and because it was very different, and more complex, than contemporary European machines. One unusual feature was the emergency control column in the rear gunner's cockpit for use if the pilot should be killed. A few DB-7s escaped to Britain, where most of the French order was diverted (increased to 270 by 1940), and over 100 were converted at Burtonwood, Lancs, into Havoc night fighters. Many Havocs had 2,700-million candlepower "Turbinlites" in the nose for finding enemy raiders by night, while 93 Sqn towed Long Aerial Mine charges on steel cables. In February 1942 the RAF began operations with the much more powerful Boston III; making daring daylight low-level raids over Europe, while production of the first US Army A-20s got into its stride. By far the most important model was the A-20G, with heavier bomb load, dorsal turret and devastating nose armament. Among many other important US Army versions were the P-70 night fighters and the transparent-nosed A-20J and K, often used as bombing lead ships by the 9th and 15th Air Forces (respectively in Northwest Europe and Italy). The RAF counterparts of the J and K were the Boston IV and V, of the 2nd Tactical Air Force and Desert AF (Italy). Total production of this hard-hitting aircraft was 7,385, of which 3,125 were supplied freely to the Soviet Union.

Left: Distinguished by its narrow, pointed vertical tail, this Havoc I was one of the first versions used by the RAF in 1940. A night intruder, in this case operated by 23 Sqn at Ford, Sussex, it retained a glazed nose; most later RAF Havocs were true night interceptors with a 'solid' nose filled with guns. The early Mk I had low-power Twin Wasp engines with locally added flame dampers, one of which is visible as a grey muff over the end of the exhaust pipe. Note old Vickers K rear gun.

Fairey Battle

Battle I to IV (data for II)

Origin: The Fairey Aviation Company; and Avions Fairey, Belgium; shadow production by Austin Motors.
Type: Three-seat light bomber.
Engine: One 1,030hp Rolls-Royce Merlin II vee-12 liquid-cooled.
Dimensions: Span 54ft 0in (16·46m); length 42ft 1¾in (12·85m); height 15ft 6in (4·72m).
Weights: Empty 6,647lb (3015kg); loaded 10,792lb (4895kg).
Performance: Maximum speed 241mph (388km/h); initial climb 920ft (280m)/min; service ceiling 25,000ft (7620m); range with bomb load at economical setting 900 miles (1448km).
Armament: One 0·303in Browning fixed in right wing and one 0·303in Vickers K manually aimed in rear cockpit; bomb load up to 1,000lb (454kg) in four cells in inner wings.
History: First flight (prototype) 10 March 1936; production Mk I, June 1937; final delivery January 1941; withdrawal from service 1949.
User: Australia, Belgium, Canada, Poland, South Africa, Southern Rhodesia, Turkey, UK (RAF).

Development: The Battle will forever be remembered as a combat aeroplane which seemed marvellous when it appeared and yet which, within four years, was being hacked out of the sky in droves so that, ever afterward, aircrew think of the name with a shudder. There was nothing faulty about the aircraft; it was simply a sitting duck for modern fighters. Designed to Specification P.27/32 as a replacement for the biplane Hart and Hind, this clean cantilever stressed-skin monoplane epitomised modern design and carried twice the bomb load for twice the distance at 50 per cent higher speed. It was the first aircraft to go into production with the new Merlin engine, taking its mark number (I, II, III or IV) from that of the engine. Ordered in what were previously unheard-of quantities (155, then 500 and then 863 from a new Austin 'shadow factory'), production built up faster than for any other new British aircraft; 15 RAF bomber squadrons were equipped between May 1937 and May 1938. When World War II began, more than 1,000 were in service and others were exported to Poland, Turkey and Belgium (where 18 were built by Avions Fairey). On 2 September 1939 ten Battle squadrons flew to France as the major offensive element of the Advanced Air Striking Force. They were plunged into furious fighting from 10 May 1940 and suffered grievously. On the first day of the Blitzkrieg in the West two members of 12 Sqn won posthumous VCs and four days later, in an all-out attack on German pontoon bridges at Sedan, 71 Battles attacked and 31 returned. Within six months all Battles were being replaced in front-line units and the survivors of the 2,419 built were shipped to Canada or Australia as trainers (many with separate instructor/pupil cockpits) or used as target tugs or test beds.

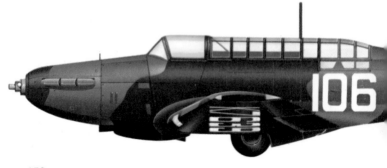

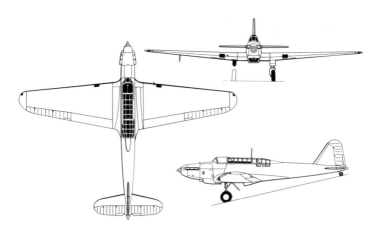

Above: Three-view of a standard Battle bomber (Mks I to IV).

Above: Flap position suggests this Battle has just landed. The yellow roundel ring was added to most Battles after the débacle in France, where the usual roundel was equal radii red, white and blue, often with striped rudder (not fin).

Left: Battle I in 1938 markings serving with 106 Sqn. Officially called Type B, the two-colour roundels were similar to those used from World War I by heavy night bombers, and were adopted to render the Battles less conspicuous. But in 1940 white had been restored – not that it made much difference.

Farman F222

F 221, 222 and 223 series

Origin: SNCA du Centre (until 1936 the Farman company).
Type: All, basically, five-seat heavy bombers.
Engines: (F 221) four 800hp Gnome-Rhône GR14Kbrs 14-cylinder two-row radials; (F 222) four 860hp GR14Kbrs; (F 222/2) four 950hp GR14N 11/15 or Kirs; (F 223) four 1,100hp Hispano-Suiza HS14Aa08/09 vee-12 liquid-cooled; NC 223.3, four 910hp HS12Y29; (NC 223.4) four 1,050hp HS12Y37.
Dimensions: Span (F 221, 222, 222/2) 118ft 1½in (36m); (F 223, NC 223) 110ft 2⅝in (33·5m); length (F 221–222/2) 70ft 8¾in (21·5m); (F 223, NC 223) 72ft 2in (22m); (NC 223.4) 77ft 1in (23·5m); height (all) 16ft 9in to 17ft 2¼in (5·22m).
Weights: Empty (F 222/2) 23,122lb (10,488kg); (NC 223.3) 23,258lb (10,550kg); (NC 223.4) 22,046lb (10,000kg); loaded (F 221) 39,242lb (17,800kg); (F 222/2) 41,226lb (18,700kg); (NC 223.3) 42,329lb (19,200kg); (NC 223.4) 52,911lb (24,000kg).
Performance: Maximum speed (F 221) 185mph (300km/h); (F 222/2) 199mph (320km/h); (NC 223.3) 248mph (400km/h) (264mph as unarmed prototype); (NC 223.4) 239mph (385km/h); service ceiling (F 221) 19,700ft (6000m); (F 222/2) 26,250ft (8000m); (NC 223.3 at maximum weight) 24,606ft (7500m); (NC 223.4 at maximum weight) 13,120ft (4000m); range with maximum bomb load (F 221) 745 miles (1200km); F 222/2) 1,240 miles (2000km); (NC 223.3) 1,490 miles (2400km); (NC 223.4) 3,107 miles (5000km).
Armament: (F 221) three manually aimed 7·5mm MAC 1934 machine guns in nose turret, dorsal and ventral positions; bomb load seldom carried; (F 222/2) same guns as 221; normal bomb load of 5,510lb with maximum internal capacity of 9,240lb (4190kg); (NC 223·3) one MAC 1934 manually aimed in nose, one 20mm Hispano 404 cannon in SAMM 200 dorsal turret, one 20mm Hispano 404 in SAMM 109 ventral turret; internal bomb load of 9,240lb. NC 223·4, one manually aimed 7·5mm Darne machine gun in entry door; internal bomb load of 4,410lb (eight 250kg bombs).
History: First flight (F 211) October 1931; (F 221) 1933; (F 222) June

Fiat B. R. 20 Cicogna

B.R.20, 20M and 20 bis

Origin: Aeronautica d'Italia SA Fiat.
Type: Heavy bomber, with normal crew of five or six.
Engines: (B.R.20) two 1,000hp Fiat A.80 RC41 18-cylinder two-row radials; (B.R.20M) as B.R.20 or two 1,100hp A.80 RC20; (B.R.20bis) two 1,250hp A.82 RC32.
Dimensions: Span, 70ft 9in (21·56m); length, (B.R.20) 52ft 9in (16·2m);

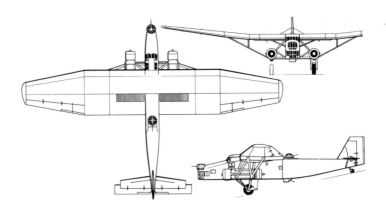

Above: Three-view of standard F 222/2.

1935; (F 222/2) October 1937; (NC 223) June 1937; (NC 223·3) October 1938; (NC 223·4) 15 March 1939.
User: France (Armée de l'Air, Aéronavale).

Development: This distinctive family formed the backbone of the Armée de l'Air heavy bomber force from 1935 until the collapse in 1940. It began with the F 210 of 1930, which set the pattern in having an angular box-like body, high-mounted wing and four engines slung on braced struts from the wing and fuselage in push/pull double nacelles. By way of the 220 came the 221, which served mainly as a 20-seat troop transport. The 222 introduced retractable landing gear, and the 36 F. 222/2 bombers of GBI/15 and II/15 served tirelessly in the dark months of 1940, often flying bombing missions by night over Germany and even Italy and as transports in North Africa until late 1944. The NC. 223.3, developed after nationalization, was a complete redesign and the most powerful and capable night bomber of 1938–40. The 223.4, a transatlantic mailplane, served with the Aéronavale as a heavy bomber, and in an epic 13hr 30min flight on 7–8 June 1940 one bombed Berlin.

(B.R.20M, 20bis) 55ft 0in (16·78m); height 15ft 7in (4·75m).
Weights: Empty (all), about 14,770lb (6700kg); loaded (B.R.20) 22,046lb (10,000kg); (B.R.20M) 23,038lb (10,450kg).
Performance: Maximum speed, (B.R.20) 264mph (425km/h); (B.R.20M) 267mph (430km/h); (B.R.20bis) 292mph (470km/h); initial climb (all) about 902ft (275m)/min; service ceiling, (B.R.20, 20M) 22,145ft (6750m); (B.R.20bis) 26,246ft (8000m); range, (B.R.20, 20M) 1,243 miles (2000km); (B.R.20bis) 1,710 miles (2750km).
Armament: (B.R.20) four 7·7mm Breda-SAFAT machine guns in nose turret (one), dorsal turret (two) and manual ventral position; bomb load 3,527lb (1600kg); (B.R.20M) as B.R.20 except nose gun 12·7mm; ▶

Left: One of the more uncommon Fiat B.R.20 Cicogna bombers was this example from a batch supplied to the Japanese Army in 1937. No fewer than 75 were delivered, seeing action in both the Chinese campaign and World War II. The aircraft illustrated served with the 1st Chutai, 12th Hikosentai. Japanese designation was Yi-shiki.

(B.R.20bis) as B.R.20M with two extra 12·7mm guns manually aimed from lateral blisters; bomb load 5,511lb (2500kg).

History: First flight (prototype) 10 February 1936; service delivery, September 1936; first flight (B.R.20M) late 1939; first flight B.R.20bis, December 1941.

Users: Hungary, Italy (RA), Japan, Spain, Venezuela.

Development: Ing Rosatelli was responsible for a great series of B.R. (Bombardamento Rosatelli) designs from 1919 onwards. Most were powerful single-engined biplanes, but in the mid-1930s he very quickly produced the B.R.20, a large monoplane with stressed-skin construction and other modern refinements. Despite its relative complexity the original aircraft was put into production within six months of the first flight and by the end of 1936 the B.R.20-equipped 13° Stormo was probably the most advanced bomber squadron in the world. Fiat also built two civil B.R.20L record-breakers, and also offered the new bomber for export, soon gaining a valuable order for 85, not from the expected China but from Japan, which needed a powerful bomber to bridge the gap caused by a delay with the Army Ki-21. In June 1937 the B.R.20 figured prominently in the Aviazione Legionaria sent to fight for the Nationalists in Spain and, with the He 111, bore the brunt of their very successful bomber operations. Spain purchased a manufacturing licence, which was not taken up, and purchased at least 25 from Fiat. An additional number were brought by Venezuela. In 1940, when Italy entered World War II, some 250 had been delivered to the Regia Aeronautica, the last 60 being of the strengthened and much more shapely M (Modificato) type. In October 1940 two groups of 37 and 38 of the M model operated against England, but they were hacked down with ease and were recalled in January 1941. During 1942 the B.R.20 began to fade, becoming used for ocean patrol, operational training and bombing where opposition was light. A large force supported the Luftwaffe in Russia, where casualties were heavy. By the Armistice only 81 of all versions were left out of 606 built. The much improved B.R.20bis never even got into bulk production.

Above: Late-production Fiat B.R.20M Cicognas of the 276th Squadriglia operating on the Eastern front in 1942. Even when assigned to relatively 'easy' sectors they suffered heavy losses.

Below: The blunter outline of the original production version can be seen in this action picture of B.R.20s of the Aviazione Legionaria operating in Spain in late 1937.

Focke-Wulf Fw 200 Condor
Fw 200C-0 to C-8

Origin: Focke-Wulf Flugzeugbau GmbH, in partnership with Hamburger Flugzeugbau (Blohm und Voss).

Type: Maritime reconnaissance bomber and (C-6 to -8) missile launcher, many used as transports.

Engines: Usually four 1,200hp BMW-Bramo Fafnir 323R-2 nine-cylinder radials.

Dimensions: Span 107ft 9½in (30·855m); length 76ft 11½in (23·46m); height 20ft 8in (6·3m).

Weights: (C-3/U-4) empty 28,550lb (12,951kg); loaded 50,045lb (22,700kg).

Performance: Maximum speed (C-3) 224mph (360km/h); (C-8) 205mph (330km/h); initial climb, about 656ft (200m)/min; service ceiling 19,030ft (5800m); range with standard fuel, 2,206 miles (3550km).

Armament: Typical C-3/C-8, one forward dorsal turret with one 15mm MG 151/15 (or 20mm MG 151/20 or one 7·92mm MG 15), one 20mm MG 151/20 manually aimed at front of ventral gondola, three 7·92mm MG 15 manually aimed at rear of ventral gondola and two beam windows (beam guns sometimes being 13mm MG 131) and one 13mm MG 131 in aft dorsal position; maximum bomb load of 4,626lb (2100kg) carried in gondola and beneath outer wings (C-6, C-8, two Hs 293 guided missiles carried under outboard nacelles).

History: First flight (civil prototype) 27 July 1937; (Fw 200C-0) January 1940; final delivery (C-8) February 1944.

User: (Fw 200C series) Germany (Luftwaffe).

Development: Planned solely as a long-range commercial transport for the German airline Deutsche Luft Hansa, the prewar Fw·200 prototypes set up impressive record flights to New York and Tokyo and attracted export orders from Denmark, Brazil, Finland and Japan. Transport prototype and production versions were also used by Hitler and Himmler as VIP executive machines and several later variants were also converted as special transports. In 1938 the Japanese asked for one Condor converted for use as a long-range ocean reconnaissance machine. The resulting Fw 200V-10 prototype introduced a ventral gondola and led to the Fw 200C-0 as the prototype of a Luftwaffe aircraft which had never been requested or planned and yet which was to prove a most powerful instrument of war. Distinguished by long-chord cowlings, twin-wheel main gears (because of the increased gross weight) and a completely new armament and equipment fit, the C-0 led to the C-1, used operationally from June 1940 by KG 40 at Bordeaux-Mérignac. By September 1940 this unit alone had sunk over 90,000 tons of Allied shipping and for the next three years the C-series Condors were in Churchill's words, "the scourge of the Atlantic". But, though the Fw 200 family continued to grow in equipment

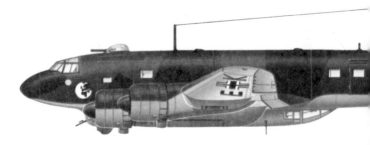

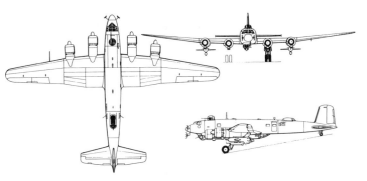

Above: The Fw 200C-8/U10, the final sub-type, with Hs 293s.

Below: One of the ultimate production variant, the Fw 200C-8, with FuG 200 Hohentwiel nose radar, HDL 151 cannon turret and racks for Hs 293 Missiles under and outboard of the engines.

and lethality, the Allies fought back with long-range Coastal Command aircraft, escort carriers and CAM (Catapult-Armed Merchantman) fighters and by mid-1944 surviving Condors were being forced into transport roles on other fronts. Total production was 276 and one of the fundamental failings of the Condor was structural weakness, catastrophic wing and fuselage failures occurring not only in the air but even on the ground, on take-off or landing.

Left: Typical of the Condors that earned the apellation 'scourge of the Atlantic' in 1940–42, this Fw 200C-3 served with KG 40 at Cognac and Bordeaux-Merignac from early 1941. The front turret had only a 7·92mm gun but a 20mm cannon was in the front of the gondola and the hand-held rear guns were often all 13mm MG131s.

Fokker C.X

C.X

Origin: NV Fokker, Netherlands; licence built by Valtion Lentokonetehdas, Finland.
Type: Two-seat bomber and reconnaissance.
Engine: (Dutch) one 650hp Rolls-Royce Kestrel V vee-12 liquid-cooled; (Finnish) one licence-built 835hp Bristol Pegasus XXI nine-cylinder radial.
Dimensions: Span, 39ft 4in (12m); length (Kestrel) 30ft 2in (9·2m); (Pegasus) 29ft 9in (9·1m); height, 10ft 10in (3·3m).
Weights: Empty (both), about 3,086lb (1400kg); loaded (Kestrel) 4,960lb (2250kg); (Pegasus) 5,512lb (2500kg).
Performance: Maximum speed (Kestrel) 199mph (320km/h); (Pegasus) 211mph (340km/h); service ceiling (Kestrel) 27,230ft (8300m); (Pegasus) 27,560ft (8400m); range (Kestrel) 516 miles (830km), (Pegasus) 522 miles (840km).
Armament: Two 7·9mm machine guns fixed in top of front fuselage and third manually aimed from rear cockpit; underwing racks for two 385lb (175kg) or four 221lb (100kg) bombs.
History: First flight 1934; service delivery (Dutch) 1937; (Finnish) 1938.
Users: Finland, Netherlands.

Development: Derived from the C.V-E and planned as a successor, the C.X was a notably clean machine typical of good military design of the mid-1930s. By this time world-wide competition was very severe and Fokker could not achieve such widespread export success. The first orders were for ten for the Royal Netherlands East Indies Army, followed by 20 for the RNethAF (then called Luchtvaartafdeling, LVA), the last 15 having enclosed cockpits and tailwheels. Further small numbers were made in Holland, at least one having a 925hp Hispano-Suiza 12Y engine with 20mm cannon firing through the propeller hub. Fokker also developed a considerably more capable C.X for Finland, with the Pegasus radial. The Finnish State Aircraft Factory at Tampere went into licence-production with this version in 1938, the engine being made at Tammerfors. The Finnish C.X had an enclosed heated cockpit, rapid cold-weather starting and either wheel or ski landing gear. All available Dutch and Finnish C.X aircraft participated in World War II. None of the LVA machines survived the "Five Day War" of 10–15 May 1940, but the Finnish aircraft continued until at least 1944 under severe conditions and finally went into action not against the Russians but in helping them drive the Germans from Finnish territory in 1944–45.

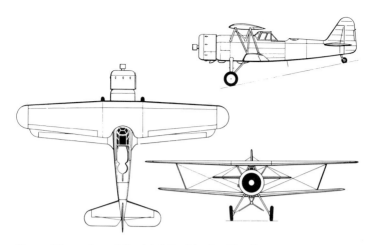

Above: Three-view of Finnish C.X with wheel landing gear.

Above: Though the pointed-nose Dutch C.X
with water-cooled Rolls-Royce Kestrel engine
saw brief action on 10 May 1940 the chief version
in World War II was this radial-engined Finnish
variant. The State Aircraft Factory at
Tammerfors delivered 30 by 1938, and then built
a further five in 1942 to replace combat losses.

Left: This illustration of one of the
special Pegasus-engined C.X bomber-
reconnaissance aircraft made under licence
in Finland shows the streamlined ski
landing gears used in winter. Though by
1939 it represented an outmoded type the
C.X was always popular with its crews.
Sadly, the last in active service was destroyed
in an accident in 1958.

Handley Page Halifax

H.P.57 Halifax I, H.P.59 Mk II Series 1A, III, H.P.61 Mk V, B.VI and VII, C.VIII and A.IX

Origin: Handley Page Ltd; also built by London Aircraft Production Group, English Electric Ltd, Rootes Securities (Speke) and Fairey Aviation Ltd (Stockport).

Type: Seven-seat heavy bomber; later ECM platform, special transport and glider tug, cargo transport and paratroop carrier.

Engines: Four Rolls-Royce Merlin vee-12 liquid-cooled or Bristol Hercules 14-cylinder two-row sleeve-valve radial (see text).

Dimensions: Span (I to early III) 98ft 10in (30·12m); (from later III) 104ft 2in (31·75m); length (I, II, III Srs 1) 70ft 1in (21·36m); (II Srs 1A onwards) 71ft 7in (21·82m); height 20ft 9in (6·32m).

Weights: Empty (I Srs 1) 33,860lb (15,359kg); (II Srs 1A) 35,270lb (16,000kg); (VI) 39,000lb (17,690kg); loaded (I) 55,000lb (24,948kg); (I Srs 1) 58,000lb (26,308kg); (I Srs 2) 60,000lb (27,216kg); (II) 60,000lb; (II Srs 1A) 63,000lb (28,576kg), (III) 65,000lb (29,484kg), (V) 60,000lb; (VI) 68,000lb (30,844kg); (VII, VIII, IX) 65,000lb.

Performance: Maximum speed (I) 265mph (426km/h); (II) 270mph (435km/h); (III, VI) 312mph (501km/h); (V, VII, VIII, IX) 285mph (460 km/h); initial climb (typical) 750ft (229m)/min; service ceiling, typically (Merlin) 22,800ft (6950m); (Hercules) 24,000ft (7315m); range with maximum load (I) 980 miles (1577km); (II) 1,100 miles (1770km); (III, VI) 1,260 miles (2030km).

Armament: See text.

History: First flight (prototype) 25 October 1939; (production Mk I) 11 October 1940; squadron delivery 23 November 1940; first flight (production III) July 1943; final delivery 20 November 1946.

Users: Australia, Canada, France (FFL), New Zealand, UK (RAF, BOAC).

Development: Though it never attained the limelight and glamour of its partner, the Lancaster, the "Halibag" made almost as great a contribution to Allied victory in World War II, and it did so in a far greater diversity of roles. Planned as a twin-Vulture bomber to Specification P.13/36 with a gross weight of 26,300lb it grew to weigh 68,000lb as a formidable weapon platform and transport that suffered from no vices once it had progressed through a succession of early changes. By far the biggest change, in the summer of 1937, was to switch from two Vultures to four Merlins (a godsend, as it turned out) and the first 100 H.P.57s were ordered on 3 September 1937. This version, the Mk I, had a 22ft bomb bay and six bomb cells in the wing centre-section. Engines were 1,280hp Merlin X and defensive armament comprised two 0·303in Brownings in the nose turret, four in the tail turret and, usually, two in manual beam positions. The first squadron was No 35 at Linton on Ouse and the first mission Le Havre on the night of 11/12 March 1942. The I Srs 2 was stressed to 60,000lb and the Srs 3 had more fuel. The Mk II had 1,390hp Merlin XX and Hudson-type twin-0·303in dorsal turret instead of beam guns. On the II Srs 1 Special the ▶

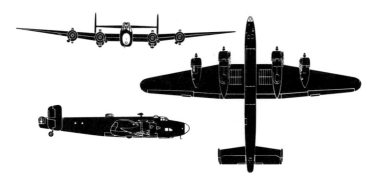

Above: Three-view of the extended-span Halifax B.111 Series II (Mk VI similar). Most had H$_2$S radar fitted.

Above: L9530 was one of the first production batch in 1940. Serving with 76 Sqn (MP-L) it had manual beam guns and prominent fuel-jettison pipes passing beneath the flaps. The photograph must have been taken from the right beam gun position of an accompanying Halifax, in mid-1941. The white object under the outer left wing is the landing light.

Left: A Halifax B.III Series II with extended wings and H$_2$S serving with 640 Sqn at Leconfield, Yorkshire. Vivid tails were common among the multi-national Halifax units which included important contributions from Canada and free France.

front and dorsal turrets and engine flame dampers were all removed to improve performance. The II Srs 1A introduced what became the standard nose, a clear Perspex moulding with manually aimed 0·303in Vickers K, as well as the Defiant-type 4×0·303in dorsal turret and 1,390hp Merlin XXII. Later Srs 1A introduced larger fins which improved bombing accuracy; one of these, with radome under the rear fuselage, was the first aircraft to use H_2S ground-mapping radar on active service. In November 1942 the GR.II Srs 1A entered service with Coastal Command, with 0·5in nose gun, marine equipment and often four-blade propellers. The III overcame all the performance problems with 1,650hp Hercules and DH Hydromatic propellers, later IIIs having the wings extended to rounded tips giving better field length, climb, ceiling and range. The IV (turbocharged Hercules) was not built. The V was a II Srs 2A with Dowty landing gear and hydraulics (Messier on other marks), used as a bomber, Coastal GR, ASW and meteorological aircraft. The VI was the definitive bomber, with 1,800hp Hercules 100 and extra tankage and full tropical equipment. The VII was a VI using old

Above: One of the first Halifax II Series 1 (the large number 9 is not explained) photographed on factory test in late 1941. Slowest of all marks, this had a Hudson-type dorsal turret instead of beam guns, plus flame-damped exhausts.

Hercules XVI. The C.VIII was an unarmed transport with large quick-change 8,000lb cargo pannier in place of the bomb bay and 11 passenger seats; it led to the post-war Halton civil transport. The A.IX carried 16 paratroops and associated cargo. The III, V, VII and IX served throughout Europe towing gliders and in other special operations, including airdropping agents and arms to Resistance groups and carrying electronic countermeasures (ECM) with 100 Group. Total production amounted to 6,176, by H.P., English Electric, the London Aircraft Production Group (London Transport), Fairey and Rootes, at a peak rate of one per hour. Final mission was by a GR.VI from Gibraltar in March 1952, the Armée de l'Air phasing out its B.VI at about the same time.

Handley Page Hampden

H.P.52 Hampden I and H.P.53 Hereford I

Origin: Handley Page Ltd; also built by English Electric Co. and Canadian Associated Aircraft.

Type: Four-seat bomber (Hampden, later torpedo bomber and minelayer).

Engines: (Hampden) two 1,000hp Bristol Pegasus XVIII nine-cylinder radials; (Hereford) two 1,000hp Napier Dagger VIII 24-cylinder H-type air-cooled.

Dimensions: Span 69ft 2in (21·98m); length 53ft 7in (16·33m); height 14ft 4in (4·37m).

Weights: Empty (Hampden) 11,780lb (5344kg); (Hereford) 11,700lb (5308kg); loaded (Hampden) 18,756lb (8508kg); (Hereford) 16,000lb (7257kg).

Performance: (Hampden) maximum speed 254mph (410km/h); initial climb 980ft (300m)/min; service ceiling 19,000ft (5790m); range with maximum bomb load 1,095 miles (1762km).

Armament: Originally, one offensive 0·303in Vickers fixed firing ahead, one 0·303in Lewis manually aimed from nose by nav/bomb aimer, one Lewis manually aimed by wireless operator from upper rear position and one Lewis manually aimed by lower rear gunner; bomb load of 4,000lb (1814kg). By January 1940 both rear positions had twin 0·303in Vickers K with increased field of fire. Hard points for two 500lb bombs added below outer wings, provision for carrying mines or one 18in torpedo internally.

History: First flight (H.P.52 prototype) 21 June 1936; (production Hampden I) May 1938; (Hereford I) December 1939; termination of production March 1942.

Users: Canada, New Zealand, UK (RAF).

Development: On paper the Hampden, the last of the monoplane bombers to enter RAF service during the Expansion Scheme of 1936–38, was a truly outstanding aircraft. The makers considered it so fast and manoeuvrable they called it "a fighting bomber" and gave the pilot a fixed gun. They judged the three movable guns gave complete all-round defence without the penalties of heavy turrets and, while the Hampden was almost the equal of the big Whitley and Wellington in range with heavy bomb load, it was much faster than either; it was almost as fast as the Blenheim, but carried four times the load twice as far (on only fractionally greater power). Thanks to its well flapped and slatted wing it could land as slowly as 73mph. Designed to B.9/32, the prototype was angular but the production machine, to 30/36, looked very attractive and large orders were placed, eight squadrons being operational at the start of World War II. Hampdens were busy in September 1939 raiding German naval installations and ships (bombing German land was forbidden), until the daylight formations encountered enemy fighters. Then casualties were so heavy the Hampden was taken off operations and re-equipped with much better armament and armour — and, ▶

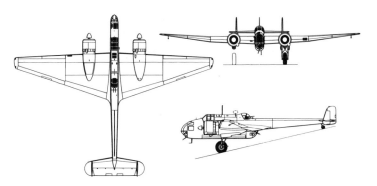

Above: Hampden I in 1940 with twin dorsal and ventral guns.

Above: This photograph taken from the upper rear gunner's position, probably in 1940, shows three other Hampdens in line astern. Though exceptionally manoeuvrable, the Hampden proved in practice to have no significant capability as a fighter, though the fixed nose gun was retained. More important was the decision, pushed by Guy Gibson, to fit twin guns at the rear.

Left: A Hampden I of No 44 (Rhodesia) Sqn, based at Waddington in 1940 and painted in that period's markings with black sides and with lettering in Dull Red. In June 1942 the white and yellow in the national insignia was made thinner (one-eighth of the total) to reduce contrast at night. By that time No 44 had become first squadron to convert to the Lancaster, a far more formidable aircraft.

more to the point, used only at night. Despite cramp and near-impossibility of getting from one crew position to another, the "Flying Suitcase" had a successful career bombing invasion barges in the summer of 1940, bombing German heartlands, mine-laying and, finally, as a long-range torpedo bomber over the North Sea and northern Russia. Handley Page built 500, English Electric built 770 and Canadian Associated Aircraft 160. Short Brothers built 100 Herefords which never became operational; many were converted to Hampdens.

Top: A Hampden I (there was only the one basic mark) of RAF No 455 Sqn, based at Leuchars in late 1941. The added external 500lb bomb rack under the right wing can be clearly seen.

Above: A fine portrait of Hampdens of No 44 (Rhodesia) Sqn, taken in early 1942. This was immediately before the squadron re-equipped with the Lancaster and became the envy of Bomber Command. Compare with the picture on pages 14–15.

Heinkel He 111

He 111 B series, E series, H series and P series

Origin: Ernst Heinkel AG; also built in France on German account by SNCASO; built under licence by Fabrica de Avione SET, Romania, and CASA, Spain.

Type: Four-seat or five-seat medium bomber (later, torpedo bomber, glider tug and missile launcher).

Engines: (He 111H-3) two 1,200hp Junkers Jumo 211D-2 12-cylinder inverted-vee liquid-cooled; (He 111P-2) two 1,100hp Daimler-Benz DB 601A-1 12-cylinder inverted-vee liquid-cooled.

Dimensions: (H-3) Span 74ft $1\frac{3}{4}$in (22·6m); length 53ft $9\frac{1}{2}$in (16·4m); height 13ft $1\frac{1}{2}$in (4m).

Weights: Empty (H-3) 17,000lb (7720kg); (P-2) 17,640lb (8000kg); maximum loaded (H-3) 30,865lb (14,000kg); (P-2) 29,762lb (13,500kg).

Performance: Maximum speed (H-3) 258mph (415km/h); (P-2) 242mph (390km/h) at 16,400ft (5000m) (at maximum weight, neither version could exceed 205mph, 330km/h); climb to 14,765ft (4500m) 30–35min at normal gross weight, 50min at maximum; service ceiling (both) around 25,590ft (7800m) at normal gross weight, under 16,400ft (5000m) at maximum; range with maximum bomb load (both) about 745 miles (1200km).

Armament: (P-2) 7·92mm Rheinmetall MG 15 machine gun on manual mountings in nosecap, open dorsal position and ventral gondola; (H-3) same, plus fixed forward-firing MG 15 or 17, two MG 15s in waist windows and

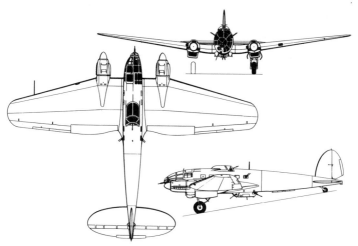

Above: A fairly late bomber variant, the He 111H-16.

(usually) 20mm MG FF cannon in front of ventral gondola and (sometimes) fixed rear-firing MG 17 in extreme tail; internal bomb load up to 4,410lb (2000kg) in vertical cells, stored nose-up; external bomb load (at expense of internal) one 4,410lb (2000kg) on H-3, one or two 1,102lb (500kg) on others; later marks carried one or two 1,686lb (765kg) torpedoes, Bv 246 glide missiles, Hs 293 rocket missiles, Fritz X radio-controlled glide bombs or one FZG-76 (''V-1'') cruise missile. *continued▶*

Left: The most numerous He 111 model was the H-6, which was often used with a 20mm MG FF firing forward from the gondola against ships. This H-6 served with II/KG 26 from Ottana, Sardinia, in 1943.

Below, left: An SC2000 bomb (4,410lb) about to be hung under a Heinkel of KG 26 on a mission over southern England in late 1940

Below: Bombs fell tail-first and tumbled wildly.

Above: He 111P-1 bombers photographed in spring 1939 serving with III/KG 255, which on 1 May 1939 was redesignated III/KG 51. Later the P-1 was supplanted by the Jumo-powered H-series.

Below: Armourers of KG 55 pulling an SC 500 bomb of 1,102lb on the Russian front soon after Operation Barbarossa in June 1941. The aircraft is an He 111H-6, the most numerous version.

History: First flight (He 111V1 prototype) 24 February 1935; (pre-production He 111B-0) August 1936; (production He 111B-1) 30 October 1936; (first He 111E series) January 1938; (first production He 111P-1) December 1938; (He 111H-1) January or February 1939; final delivery (He 111H-23) October 1944; (Spanish C.2111) late 1956.

Users: China, Germany (Luftwaffe, Luft Hansa), Hungary, Iraq, Romania, Spain, Turkey.

Development: A natural twin-engined outgrowth of the He 70, the first He 111 was a graceful machine with elliptical wings and tail, secretly flown as a bomber but revealed to the world a year later as a civil airliner. Powered by 660hp BMW VI engines, it had typical armament of three manually aimed machine guns but the useful bomb load of 2,200lb (1000kg) stowed nose-up in eight cells in the centre fuselage. In 1937 a number of generally similar machines secretly flew photo-reconnaissance missions over Britain, France and the Soviet Union, in the guise of airliners of Deutsche Luft Hansa. In the same year the He 111B-1 came into Luftwaffe service, with two 880hp Daimler-Benz DB 600C engines, while a vast new factory was built at Oranienburg solely to make later versions. In February 1937 operations began with the Legion Kondor in Spain, with considerable success, flight performance being improved in the B-2 by 950hp DB 600CG engines which were retained in the C series. The D was faster, with the 1,000hp Jumo 211A-1, also used in the He 111 F in which a new straight-edged wing was introduced. To a considerable degree the success of the early elliptical-winged He 111 bombers in Spain misled the Luftwaffe into considering that nothing could withstand the onslaught of their huge fleets of medium bombers. These aircraft — the trim Do 17, the broad-winged He 111 and the

Above: The pale theatre band ahead of the tail (yellow for the Eastern front, white for the Mediterranean) shows that this photo, taken from alongside the pilot, dates from later than 1940. The slow Heinkel never did find satisfactory defensive armament.

high-performance Ju 88 — were all extremely advanced by the standards of the mid-1930s when they were designed. They were faster than the single-seat fighters of that era and, so the argument went, therefore did not need much defensive armament. So the three machine guns carried by the first He 111 bombers in 1936 stayed unchanged until, in the Battle of Britain, the He 111 was hacked down with ease, its only defence being its toughness and ability to come back after being shot to pieces. The inevitable result was that more and more defensive guns were added, needing a fifth or even a sixth crew-member. Coupled with incessant growth in equipment and armour the result was deteriorating performance, so that the record-breaker of 1936–38 became the lumbering sitting duck of 1942–45. Yet the He 111 was built in ever-greater numbers, virtually all the later sub-types being members of the prolific H-series. Variations were legion, including versions with large barrage-balloon deflectors, several kinds of missiles (including a V-1 tucked under the left wing root), while a few were completed as saboteur transports. The most numerous version was the H-6, and the extraordinary He 111Z (Zwilling) glider tug of 1942 consisted of two H-6s joined by a common centre wing carrying a fifth engine. Right to the end of the war the RLM and German industry failed to find a replacement for the old "Spaten" (spade), and the total produced in Germany and Romania was at least 6,086 and possibly more than 7,000. Merlin-engined C.2111 versions continued in production in Spain until 1956.

Heinkel He 177 Greif

He 177A-0 to A-5, He 277 and He 274

Origin: Ernst Heinkel AG; also built by Arado Flugzeugwerke.

Type: He 177, six-seat heavy bomber and missile carrier.

Engines: Two 2,950hp Daimler-Benz DB 610A-1/B-1, each comprising two inverted-vee-12 liquid-cooled engines geared to one propeller.

Dimensions: Span 103ft 1¾in (31·44m); length 72ft 2in (22m); height 21ft (6·4m).

Weights: Empty 37,038lb (16,800kg); loaded (A-5) 68,343lb (31,000kg).

Performance: Maximum speed (at 41,000lb, 18,615kg) 295mph (472 km/h); initial climb 853ft (260m)/min; service ceiling 26,500ft (7080m); range with FX or Hs 293 missiles (no bombs) about 3,107 miles (5000km).

Armament: (A-5/R2) one 7·92mm MG 81J manually aimed in nose, one 20mm MG 151 manually aimed at front of ventral gondola, one or two 13mm MG 131 in forward dorsal turret, one MG 131 in rear dorsal turret, one MG 151 manually aimed in tail and two MG 81 or one MG 131 manually aimed at rear of gondola; maximum internal bomb load 13,200lb (6000kg), seldom carried; external load, two Hs 293 guided missiles, FX 1400 guided bombs, mines or torpedoes (more if internal bay blanked off and racks added below it).

History: First flight (He 177V-1) 19 November 1939; (pre-production He 177A-0) November 1941; service delivery (A-1) March 1942; (A-5) February 1943; first flight (He 277V-1) December 1943; (He 274, alias AAS 01A) December 1945.

User: Germany (Luftwaffe).

Development: The Heinkel 177, Germany's biggest bomber programme in World War II, is remembered as possibly the most troublesome and unsatisfactory aircraft in military history, and it was only through dogged courage and persistence that large numbers were put into service. Much of the fault lay in the stupid 1938 requirement that the proposed heavy bomber and anti-ship aircraft should be capable of dive bombing. Certainly the wish to reduce drag by using coupled pairs of engines was mistaken, because no engines in bomber history have caught fire so often in normal cruising flight. Six of the eight prototypes crashed and many of the 35 pre-production A-0s (built mainly by Arado) were written off in take-off swings

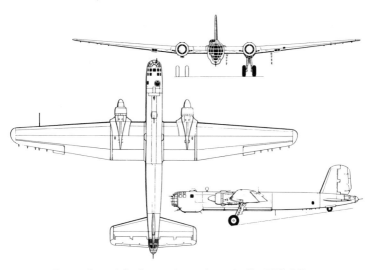

Above: Three-view of the first major variant, the He 177A-1/R1.

or in-flight fires. Arado built 130 A-1s, followed by 170 Heinkel-built A-3s and 826 A-5s with repositioned engines and longer fuselages. About 700 served on the Eastern Front, many having 50mm and 75mm guns for tank-busting; a few nervously bombed Britain in 400mph shallow dives, without any proper aiming of their bombs. So bothersome were these beasts that Goering forbade Heinkel to pester him any more with plans to use four separate engines, but Heinkel secretly flew the He 277, with four 1,750hp DB 603A, at Vienna, as the first of a major programme. The almost completely redesigned He 274 was a high-altitude bomber developed at the Farman factory at Suresnes, with four 1,850hp engines, a 145ft wing and twin fins. After the liberation it was readied for flight and flown at Orléans-Bricy.

Below: Main operational model was the A-5, of which 826 were built. This A-5/R2 has external racks for Fritz-X and Hs 293 guided missiles under its wings and on the centreline.

Ilyushin Il-4

TsKB-26, TsKB-30, DB-3 and DB-3F (Il-4)

Origin: Design bureau of Sergei Ilyushin, Soviet Union.
Type: Four-seat bomber and torpedo carrier.
Engines: Final standard, two 1,100hp M-88B 14-cylinder two-row radials.
Dimensions: Span 70ft 4¼in (21·44m); length 48ft 6½in (14·8m); height approximately 13ft 9in 4·2m).
Weights: About 13,230lb (6000kg); loaded 22,046lb (10,000kg).
Performance: Maximum speed 255mph (410km/h); initial climb 886ft (270m)/min; service ceiling 32,808ft (10,000m); range with 2,205lb of bombs 1,616 miles (2600km).
Armament: Three manually aimed machine guns, in nose, dorsal turret and periscopic ventral position, originally all 7·62mm ShKAS and from 1942 all 12·7mm BS; internal bomb bay for ten 220lb (100kg) bombs or equivalent, with alternative (or, for short ranges, additional) racks for up to three 1,102lb (500kg) or one 2,072lb (940kg) torpedo or one 2,205lb (1000kg) bomb, all under fuselage.
History: First flight (TsKB-26) 1935; (production DB-3) 1937; (DB-3F) 1939; final delivery 1944.
User: Soviet Union (DA, VMF).

Development: Though much less well-known around the world than such Western bombers as the B-17 and Lancaster, the Il-4 was one of the great bombers of World War II and saw service in enormous numbers in all roles from close support to strategic bombing of Berlin and low-level torpedo attacks. Originally known by its design bureau designation of TsKB-26 (often reported in the West as CKB-26), it was officially designated DB-3 (DB for Dalni Bombardirovshchik, long-range bomber) and went into production in early 1937. Powered by two 765hp M-85 engines, soon replaced by 960hp M-86, it was roughly in the class of the Hampden, with excellent speed, range, load and manoeuvrability but poor defensive armament (which was never changed, apart from increasing the calibre of the three guns). In 1939, when 1,528 had been delivered, production switched to the DB-3F with blunt nose turret replaced by a long pointed nose. In 1940, when over 2,000 were delivered, the designation was

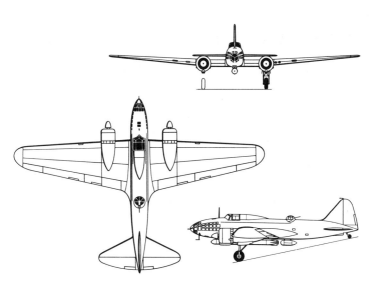

Above: Three-view of an Il-4 of the type used by the VVS-VMF for bombing and (as shown) torpedo attacks.

changed to Il-4, conforming with the new scheme in which aircraft were named for their designers (in this case Sergei Ilyushin). After the German invasion desperate materials shortage nearly halted production but by 1942 new plants in Siberia were building huge numbers of Il-4s with a redesigned airframe incorporating the maximum amount of wood. More than 6,800 had been delivered when production was stopped in 1944. Il-4s bombed Berlin many times, the first time by a force of VVS-VMF (Soviet Navy) Il-4s on 8 August 1941. By 1943 reconnaissance and glider towing were additional duties for these hard-worked aircraft.

Below: This was one of the many Il-4s used by the VVS-VMF, the Soviet naval air force. It could carry a weapon load of 2500kg.

Junkers Ju 86

Ju 86D, E, G, K, P and R

Origin: Junkers Flugzeug und Motorenwerke AG; also built by Henschel, and built under licence by Saab, Sweden.
Type: (D, E, G and K) bomber; (P) bomber/reconnaissance; (R) reconnaissance.
Engines: (D) two 600hp Junkers Jumo 205C six opposed-piston cylinder diesels; (E, G) two 800 or 880hp BMW 132 nine-cylinder radials; (K) two 905hp Bristol Mercury XIX nine-cylinder radials; (P, R) two 1,000hp Jumo 207A-1 or 207B-3/V turbocharged opposed-piston diesels.
Dimensions: Span 73ft 10in (22·6m); (P) 84ft (25·6m); (R) 105ft (32m); length (typical) 58ft 8½in (17·9m); (G) 56ft 5in; (P, R) 54ft; height (all) 15ft 5in (4·7m).
Weights: Empty (E-1) 11,464lb (5200kg); (R-1) 14,771lb (6700kg); loaded (E-1) 18,080lb (8200kg); (R-1) 25,420lb (11,530kg).
Performance: Maximum speed (E-1) 202mph (325km/h); (R-1) 261mph (420km/h); initial climb (E) 918ft (280m)/min; service ceiling (E-1) 22,310ft (6800m); (R-1) 42,650ft (13,000m); range (E) 746 miles (1200m); (R-1) 980 miles (1577km).
Armament: (D, E, G, K) three 7·92mm MG 15 manually aimed from nose, dorsal and retractable ventral positions; internal bomb load of four 551lb (250kg) or 16 110lb (50kg) bombs; (P) single 7·92mm fixed MG 17, same bomb load; (R) usually none.
History: First flight (Ju 86V-1) 4 November 1934; (V-5 bomber prototype) January 1936; (production D-1) late 1936; (P-series prototype) February 1940.
Users: Bolivia, Chile, Germany (Luftwaffe, Lufthansa), Hungary, Portugal, South Africa, Spain, Sweden.

Development: Planned like the He 111 as both a civil airliner and a bomber, the Ju 86 was in 1934 one of the most advanced aircraft in Europe. The design team under Dipl-Ing Zindel finally abandoned corrugated skin

Above: One of the colourful Ju 86K-2 bombers of the Hungarian 3./I Bombázó Oszatály, based at Tapolca in 1938.

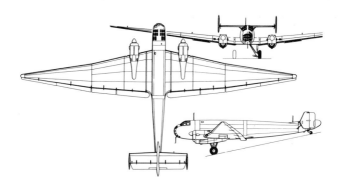

Above: Three-view of the extreme-altitude Ju 86R-1.

and created a smooth and efficient machine with prominent double-wing flaps and outward-retracting main gears. The diesel-engined D-1 was quickly put into Luftwaffe service to replace the Do 23 and Ju 52 as the standard heavy bomber, but in Spain the various· D-versions proved vulnerable even to biplane fighters. The E-series bombers, with the powerful BMW radial, were faster and the fastest of all were the Swedish Bristol-engined Ks, of which 40 were built by Junkers (first delivery 18 December 1936) and 16 by Saab (last delivery 3 January 1941). Many D and E bombers were used against Poland, but that was their swan-song. By 1939 Junkers was working on a high-altitude version with turbocharged engines and a pressure cabin and this emerged as the P-1 bomber and P-2 bomber/reconnaissance which was operational over the Soviet Union gathering pictures before the German invasion of June 1941. The R series had a span increased even beyond that of the P and frequently operated over southern England in 1941–2 until — with extreme difficulty — solitary Spitfires managed to reach their altitude and effect an interception. Total military Ju 86 production was between 810 and 1,000. Junkers schemed many developed versions, some having four or six engines.

Below: A Ju 86A-1 of KG 253 on manoeuvres in winter 1936-37, when this was still a very modern bomber. No guns are fitted to this aircraft, though the dustbin turret is extended.

Junkers Ju 188

Ju 188A, D and E series, and Ju 388, J, K and L

Origin: Junkers Flugzeug und Motorenwerke AG; with subcontract manufacture of parts by various French companies.
Type: Five-seat bomber (D-2, reconnaissance).
Engines: (Ju 188A) two 1,776hp Junkers Jumo 213A 12-cylinder inverted-vee liquid-cooled; (Ju 188D) same as A; (Ju 188E) two 1,700hp BMW 801G-2 18-cylinder two-row radials.
Dimensions: Span 72ft 2in (22m); length 49ft 1in (14·96m); height 16ft 1in (4·9m).
Weights: Empty (188E-1) 21,825lb (9900kg); loaded (188A and D) 33,730lb (15,300kg); (188E-1) 31,967lb (14,500kg).
Performance: Maximum speed (188A) 325mph (420km/h) at 20,500ft (6250m); (188D) 350mph (560km/h) at 27,000ft (8235m); (188E) 315mph (494km/h) at 19,685ft (6000m); service ceiling (188A) 33,000ft (10,060m); (188D) 36,090ft (11,000m); (188E) 31,170ft (9500m); range with 3,300lb (1500kg) bomb load (188A and E) 1,550 miles (2480km).
Armament: (A, D-1 and E-1) one 20mm MG 151/20 cannon in nose, one MG 151/20 in dorsal turret, one 13mm MG 131 manually aimed at rear dorsal position and one MG 131 or twin 7·92mm MG 81 manually aimed at rear ventral position; 6,614lb (3000kg) bombs internally or two 2,200lb (1000kg) torpedoes under inner wings.
History: First flight (Ju 88B-0) early 1940; (Ju 88V27) September 1941; (Ju 188V1) December 1941; (Ju 188E-1) March 1942; (Ju 388L) May 1944.
User: Germany (Luftwaffe).

Above: One of the best anti-shipping aircraft of World War II, the Ju 188E-2 was equipped with FuG 200 Hohentwiel radar and could carry two of the advanced LT 1B or LT F5b torpedoes. Not all E-2 aircraft had the EDL 131 dorsal turret, but the G even had a manned turret (with two MG 131s) in the extreme tail.

Right: Painted in 72/73 green shades with a wavy line of 65 light blue, this Ju 188D-2 operated from Kirkenes, Norway, in 1944 with 1(F)/124. The D-2 was a maritime reconnaissance aircraft with FuG 200 radar.

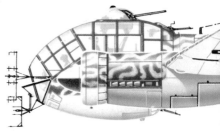

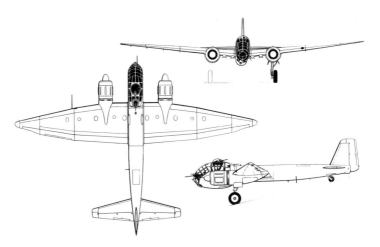

Above: Three-view of the Ju 188E-1 bomber, one of the versions with the BMW 801G-2 radial engine.

Development: In 1939 Junkers had the Jumo 213 engine in advanced development and, to go with it, the aircraft side of the company prepared an improved Ju 88 with a larger yet more streamlined crew compartment, more efficient pointed wings and large squarish tail. After protracted development this went into production as the Ju 188E-1, fitted with BMW 801s because the powerful Jumo was still not ready. The plant at Bernburg delivered 120 E-1s and a few radar-equipped turretless E-2s and reconnaissance F versions before, in mid-1943, finally getting into production with the A-1 version. Leipzig/Mockau built the A-2 with flame-damped exhaust for night operations and the A-3 torpedo bomber. The D was a fast reconnaissance aircraft, and the Ju 188S was a family of high-speed machines, for various duties, capable of up to 435mph (696km/h). Numerous other versions, some with a remotely controlled twin-MG 131 tail turret, led to the even faster and higher-flying Ju 388 family of night fighters (J), reconnaissance (L) and bomber aircraft (K). Altogether about 1,100 Ju 188 and about 120 388s were delivered, while at the war's end the much larger and markedly different Ju 288 had been shelved and the Ju 488, a much enlarged four-engined 388, had been built at Toulouse. All these aircraft, and the even greater number of stillborn projects, were evidence of the increasingly urgent need to make up for the absence of properly conceived new designs by wringing the utmost development out of the obsolescent types with which the Luftwaffe had started the war.

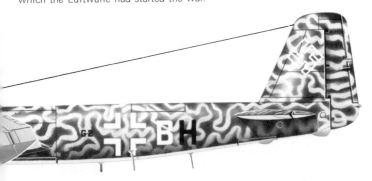

Junkers Ju 290

Ju 290A-1 to A-8 and B-1, B-2 and C

Origin: Junkers Flugzeug und Motorenwerke; design and development at Prague-Letnany, prototypes at Dessau and production at Bernberg.

Type: Long-range transport and reconnaissance bomber.

Engines: Four BMW 801 14-cylinder radials, (A) usually 1,700hp 801D, (B) 1,970hp 801E.

Dimensions: Span 137ft 9½in (42·00m); length 92ft 1in to 97ft 9in (A-5, 93ft 11½in, 28·64m); height 22ft 4¾in (6·83m).

Weights: Empty, not known (published figures cannot be correct); maximum (A-5) 99,141lb (44,970kg), (A-7) 101,413lb (45,400kg), (B-2) 111,332lb (50,500kg).

Performance: Maximum speed (all, without missiles) about 273mph (440km/h); maximum range (typical) 3,700 miles (5950km), (B-2) 4,970 miles (8000km).

Armament: See text.

History: First flight (rebuilt Ju 90V5) early 1939, (production 290A-0) October 1942; programme termination October 1944.

User: Germany (Luftwaffe).

Development: In 1936 Junkers considered the possibility of turning the Ju 89 strategic bomber into the Ju 90 airliner. With the death of Gen Wever the Ju 89 was cancelled and the Ju 90 became the pride of Deutsche Lufthansa. By 1937 the civil Ju 90S (Schwer = heavy) was in final design, with the powerful BMW 139 engine. By 1939 this had flown, with a new

Above: Taken at the Junkers plant at Bernburg, the centre for Ju 290 development, this shows the first production A-7 (Werk-Nr 0186) being readied for flight in May 1944.

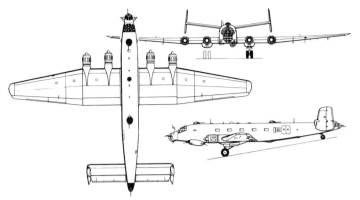

Above: Three-view of the Ju 290A-7 (photograph opposite).

wing and BMW 801 engines, and via a string of development prototypes led to the Ju 290A-0 and A-1 transports first used at Stalingrad. The A-2 was an Atlantic patrol machine, with typical armament of five 20mm MG 151 (including two power turrets) and six 13mm MG 131. There were many other versions, and the A-7 introduced a bulbous glazed nose; armament of the A-8 series was ten MG 151 and one (or three) MG 131, the most powerful carried by any bomber of World War II. The B carried more fuel and pressurized crew compartments, and like some A versions had radar and could launch Hs 293 and other air/surface missiles. In 1944 three A-5 made round trips to Manchuria.

Above: A Ju 290A-5 of FAGr 5 ocean-recon geschwader, 1943.

Below: The first Ju 290A-3 transport, also used by FAGr 5.

Kawasaki Ki-48 "Lily"

Ki-48-I, -IIa, -IIb and -IIc
(Allied code-name "Lily")

Origin: Kawasaki Kokuki Kogyo KK.
Type: Four-seat light bomber.
Engines: Two 14-cylinder radials, (-I) 980hp Nakajima Ha-25 (Army Type 99), (-II) 1,150hp Nakajima Ha-115 (Army Type 1).
Dimensions: Span 57ft 3¾in (17·47m); length (-I) 41ft 4in (12·60m), (-II) 41ft 10in (12·75m); height 12ft 5½in (3·80m).
Weights: Empty (-I) 8,928lb (4050kg), (-II) 10,030lb (4550kg); loaded (-I) 13,337lb (6050kg), (-II) 14,880lb (6750kg).
Performance: Maximum speed (-I) 298mph (480km/h), (-II) 314mph (505km/h); range (both, bomb load not specified) 1,491 miles (2400km).
Armament: (most) three 7·7mm Type 89 manually aimed from nose, dorsal and ventral positions, (-IIc) two Type 89 in nose, one ventral and manually aimed 12·7mm Type 1 dorsal; (all) internal bay for bomb load of up to 882lb (400kg), with normal load of 661lb (300kg) (-II capable of carrying 1,764lb, 800kg, but seldom used).
History: First flight July 1939; service delivery July or August 1940; final delivery October 1944.
User: Japan (Imperial Army).

Development: The Imperial Army's procurement organization tended to plan aircraft to meet existing, rather than future, threats. This straightforward bomber was requested in answer to the Soviet Union's SB-2. The latter was designed in 1933 and in action in Spain in 1936, but the Ki-48 (which was inferior in bomb load and only slightly faster) was a World War II machine. Entering service in China, it did well and proved popular, and it soon became the most important light bomber in the south-west Pacific with 557 -I built by June 1942. But its deficient performance and protection forced it to operate by night, which reduced the effectiveness of the small bomb load. The lengthened and more powerful -IIa had armour and protected tanks, and the -IIb had dive-bombing airbrakes; later examples of both had a dorsal fin. The -IIc had better armament, with provision also for machine guns fired

Lockheed Model 414 (A-29, PBO) Hudson

Hudson I to VI, A-28, A-29, AT-18, C-63 and PBO-1

Origin: Lockheed Aircraft Corporation.
Type: Reconnaissance bomber and utility.
Engines: (Hudson I, II) two 1,100hp Wright GR-1820-G102A nine-cylinder radials; (Hudson III, A-29, PBO-1) two 1,200hp GR-1820-G205A, (Hudson IV, V, VI and A-28) two 1,200hp Pratt & Whitney R-1830-S3C3-G, S3C4-G or -67 14-cylinder two-row radials.
Dimensions: Span 65ft 6in (19·96m); length 44ft 4in (13·51m); height 11ft 10½in (3·62m).
Weights: Empty (I) 12,000lb (5443kg); (VI) 12,929lb (5864kg); maximum loaded (I) 18,500lb (8393kg); (VI) 22,360lb (10,142kg).
Performance: Maximum speed (I) 246mph (397km/h); (VI) 261mph (420km/h); initial climb 1,200ft (366m)/min; service ceiling 24,500ft

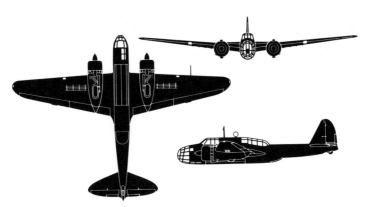

Above: Three-view of Ki-48-IIb (IIc similar).

Below: The Ki-48-IIb was fitted with snow-fence type dive-bombing airbrakes above and below the wings.

from each side of the nose, but the Ki-48 was inherently obsolete and after a total of 1,977 of all versions production stopped in 1944. Many were used for suicide attacks and as test-beds for missiles and the Ne-00 turbojet (carried on a pylon under the bomb bay).

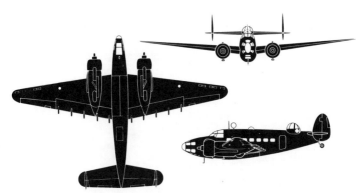

Above: Three-view of Hudson I (all Cyclone-powered similar).

(7468m); range (I) 1,960 miles (3150km); (VI) 2,160 miles (3475km).
Armament: (Typical RAF Hudson in GR role) seven 0·303in Brownings in nose (two, fixed), dorsal turret (two), beam windows and ventral hatch; internal bomb/depth charge load up to 750lb (341kg). *continued* ▶

History: First flight (civil Model 14) 29 July 1937; (Hudson I) 10 December 1938; squadron delivery February 1939; USAAC and USN delivery, October 1941.

Users: Australia, Brazil, Canada, China, Netherlands, New Zealand, UK (RAF, BOAC), US (AAC/AAF, Navy).

Development: In 1938 the British Purchasing Commission was established in Washington to seek out US aircraft that could serve with the RAF and Royal Navy and help bolster British strength beyond the then-small capacity of the British aircraft industry. One of the urgent needs was for a modern long-range reconnaissance and navigation trainer aircraft and Lockheed Aircraft, at Burbank — just climbing out of the Depression — hastily built a mock-up of their Model 14 airliner to meet the requirement. An order for 200 aircraft, many times bigger than any previous order ever received by

Right: One of a batch of 390 Lockheed Hudson GR.V reconnaissance-bombers delivered in 1940-41. This version had the two-row Twin Wasp engine with a long-chord cowling with cooling gills (seen fully open in the photograph below). Some of this batch went to the Middle East, some to the UK and some direct to New Zealand.

Below: As it was derived from a civil airliner the Hudson naturally made a good transport, and it was in this role that the majority were eventually used (though many stayed in action with such later extras as radar and underwing rocket rails). This is a GR.VI, which despite the general-recon designation was serving in West Africa on transport duties from 1941 onwards. Note the open bomb doors.

Lockheed, was fulfilled swiftly and efficiently. The order was many times multiplied and the versatile Hudson served with several RAF commands in many theatres of war. On 8 October 1939 a Hudson over Jutland shot down the first German aircraft claimed by the RAF in World War II. In February 1940 another discovered the prison ship *Altmark* in a Norwegian fjord and directed naval forces to the rescue. Over Dunkirk Hudsons acted as dog-fighters, in August 1941 one accepted the surrender of U-boat *U-570*, and from 1942 many made secret landings in France to deliver or collect agents or supplies. Hudsons of later marks carried ASV radar, rocket launchers and lifeboats. Total deliveries were 2,584 including about 490 armed versions for the US Army, 20 PBOs for the Navy and 300 AT-18 crew trainers. From this fine basic design stemmed the more powerful Vega Ventura bomber and ocean patrol aircraft and the PV-2 Harpoon at almost twice the weight of the Hudson I.

Lockheed PV-1/B-34 Ventura
Vega 37, Ventura I to V, B-34 Lexington, B-37, PV-1 and -3 and PV-2 Harpoon

Origin: Vega Aircraft Corporation, Burbank, California.
Type: Bomber and reconnaissance aircraft.
Engines: Two Pratt & Whitney R-2800 Double Wasp 18-cylinder radials, (Ventura I) 1,850hp R-2800-S1A4-G, (most others) 2,000hp R-2800-31.
Dimensions: Span 65ft 6in (19·96m), (H) 75ft 0in (22·86m); length 51ft 5in to 51ft 9in (15·77m); height 13ft 2in to 14ft 1in (4·29m).
Weights: Empty (PV-1, typical) 19,373lb (8788kg), (H) about 24,000lb (10,886kg); maximum (V) 31,077lb (14,097kg), (H) 40,000lb (18,144kg).
Performance: Maximum speed (V) 300mph (483km/h), (H) 282mph (454km/h); maximum range with max bomb load (all) about 900 miles (1448km).
Armament: See text.
History: First flight (RAF) 31 July 1941; service delivery (RAF) June 1942; final delivery (H) 1945.
Users: (WWII) Australia, Italy (CB), New Zealand, Portugal, South Africa, UK (RAF), US (AAF, Navy).

Development: Vega Aircraft, a 1940 subsidiary of Lockheed, was awarded a contract by the British Purchasing Commission in June 1940 for 875 of a new design of bomber derived from the Lockheed 18 airliner. Called Lockheed V-146, or Vega 37, it resembled a more powerful Hudson, with

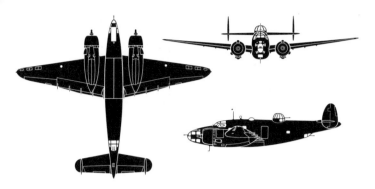

Above: Three-view of all Venturas (B-34 similar)ʻ.

longer fuselage provided with a rear ventral position with two 0·303in Brownings. Two (later four) more were in the dorsal turret, and the nose had two fixed 0·5in and two manually aimed 0·303in. Bomb load was 2,500lb (1134kg). In October 1942 Bomber Command's No 21 Sqn swept into action with a gallant daylight attack on the Phillips works at Eindhoven, but the Ventura proved a mediocre bomber and deliveries stopped at about ▶

Below: Final model of the 14/Hudson/Ventura family, the PV2 Harpoon was redesigned with a new wing and tail and many other changes, including three extra nose guns under the new radar.

300. The B-34 Lexington absorbed many of the unwanted machines, though the Army Air Force never used them operationally. The B-34B trainer, Ventura II and IIA were reconnaissance models (originally O-56), but the bulk of the 1,600 Venturas were Navy PV-1 patrol bombers with up to eight 0·5in, more fuel and ability to carry mines and torpedoes. About 380 similar aircraft served Commonwealth forces as Ventura V, surviving in South Africa to the 1970s. The PV-2 Harpoon was redesigned as a much better Navy bomber, with larger wings, new tail and up to ten 0·5in, rockets and 4,000lb (1814kg) of bombs or torpedoes. The 535 built saw brief service before being passed to Allies.

Right: This PV-1 Ventura patrol bomber of the US Navy was photographed at the Vega plant mounted on a rotatable platform having its compass swung. By 1943 many PVs had ASV radar.

Martin 167 Maryland

Model 167 Maryland I and II

Origin: The Glenn L. Martin Company.
Type: Three-seat reconnaissance bomber.
Engines: Two Pratt & Whitney Twin Wasp 14-cylinder two-row radials; (Maryland I) 1,050hp R-1830-S1C3-G; (II) 1,200hp R-1830-S3C4-G.
Dimensions: Span 61ft 4in (18·69m); length 46ft 8in (14·22m); height 10ft 1in (3·07m).
Weights: Empty 11,213lb (RAF Mk II); maximum loaded (I) 15,297lb; (II) 16,809lb (7694kg).
Performance: Maximum speed (prototype) 316mph; (I) 304mph; (II) 280mph (451km/h); initial climb 1,790ft (545m)/min; service ceiling (I) 29,500ft (8992m); (II) 26,000ft (7925m); range with bomb load 1,080 miles (1738km).
Armament: Four 0·303in Browning (France, 7·5mm MAC 1934) fixed in outer wings, two 0·303in Vickers K (France, MAC 1934) manually aimed

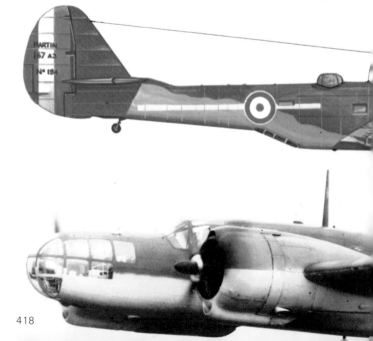

from dorsal turret and rear ventral position; internal bomb load of 2,000lb (907kg) (France 1,874lb, 850kg; Maryland I, 1,250lb, 567kg).
History: First flight 14 March 1939; (production 167F) 7 August 1939; service delivery (France) October 1939; final delivery 1941.
Users: France, South Africa, UK (RAF, RN).

Development: Designed as the US Army XA-22 attack bomber, the Martin 167 was not adopted but immediately attracted a big French order for the Armée de l'Air as the 167F, with Armée de l'Air designation 167A-3. Of 215 purchased, about 75 reached France before the June 1940 capitulation, squadrons GB I/62 and I/63 completing conversion and, despite being chosen for dangerous missions, suffering only 8 per cent casualties (the lowest of any French bomber type). Some survivors and undelivered aircraft went to the RAF, while most surviving French aircraft served the Vichy Air Force and operated against the Allies over Gibraltar, North Africa and Syria. The RAF accepted 75 ex-French machines and bought a further 150 with two-stage supercharged engines as the Maryland II, using all 225 as reconnaissance bombers in Cyrenaica, Malta and other Middle East areas. A few went to the Fleet Air Arm (one gave first warning of the departure of *Bismarck*) and four squadrons served with the South African AF. In basic arrangement rather like Luftwaffe bombers, the Maryland was quite fast, nice to fly, but cramped and inadequately armed.

Left: This aircraft, designated Martin 167A-3 by the French, was used by GB I/63 of the Vichy forces against Gibraltar.

Below: The first Maryland I, built to a French order and taken over by the RAF. This mark had US equipment.

Martin 179 B-26 Marauder

Model 179, B-26A to G, Marauder I to III

Origin: The Glenn L. Martin Company.

Type: Five- to seven-seat medium bomber.

Engines: Two Pratt & Whitney Double Wasp 18-cylinder two-row radials; (B-26) 1,850hp R-2800-5; (A) 2,000hp R-2800-39; (B, C, D, E, F, G) 2,000hp R-2800-43.

Dimensions: Span (B-26, A and first 641 B-26B) 65ft (19·8m); (remainder) 71ft (21·64m); length (B-26) 56ft, (A, B) 58ft 3in (17·75m); (F, G) 56ft 6in (17·23m); height (up to E) 19ft 10in (6·04m); (remainder) 21ft 6in (6·55m).

Weights: Empty (early, typical) 23,000lb (10,433kg); (F, G) 25,300lb (11,490kg); maximum loaded (B-26) 32,000lb; (A) 33,022lb; (first 641 B) 34,000lb, then 37,000lb (16,783kg); (F) 38,000lb (G) 38,200lb (17,340kg).

Performance: Maximum speed (up to E, typical) 310mph (500km/h); (F, G) 280mph (451km/h); initial climb 1,000ft (305m)/min; service ceiling (up to E) 23,000ft (7000m); (F, G) 19,800ft (6040m); range with 3,000lb (1361kg) bomb load (typical) 1,150 miles (1850km).

Armament: (B-26, A) five 0·30in or 0·50in Browning in nose (1 or 2), power dorsal turret (2), tail (1, manual) and optional manual ventral hatch; (B to E) one 0·5in manually aimed in nose, twin-gun turret, two manually aimed 0·5in waist guns, one "tunnel gun" (usually 0·5in), two 0·5in in power tail turret and four 0·5in fixed as "package guns" on sides of forward fuselage; (F, G) same but without tunnel gun; some variations and trainer and Navy versions unarmed. Internal bomb load of 5,200lb (2359kg) up to 641st B, after which rear bay was disused (eliminated in F, G) to give maximum load of 4,000lb (1814kg). Early versions could carry two torpedoes.

History: First flight 25 November 1940; service delivery 25 February 1941; final delivery March 1945.

Users: France, South Africa, UK (RAF), US (AAF, Navy).

Development: With its background of leadership in bomber design, Martin pulled out all the stops to win the 1939 Medium Bomber competition of the US Army, and boldly chose a wing optimised for high-speed cruise efficiency rather than for landing. Though the Model 179 won the competition — 201 being ordered "off the drawing board" on 5 July 1939 — the actual hardware proved too much for inexperienced pilots to handle, with unprecedented wing loading. In fact there were no real problems, but the newness of the first B-26 versions, coupled with their reputation of being a

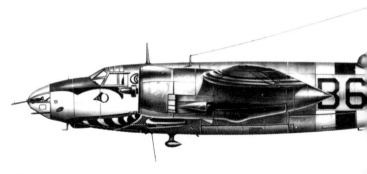

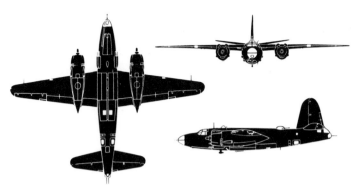

Above: Three-view of B-26C (Marauder III similar).

"widow maker", created a vicious circle of high casualties. Production B-26A models, with torpedo shackles between the bomb doors, were deployed to Australia the day after Pearl Harbor (8 December 1941), and later B models saw extensive South West Pacific service with the rear bomb bay used as a fuel tank (maximum bomb load 2,000lb). From the 641st B the wing and vertical tail were extended and on 14 May 1943 the Marauder began its career as the chief medium bomber of the 9th AF in the ETO (European Theatre of Operations). By VE-day the B-26 had set a record for the lowest loss-rate of any US Army bomber in Europe. About 522 also ▶

Above: Among the lesser-known sub-types of Marauder were the JM-1 target tugs of the US Navy, which were painted yellow. The Navy had 225 JM-1s (ex-USAAF AT-23B crew trainers converted from B-26Cs, as illustrated) and 47 JM-2s converted from the TB-26G.

Left: By far the most important B-26 operator in Europe was the 9th Air Force, whose B-26s served alongside the A-20 and new A-26 Invader in pounding enemy targets by day. This B-26B-55, painted in D-day invasion stripes, was assigned to the 9th AAF 397th Bombardment Group.

served with the RAF and South African AF in Italy. Total production amounted to 5,157 for the US Army (including Allied forces) plus a few dozen JM-1 and -2 target tug, reconnaissance and utility versions for the US Navy and about 200 AT-23 (later called TB-26) trainers. In 1948 the Marauder was withdrawn, and the B-26 designation passed to the Douglas Invader.

Above: A B-26B-55, one of a formation of various Marauder sub-types heading out over Florence to bomb Kesselring's Italian front.

Below: A Bomb Group of the 8th (not the 9th) Army Air Force streaming round a taxiway in southern England for a mission in 1944. As far as can be seen, the aircraft are B-26Cs.

Martin 187 Baltimore

Model 187, Baltimore I to V
(US Army A-30)

Origin: The Glenn L. Martin Company.
Type: Four-seat light bomber.
Engines: Two Wright Cyclone 14-cylinder two-row radials; (I, II) 1,600hp R-2600-A5B; (III, IV) 1,660hp R-2600-19; (V) 1,700hp R-2600-29.
Dimensions: Span 61ft 4in (18·69m); length 48ft 6in (14·78m); height 17ft 9in (5·41m).
Weights: Empty (III) 15,200lb (6895kg); maximum loaded (I) 22,958lb; (III) 23,000lb (10,433kg); (V) 27,850lb (12,632kg).
Performance: Maximum speed (I) 308mph; (III, IV) 302mph; (V) 320mph (515km/h); initial climb 1,500ft (457m)/min; service ceiling (typical) 24,000ft (7315m); range with 1,000lb bomb load (typical) 1,060 miles (1700km).
Armament: Four 0·303in Brownings fixed in outer wings; mid-upper position with manually aimed 0·303in Vickers K (I), twin Vickers (II), Boulton Paul turret with two or four 0·303in Browning (III), Martin turret with two 0·5in Browning (IV, V); rear ventral position with two 0·303in

Right: Seldom hitting the headlines, the Baltimore worked hard by day and night from Libya through Tunisia and Sicily to Italy and the Balkans. This formation of Mk V (ex-USAAF A-30) bombers belonged to the Italian Stormo Baltimore, a major element of the Co-Belligerent AF formed in early 1943.

Below: Another Co-Belligerent Baltimore (a Mk IV or V) is seen in this photograph taken on an Italian airfield in early 1944.

Vickers K; optional four or six fixed 0·303in guns firing directly to rear or obliquely downward. Internal bomb load up to 2,000lb (907kg).

History: First flight 14 June 1941; service delivery October 1941; final delivery May 1944.

Users: Australia, France, Italy, South Africa, Turkey, UK (RAF, RN).

Development: Martin received an RAF order in May 1940 for 400 improved Maryland bombers with deeper fuselages to allow intercommunication between crew members. In the course of design the more powerful R-2600 engine was adopted and the final aircraft marked an appreciable all-round improvement. The 400 were made up of 50 Mk I, 100 Mk II and 250 Mk III differing mainly in mid-upper armament. To facilitate Lend-Lease contracts, under which additional machines were ordered, the Model 187 was given the US Army designation A-30, but none were supplied for American use. After 281 Mk IIIA, identical to the III but on US Lend-Lease account, and 294 Mk IV, production completed with 600 Mk V (A-30A), the total being 1,575 all for the RAF. Many were passed on to the South African AF, and a few to the Royal Navy, all being worked very hard in Cyrenaica, Tunisia, Sicily and Italy in bombing and close-support missions. In 1944 units of the co-belligerent Italian forces received ex-RAF machines and formed the Stormo Baltimore which was active over Jugoslavia and the Balkans.

Mitsubishi G3M "Nell"
G3M1, G3M2 and G3M3; some rebuilt as L3Y

Origin: Mitsubishi Jukogyo KK, Nagoya; also built by Nakajima Hikoki KK at Koizumi.

Type: Long-range land-based bomber (L3Y, transport).

Engines: Two Mitsubishi Kinsei 14-cylinder two-row radials, (G3M1, L3Y1) 910hp Kinsei 3, (G3M2, L3Y2) 1,075hp Kinsei 42 or 45, (G3M3) 1,300hp Kinsei 51.

Dimensions: Span 82ft 0¼in (25·00m); length 53ft 11½in (16·45m); height 12ft 1in (3·685m).

Weights: Empty (1) 10,516lb (4770kg), (3) 11,551lb (5243kg); max loaded (1) 16,848lb (7642kg), (3) 17,637lb (8000kg).

Performance: Maximum speed (1) 216mph (348km/h), (2) 232mph (373km/h), (3) 258mph (415km/h); service ceiling (3) 33,730ft (10,280 m); maximum range (3) 3,871 miles (6228km).

Armament: (1 and 2) up to four 7·7mm Type 92 manually aimed from two retractable dorsal positions, ventral position and cockpit, (3) one 20mm Type 99 in dorsal fairing and three 7.7mm in side blisters, and retractable dorsal turret; external bomb load or torpedo of 1,764lb (800kg).

History: First flight (Ka-15 prototype) July 1935; service delivery late 1936.

User: Imperial Japanese Navy.

Development: Derived from the Ka-9 of April 1934, the Ka-15 series of prototypes were among the first outstanding Japanese warplanes superior to Western types. Designed by a team under Prof Kiro Honjo, the Ka-15 was

Right: Mitsubishi G3M2 bombers, probably of the Mihoro Kokutái, photographed whilst releasing their bombs in a stick. All aircraft in the picture are of the Model 22 sub-type with a large turtle-back dorsal gun position equipped with a 20mm cannon. The Mihoro Kokutai provided high-level bombers which sank the British capital ships *Prince of Wales* and *Repulse* on 10 December 1941.

Below: A formation of G3M3 bombers (the final G3M3 sub-type, the Model 22 had similar armament) with dorsal turrets extended and machine gun deployed ahead of the prominent dorsal canopy over the gunner who manned the cannon. Note the landing wheel on the nearest aircraft, which only retracted partially.

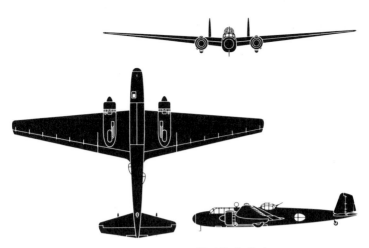

Above: Three-view of G3M3 Model 23 (G3M2 similar).

a smooth stressed-skin machine, with exceptional range. On 14 August 1937 the Kanoya air corps based on Taipei made the world's first trans-oceanic raid when a large force of G3M2 hit targets 1,250 miles away in China. Many other great raids were made, but the most famous action was the sinking of HMS *Prince of Wales* and *Repulse* (which thought they were out of range) on 10 December 1941. By 1943 most were in second-line service, though known to the Allies as "Nell". The L3Y transport conversion was code-named "Tina".

Mitsubishi G4M "Betty"

G4M1 to G4M3c and G6M

Origin: Mitsubishi Jukogyo KK.

Type: Land-based naval torpedo bomber and missile carrier.

Engines: (G4M1) two 1,530hp Mitsubishi Kasei 11 14-cylinder two-row radials; (subsequent versions) two Kasei 22 rated at 1,850hp with water/methanol injection.

Dimensions: Span 81ft 7¾in (24·89m); length (1) 65ft 6¼in; (later versions) 64ft 4¾in (19·63m); height (1) 16ft 1in; (later versions) 13ft 5¾in (4·11m).

Weights: Empty (1) 14,860lb (6741kg); (2) 17,623lb (7994kg); (3) 18,500lb (8391kg); loaded (1) 20,944lb (9500kg); (2, 3) 27,550lb (12,500kg); max overload (1) 28,350lb (12,860kg); (2, 3) 33,070lb (15,000kg).

Performance: Maximum speed (1) 265mph (428km/h); (2) 271mph (437km/h); (3) 283mph (455km/h); initial climb (1) 1,800ft (550m)/min; (2, 3) 1,380ft (420m)/min; service ceiling (all) about 30,000ft (9144m); range (with bombs at overload weight) (1) 3,132 miles (5040km); (2) 2,982 miles (4800km); (3) 2,262 miles (3640km). ***continued ▶***

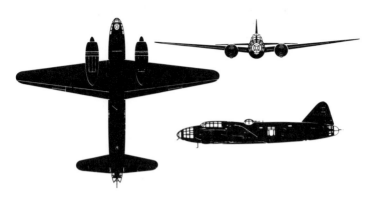

Above: Three-view of G4M2, without bulged weapon-bay doors.

Left: A G4M2a of the 763rd Kokutai (Air Corps). This aircraft was found abandoned in the Philippines. Finish was dark green above and natural metal on underside.

Below: Aircrew of a Navy kokutai (air corps) photographed near the end of World War II when the desperate situation had led to widespread suicide missions. The aircraft is a G4M2e carrying an MXY-7 Ohka piloted missile under its belly.

Armament: (1) three manually aimed 7·7mm in nose, dorsal and ventral positions and 20mm manually aimed in tail; internal bomb load of 2,205lb (1000kg) or 1,764lb (800kg) torpedo externally; (2) as before but electric dorsal turret (one 7·7mm) and revised tail position with increased arc of fire; (2e, and, retro-actively, many earlier G4M2) one 7·7mm in nose, one 20mm in dorsal turret and manual 20mm in tail and two beam windows. (G4M2e) adapted to carry Ohka piloted missile.
History: First flight October 1939; service delivery April 1941; first flight (G4M2) November 1942.
User: Japan (Imperial Navy).

Development: Designed to an incredibly difficult 1938 Navy specification, the G4M family (Allied name, "Betty") was the Imperial Japanese Navy's premier heavy bomber in World War II; yet the insistence on the great range of 2,000 nautical miles (3706km) with full bomb load made the saving of weight take priority over defence and the aircraft was highly vulnerable and not very popular. The wing was of the same Mitsubishi 118 section as the Zero-Sen and boldly designed as an integral fuel tank to accommodate no less than 5,000 litres (1,100gal). The company kept recommending four engines and being overruled by the Navy, which, during the early flight-test stage, wasted more than a year, and 30 aircraft, in trying to make the design into the G6M bomber escort with crew of ten and 19 guns. Eventually the G4M1 was readied for service as a bomber and flew its first missions in South East China in May 1941. More than 250 operated in the Philippines and Malayan campaigns, but after the Solomons battle in August 1942 it began to be apparent that, once intercepted and hit, the unprotected bomber went up like a torch (hence the Allied nickname "one-shot lighter").

Mitsubishi Ki-21 "Sally"

Ki-21-I, -IIa and -IIb

Origin: Mitsubishi Jukogyo KK; also built by Nakajima Hikoki KK.
Type: Seven-seat heavy bomber.
Engines: (I) two 850hp Nakajima Ha-5-Kai 14-cylinder two-row radials; (II) two 1,490hp Mitsubishi Ha-101 of same layout.
Dimensions: Span 73ft 9¾in (22·5m); length 52ft 6in (16·0m); height 15ft 11in (4·85m).
Weights: Empty (I) 10,341lb (4691kg); (II) 13,382lb (6070kg); maximum loaded (I) 16,517lb (7492kg); (II) 21,395lb (9710kg).
Performance: Maximum speed (I) 268mph (432km/h); (II) 297mph (478km/h); initial climb (I) 1,150ft (350m)/min; (II) 1,640ft (500m)/min; service ceiling (I) 28,220ft (8600m); (II) 32,800ft (10,000m); range with full bomb load (I) 1,678 miles (2700km); (II) 1,370 miles (2200km).
Armament: See text for defensive armament; internal bomb bay in fuselage for load of (I) 1,653lb (750kg) or (II) 2,205lb (1000kg).

Above: Dark green and sky grey G4M1s over China in 1941.

Total production reached the exceptional quantity of 2,479, most of them in the many sub-types of G4M2 with increased fuel capacity and power. Finally the trend of development was reversed with the G4M3 series with full protection and only 968gal fuel.

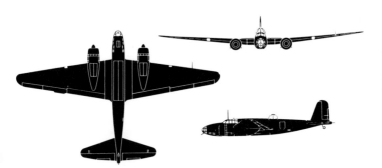

Above: Three-view of the Ki-21-IIb.

Left: This Ki-21-Ia of the 2nd Chutai, 60th Hikosentai, was painted in one of the more colourful Army finishes in which upper surfaces were olive green and brown separated by white strips, the undersurfaces of wings and tail-plane being light grey (rather like the Navy sky grey). In 1937, when this initial version entered service, the Ki 21 outperformed every other bomber except the B-17 then also just entering service. After Pearl Harbor, however, it was gradually recognised as obsolescent, though production continued until September 1944.

431

History: First flight November 1936; service delivery 1937; first flight (Ki-21-II) mid-1940; final delivery September 1944.
User: Japan (Imperial Army).

Development: In 1936 the Imperial Japanese Army issued a challenging specification for a new heavy bomber, demanding a crew of at least four, an endurance of five hours, a bomb load of 750kg and speed of 400km/h. Mitsubishi won over the Nakajima Ki-19 and built five prototypes powered by the company's own A.14 (Kinsei Ha-6) engine. The fields of fire of the three manually aimed 7·7mm machine guns were inadequate and the Army also requested a switch to the Ha-5 engine. With various modifications it was accepted as the Type 97 (also called OB-97; omoshi bakudanki meaning heavy bomber) and put into production not only by Mitsubishi but also, in 1938, by Nakajima. It rapidly became the premier Japanese Army heavy bomber and served throughout the "Chinese incident", the operational results being efficiently fed back to the procurement machine and the manufacturer. This led to the defensive armament being increased to five guns, one remotely controlled in the extreme tail, the crew being increased to seven. The bomb bay was enlarged, the flaps were increased in size and crew armour was dramatically augmented. The result was the Ki-21-Ib. Increase in fuel capacity and addition of a sixth (beam) gun resulted in the -Ic variant. In 1939 work began on the much more powerful -II, with increased-span tailplane. Several hundred of both versions were in use in December 1941 and they were met on all fronts in the Pacific war (being fairly easy meat for Hurricanes in Burma). Code-named "Sally" they faded from front-line service in 1943, though the -IIb with "glasshouse" replaced by a dorsal turret (one 12·7mm) improved defence when it entered service in 1942. Total production was 2,064 (351 by Nakajima), plus 500 transport versions (called MC-20, Ki-57 and "Topsy").

Below: Taken over Japan in 1941 or 1942, this photograph shows Ki-21-IIa bombers of the Hammamatsu Bomber School whose emblem appears on the tail of the nearest machine. As this model had no turret its chief role must have been to train pilots, navigators and bomb-aimers.

Above: After 1942 Japan had lost air supremacy almost everywhere and even front-line bombers such as this Ki-21-IIb of the 14th Sentai had to hug the treetops to try to evade Allied fighters. This olive green and light grey machine, with scarlet tail badge, was over the Philippines in 1944.

Mitsubishi Ki-30 "Ann"

Ki-30

Origin: Mitsubishi Jukogyo KK; also built by Tachikawa Dai-Ichi Rikugun Kokusho.
Type: Two-seat light bomber.
Engine: One 950hp Mitsubishi Ha-5 Zuisei 14-cylinder two-row radial.
Dimensions: Span 47ft 8¾in (14·55m); length 33ft 11in (10·34m) height 11ft 11¾in (3·65m).
Weights: Empty 4,915lb (2230kg); maximum loaded 7,324lb (3322kg).
Performance: Maximum speed 263mph (423km/h); initial climb 1,640ft (500m)/min; service ceiling 28,117ft (8570m); range (bomb load not stated) 1,056 miles (1700km).
Armament: One 7·7mm Type 89 machine gun fixed in wing (sometimes both wings) and one manually aimed from rear cockpit; internal bomb bay for three 220lb (100kg) or equivalent bomb load.
History: First flight February 1937; service delivery October 1938; final delivery 1941.
Users: Japan (Imperial Army), Thailand.

Development: With the Ki-32, Ki-27 fighter and Ki-21 heavy bomber, the Ki-30 was one of the important new stressed-skin monoplanes ordered by the Imperial Army under its modernisation plan of 1935. It was the first in Japan to have a modern two-row engine, as well as internal bomb bay, flaps and constant-speed propeller. It was notably smaller than the otherwise similar Fairey Battle produced in Britain. Unlike the British bomber the bomb bay was in the fuselage, resulting in a mid-wing and long landing gear (which was fixed). The pilot and observer/bomb aimer had a good view but were unable to communicate except by speaking tube. The Ki-30 was in service in numbers in time to be one of the major types in the Sino-Japanese war. In 1942 surviving aircraft played a large part in the advance to the Philippines, but then swiftly withdrew from first-line operations. Mitsubishi built 638 at Nagoya and 68 were completed at the Tachikawa Army Air Arsenal. In conformity with the Allied system of code-naming bombers after girls, the Ki-30 was dubbed "Ann". It was the ultimate development of the Karigane family of high-performance monoplanes. In the mid-1930s these had been the epitome of advanced technology, and until 1941 resulted in effective, reliable warplanes, but after that year the concept was obsolescent, and vulnerable to Allied fighters.

Left: A Ki-30 of the 2nd Chutai of the 10th Hikosentai. This was an excellent light bomber in the war against China, and saw much action in that theatre. From 1940 many were supplied to the Royal Thai Air Force for use against the Vichy French forces in Indo-China in a campaign begun in January 1941.

Below: Pilots and observers of a Ki-30 Chutai relax before a combat mission, probably in China before the start of World War II. At this period the Army painted its bombers pale grey or left them in natural metal finish. Note the projecting tube ahead of the spinner for the traditional Hucks starter.

Mitsubishi Ki-67 Hiryu "Peggy"

Ki-67-Ia, Ib and II and Ki-109

Origin: Mitsubishi Jukogyo KK; also built by Kawasaki and (assembly only) Nippon Kokusai Koku Kogyo KK, plus one by Tachikawa.

Type: Heavy bomber and torpedo dropper; Ki-109 heavy escort fighter.

Engines: Two 1,900hp Mitsubishi Ha-104 18-cylinder two-row radials.

Dimensions: Span 73ft 9¾in (22·5m); length 61ft 4¼in (18·7m); height 18ft 4½in (5·60m).

Weights: (lb) empty 19,068lb (8649kg); loaded 30,346lb (13,765kg).

Performance: (lb) Maximum speed 334mph (537km/h); initial climb 1,476ft (450m)/min; service ceiling 31,070ft (9470m); range with full bomb load 621 miles (1000km) plus 2hr reserve, also reported as total range 1,740 miles (2800km).

Armament: Standard on Ia, Ib, one 20mm Ho-5 in electric dorsal turret and single 12·7mm Type 1 manually aimed from nose, tail and two beam positions; internal bomb load 1,764lb (800kg); suicide attack 6,393lb (2900kg).

History: First flight "beginning of 1943"; service delivery April 1944; first flight (Ki-109) August 1944.

User: Japan (Imperial Army and Navy).

Development: Designed by a team led by Dr Hisanojo Ozawa to meet a February 1941 specification, this Army bomber not only met the demand for much higher speed but also proved to have the manoeuvrability of a fighter. It also lacked nothing in armour and fuel-tank protection, and was probably the best all-round bomber produced in Japan during World War II. With a crew of six/eight, it was often looped and shown to have excellent turning power, better than that of several Japanese fighters. Indeed the Ki-69 escort fighter version was developed in parallel with the bomber

Below: This Ki-67-Ib was painted dark olive and pale grey and was serving with the 74th Sentai in 1944.

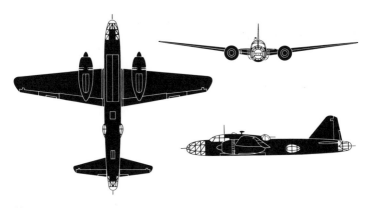

Above: Three-view of Ki-67-Ib.

during 1942 but had to be shelved as delays to the bomber were becoming serious. These delays were due to inefficiency, material shortage and continual changes requested by the customer. By 1944 only 15 (all different) had been built, but production was then allowed to begin in earnest and by VJ-day the creditable total of 727 had been delivered, 606 by Mitsubishi and the rest by Kawasaki, Nippon and (one only) the Tachikawa arsenal. At first the Ki-67 Hiryu (Flying Dragon) was used as a torpedo bomber in the Philippine Sea battle, receiving the Allied name "Peggy". Later it operated against Iwo Jima, the Marianas and Okinawa and in the defence of Japan. There were only two versions used, the Ib having bulged waist blisters. Of many projected versions, of which the Ki-67-II with 2,500hp Ha-214 engines marked the biggest advance, only the Ki-109 reached the service trials stage. Armed with a 75mm gun with 15 hand-loaded rounds, plus a 12·7mm in the tail, this was meant to have 2,000hp turbocharged Ha-104 engines but none were available. With ordinary Ha-104s the Ki-109 could not get up to B-29 altitude!

Below: This Mitsubishi Ki-67-Ib is in the hands of a combat unit but does not appear to have been painted in unit markings and may be new from the manufacturer. In general the Ki-67 was an excellent aircraft, and extremely popular with its crews, though internal bomb load was surprisingly small.

Nakajima Ki-49 Donryu "Helen"

Ki-49-I, IIa, IIb, III and Ki-58

Origin: Nakajima Hikoki KK; also built by Tachikawa Hikoki KK and (few) Mansyu Hikoki.

Type: Eight-seat heavy bomber; Ki-58, escort fighter.

Engines: (I) two 1,250hp Nakajima Ha-41 14-cylinder two-row radials; (II) two 1,450hp Nakajima Ha-109-II of same layout; (III) two 2,500hp Nakajima Ha-117 18-cylinder two-row radials.

Dimensions: Span 66ft 7¼in (20·3m); length 53ft 1¾in (16·2m); height 13ft 11½in (4·25m).

Weights: Empty (II) 15,653lb (7100kg); normal loaded 23,545lb (10,680kg).

Performance: Maximum speed (II) 304mph (490km/h); initial climb 1,312ft (400m)/min; service ceiling 26,772ft (8160m); range with bomb load, 1,491 miles (2400km).

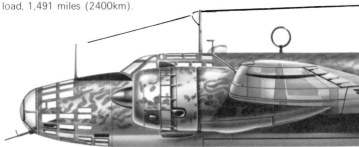

Armament: (I) one 20mm cannon manually aimed in dorsal position, single 7·7mm manually aimed at nose and tail; (IIa) as (I) plus extra 7·7mm in ventral and two beam positions (total five); (IIb) as IIa but with all 7·7mm replaced by 12·7mm, thus 20mm dorsal and single 12·7mm in nose, tail, ventral and two beam positions; all versions, internal bay for bomb load up to 2,205lb (1,000kg).

History: First flight August 1939; (production Ki-49-I) probably May 1940; (II) 1942; final delivery December 1944.

User: Japan (Imperial Army).

Development: Designed to a late 1938 specification aimed at replacing the Mitsubishi Ki-21, the Ki-49 was the first Japanese bomber to mount a 20mm cannon; but it was at first only slightly faster than the Ki-21, had a poor ceiling and never did achieve any advance in range and bomb load. The 1,160hp Nakajima Ha-5B engines of the prototype were replaced by the Ha-41, and 129 of the -I model were built at Ohta, after whose Donryu (Dragon Swallower) shrine the type was named. The production machine was the Type 100 heavy bomber, and the Allied code name was "Helen". Its first mission was a raid on Port Darwin from a New Guinea base on 19 February 1942. The main model was the better-armed -II series, of which 649 were built by Nakajima, 50 by Tachikawa and a few by Mansyu in Harbin, Manchuria. Though met in all parts of the Japanese war, the Ki-49 was not very effective; many were destroyed at Leyte Gulf, and by late 1944 all were being used either for non-combatant purposes or as suicide machines or, with ASV radar or magnetic-mine detectors, for ocean patrol. As it was a poor bomber three were converted as Ki-58 fighters with five 20mm cannon and three 12·7mm guns, while two were rebuilt as Ki-80 leadships for attack by fighter-bomber or suicide aircraft. The much more powerful III model was not ready by August 1945, though six were built.

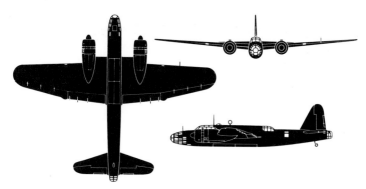

Above: Three-view of Ki-49-I (II has oil coolers under engines).

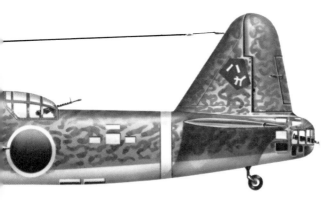

Above: The Ki-49-IIb was the main production version, and this example is typical. It was left in New Guinea but the unit to which it belonged has not been identified. The most probable colour scheme was a mottled light grey and olive green on the sides and upper surfaces and paler grey or sky underneath. No really good specimen of this important Army bomber exists today, though there are many wrecks.

Below: This excellent photograph shows a Ki-49-I in the home-based training role. It is probably finished in bright training orange overall, and carries on its tail stylised representations of the three Kanji characters spelling Hammamatsu, home of the Hammamatsu Army Bomber Training School. It is apparently not fitted with defensive armament.

North American NA-62 B-25 Mitchell

B-25 to TB-25N, PBJ series, F-10

Origin: North American Aviation Inc, Inglewood and Kansas City.

Type: Medium bomber and attack with crew from four to six (see text).

Engines: (B-25, A, B), two 1,700hp Wright R-2600-9 Double Cyclone 14-cylinder two-row radials; (C, D, G) two 1,700hp R-2600-13; (H, J, F-10), two 1,850hp (emergency rating) R-2600-29.

Dimensions: Span 67ft 7in (20·6m); length (B-25, A) 54ft 1in; (B, C, J) 52ft 11in (16·1m); (G, H) 51ft (15·54m); height (typical) 15ft 9in (4·80m).

Weights: Empty (J, typical) 21,100lb (9580kg); maximum loaded (A) 27,100lb; (B) 28,640lb; (C) 34,000lb (15,422kg); (G) 35,000lb (15,876kg); (H) 36,047lb (16,350kg); (J) normal 35,000lb, overload 41,800lb (18,960 kg).

Performance: Maximum speed (A) 315mph; (B) 300mph; (C, G) 284mph (459km/h); (H, J) 275mph (443km/h); initial climb (A, typical) 1,500ft (460m)/min; (late models, typical) 1,100ft (338m)/min; service ceiling (A) 27,000ft (8230m); (late models, typical) 24,000ft (7315m); range (all, typical) 1,500 miles (2414km).

Armament: See text.

History: First flight (NA-40 prototype) January 1939; (NA-62, the first production B-25) 19 August 1940; (B-25G) August 1942.

Users: (Wartime) Australia, Brazil, China, France (FFL), Italy (Co-Belligerent), Mexico, Netherlands (1944), Soviet Union, UK (RAF, RN), US (AAC/AAF, Navy).

Development: Named in honour of the fearless US Army Air Corps officer who was court-martialled in 1924 for his tiresome (to officialdom) belief in air power, the B-25 — designed by a company with no previous experience of twins, of bombers or of high performance warplanes — was made in larger quantities than any other American twin-engined combat ▶

Below: One of the most heavily armed twin-engined aircraft of the war, this B-25J belonged to the 345th BG in the Philippines.

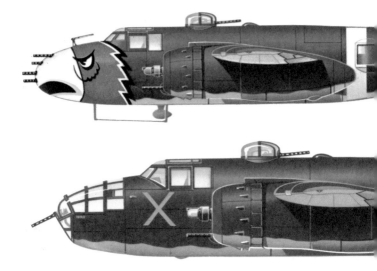

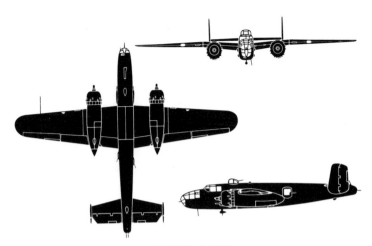

Above: Three-view of B-25J (RAF, Mitchell III).

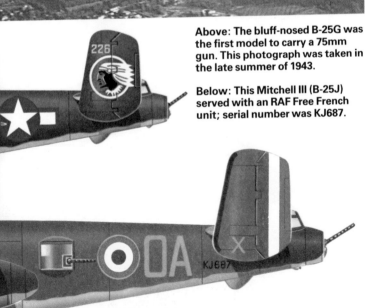

Above: The bluff-nosed B-25G was the first model to carry a 75mm gun. This photograph was taken in the late summer of 1943.

Below: This Mitchell III (B-25J) served with an RAF Free French unit; serial number was KJ687.

aircraft and has often been described as the best aircraft in its class in World War II. Led by Lee Atwood and Ray Rice, the design team first created the Twin Wasp-powered NA-40, but had to start again and build a sleeker and more powerful machine to meet revised Army specifications demanding twice the bomb load (2,400lb, 1089kg). The Army ordered 184 off the drawing board, the first 24 being B-25s and the rest B-25A with armour and self-sealing tanks. The defensive armament was a 0·5in manually aimed in the cramped tail and single 0·3in manually aimed from waist windows and the nose; bomb load was 3,000lb (1361kg). The B had twin 0·5in in an electrically driven dorsal turret and a retractable ventral turret, the tail gun being removed. On 18 April 1942 16 B-25Bs led by Lt-Col Jimmy Doolittle made the daring and morale-raising raid on Tokyo,

having made free take-offs at gross weight from the carrier *Hornet* 800 miles distant. Extra fuel, external bomb racks and other additions led to the C, supplied to the RAF, China and Soviet Union, and as PBJ-1C to the US Navy. The D was similar but built at the new plant at Kansas City. In 1942 came the G, with solid nose fitted with a 75mm M-4 gun, loaded manually with 21 rounds. At first two 0·5in were also fixed in the nose, for flak suppression and sighting, but in July 1943 tests against Japanese ships showed that more was needed and the answer was four 0·5in "package guns" ▶

Below: Shadows race across the Tunisian desert as a squadron of USAAF B-25C Mitchells of the newly formed 12th Air Force head for a daytime target. Note RAF-style fin flashes.

Above: This B-25J was one of 870 of various sub-types supplied freely under Lend-Lease to the Soviet Union in 1941–44. The B-25 was supplied in greater numbers than any other Allied offensive aircraft, though the various A-20 versions ran it close.

Right: A dramatic photograph taken on 18 April 1942 as one of Lt-Col James H. Doolittle's B-25Cs staggers into the air from USS *Hornet* bound for Tokyo. The lead aircraft on this intrepid mission had a run of only 467 feet along the pitching deck.

on the sides of the nose. Next came the B-25H with the fearsome armament of a 75mm, 14 0·5in guns (eight firing ahead, two in waist bulges and four in dorsal and tail turrets) and a 2,000lb (907kg) torpedo or 3,200lb (1451kg) of bombs. Biggest production of all was of the J, with glazed nose, normal bomb load of 4,000lb (1814kg) and 13 0·5in guns supplied with 5,000 rounds. The corresponding attack version had a solid nose with five additional 0·5in guns. Total J output was 4,318, and the last delivery in August 1945 brought total output to 9,816. The F-10 was an unarmed multi-camera reconnaissance version, and the CB-25 was a post-war transport model. The wartime AT-24 trainers were redesignated TB-25 and, after 1947, supplemented by more than 900 bombers rebuilt as the TB-25J, K, L and M. Many ended their days as research hacks or target tugs and one carried the cameras for the early Cinerama films.

Petlyakov Pe-2 and Pe-3

Pe-2, 2I, 2R, 2U and 3bis

Origin: The design bureau of V. M. Petlyakov.
Type: (2) attack bomber; (2I) interceptor fighter; (2R) reconnaissance; (2U) dual trainer; (3bis) fighter reconnaissance.
Engines: Two Klimov (Hispano-Suiza basic design) vee-12 liquid-cooled; (2, pre-1943) 1,100hp M-105R or RA; (2, 1943 onwards, 2R, 2U, 3bis) 1,260hp M-105PF; (2I) 1,600hp M-107A.
Dimensions: Span 56ft 3$\frac{1}{2}$in (17·2m); length 41ft 4$\frac{1}{4}$in to 41ft 6in (12·6–12·66m); height 11ft 6in (3·5m).
Weights: Empty (typical) 12,900lb (5870kg); normal loaded 16,540–16,976lb (7700kg); maximum loaded (all versions) 18,780lb (8520kg).
Performance: Maximum speed (typical, 105R) 336mph (540km/h); (105PF) 360mph (580km/h); (107A) 408mph (655km/h); initial climb (typical) 1,430ft (436m)/min; service ceiling (except 2I) 28,870ft (8800 m); (2I) 36,100ft (11,000m); range with bomb load (105R) 746 miles (1200km); (105PF) 721 miles (1160km).
Armament: See text.
History: First flight (VI-100) 1939; (production Pe-2) June 1940; final delivery, probably January 1945.
User: Soviet Union (post-war, Czechoslovakia, Poland).

Development: Not until long after World War II did Western observers appreciate the importance of the Pe-2. Built throughout the war, it was one of the outstanding combat aircraft of the Allies and, by dint of continual improvement, remained in the front rank of tactical fighting along the entire Eastern front right up to the German surrender. It was planned by Vladimir M. Petlyakov's design team in 1938 as a high-altitude fighter designated

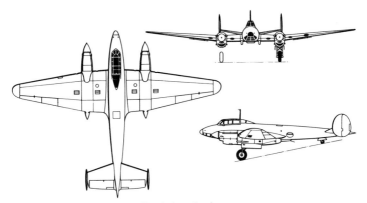

Above: Three-view of Pe-2 (basic bomber).

VI-100. When adapted to high-level bombing it kept the fighter's slim fuselage and this feature, coupled with intensive aerodynamic refinement, always made it fast enough to be difficult for German fighters to intercept it. Level bombing at height proved inaccurate, so dive brakes were added under the wings and the Pe-2 went into service in August 1940 as a multi-role dive and attack bomber, with crew of three and four 7·62mm ShKAS machine guns, two fixed firing ahead above the nose, one aimed from the upper rear position and one aimed from a retracting ventral mount with periscopic sight. Up to 2,205lb (1000kg) of bombs could be carried, either ▶

Below: Though it could not carry a 4,000lb bomb, as could some British Mosquitoes, the Pe-2 had a remarkably long weapon bay (with doors open in this picture) plus bays in the engine nacelles.

all externally or partly in the bomb bay and part in the rear of the long nacelles. The Pe-3bis fighter of 1941 had manoeuvre flaps instead of dive brakes, and additional fixed 20mm ShVAK and 12·7mm BS guns. During 1942 a 12·7mm power turret replaced the upper rear gun, the lower rear gun was made 12·7mm calibre and two 7·62mm beam guns were added. Extra armour, self-sealing tanks with cold exhaust-gas purging, detail drag-reduction and PF engines followed. The final versions had M-107 (VK-107) engines, various heavier armament and up to 6,615lb (3000kg) bomb load. Total production was just over 11,400.

From the basic three-seat low-level attack bomber, itself derived from a high-altitude fighter, stemmed numerous research or stillborn develop-ments. One was the Pe-2VI high-altitude fighter, for which Dr M. N. Petrov's pressure cabin (planned for the original fighter) was resurrected. It had a heavy nose armament, but the high-flying threat (which was

Probably taken in 1943 this photo shows Pe-2FT bombers (FT stood for front-line request and added extra rear-firing guns and armour) which cruised so fast that escorting Hurricanes could not keep up!

expected to include the Ju 288) never materialised. One of the leaders on the VI team was Myasishchev, who later accomplished important designs in his own right. Another fighter version, about two years later in timing than the Pe-3bis, was the Pe-2I with direct-injection M-107A engines and a speed comfortably in excess of 400mph. Other versions included the Pe-2R long-range low- and high-level reconnaissance aircraft, with a large camera installation instead of a bomb bay, and the Pe-2UT trainer with tandem dual controls. In 1943–45 a Pe-2R was also used for ground and flight rocket tests by the RD-1 nitric acid/kerosene engine, installed in the tail; 169 firings were made.

Petlyakov Pe-8

ANT-42, TB-7, Pe-8 (various sub-types)

Origin: The design bureau of A. N. Tupolev, with team headed by V. M. Petlyakov.

Type: Heavy bomber with normal crew of nine.

Engines: (Prototype) see text; (first production) four 1,300hp Mikulin AM-35A vee-12 liquid-cooled; (second production) four 1,475hp Charomski M-30B vee-12 diesels; (third production) four 1,630hp Shvetsov ASh-82FNV 14-cylinder two-row radials.

Dimensions: Span 131ft 0½in (39·94m); length 73ft 8¾in (22·47m); height 20ft (6·1m).

Weights: Empty (first production) 37,480lb (17,000kg); (typical late production) about 40,000lb (18,000kg); maximum loaded (early) 63,052lb (28,600kg); (late, M-30B) 73,469lb (33,325kg); (ASh-82) 68,519lb (31,080kg).

Performance: Maximum speed (AM-35) 276mph (444km/h); (M-30B) 272mph (438km/h); (ASh-82) 280mph (451km/h); initial climb (typical) 853ft (260m)/min; service ceiling (AM-35, M-30B) about 22,966ft (7000m); (ASh-82) 29,035ft (8850m); range, see text.

Armament: (Typical) one 20mm ShVAK in dorsal and tail turrets, two 7·62mm ShKAS in nose turret and one 12·7mm BS manually aimed from rear of each inner nacelle; bomb load, see text.

History: First flight (ANT-42) 27 December 1936; (production TB-7) early 1939; (ASh-82 version) 1943; final delivery 1944.

User: Soviet Union (ADD).

Development: Despite the Soviet Union's great heritage of impressive heavy bombers the TB-7 was the only aircraft in this category in World War II and only a few hundred were built. This resulted from a Germanic concentration on twin-engined tactical machines rather than any shortcoming in the Pe-8 and there was at no time any serious problem with propulsion, though the type of engine kept changing. The prototype, built

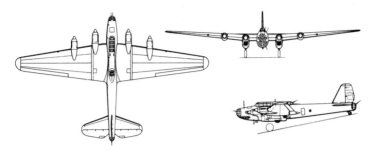

Above: Three-view of Pe-8 first series with AM-35 engines.

to a 1934 specification, had four 1,100hp M-105 engines supercharged by a large blower driven by an M-100 engine in the rear fuselage. Another had AM-34FRN engines, but the AM-35A was chosen for production at Kuznets in 1939, by which time the complex ACN-2 supercharging system had been abandoned. Performance at 8000m (26,250ft, double the maximum-speed height for earlier Soviet heavies) was outstanding and faster than the Bf 109B. In 1940, in line with the new Soviet designation system, the TB-7 was credited to Petlyakov, leader of the design team. Unfortunately he was killed in a crash two years later and most of the wartime development was managed by I. F. Nyezeval. Maximum bomb load was 8,818lb (4000kg), the range of 2,321 miles being raised to over 3,000 miles by the diesel engines substituted when AM-35 production ceased. The final radial-engined version could carry 11,600lb for 2,500 miles and many long missions were made into Hungary, Romania and East Germany the first major mission being on Berlin in mid-1941.

Below: The final Nyezeval-managed variant had direct-injection Ash-82FNV engines with slim inner nacelles, but not many were built owing to concentration on tactical bombers. The 4,410lb (2000kg) bomb was carried internally – but not very often.

PZL P.23 and 43 Karaś

P.23A and B, P.43A and B

Origin: Panstwowe Zaklady Lotnicze, Poland.
Type: Three-seat reconnaissance bomber.
Engine: (P.23A) one 580hp PZL (Bristol-licence) Pegasus II nine-cylinder radial; (P.23B) 680hp PZL Pegasus VIII; P.43A, 930hp Gnome-Rhône 14 Kfs 14-cylinder two-row radial; (P.43B) 980hp G-R 14N1.
Dimensions: Span 45ft 9in (13·95m); length (23) 31ft 9in (9·68m); (43) 32ft 10in; height 11ft 6in (3·5m).
Weights: Empty (23, typical) 4,250lb (1928kg); loaded (23) 6,918lb (3138kg); maximum overload 7,774lb (3526kg).
Performance: Maximum speed (23A) 198mph (320km/h); (23B) 217mph (350km/h); (43B) 227mph (365km/h); initial climb (typical) 985ft (300m)/min; service ceiling (typical) 24,600ft (7500m); range with bomb load, 410 miles (660km) (overload, 932 miles, 1500km).
Armament: (23) one 7·7mm Browning or KM Wz 33 firing forward, one on PZL hydraulically assisted mount in rear cockpit and third similarly mounted in rear ventral position; external bomb load of up to 1,543lb (700kg); (43) as 23 but with two forward-firing guns, one on each side of cowling.
History: First flight (P.23/I) August 1934; (production Karaś A) June 1936; (P.43A) 1937.
Users: Bulgaria, Poland, Romania.

Development: Designed by a team led by Stanisław Prauss, the P.23 was hardly beautiful yet it provided the tactical attack capability of one of Europe's largest air forces in the late 1930s. By the outbreak of World War II, 14 of the bomber regiments of the Polish Air Force had been equipped with the Karaś (Carp); its successor, the greatly improved Sum, was about to enter service. When designed, in 1931–32, the Karaś was an outstandingly

Below: The Karaś entered service in late 1936 and eventually equipped 14 squadrons, at least two of which are seen in this 1938 photograph on parade for inspection. When the Germans invaded Poland in 1939 the type equipped 12 squadrons, seven of them attached to the land armies and five forming the independent Bomber Brigade. During the desperate four-week campaign they were flown with great gallantry though they suffered severe losses.

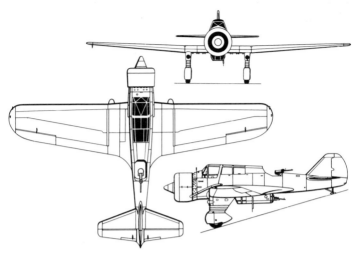

Above: Three-view of P.23A (P.23B almost identical).

modern aircraft, one of its radical features being the use of smooth skin of light-alloy/balsa sandwich construction. It carried a bomb load far heavier than any of its contemporaries and had no defence "blind spots", though its firepower was meagre. The more powerful P.43 was built for Bulgaria, 12 43A being followed by an order for 42 of the B model of which nearly all were delivered by the start of World War II. Despite skill and heroism the Polish squadrons were soon overwhelmed, but a handful of Karaś managed to reach Romania, where they were refurbished, put into service with Romanian crews and used on the Bessarabian front in the invasion of the Soviet Union in 1941.

Below: The national eagle on a pentagon badge shows that this Karaś B served with the same regiment as the aircraft in the foreground opposite; all regiments displayed their badges in this position, except for Karaś A aircraft at training schools. Colour was dark olive green with pale grey underside. The P.23 Karaś was an outstandingly fine attack bomber when it first flew in the mid-1930s, but it was obsolescent by 1939 and was an easy prey for German fighters.

PZL P.37 Łoś

P.37-I Łoś A and P.37-II Łoś B (Łoś = Elk).

Origin: Panstwowe Zaklady Lotnicze, Poland.
Type: Medium bomber.
Engines: Two PZL-built Bristol Pegasus nine-cylinder radials, (Łoś A) 875hp Pegasus XIIB, (B) 925hp Pegasus XX.
Dimensions: Span 58ft 8¾in (17·90m); length 42ft 4in (12·90m); height 16ft 8in (5·08m).
Weights: Empty 9,293lb (4213kg); normal loaded 18,739lb (8500kg); max overload 19,577lb (8880kg).
Performance: Maximum speed 273mph (440km/h); service ceiling 19,685ft (6000m); range with 3,880lb (1760kg) bomb load 1,616 miles (2600km).
Armament: Single manually aimed 7·7mm KM Wz.37 machine guns in nose, dorsal and ventral positions; internal (fuselage and wing) bays for bomb load of up to 5,688lb (2580kg).
History: First flight June 1936; service delivery, spring 1938.
Users: Poland, Romania.

Development: Designed by a team led by Jerzy Dabrowski in 1934, this bomber (extraordinarily efficient in its ratio of empty to gross weight) was the subject of unwarranted political criticism instigated by the Army ground forces. Nevertheless by the outbreak of war four squadrons, with nine Łoś B each, were operational with the Bomber Brigade and they proved extremely effective in the few days they were able to operate. About 100 had been delivered, and a dozen more were readied for combat during the Polish campaign, some 40 Łoś A and B finally escaping to Romania. There they were taken over and in 1941 used against the Soviet Union, a few still serving as target tugs in the late 1950s. By 1938 the dramatic performance of the Łoś resulted in intense international interest, and had war not supervened PZL would have fulfilled export contracts for at least five, and probably nine, countries.

Below: Air and ground crews parade with their Los A bombers at the IIIrd Dyon (Conversion Unit) in late 1938.

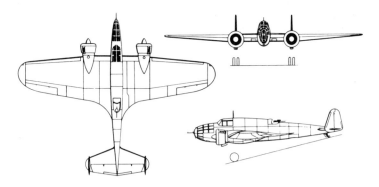

Above: Three-view of P.37 Łoś A (Łoś B outwardly identical).

Below: One of the first Łoś B bombers, pictured with a regiment of P.11c fighters shortly before the German attack on 1 September 1939. The P.37 Łoś was possibly the best bomber in the world in service at that time, yet it was unwanted by the Army chiefs who sought by every means possible to stop production and disrupt training. Despite this the Bomber Brigade had managed to form four Dyons (each equivalent to a squadron), Nos 211, 212, 216 and 217, with nine aircraft each, and complete initial training.

Savoia-Marchetti S.M.79 Sparviero

S.M.79-I, II and III, 79B and 79-JR

Origin: SIAI "Savoia-Marchetti"; built under licence (79-II) by Aeronautica Macchi and OM "Reggiane"; (79 JR) Industria Aeronautica Romana.
Type: 4/5-seat bomber, torpedo bomber and reconnaissance.
Engines: (I) three 780hp Alfa-Romeo 126 RC34 nine-cylinder radials; (II) three 1,000hp Piaggio P.XI RC40 14-cylinder two-row radials (one batch, 1,030hp Fiat A.80 RC41); (79-JR) two 1,220hp Junker Jumo 211Da inverted-vee-12 liquid-cooled.
Dimensions: Span 69ft 6½in (21·2m); length (I) 51ft 10in; (II) 53ft 1¾in (16·2m); (B -JR) 52ft 9in; height'(II) 13ft 5½in (4·1m)   *continued* ▶

456

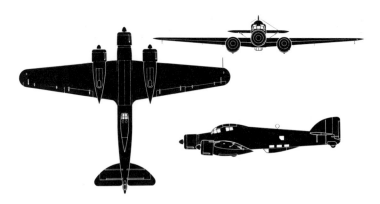

Above: Three-view of a typical S.M. 79-II.

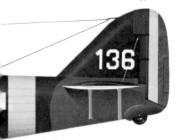

Left: In appearance and character quite unlike the familiar tri-motor bomber of the Regia Aeronautica, the S.M.79-JR of the Royal Air Forces of Romania was powered by the same engines as a Heinkel 111H, two Jumo 211 liquid-cooled units. This example served with the 3rd Air Corps on the Eastern front in 1943, by which time it was operating mainly by night.

Below: Early S.M.79-I bombers of the Regia Aeronautica's 52° Squadriglia, photographed shortly before Italy entered the war in 1940. The upper surface colours were dark green and khaki.

Weights: Empty (I) 14,990lb (6800kg); (II) 16,755lb (7600kg); (-JR) 15,860lb (7195kg); maximum loaded (I) 23,100lb (10,500kg); (II) 24,192lb (11,300kg); (-JR) 23,788lb (10,470kg).

Performance: Maximum speed (I) 267mph; (II) 270mph (434km/h); (B) 255mph; (-JR) 276mph; initial climb (typical) 1,150ft (350m)/min; service ceiling (all) 21,325–23,300ft (7000m); range with bomb load (not torpedoes), typical, 1,243 miles (2000km).

Armament: (Typical) one 12·7mm Breda-SAFAT fixed firing ahead from above cockpit, one 12·7mm manually aimed from open dorsal position, one 12·7mm manually aimed from rear of ventral gondola and one 7·7mm Lewis manually aimed from either beam window; internal bomb bay for up to 2,200lb (1000kg) or two 450mm torpedoes slung externally; (79B and -JR) no fixed gun, typically three/five 7·7mm guns and bomb load up to 2,640lb (1200kg).

History: First flight (civil prototype) late 1934; service delivery (I) late 1936; (II) October 1939; final delivery (III) early 1944.

Users: Brazil, Iraq, Italy (RA, CB, ARSI), Jugoslavia, Romania, Spain (Nationalist).

Development: Though often derided – as were most Italian arms in World War II – the S.M.79 Sparviero (Hawk) was a fine and robust bomber that unfailingly operated in the most difficult conditions with great reliability. The prototype, fitted with various engines and painted in civil or military liveries, set various world records in 1935–36, despite its mixed structure of steel tube, light alloy, wood and fabric. Built at unprecedented rate for the Regia Aeronautica, the 79-I established an excellent reputation with

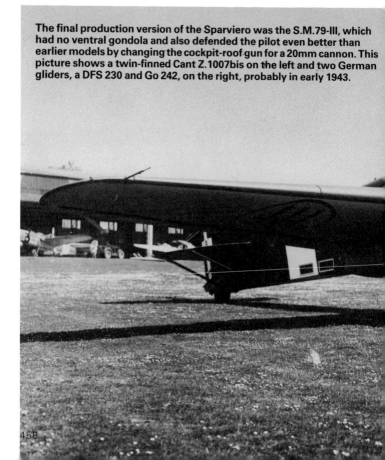

The final production version of the Sparviero was the S.M.79-III, which had no ventral gondola and also defended the pilot even better than earlier models by changing the cockpit-roof gun for a 20mm cannon. This picture shows a twin-finned Cant Z.1007bis on the left and two German gliders, a DFS 230 and Go 242, on the right, probably in early 1943.

Above: A rare colour photograph of S.M.79-II torpedo bombers of the famous and courageous Squadriglie Aerosiluranti.

the Aviación Legionaria in the Spanish civil war, while other Stormi laid the basis for great proficiency with torpedoes. Altogether about 1,200 of all versions served with the Regia Aeronautica, while just over 100 were exported. Most exports were twin-engined 79B versions, but the Romanian-built 79-JR was more powerful and served on the Russian front in 1941–44.

Savoia-Marchetti S.M.81 Pipistrello

S.M.81 Pipistrello (Bat) of many serie

Origin: SIAI "Savoia-Marchetti".
Type: Multi-role bomber, transport and utility.
Engines: (Most) three aircooled radials, usually 700hp Piaggio P.X nine-cylinder; others 580hp Alfa Romeo 125, 680hp Piaggio P.IX, 900hp Alfa Romeo 126 and 1,000hp Gnome-Rhône K-14; (81B, two engines, various).
Dimensions: Span 78ft 8¾in (24·00m); length (typical) 58ft 4¾in (17·80 m); height 14ft 7¼in (4·45m).
Weights: Empty (typical) 13,890lb (6300kg); max loaded 23,040lb (10,450kg).
Performance: Maximum speed 211mph (340km/h); typical range with bomb load 932 miles (1500km).
Armament: Varied or absent, but usually two 7·7mm Breda-SAFAT in powered dorsal turret, two more in retractable ventral turret and two more aimed manually from beam windows; internal weapon bay for up to 2,205lb (1000kg) of bombs.
History: First flight 1935; service delivery, autumn 1935; final delivery, possibly 1941.
Users: Italy (RA, CB, ARSI, post-war AF), Spain.

SNCASE LeO 451

LeO 45, 451 B4 and derivatives

Origin: Soc Lioré et Olivier, Argenteuil, in 1937 nationalized as part of SNCASE; production see text.
Type: Medium bomber, later transport.
Engines: Two 1,140hp Gnome-Rhône 14N 48/49 14-cylinder radials.
Dimensions: Span 73ft 10¾in (22·52m); length 56ft 4in (17·17m); height 14ft 9¼in (4·50m).
Weights: Empty 17,225lb (7813kg); normal loaded 25,133lb (11,400kg); max 26,455lb (12,000kg).
Performance: Maximum speed 307mph (495km/h); service ceiling 29,530ft (9000m); range with 1,102lb (500kg) bomb load 1,430 miles (2300km).
Armament: One 20mm Hispano-Suiza 404 cannon in SAMM retractable dorsal turret, 7·5mm MAC 1934 in retractable ventral turret and MAC 1934 fixed in nose firing ahead; internal bay for up to 4,410lb (2000kg) of bombs.
History: First flight 16 January 1937; service delivery 16 August 1939; final delivery 1943.
Users: France (Armée de l'Air, Vichy French and post-war AF), Germany (Luftwaffe), Italy (RA and CB), UK (RAF) and US (AAF).

Development: Beyond doubt the best bomber developed in France in the final years before the war, the LeO 45 was also available in substantial numbers. Despite chaotic conditions caused by nationalization of the airframe industry and widespread sabotage, production at Paris (Clichy and Levallois) and assembly at Villacoublay got into its stride by the spring of 1939. To provide the stipulated catwalk past the bomb bay small secondary bays were added in the inner wing and the main bay made even narrower than the slim fuselage. Production was dispersed to take in factories

Above: Most of the large force of S.M.81 bomber/transports prior to World War II were silver or cream, but this example was one of many whose wing upper surfaces were banded with red.

Development: A military version of the very successful S.M.73 airliner, the S.M.81 was one of the world's best multi-role bomber/transport aircraft in 1935, but when Italy entered World War II in June 1940 (by which time about 100 were in service, plus about 40 in Spain) it was becoming obsolescent. Despite this its serviceability and popularity resulted in it appearing in every theatre in which Italy was engaged, from Eritrea to the Soviet Union. Until 1942 it was an important night bomber in the eastern Mediterranean, and it became the most important Italian transport in terms of numbers (though much inferior to the S.M.82 in capability). A few served with the post-war Aeronautica Militare until about 1951.

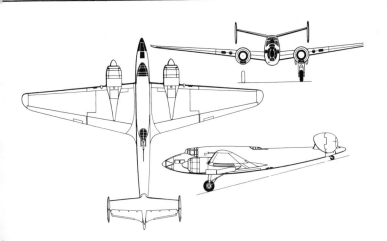

Above: Three-view of LeO 451 B4 with armament retracted.

around Lyons, a second assembly-line at Ambérieu (Ain) and a third line at Marignane (Marseilles), and the evacuated Villacoublay plant was hastily moved to an underground works at Cravant near Auxerre in May 1940. The 451 B4 had been in action from the first day of war, and by May 1940 some 472 equipped eight Armée de l'Air groups. Missions could not have been more impossible, negating all the type's brilliant qualities, 47 being lost in the first 288 sorties (though on one mission the dorsal gunner destroyed two Bf 110s). Several sub-types served the Vichy forces and Luftwaffe, one Gruppe switching from Stalingrad to equip with the LeO 451T. Italy, the RAF and USAAF used the aircraft chiefly as a utility transport.

Short S.29 Stirling

Stirling I to V

Origin: Short Brothers, Rochester and Belfast.
Type: (I–III) heavy bomber with crew of 7/8; (IV) glider tug and special transport; (V) strategic transport.
Engines: (I) four 1,595hp Bristol Hercules XI 14-cylinder sleeve-valve radials; (II) 1,600hp Wright R-2600-A5B Cyclone; (III, IV, V) 1,650hp Bristol Hercules XVI.
Dimensions: Span 99ft 1in (30·2m); length (except V) 87ft 3in (26·6m); (V) 90ft 6¾in (27·6m); height 22ft 9in (6·94m).
Weights: Empty (I) 44,000lb (19,950kg); (III) 46,900lb (21,273kg); (IV, V, typical) 43,200lb (19,600kg); maximum loaded (I) 59,400lb (26,943kg); (III, IV, V) 70,000lb (31,750kg).
Performance: Maximum speed (I–III) 270mph (435km/h); (IV, V) 280mph (451km/h); initial climb (typical) 800ft (244m)/min; service ceiling (I–III) 17,000ft (5182m); range (III) 590 miles (950km) with 14,000lb bombs or 2,010 miles (3235km) with 3,500lb; range (IV, V) 3,000 miles (4828km).
Armament: (I) two 0·303in Brownings in nose and dorsal turrets and four in tail turret, plus (early batches) two in remote control ventral turret; ▶

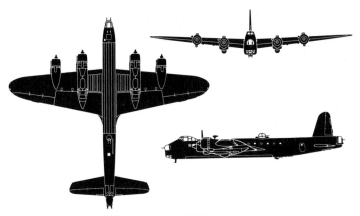

Above: Three-view of Stirling I with FN.64 ventral turret.

Below: One of an outstanding series of colour photographs taken in 1941 on a visit to 149 Sqn, one of the first Stirling users. At this time the RAF was still trying to make deep penetrations of the Continent in daylight —not a good idea with Stirlings.

maximum bomb load 18,000lb (8165kg) in fuselage and inner wings; (II, III) as (I) but different dorsal turret; (IV) sole armament, tail turret; (V) none.

History: First flight 14 May 1939; (production Mk I) May 1940; final delivery (V) November 1945.

User: UK (RAF).

Development: Though extremely impressive, with vast length, unprecedented height and even two separate tailwheels, the Stirling was unpopular. Partly owing to short wing span it had a poor ceiling and sluggish manoeuvrability except at low level. Though it carried a heavy bomb load,

Below: This Stirling I is of the intermediate series of 1941 between the first Series I (no dorsal turret) and the Mk I Series III with the Lancaster-type dorsal turret as also fitted to the Mk III. This Series II had the unpopular F.N.7-mod dorsal turret similar to that of the Botha and Manchester I.

it could not carry bombs bigger than 2,000lb (the largest size when the design was completed in 1938). Operations began with daylight attacks in February 1941, soon switched to night, and by 1943 the Stirling was regarded mainly as a tug and transport and carrier of ECM jamming and spoofing devices for 100 Group. The RAF received 2,221 bomber versions, excluding the two Mk II conversions, and Short's new Belfast plant finally built 160 of the streamlined Mk V transports which carried 40 troops or heavy freight.

Below: A late-production Stirling I Series III with definitive dorsal turret, serving with 214 Sqn based at Stradishall in late 1942.

Tupolev SB-2
ANT-40, SB-1, -2 and -2bis (ANT-41)

Origin: The design bureau of A. N. Tupolev.
Type: Medium bomber with usual crew of three.
Engines: Two vee-12 liquid-cooled; (early -2 versions) 750hp VK-100 (M-100) derived from Hispano-Suiza 12Y; (late -2 versions) 840hp M-100A; (-2bis versions) 1,100hp M-103.
Dimensions: Span 66ft 8½in (20·34m); length (with very few exceptions) 40ft 3¼in (12·29m); height 10ft 8in (3·28m).
Weights: Empty (early -2) 8,267lb (3750kg); (M-100A) typically 8,820lb (4000kg); (-2bis) about 10,800lb (4900kg); maximum loaded (early -2) 13,449lb (6100kg); (M-100A) 13,955lb (6330kg), (-2bis) normally 17,196lb (7800kg); overload 21,165lb (9600kg).
Performance: Maximum speed (early) 255mph (410km/h); (M-100A) 263mph (425km/h); (-2bis) 280mph (450km/h); initial climb (-2bis) 1,310ft (400m)/min; service ceiling (typical later version) 31,000–35,000ft (9500–10,500m); range with bomb load (typical -2) 746 miles (1200km); (-2bis, max fuel) 994 miles (1600km).
Armament: (Normal for all versions) four 7·62mm ShKAS machine guns, two manually aimed through vertical slits in nose, one from dorsal position and one from rear ventral position; internal bomb bay for six 220lb (100kg) or single 1,100lb (500kg).
History: First flight (SB-1) 7 October 1934; service delivery (-2) early 1936; (-2bis) probably late 1938; final delivery, probably 1942.
Users: China, Soviet Union, Spain (Republican).

Below: When it entered service in January 1936 the SB-2 outperformed every other bomber. This was one of more than 200 supplied to the Republican forces in Spain (Grupo de Bombardeo 24).

Right: This SB-2, again one of the 1936-37 vintage with flat-fronted radiators but in this case fitted with propeller spinners, was one of a considerable number supplied to the Chinese Central Government in early 1938. It formed the core of Chinese bomber strength.

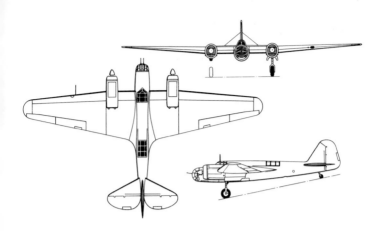

Above: Three-view of early SB-2 as used from 1936.

Development: Like the TB-3, the SB-2 was built in great numbers in the 1930s and bore a heavy burden in "the Great Patriotic War" from June 1941 until long after it was obsolescent. Though built to a 1933 specification it was actually much superior to Britain's later Blenheim and it was the Soviet Union's first stressed-skin bomber. The SB-1 prototype had M-25 radials, but performance was even better with the VK-100 in-lines and service in the Spanish civil war in 1936–39 initially found the Nationalists lacking any fighters able to catch the speedy, high-flying SB. In speed and rate of ▶

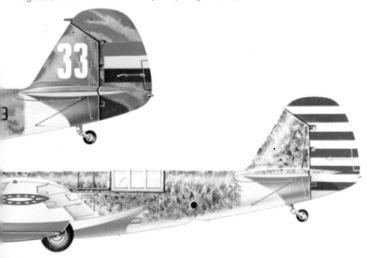

Left: Though retaining the same basic airframe as earlier versions, with local reinforcement for increased weights and speeds, this SB-2bis was one of the later series (bis suffix) with streamlined cowlings incorporating ducted radiators. A dorsal turret was added and the rear ventral position was improved. The aircraft depicted was wrecked at Lvov in the first days of the German invasion.

climb even the first service versions surpassed contemporary fighters and, despite a considerable increase in fuel capacity and weight, performance was improved with the more streamlined M-103, without the original bluff frontal radiators. Total production exceeded 6,000 of all versions, and the type served against Japan in 1938–39, in Finland and against German forces until 1943, the last two years mainly in the role of a night bomber.

Tupolev TB-3

ANT-6, TB-3 Types 1932, 1934 and 1936

Origin: The design bureau of A. N. Tupolev.
Type: Heavy bomber with crew of ten (Type 1932) and later six.
Engines: Four vee-12 liquid-cooled; (1932) 730hp M-17; (1934) 900hp M-34R (derived from BMW VI); later 950–1,280hp M-34RN or RNF.
Dimensions: Span 132ft 10½in (40·5m); (1936) 137ft 1½in (41·8m); length (early) 81ft (24·69m); (1934 onward) 82ft 8¼in (25·21m); height, not available but about 18ft.
Weights: Empty, 22,000–26,450lb (11,000–12,000kg); maximum loaded (1932) 38,360lb (17,500kg); (1934) 41,021lb (18,606kg); (1936) 41,226lb (18,700kg), with overload of 54,020lb (24,500kg).
Performance: Maximum speed (M-17, 1932) 134mph (215km/h); (M-34R, 1934) 144mph (232km/h); (M-34RN, 1936) 179mph (288km/h); initial climb, not available; service ceiling (1932) 12,467ft (3800m); (1934) 15,090ft (4600m); (1936) 25,365ft (7750m); range with bomb load (typical of all) 1,550 miles (2500km).
Armament: (1932, 1934) five pairs of 7·62mm DA-2 machine guns in nose, two dorsal mountings and two underwing positions, all manually aimed; internal bomb cells for maximum load of 4,850lb (2200kg); (1936) five (later three or four) 7·62mm ShKAS manually aimed, by 1936 without wing positions; bomb load up to 12,790lb (5800kg) carried on 26 fuselage racks and 12 external racks under fuselage and wings.
History: First flight (ANT-6) 22 December 1930; (production TB-3) probably late 1931; (M-34 prototype) March 1933; final delivery, probably 1939.
Users: China, Soviet Union.

Development: Though seemingly archaic in appearance – and its basic design dated from 1926 – the TB-3 was a large and formidable aircraft with capabilities outstripping those of any other bomber in service in other

Above: In the first week following the German invasion of the Soviet Union on 22 June 1941 more than two-thirds of Russian aircraft were destroyed, mostly on the ground. Here a surviving SB-2 of the early series is pushed into a wood for cover. Once a world-beater, Tupolev's speedy tactical bomber had by this time become obsolescent, though still extremely useful.

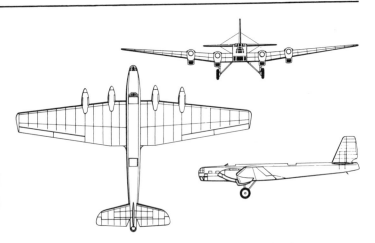

Above: Three-view of 1936 version with single mainwheels.

countries. Though not a stressed-skin design it was a cantilever monoplane with corrugated metal skin using Junkers technology and, thanks to generous stressing, had a considerable "stretching" capability that was put to good use during its long career. A leader in the Tupolev design team was young V. M. Petlyakov, later to produce bombers in his own right, but the aircraft was always known by its functional designation. The 1934 version had brakes on the tandem wire-spoked wheels, a tail turret in place of the underwing positions, and geared engines, which in 1935 were super-charged RN type. Altogether at least 800 of these fine machines were built, final models having smooth skin, single-wheel main gears and only three gunners in enclosed manual turrets. TB-3s saw much action against Japan, Poland, Finland and the German invader and served until 1944 as freight and paratroop transports.

Tupolev Tu-2

ANT-58, Tu-2 (many sub-variants), Tu-6

Origin: The design bureau of A. N. Tupolev.
Type: Attack bomber with normal crew of four.
Engines: Two 1,850hp Shvetsov ASh-82FN or FNV 14-cylinder two-row radials.
Dimensions: Span 61ft 10½in (18·86m); length 45ft 3¾in (13·8m); height 13ft 9½in (4·20m).
Weights: Empty 18,240lb (8273kg); maximum loaded 28,219lb (12,800kg).
Performance: Maximum speed 342mph (550km/h); initial climb 2,300ft (700m)/min;' service ceiling 31,168ft (9500m); range with 3,307lb (1500kg) bombs 1,553 miles (2500km).
Armament: Typically three manually aimed 12·7mm Beresin BS, one in upper rear of crew compartment, one in rear dorsal position and one in rear ventral position, and two 20mm ShVAK, each with 200 rounds, fixed in wing roots for ground attack (later, often 23mm); internal bomb bay for maximum load of 5,000lb (2270kg), later 6,615lb (3000kg).
History: First flight (ANT-58) October 1940; (production Tu-2) August 1942; final delivery 1948.
User: (Wartime) Soviet Union.

Development: Though it was undoubtedly one of the outstanding designs of World War II, the Tu-2 had the misfortune to emerge into a Soviet Union teeming with the Pe-2, and the older and smaller machine continued to be

Below: In 1950 about 200 Tu-2s were supplied to the newly formed People's Republic of China air force. This example is from the batch with three rear windows on each side.

Below: Numerous Tu-2s were supplied in the immediate post-war era to satellite air forces; this aircraft served with Poland.

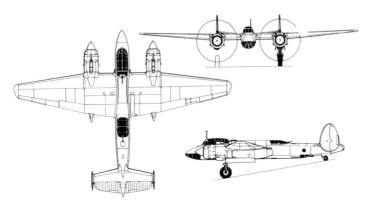

Above; Three-view of typical Tu-2.

produced at just ten times the rate of its supposed replacement (much the same happened with German bombers). It was formidable and reliable in service, extremely popular and hardly needed any major modification in the course of a career which extended right through the nervous Berlin Airlift (1948), Korea (1950–53, in North Korean service) and up to 1961 with several Communist nations. Known to NATO as "Bat", the post-war variants included a close-support type with 37mm cannon, a radar-equipped (night fighter?) variant and the high-altitude Tu-6 with long span and bigger tail.

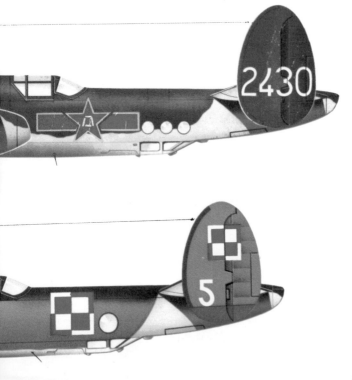

Vickers Wellesley

Type 287, Wellesley I and II

Origin: Vickers (Aviation) Ltd.
Type: Two-seat general-purpose bomber.
Engine: One 925hp Bristol Pegasus XX nine-cylinder radial.
Dimensions: Span 74ft 7in (22·73m); length 39ft 3in (11·96m); height 12ft 4in (3·75m).
Weights: Empty 6,369lb (2889kg); maximum loaded (except record flight) 11,100lb (5035kg).
Performance: Maximum speed 228mph (369km/h); initial climb 1,200ft (366m)/min; service ceiling 33,000ft (10,060m); range with bomb load 1,110 miles (1786km).
Armament: One 0·303in belt-fed Vickers in right wing firing ahead, one Vickers K manually aimed from rear cockpit; four 500lb (227kg) or eight 250lb bombs in streamlined containers, originally fitted with bomb doors, under wings.

History: First flight 19 June 1935; service delivery April 1937; final delivery May 1938.

User: UK (RAF), possibly passed on to other Middle East countries.

Development: Vickers built a large biplane to meet the RAF G.4/31 specification, but it was so humdrum the company board decided at their own risk to build a monoplane using the radical geodetic (metal basketwork) construction developed for airships by their structural wizard B.N. (later Sir Barnes) Wallis. The result was so dramatically superior the Air Ministry lost its fear of monoplanes and bought 176 as the Wellesley. Distinguished by great span, high aspect ratio, extreme cruise efficiency and a most reliable engine (identical in size to the Jupiter but of virtually twice the power) it was natural to form a special Long-Range Development Flight. Three aircraft, with three seats, extra fuel and long-chord cowlings, took off from Ismailia, Egypt, on 5 November 1938; one landed at Koepang and the other two reached Darwin, 7,162 miles (11,525km) in 48 hours non-stop. In World War II Wellesleys were extremely active in East Africa, Egypt, the Middle East and surrounding sea areas until late 1942.

Left: One of the very first Wellesleys to reach the RAf was this example delivered to 76 Sqn at RAF Finningley, Yorkshire, in April 1937.

Below: The Wellesley saw most of its service in east and north-east Africa in 1940-42. This example, pictured in 1940, has the hood of the rear cockpit swung open and the gun ready for action. The containers housed the bombs.

Vickers-Armstrongs Wellington
Type 415 and 440, Wellington I to T.19

Origin: Vickers-Armstrongs (Aircraft) Ltd.

Type: Originally long-range bomber with crew of six; later, see text.

Engines: Variously two Bristol Pegasus nine-cylinder radials, two Rolls-Royce Merlin vee-12 liquid-cooled, two Pratt & Whitney Twin Wasp 14-cylinder two-row radials or two Bristol Hercules 14-cylinder two-row sleeve-valve radials; for details see text.

Dimensions: Span 86ft 2in (26·26m); (V, VI) 98ft 2in; length (most) 64ft 7in (19·68m), (some, 60ft 10in or, with Leigh light, 66ft); height 17ft 6in (5·33m), (some 17ft).

Weights: Empty (IC) 18,556lb (8417kg); (X) 26,325lb (11,940kg); maximum loaded (IC) 25,800lb (11,703kg); (III) 29,500lb (13,381kg); (X) 36,500lb (16,556kg).

Performance: Maximum speed (IC) 235mph (379km/h); (most other marks) 247–256mph (410km/h); (V, VI) 300mph (483km/h); initial climb (all, typical) 1,050ft (320m)/min; service ceiling (bomber versions, typical) 22,000ft (6710m); (V, VI) 38,000ft (11,600m); range with weapon load of 1,500lb (680kg), typically 2,200 miles (3540km).

Armament: See text.

History: First flight (B.9/32) 15 June 1936; (production Mk I) 23 December 1937; service delivery (I) October 1938; final delivery (T.10) 13 October 1945.

Users: (Wartime) Australia, Czechoslovakia, France, New Zealand, Poland. UK (RAF).

Development: It was natural that Vickers (Aviation), from October 1938 Vickers-Armstrongs (Aircraft), should have followed up the success of the Wellesley with a larger bomber using the geodetic form of construction. There were difficulties in applying it to wings, cut-out nacelles and fuselages with large bomb-doors and turrets, but the B.9/32 prototype was obviously efficient, and by September 1939 had been developed into Britain's most formidable bomber. The following were chief versions:

I Powered by 1,050hp Pegasus XVIII and originally with twin 0·303in Brownings in simple Vickers turrets at nose and tail; internal bomb load 4,500lb (2041kg). Built one-a-day at Weybridge, later a further 50 per month at Chester and, later still, about 30 a month at Squire's Gate, Blackpool. Mk IA had Nash and Thompson power turrets, and the main IC version had two beam guns (some earlier had a ventral barbette). Production: 180+ 183+ 2,685.

II Had 1,145hp Merlin X, otherwise as IC. Production: 400.

III Main Bomber Command type in 1941–2, with 1,375hp Hercules III or XI, and four-gun tail turret. Production: 1,519.

IV Flown by two Polish squadrons, powered by 1,200hp Twin Wasp R-1830-S3C4-G. Production: 220.

continued▶

Right: One of the 2,685 Wellington IC bombers, in this case from the Shadow Factory at Chester. It is depicted as it was in 1940, serving with 150 Sqn at Newton, near Nottingham. All later bomber versions had greater power and increased armament.

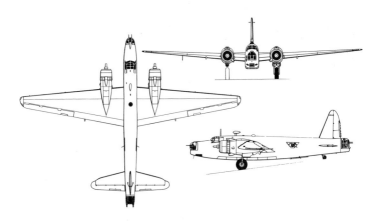

Above: Three-view of Wellington III (other Hercules versions similar).

Above: Although the colour has faded with age, this is an original photograph dating from 1940–41, showing 20 bombs of nominal 250lb size going aboard a Wellington IC. At the time, this was the RAF's most formidable bomber, but bigger ones were in prospect.

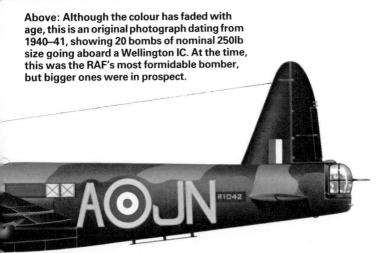

Above: Wellington I series 1 bombers of the only two squadrons then equipped with the new bomber (9 and 149) took part in air exercises in summer 1939. This early model had four machine guns in "roll-top desk" fairings at nose and tail.

Below: One of the first batch of 200 Merlin-engined Wellington IIs, of which 585 were built in all (all at Weybridge). This photograph was taken in 1941, by which time the new standard mark was the Hercules-engined III with four-gun rear turret.

V Experimental pressurised high-altitude, turbocharged Hercules VIII. Three built, converted to VI.

VI Long-span pressurised, with 1,600hp Merlin R6SM engines, no guns and special equipment. Used by 109 Sqn and as Gee trainers. Production 63.

VII One only, Merlin engines, tested large 40mm Vickers S gun turret for P.92 fighter, later with twin fins.

VIII Conversion of IC as Coastal reconnaissance version, with ASV radar arrays, Leigh light in long nose, and two 18in torpedoes or anti-submarine weapons. Some, huge hoops for detonating magnetic mines.

IX Conversion of IC for special trooping.

X Standard bomber, similar to III but 1,675hp Hercules VI or XVI. Peak production rate per month in 1942 was Weybridge 70, Chester 130 and Blackpool 102. Production: 3,804.

XI Advanced Coastal version of X, no mast aerials but large chin radome, torpedoes, retractable Leigh light.

XII Similar to XI, with Leigh light ventral.

XIII Reverted to ASV Mk II with masts, and nose turret.

XIV Final Coastal, ASV.III chin radome, wing rocket rails, Leigh light in bomb bay.

XV, XVI Unarmed Transport Command conversions of IC.

Total production of this outstanding type amounted to 11,461. After World War II hundreds were converted for use as trainers, the main variant being the T.10 which remained in service until 1953. The T.19 was a specialised navigation trainer. The Vickers successor to the Wellington, the bigger Warwick, was inferior to four-engine machines, and was used mainly in Coastal and transport roles.

Above: By 1943 almost all the new-built (as distinct from converted) Wellingtons were maritime variants with anti-ship radar, Leigh light (for seeing surfaced U-boats at night) and rockets, torpedoes and depth bombs. HZ258 was a Mk XI built at Squire's Gate in 1943, seen off the Cornish coast.

Below: This Wimpey from a Polish squadron had completed more than 60 'ops' (operational missions) when this photograph was taken in 1942. It might be a Mk IV, flown by Polish squadrons 300 and 301.

PRINTED IN BELGIUM BY

proost
INTERNATIONAL BOOK PRODUCTION